The Law in War

A Concise Overview

This book provides a comprehensive yet concise overview of the law that regulates armed hostilities between States, and between States and non-State groups.

The text explains the conditions that result in the applicability of international humanitarian law, and then subsequently addresses how the law influences a broad range of operational, humanitarian, and accountability issues that arise during military operations.

Each chapter provides a clear and comprehensive explanation of humanitarian law, focusing especially on how it impacts operations. The chapters also highlight both contemporary controversies in the field and potentially emerging norms of the law.

This book is an ideal companion for students studying international humanitarian law and military and civilian attorneys engaged in humanitarian law practice, as well as an excellent introduction for students and practitioners of public international law and international relations.

Geoffrey Corn is the Vinson & Elkins Professor of Law at the South Texas College of Law Houston. Prior to joining the South Texas faculty in 2005, Professor Corn served in the U.S. Army for 21 years, retiring in the rank of Lieutenant Colonel. Following retirement from active duty, Professor Corn served an additional year as the Army's senior civilian law of war expert in the Office of the Judge Advocate General and Chief of the Law of War Branch in the International Law Division.

Ken Watkin served for 33 years in the Canadian Forces, including four years as the Judge Advocate General. In 2002 he was appointed to the Order of Military Merit, in 2006 a Queen's Counsel, and in 2010 he received the Canadian Bar Association President's Award. Ken was responsible for providing operational law advice regarding Canada's military operations post-9/11, and worked as government counsel for various inquiries arising from the 1994 Rwandan genocide. Since his retirement in 2010, he has served as a foreign observer to the Israeli Independent Commission investigating the 2010 Gaza blockade incident, and as the Charles H. Stockton Professor of International Law at the United States Naval War College. He is the author of *Fighting at the Legal*

Boundaries: Controlling the Use of Force in Contemporary Conflict (Oxford University Press, 2016), which was awarded the 2017 Francis Lieber Prize by the American Society of International Law.

Jamie Williamson is the executive director of the International Code of Conduct for Private Security Providers Association. He previously worked with the International Committee of the Red Cross in a number of legal, operational, and managerial positions in Geneva, Washington, D.C., and southern Africa. He also served from 1996–2005 with the UN ad hoc international criminal tribunals in Tanzania and the Netherlands, and with the Special Court for Sierra Leone. Jamie is on the faculty of the American University's Program of Advanced Studies of the Academy on Human Rights and Humanitarian Law.

The Law in War

A Concise Overview

Geoffrey Corn
Ken Watkin
Jamie Williamson

LONDON AND NEW YORK

First published 2018
by Routledge
2 Park Square, Milton Park, Abingdon, Oxon OX14 4RN

and by Routledge
711 Third Avenue, New York, NY 10017

Routledge is an imprint of the Taylor & Francis Group, an informa business

British Library Cataloguing-in-Publication Data
A catalogue record for this book is available from the British Library

Library of Congress Cataloging-in-Publication Data
Names: Corn, Geoffrey S., author. | Watkin, Kenneth, author. |
Williamson, Jamie (Jamie A.), author.
Title: The law in war : a concise overview / by Geoffrey Corn,
Ken Watkin, Jamie Williamson.
Description: Abingdon, Oxon [UK]; New York, NY : Routledge,
2018. | Includes bibliographical references and index.
Identifiers: LCCN 2018002753 | ISBN 9781138910478 (hbk) |
ISBN 9781138910485 (pbk) | ISBN 9781317436201 (epub) |
ISBN 9781317436195 (mobipocket)
Subjects: LCSH: War (International law). | Humanitarian law. |
War victims—Legal status, laws, etc. | Prisoners of war—Legal status,
laws, etc. | Detention of persons. | War crimes.
Classification: LCC KZ6355.C67 2018 | DDC 341.6—dc23
LC record available at https://lccn.loc.gov/2018002753

ISBN: 978-1-138-91047-8 (hbk)
ISBN: 978-1-138-91048-5 (pbk)
ISBN: 978-1-315-69340-8 (ebk)

Typeset in Galliard
by Florence Production Ltd, Stoodleigh, Devon, UK

Contents

Foreword

International humanitarian law, or the law of armed conflict, has never been more relevant than it is today. Even those with no military or legal background understand that international law imposes limits on the conduct of armed forces and organized armed groups engaged in hostilities, and requires respect for the fundamental human rights of war victims. This book is intended to contribute to a more informed understanding of this important branch of international law.

In deciding to collaborate on this project, we three authors sought to leverage a variety of perspectives and experiences to this book. International humanitarian law has been a central focus of each of our professional experiences. Our collective interest in the law is therefore grounded in practical experience, but from quite different perspectives. We hope this results in not only a comprehensive overview of the law but one that is reflective of these different perspectives.

We know that anyone considering this book will have the choice of many excellent options. Our goal was to provide a concise overview of international humanitarian law, one that is equally accessible to the non-lawyer as it is to the lawyer; and that is equally valuable to the practitioner as it is to the interested member of society. To that end, we have selected the aspects of the law we believe are most essential for providing such an overview. While a more extensive treatment of many of these aspects of the law would certainly have been possible, our goal was to provide an outline of the law. Nonetheless, we believe our overview is sufficiently comprehensive to substantially contribute to a meaningful understanding of how international humanitarian law actually impacts military operations.

Finally, we must commend our research assistant, Andrew Culliver, who graduated with his Juris Doctor degree from the South Texas College of Law Houston in May 2017 and began his career as First Lieutenant in the U.S. Army Judge Advocate General's Corps in January 2018. Andrew's contribution to this book was essential in its completion, and his diligence and selflessness deserves our highest praise. It is especially meaningful for us that his efforts were so central to completing a project that will hopefully contribute to his own professional development and that of his JAG peers.

Abbreviations

Additional Protocol I *or* AP I *or* 1977 Protocol I	Protocol (I) Additional to the Geneva Conventions of 12 August 1949, and Relating to the Protection of Victims of International Armed Conflicts, 8 June 1977
Additional Protocol II *or* AP II *or* 1977 Protocol II	Protocol (II) Additional to the Geneva Conventions of 12 August 1949, and Relating to the Protection of Victims of International Armed Conflicts, 8 June 1977
Additional Protocol III *or* AP III	Protocol (III) Additional to the Geneva Conventions of 12 August 1949, and Relating to the Adoption of an Additional Distinctive Emblem, 8 December 2005
AP Commentary	Commentary on the Additional Protocols of 8 June 1977 to the Geneva Conventions of 12 August 1949
AFRC	Armed Forces Revolutionary Council (a rebel group formerly in Sierra Leone)
AR	Army Regulation (United States)
ATACMS	Army Tactical Missile System (United States)
AUMF	Authorization for Use of Military Force (United States)
BWC	Convention on the Prohibition of the Development, Production and Stockpiling of Bacteriological (Biological) and Toxin Weapons and on Their Destruction, 10 April 1972
Common Article 2 *or* CA2	Article 2 common to all four of the Geneva Conventions, 12 August 1949
Common Article 3 *or* CA3	Article 3 common to all four of the Geneva Conventions, 12 August 1949
CAT	Convention Against Torture and Other Cruel, Inhuman or Degrading Treatment or Punishment, 10 December 1984

CCW	Convention on Prohibitions or Restrictions on the Use of Certain Conventional Weapons Which May Be Deemed to Be Excessively Injurious or to Have Indiscriminate Effects, 10 October 1980
CDF	Civil Defense Force (a paramilitary organization that operated during the Sierra Leone Civil War)
CIL	Customary international law
CIWS	(Phalanx) Close-In Weapons System (United States)
CNA	Computer network attack
CPL	Civilian Protection Law
CRC	Convention on the Rights of the Child, 20 November 1989
CS gas	2-chlorobenzalmalononitrile (a component of tear gas)
CSRT	Combatant Status Review Tribunals (United States)
CWC	Convention on the Prohibition of the Development, Production, Stockpiling and Use of Chemical Weapons and on Their Destruction, 13 January 1993
DoD	Department of Defense (U.S.)
DPH	Direct participation in hostilities
ECCC	Extraordinary Chambers in the Courts of Cambodia
EEZ	Exclusive economic zone
ENMOD	Convention on the Prohibition of Military or Any Other Hostile Use of Environmental Modification Techniques, 18 May 1977
EPW	Enemy prisoners of war
ERW	Explosive remnants of war
European Convention on Human Rights *or* ECHR	Convention for the Protection of Human Rights and Fundamental Freedoms, 3 September 1953
EU	European Union
FARC	Revolutionary Armed Forces of Columbia *or* Fuerzas Armadas Revolucionarias de Colombia
Geneva Law	Law attributable to the protection of victims of armed conflict
1864 Geneva Convention	Geneva Convention for the Amelioration of the Condition of the Wounded in Armies in the Field, 22 August 1864

GWS *or* First Geneva Convention *or* Geneva I *or* GC I	Geneva Convention for the Amelioration of the Condition of the Wounded and Sick in Armed Forces in the Field, 12 August 1949
1906 GWS *or* 1906 Geneva Convention	Geneva Convention for the Amelioration of the Condition of the Wounded and Sick in Armies in the Field, 6 July 1906
1929 GWS	Geneva Convention for the Amelioration of the Condition of the Wounded and Sick of Armies in the Field, 27 July 1929
GWS-Sea *or* Second Geneva Convention *or* Geneva II *or* GC II	Geneva Convention for the Amelioration of the Condition of Wounded, Sick, and Shipwrecked Members of the Armed Forces at Sea, 12 August 1949
GPW *or* Third Geneva Convention *or* Geneva III *or* GC III	Geneva Convention Relative to the Treatment of Prisoners of War, 12 August 1949
1929 GPW	Geneva Convention Relative to the Treatment of Prisoners of War, 27 July 1929
GC *or* Fourth Geneva Convention *or* Geneva IV *or* GC IV	Geneva Convention Relative to the Protection of Civilian Persons in Time of War, 12 August 1949
Hague Law	Law attributable to the conduct of hostilities
1907 Hague IV Regulations *or* 1907 Hague Regulations *or* 1907 Hague Land Warfare Regulations *or* Hague IV *or* 1907 Regulations	Convention (IV) Respecting the Laws and Customs War on Land and its annex: Regulations concerning the Laws and Customs of War on Land, 18 October 1907
HIMARS	High Mobility Artillery Rocket (United States)
HPCR Air and Missile Warfare Manual *or* HPCR AMWM	Program on Humanitarian Policy and Conflict Research *Manual on International Law Applicable to Air and Missile Warfare*
IAC	International armed conflict
ICC	International Criminal Court
ICCPR	International Covenant on Civil and Political Rights, 16 December 1966
ICJ	International Court of Justice
ICL	International criminal law

ICRC	International Committee of the Red Cross
ICTR	International Criminal Tribunal for the Prosecution of Persons Responsible for Genocide and Other Serious Violations of International Humanitarian Law Committed in the Territory of Rwanda and Rwandan Citizens Responsible for Genocide and Other Such Violations Committed in the Territory of Neighbouring States, between 1 January 1994 and 31 December 1994
ICTY	International Tribunal for the Prosecution of Persons Responsible for Serious Violations of International Humanitarian Law Committed in the Territory of the Former Yugoslavia since 1991 *or* International Criminal Tribunal for the former Yugoslavia
IDF	Israeli Defense Forces
IED	Improvised explosive device
IHFFC	International Humanitarian Fact-Finding Commission
IHL	International humanitarian law (synonymous with law of armed conflict or LOAC)
IHRL	International human rights law
ISIS *or* ISIL	Islamic State of Iraq and Syria *or* Islamic State of Iraq and the Levant
JNA	Yugoslav People's Army
KLA	Kosovo Liberation Army
LOAC	Law of armed conflict (synonymous with international humanitarian law or IHL)
LRM	Least restrictive means (theory)
MICT	International Residual Mechanism for Criminal Tribunals
MOOTW	Military operations other than war
MRLS	Multiple Rocket Launch System (United States)
NATO/OTAN	North Atlantic Treaty Organization/Organisation du Traité de l'Atlantique Nord
NEO	Non-combatant evacuation operation
NIAC	Non-international armed conflict
NOTAM	Notice to airmen

Ottawa Convention *or* 1997 Ottawa Convention	Convention on the Prohibition of the Use, Stockpiling, Production and Transfer of Anti-Personnel Mines and on Their Destruction, 18 September 1997
PFLP	Popular Front for the Liberation of Palestine
PLO	Palestine Liberation Organization
POW	Prisoner of war
ROE	Rules of engagement
1998 Rome Statute *or* Rome Statute	Rome Statute of the International Criminal Court, 17 July 1998
RP	Retained person(s) *or* retained personnel
RSCSL	Residual Special Court for Sierra Leone
RUF	Revolutionary United Front (a rebel group formerly in Sierra Leone)
SAS	Special Air Service (United Kingdom)
SBS	Special Boat Service (United Kingdom)
SCSL	Special Court for Sierra Leone
SEALs	"Sea, Air, Land" special forces (United States)
SROE	Standing rules of engagement
THAAD	Terminal High Altitude Area Defense (United States)
UAV/UCAV	Unmanned aerial vehicle/unmanned combat aerial vehicle
UN	United Nations
UNGA	United Nations General Assembly
UDHR *or* 1948 Universal Declaration on Human Rights	Universal Declaration on Human Rights, 10 December 1948
UNSC	United Nations Security Council
UK	United Kingdom of Great Britain and Northern Ireland
US *or* U.S.	United States
USA	United States Army
USN	United States Navy
UXO	Unexploded ordinance
VJ	Army of the Federal Republic of Yugoslavia

VRS	Army of the Serbian Republic of Bosnia and Herzegovina/Republika Srpska
9/11	11 September 2001 terror attacks in the United States

Introduction

War has been an unfortunate part of human existence from the beginning of recorded history, despite periodic efforts to eliminate war from human relations. While the very nature of warfare is inherently chaotic, for as long as warfare has been a reality, man has tried to inject a certain degree of order. What can very generally be labeled as *rules and customs of war* have and remain a defining characteristic of warfare, in a very real sense the thing that distinguishes war from total chaos.

These rules have taken different forms, included different content, and were derived from differing sources throughout history. But, as international law emerged as a source of regulation for relations between sovereign States, rules of war took a prominent place in the emerging body of customary international law. This was most notably the case for the nations of Europe, and to a lesser extent the new nations in North and South America that grew out of the seeds of European colonization. For centuries, a handful of highly respected international law scholars provided treatises that detailed the accepted rules of conduct in warfare.

The American Civil War proved to be a transformative event in the evolution of the laws and customs of war. Unlike European nations, neither the United States nor the newly formed Confederate States of America could call on a large professional military steeped in the customs of the professional warrior. Instead, consistent with the American aversion for standing armies, this massive and brutal conflict would be fought primarily by citizen-soldiers on both sides of the battle lines. Recognizing that this rapid formation of a massive unprofessional army necessitated more concrete rules of conduct, General Henry Halleck, the commander of all Union armed forces, commissioned Professor Francis Lieber of Columbia University to draft what was in essence a code of conduct for the Union armed forces that enumerated rules of customary international law. Lieber's effort would be issued as General Order Number 100, and known thereafter as the Lieber Code. The idea of enumerating rules of war for the force also appealed to the Confederacy, which also adopted Lieber's Code.

This initiated what is best understand as an era of codification, which progressed along two related but somewhat distinct tracks. On one track was the effort to ameliorate the suffering of victims of war, which began with the First Geneva

Convention of 1864, devoted to the protection, collection, and care for the wounded and sick on the battlefield. Over the next approximatly 80 years, this Geneva tradition would bear fruit in the form of multiple treaties devoted to the protection of distinct classes of war victims: the wounded and shipwrecked at sea, prisoners of war, and civilians under enemy control. These four Geneva Conventions would earn the distinct status of the only treaties universally ratified by the community of nations. On the other track were efforts to regulate the conduct of hostilities—how armies fought one another. This began modestly with a treaty banning what was at the time considered an especially pernicious weapon—the bullet that exploded upon impact. But this was a landmark treaty, for it initiated the process of developing multilateral treaty regulations related to both the means (weapons) and methods (tactics) of warfare. In 1899, and again in 1907, such regulations were adopted as part of The Hague Convention IV.

Since that time, treaty law and customary law have continued to evolve, creating what is often a complex and in many ways symbiotic relationship with one another. Many rules considered customary in nature have been incorporated into specific treaty provisions; other new rules adopted in treaties have been so pervasively followed that they are today considered customary in nature, therefore binding on even non-treaty States. Other treaty rules are, as the result of rejection by non-treaty States or through reservations lodged by States upon treaty ratification, binding only on those States that have expressly agreed to them. This relationship between treaty and customary international law will be a consistent feature of the chapters that follow.

Collectively, these efforts to create a body of law governing armed conflict have resulted in the creation of a body of law historically called the law of war, but today more commonly referred to as the law of armed conflict (LOAC) or international humanitarian law (IHL). These designations are synonymous in terms of the law they refer to, but as IHL is the more common characterization today it will be the primary characterization used throughout this text.

One especially significant IHL evolution has been in relation to the regulation of what are known as non-international armed conflicts (NIACs). Prior to 1949, international law played little to no role in the regulation of conflicts other than those between States: so-called international armed conflicts (IACs). There were some civil wars that fell within the scope of this international legal regulation by operation of a doctrine called recognition of belligerency, whereby both parties to the conflict, because they manifested indications of statehood, were treated as States for purposes of both international legal regulation, and so that neutral States could rely in the international law of neutrality when dealing with them. For example, a number of European nations recognized the Confederate States of America as a belligerent during the American Civil War. However, this was a rare exception to the more general reality that conflicts between States and non-State belligerent groups were not considered "wars" within the meaning of international law, and therefore beyond the scope of the international laws and customs of war.

The International Committee of the Red Cross, the organization created by the First Geneva Convention and vested with the specific mandate to monitor compliance with the Conventions and facilitate implementation of the Conventions, sought to address this humanitarian gap during the conference called to revise the 1929 Geneva Conventions that resulted in the 1949 version of these treaties. It proposed extending application of the four Conventions to any armed conflict, whether international (inter-State) or non-international (generally understood at that time as intra-State). The assembled State delegations ultimately rejected this proposal, but did agree to include within the four Conventions a single Article imposing on parties to a NIAC the obligation to treat humanely any individual not actively participating in hostilities. The first express imposition of humanitarian regulation to NIACs, this "common article" provided a foundation for subsequent efforts to provide humanitarian constraints and obligations on parties involved in such armed conflicts, a process that continues to this day and will be addressed in Chapter 1 of this text.

Another important evolution of IHL occurred in relation to accountability for violations. As will be explored, prior to World War I international law was understood as imposing obligations exclusively upon States, and not on individuals. As a result, remedies for violations of the laws and customs of war involved actions by one State directed against another. Beginning with the Treaty of Versailles, this changed. In order to enhance the effectiveness of the law, individuals were subjected to accountability for their violations of what is today IHL. This notion of individual responsibility advanced in fits and starts, but today is firmly rooted in the fabric of international criminal law (ICL). Nonetheless, there are important and complex questions abound where IHL intersects with ICL, ranging from the relationship between State and international criminal jurisdiction, to requisite criminal state of mind for transforming a violation of regulatory norms into a basis for criminal responsibility, to liability of leaders for their failure to ensure compliance with the law.

All of these issues, and many more, will be addressed in the chapters that follow. Our goal is not to provide a comprehensive restatement of the law, or even a comprehensive treatise on the law. Instead, we hope to provide an accessible overview of the law, exposing the reader to the most important legal concepts, lingering and emerging areas of uncertainty, and an appreciation of how law impacts the planning and execution of military operations.

1 International humanitarian law application

1 Introduction

Understanding how international humanitarian law (IHL) regulates hostilities begins with assessing the conditions that bring this body of international law into force. Unlike most areas of domestic law, IHL is not constantly in force. IHL only applies when there is an armed conflict in existence.[1] The existence of an armed conflict is dependent upon certain conditions being satisfied—conditions that indicate a need for the regulatory effect of this law—that it will become obligatory on those engaged in hostilities, and to a lesser extent even neutral States.

2 Origins of the conflict classification paradigm

Prior to 1949, the laws and customs of war, in the form of both treaty obligations and customary international law, applied during war. *War*, in turn, was understood not in the pragmatic sense of hostilities between organized armed enemies but instead in the legal sense. Following World War II, this legally technical condition precedent to the applicability of the laws of war was identified as undermining the humanitarian objectives of the law. States engaged in hostilities that undoubtedly necessitated the regulatory benefit of the law could hide behind these technicalities to avoid the law and expand their zone of operational impunity.

The response to this impediment was a central focus during the two-year process of revising the 1929 Geneva Conventions. The drafters of these IHL treaties were determined to link application of these humanitarian protection treaties to situations of de facto hostilities and decouple application from formalistic legal concepts. Accordingly, each of the four treaties that emerged from the revision effort—the four Geneva Conventions of 1949—included two *Common Articles* dictating treaty application. Armed conflict, and not war, became the focal point for this applicability. Common Article 2 of the treaties addressed situations of inter-State hostilities, indicating that each treaty applied to all cases of declared war, belligerent occupation, or any other armed conflict between contracting parties, or States—so-called *international armed conflicts*

(IACs). The effort to link applicability of humanitarian regulation to de facto hostilities did not end there. Instead, in an even more progressive development, Common Article 3 of each treaty extended basic humanitarian protection to armed conflict not of an international character, in other words hostilities between States and non-State groups—so-called *non-international armed conflicts* (NIACs). Subsequent treaties, such as the 1977 Protocols Additional to the 1949 Geneva Conventions also contain provisions that help identify the scope and nature of an armed conflict.

2.1 The triggers—Common Articles 2 and 3

The significance of the law-triggering threshold established by these two treaty provisions has evolved substantially since 1949. At that time, they only impacted the applicability of the Geneva Conventions. Today, however, they are recognized as establishing the triggering standard for IHL at large, to include not only the Geneva Conventions, but other provisions of treaty and customary IHL.

As noted above, Common Article 2 addressed situations of formal and de facto inter-State hostilities,[2] providing that:

> The present Convention shall apply to all cases of declared war or of any other armed conflict which may arise between two or more of the High Contracting Parties, even if the state of war is not recognized by one of them.
>
> The Convention shall also apply to all cases of partial or total occupation of the territory of a High Contracting Party, even if the said occupation meets with no armed resistance.[3]

Like all other Geneva Convention Articles, the Commentary to the treaties prepared by the International Committee of the Red Cross provides important insight into the intended meaning and effect of Common Article 2. Specifically, the Commentary confirms that the inclusion of both a de jure and de facto law trigger was adopted to foreclose law avoidance at the peril of those most in need of humanitarian protection:

> Article 2(1) encompasses the concepts of "declared war" and "armed conflict". Both trigger the application of the Geneva Conventions but cover different legal realities, the latter being more flexible and objective than the former. However, they are complementary, may even overlap, and cover a larger spectrum of belligerent relationships than was the case in the law prior to the 1949 Geneva Conventions.
>
> The rationale of Article 2(1) is to extend the scope of application of the Geneva Conventions so that their provisions come into force even when hostilities between States do not result from a formal declaration of war. In this way, Article 2(1) serves the humanitarian purpose of the Geneva Conventions by minimizing the possibility for States to evade their

obligations under humanitarian law simply by not declaring war or refusing to acknowledge the existence of an armed conflict.[4]

The Commentary also indicates that, consistent with the humanitarian objective of the treaties, even hostilities of short duration, limited geographic scope, or limited intensity trigger the law:

> For international armed conflict, there is no requirement that the use of armed force between the Parties reach a certain level of intensity before it can be said that an armed conflict exists. Article 2(1) itself contains no mention of any threshold for the intensity or duration of hostilities. Indeed, in the frequently cited 1958 commentary on common Article 2, Pictet stated:
>
> Any difference arising between two States and leading to the intervention of members of the armed forces is an armed conflict within the meaning of Article 2, even if one of the Parties denies the existence of a state of war. It makes no difference how long the conflict lasts, or how much slaughter takes place. The respect due to the human person as such is not measured by the number of victims.[5]

As noted above, the Conventions did not restrict application of humanitarian protections to inter-State hostilities. Instead, they expanded the scope of IHL coverage to the realm of what was characterized as armed conflicts not of an international character. While the prevalence of this type of conflict since 1949 may suggest this was unremarkable, at that time it was anything but. While pressed by advocates of humanitarian protection based on the sheer logic that the nature of the parties to an armed conflict in no way impacts the necessity of conflict regulation, States perceived this extension as a serious intrusion into their sphere of sovereign prerogative, and resisted proposals to make the law applicable to these conflicts co-extensive with the law applicable to IACs.

The compromise that emerged took the form of Common Article 3. Like Common Article 2, it established the trigger for the much more limited humanitarian regulation extended to this type of armed conflict. These regulations were included within Common Article 3 itself, which explains why it was referred to as a "Convention in miniature."[6] According to the Article, this limited regulation applies "[i]n the case of armed conflict not of an international character occurring in the territory of one of the High Contracting Parties."[7]

Ultimately, Common Articles 2 and 3 evolved to function as *triggering* conduits for assessing the applicability of the law governing these two categories of armed conflicts, meaning all applicable IHL treaty provisions and applicable IHL customary international law. Common Article 3 indicates situations that require application of the Article's substantive obligation to provide humane treatment to any individual not actively participating in hostilities,[8] and other customary IHL obligations now applicable to NIACs. In contrast, Common

Article 2 indicates when the substantive rules contained in all the other Articles of the Geneva Conventions become applicable,[9] as well as other treaty and customary IHL obligations applicable to IACs. Accordingly, contemporary IHL application is contingent on two essential factors: first, the existence of armed conflict; second, the nature of the armed conflict.[10]

2.2 *The existence of an armed conflict*

Armed conflict is the common requirement for both Common Articles 2 and 3. The term *armed conflict* was not, however, defined in the Conventions, although the ICRC Commentary is considered instructive on the meaning of this term. Based on the Commentary and the pragmatic purpose of Articles 2 and 3, assessing the existence of armed conflict involves consideration of a range of factors, with no single factor playing a dispositive role. These factors should be assessed on a case-by-case basis in order to link law applicability with de facto reality.[11]

With respect to IAC, neither motive for nor characterization of disputes between two States should influence the assessment of armed conflict, so long as the underlying use of military force is in response to an inter-State dispute. And, in practice, the dispute element itself may be inferred from the break out of hostilities between the armed forces of two States. This may, however, justify denying an armed conflict characterization for an inadvertent cross-border incursion by armed forces into the territory of another State, so long as the incursion does not result in actual hostilities. But where even an inadvertent incursion results in actual hostilities between armed forces, an armed conflict occurs. For example, the United States asserted the existence of an armed conflict after four U.S. soldiers serving as part of a United Nations peacekeeping mission in Macedonia were placed under fire and captured by Serbian forces after allegedly crossing the border into Serbia without authority.[12]

The Commentary to Article 2 indicates that an armed conflict exists whenever two or more States resort to the use of military forces in response to a dispute between them. Even confrontations of short duration or minimal intensity qualify as such, a point emphasized above from the ICRC Commentary:

> For international armed conflict, there is no requirement that the use of armed force between the Parties reach a certain level of intensity before it can be said that an armed conflict exists. Article 2(1) itself contains no mention of any threshold for the intensity or duration of hostilities.[13]

Since 1949, States have frequently invoked this expansive definition of armed conflict, especially when seeking humanitarian protection for their service personnel during inter-State conflict. Thus, for the purposes of assessing the existence of an IAC within the meaning of Common Article 2, duration and intensity of hostilities should play virtually no role, so long as the hostilities are the result of a dispute between the States. Furthermore, from a pragmatic perspective, it is difficult to see how actual fighting between the armed forces of two States can be attributed to anything other than a dispute. Accordingly, while an inadvertent confrontation between armed forces that does not escalate into hostilities can arguably be excluded from the definition of armed conflict, any actual outbreak of hostilities should fall within that definition.

In contrast, as international law has developed, the intensity and duration of hostilities appear to be essential considerations when assessing the existence of NIACs—armed conflicts between a State and a non-State organized armed group, or between such organized armed groups.[14] Although by 1949 there was sufficient State support for extending basic humanitarian protection to this category of hostilities, there was no consensus on the extent of such protection, or the point at which an armed conflict arose.[15]

States quickly rejected the ICRC's initial proposal to apply all Geneva Convention provisions to both IAC and NIAC.[16] States were not indicating an indifference to the human suffering associated with such hostilities. Instead, they were hesitant to cede their sovereign prerogative to deal with internal armed dissident challenges (the primary focus of the NIAC debate) by committing to extensive international legal regulation.[17] Central to this resistance was the concern that adopting the ICRC proposal might contribute to the legitimacy of domestic dissident violence.[18]

What emerged from the revision conference was a humanitarian compromise: extend a humane treatment obligation to all individuals taking no active part in hostilities, whether because they are not participants in hostilities or because they have been rendered *hors de combat* (out of the fight) as the result of wounds, sickness, or capture.[19] Because this obligation was imposed on "each party to the conflict," it was clear that the existence of armed conflict was the necessary triggering requirement.[20] However, by recognizing a legal category of armed conflict outside the inter-State context, a new level of complexity was added to the definitional challenge: what indicates the existence of a NIAC?

This question has always been complicated by the fact that disturbances within a State range across a spectrum from sporadic disorganized violence to hostilities between highly organized armed groups bearing the traditional indicia of regular armed forces. In the latter situation, the existence of armed conflict will be difficult to dispute. However, because insurgencies routinely involve a progression from criminal activity to more concerted military-type challenges to government authority, identifying at what stage of development a non-State threat becomes an armed conflict is always difficult.

There is simply no easy answer to this complex question. What is clear is that an armed conflict requires at least two competing parties (i.e., organized armed groups) involved in armed violence of sufficient intensity, as only such a situation justifies IHL application.[21] It is equally clear that many internal threats will fail to rise to this level, and therefore fall below the threshold of IHL regulation. So much was emphasized by both the original 1952 and current 2016 ICRC Commentaries:

The threshold for NIACs is different to that for IACs . . .

Pictet's 1952 Commentary on the First Geneva Convention, referring to the absence of a definition of the term *armed conflict not of an international character*, stated:

[M]any of the delegations feared that it might be taken to cover any act committed by force of arms—any form of anarchy, rebellion, or even plain banditry. For example, if a handful of individuals were to rise in rebellion against the State and attack a police station, would that suffice to bring into being an armed conflict within the meaning of the Article?

These concerns relating to sovereignty help to explain the higher threshold for the applicability of humanitarian law in non-international armed conflict than in international armed conflict.[22]

It would therefore be wrong to focus on any single factor to assess this demarcation point. Instead, as is proposed by the 1952 Commentary, a totality approach that considers all relevant factors is required:

[T]hese different conditions, although in no way obligatory, constitute convenient criteria, and we therefore think it well to give a list of those contained in the various amendments discussed; they are as follows:

(1) That the Party in revolt against the de jure Government possesses an organized military force, an authority responsible for its acts, acting within a determinate territory and having the means of respecting and ensuring respect for the Convention.

(2) That the legal Government is obliged to have recourse to the regular military forces against insurgents organized as military and in possession of a part of the national territory.

(3) (a) That the de jure Government has recognized the insurgents as belligerents; or

(b) that it has claimed for itself the rights of a belligerent; or

(c) that it has accorded the insurgents recognition as belligerents for the purposes only of the present Convention; or

(d) that the dispute has been admitted to the agenda of the Security Council or the General Assembly of the United Nations as being a threat to international peace, a breach of the peace, or an act of aggression.

(4) (a) That the insurgents have an organisation purporting to have the characteristics of a State.

(b) That the insurgent civil authority exercises de facto authority over persons within a determinate territory.

(c) That the armed forces act under the direction of the organized civil authority and are prepared to observe the ordinary laws of war.

(d) That the insurgent civil authority agrees to be bound by the provisions of the Convention.[23]

The 2016 Commentary adds the following:

> Since common Article 3 as finally adopted abandoned the idea of a full application of the Geneva Conventions to non-international armed conflicts, in exchange for a wide scope of application, not all of these criteria are fully adapted to common Article 3. Nonetheless, if met, the "convenient criteria" may certainly indicate the existence of a non-international armed conflict.
>
> Over time, of the criteria enumerated in the Pictet Commentaries, two are now widely acknowledged as being the most relevant in assessing the existence of a non-international armed conflict: that the violence needs to have reached a certain intensity and that it must be between at least two organized Parties/armed groups. The existence of a non-international armed conflict thus needs to be assessed according to these specific criteria.[24]

In practice, the combined effect of factors (2), and (4)(a) and (c) have been particularly instructive: "the legal Government is obliged to have recourse to the regular military forces against insurgents organized as military"; "insurgents have an organisation purporting to have the characteristics of a State"; and those State armed forces "are prepared to observe the ordinary laws of war" even when acting under civil authority.[25] These three factors focus on an apparent difference between normal law enforcement activities and armed conflict. When the State resorts to the combat capabilities of regular armed forces, it certainly suggests the situation has crossed the demarcation into the realm of armed conflict, and the violence involves those armed forces fighting an opposing force that threatens violence above that associated with simple banditry.

This is especially true when the ensuing violence is protracted, a consideration emphasized by the International Criminal Tribunal for the former Yugoslavia (ICTY)—the ad hoc international tribunal created by the UN Security Council to prosecute individuals who committed genocide, war crimes, and crimes against humanity following the breakup of the former Yugoslavia. In *Prosecutor v. Tadić*, the Tribunal concluded that "an armed conflict exists whenever there is a resort to armed force between States or protracted armed violence between governmental authorities and organised armed groups or between such groups within a State."[26] In *Prosecutor v. Haradinaj*, the ICTY later concluded that the notion of *protracted armed violence* must be understood to include not only the duration of the violence but also all aspects that would enable the degree of intensity to be evaluated.[27]

This protraction/intensity equation is consistent with Common Article 3 because it facilitates distinction between civil strife or other acts of general lawlessness and actual armed hostilities (although it should be noted that today the substantive humane treatment obligation of Common Article 3 would be obligatory even outside the context of armed conflict by operation of fundamental human rights obligations, a point emphasized by the ICRC Commentary to Common Article 3).[28] However, although these additional factors are significant, they should not be understood as altering the totality of the circumstances analysis proposed by the ICRC Commentary. Instead, as one commentator has said, these judgments reinforce the need to consider a variety of relevant indicia, including

> the collective nature of the fighting or the fact that the State is obliged to resort to its army as its police forces are no longer able to deal with the situation on their own. The duration of the conflict, the frequency of the acts of violence and military operations, the nature of the weapons used, displacement of civilians, territorial control by opposition forces, the number of victims (dead, wounded, displaced persons, etc.) are also pieces of information that may be taken into account.[29]

Ultimately, no formula can guarantee a perfect symmetry between ground truth and recognition or acknowledgment of the same. However, the Commentary, jurisprudence of international tribunals, and an ever-increasing body of scholarly treatment of this issue have all contributed to providing additional clarity to the meaning of NIAC. This clarity has in turn contributed to greater predictability that Common Article 3's humanitarian protections will apply during conflicts that often involve a level of brutality that rival if not exceed that associated with inter-State conflicts.

2.3   The nature of the armed conflict

The second element in the IHL application equation is assessing the nature of the armed conflict: international or non-international, which in turn dictates the extent of IHL regulation. As noted, Common Article 2 IACs trigger the full corpus of IHL, whereas Common Article 3 NIACs trigger a much more limited set of IHL protections under both treaty[30] and customary law.[31] While the customary law rules do provide as broad a protection in internal conflict, they have been recognized to

> cover such areas as protection of civilians from hostilities, in particular from indiscriminate attacks, protection of civilian objects, in particular cultural property, protection of all those who do not (or no longer) take active part in hostilities, as well as prohibition of means of warfare proscribed in international armed conflicts and ban of certain methods of conducting hostilities.[32]

Although not explicitly defined in Common Articles 2 or 3, defining *international* and *non-international* has been much less problematic than defining armed conflict. Reference to the Geneva Conventions and discussion of these terms in the ICRC Commentary indicates *international* is a synonym for *inter-State*.[33] This includes situations where one State involved in the dispute refuses to recognize the legitimacy of the opposing State, or that the intervention of armed forces by one State meets no military resistance by the other State. As long as the use of armed force is the product of an underlying inter-State dispute, the conflict is considered an IAC.[34]

This broad meaning of international has not, however, eliminated all uncertainty. Where one State intervenes in the territory of another to conduct operations against a non-State group in that territory with no opposition from the territorial State,[35] or where the territorial State is considered a *failed State* with no functioning central government,[36] there may be assertions that the intervention is not the result of an inter-State dispute.[37] These, however, are rare exceptions to the general rule. Since 1949, identifying when an armed conflict qualifies as international within the meaning of Common Article 2 has not been particularly challenging.

As for the term *non-international*, in 1949 it generated little uncertainty—it simply meant intra-State. Today, however, the meaning of this term is has attracted considerable additional scrutiny. This scrutiny was generated in large measure by the U.S.-led military response to the terrorist attacks of 11 September 2001. These military operations, and those of other States such as Israel in respect of terrorist threats largely in territory adjacent to its borders, led to debates over the proper characterization of an armed conflict against non-State belligerent groups operating not in the territory of the State conducting the operations but transnationally.[38]

Common Article 3 indicates that these armed conflicts occur "within the territory of one of the High Contracting Parties."[39] This provides some support for the conclusion that a non-international is a synonym for intra-State, or internal. This original understanding of Common Article 3, coupled with the reality that the vast majority of NIACs between 1949 and 2001 were predominantly intra-State, produced an either/or law-triggering equation: armed conflicts were either *inter*-State, falling under Common Article 2, or *intra*-State, falling under Common Article 3.[40]

However, once the Geneva Conventions became universally ratified, it became apparent that *any* armed conflict between a State and a non-State opponent would ipso facto occur "in the territory of one of the High Contracting Parties." It was, however, the U.S. characterization of its response against al Qaeda as an armed conflict that fundamentally challenged this either/or assumption. Because al Qaeda was not a State, the United States did not consider the conflict international.[41] Nor, however, was the conflict internal, as al Qaeda operated transnationally. The Bush administration initially sought to treat the operations as an armed conflict outside the scope of either Common Article 2 or 3.[42] However, the United States would ultimately adopt an alternative legal position: this was (and remains) a NIAC within the meaning of Common Article 3, but one of international scope; or the less confusing characterization of transnational armed conflict. The Supreme Court affirmed this expanded interpretation of Common Article 3 in *Hamdan v. Rumsfeld*,[43] when it rejected the Government's argument that consistent with the original purpose of Common Article 3, non-international meant only intra-State:

The Court of Appeals thought, and the Government asserts, that Common Article 3 does not apply to Hamdan because the conflict with al Qaeda, being "international in scope," does not qualify as a "conflict not of an international character." That reasoning is erroneous. The term "conflict not of an international character" is used here in contradistinction to a conflict between nations. So much is demonstrated by the "fundamental logic [of] the Convention's provisions on its application." Common Article 2 provides that "the present Convention shall apply to all cases of declared war or of any other armed conflict which may arise between two or more of the High Contracting Parties." High Contracting Parties (signatories) also must abide by all terms of the Conventions vis-a-vis one another even if one party to the conflict is a nonsignatory "Power," and must so abide vis-a-vis the nonsignatory if "the latter accepts and applies" those terms. Common Article 3, by contrast, affords some minimal protection, falling short of full protection under the Conventions, to individuals associated with neither a signatory nor even a nonsignatory "Power" who are involved in a conflict "in the territory of" a signatory. The latter kind of conflict is distinguishable from the conflict described in Common Article 2 chiefly because it does not involve a clash between nations (whether signatories or not). In context, then, the phrase "not of an international character" bears its literal meaning.[44]

This interpretation of NIAC remains controversial. Many international legal experts reject this notion of a NIAC of transnational scope. These experts are especially skeptical about characterizing counterterror operations as an armed conflict owing to their sporadic nature.[45] Nonetheless, it is increasingly difficult to dismiss this interpretation, especially as States continue to confront similar types of transnational armed non-State threats (*see* Chapter 2: *Non-international armed conflict*).

3   The impact of the 1977 Additional Protocols

In 1977, two treaties were created to update the 1949 Geneva Conventions: Additional Protocol I (AP I) supplemented the law applicable to IACs;[46] Additional Protocol II (AP II) supplemented the law applicable to NIACs.[47] And, unlike the Geneva Conventions they complemented, both treaties addressed both the humanitarian protection of victims of armed conflict *and* the regulation of means (weapons) and methods (tactics) of warfare.[48] Furthermore, each new treaty included an Article defining its scope of application, adding an additional dimension to the Common Article 2/3 law-triggering equation.

Article 1 of AP I indicates that the Protocol applies to all situations referred to in Common Article 2 of the Geneva Conventions.[49] However, it also included within the scope of application:

> Armed conflicts in which peoples are fighting against colonial domination and alien occupation and against racist régimes in the exercise of their right

of self-determination, as enshrined in the Charter of the United Nations and the Declaration on Principles of International Law concerning Friendly Relations and Co-operation among States in accordance with the Charter of the United Nations.[50]

By effectively redefining what had before been considered a NIAC as international based on the *causus belli* of the non-State Party, this provision of Article 1 substantially altered the definition of IAC. This initially led to significant resistance, as some States considered this inconsistent with the underlying purpose of Common Article 2: extracting political considerations from the law applicability determination.[51] Although in 1949 these conflicts would almost certainly have been understood as falling into the category of non-international,[52] by 1975 many States were prepared to extend the full protection of IHL to limited wars for national liberation.

In 2014, nearly 90 percent of States were reported to be parties to AP I,[53] although there remained a number of major military powers, such as China, India, Iran, Pakistan, and the United States, that had not ratified this treaty (although, as will be explained in the subsequent chapters, even these States consider many of Articles of the treaty binding as customary international law).[54] States that have opposed this expansion either refused to commit to the Protocol, or opted out of the expansion by treaty reservation.[55] Nonetheless, States bound by AP I without qualification must treat these objective NIACs as IACs for purposes of law applicability, although overall it has been suggested to have been a relatively minor change to existing law.[56] The scope for its application appears limited because the right of self-determination has been so narrowly interpreted.[57]

Like AP I, AP II also includes a scope of application provision that indicates the treaty supplements Common Article 3 without "modifying its existing conditions of application." This assertion, however, is dubious. In fact, Article 1 of AP II deviated from Common Article 3's broad totality approach for assessing the existence of a NIAC, and instead restricted application of AP II to only a certain type of NIAC: a purely internal armed conflict in which the dissident forces establish and maintain control over a portion of the national territory. This is expressly acknowledged in the ICRC Commentary, which notes:

> At first sight the article seems to be based on complicated concepts. In fact, the Protocol only applies to conflicts of a certain degree of intensity and does not have exactly the same field of application as common Article 3, which applies in all situations of non-international armed conflict.[58]

The Commentary further notes that:

> The ICRC proposed a broad definition based on material criteria: the existence of a confrontation between armed forces or other organized armed groups under responsible command, i.e., with a minimum degree of organization. . . . The three criteria that were finally adopted on the side

of the insurgents i.e.—a responsible command, such control over part of the territory as to enable them to carry out sustained and concerted military operations, and the ability to implement the Protocol—restrict the applicability of the Protocol to conflicts of a certain degree of intensity. This means that not all cases of non-international armed conflict are covered, as is the case in common Article 3.[59]

Protocol II included an important threshold criterion for the establishment of an armed conflict in identifying that its provisions did "not apply to situations of internal disturbances and tensions, such as riots, isolated and sporadic acts of violence and other acts of a similar nature, as not being armed conflict."[60]

This more restrictive definition of NIAC also met resistance, including initially from States that at the time had newly won their independence.[61] In the late 1980s, President Reagan of the United States indicated a willingness to ratify AP II, and apply it more broadly to all conflicts not covered by Common Article 3, but the United States has not done so to date.[62] As of 2017, there are 168 States Parties to AP II.[63]

4 A few wrinkles

4.1 External intervention in an internal armed conflict

An armed conflict may involve multiple States. As the unique jurisdictional provisions of AP I are ordinarily not relevant, the determination that an armed conflict is international in character will turn on the existence of a dispute between at least two of the States. Thus, if one or more States intervene in an armed conflict to assist another State to prevail over a non-State group, the participation of multiple States does not indicate the existence of an IAC. If, however, one State were to intervene with military force in an existing armed conflict between a non-State group and State armed forces *in order to assist the non-State group*, this would qualify as an IAC. This is because in such a situation the intervention results in armed conflict *between* two States.

Third-party State interventions into ongoing NIACs often produce other complications. For example, what effect does the intervention have on the status of the original NIAC between the State and the insurgent forces? If the insurgents are incorporated—formally or functionally—into the armed forces of the intervening State, they could be considered participants to an IAC. However, this is not an automatic consequence of such external State intervention. It is just as likely that the intervening State or States will assert an independent justification for conducting operations against a common State enemy, and disavow any operational relationship to the non-State forces. For example, NATO launched an air campaign against Serbia in 1998 to force the Milošević regime to cease the ethnic cleansing in the Kosovo. Although these operations certainly aided the nascent Kosovo Liberation Army (KLA) against the common Serb enemy, the alliance emphasized the intervention was not conducted for that purpose, and that the KLA was distinct from NATO forces.[64] As a result, there were two distinct armed conflicts, one international, and one non-international. NATO's air campaign against Libya nearly a decade later reflected a similar conflict bifurcation.

4.2   Straddling the armed conflict threshold

Another area of uncertainty is the extent of external involvement that qualifies as an armed conflict. At what point does the external State become a party to the armed conflict as the result of its support to a dissident group engaged in a NIAC? The ICTY addressed this issue in *Prosecutor v. Tadić*, noting that:

> It is indisputable that an armed conflict is international if it takes place between two or more States. In addition, in case of an internal armed conflict breaking out on the territory of a State, it may become international (or, depending upon the circumstances, be international in character alongside an internal armed conflict) if (i) another State intervenes in that conflict through its troops, *or alternatively if (ii) some of the participants in the internal armed conflict act on behalf of that other State.*[65]

The Tribunal then undertook the task of defining what "on behalf of that other state" means or, in other words, to "identify the conditions under which those forces may be assimilated to organs of a State other than that on whose territory they live and operate."[66] The focal point of that analysis was *overall* control.[67] In conducting this assessment, the Tribunal considered evidence that the army of the Federal Republic of Yugoslavia, the VJ, exercised operational control over the army of the Serbian Republic of Bosnia and Herzegovina/ Republika Srpska, or VRS, the dissident Serb forces of Bosnia, in their fight against Bosnian Government forces. The Tribunal concluded that "the VRS and VJ did not, after May 1992, comprise two separate armies in any genuine sense."[68]

Central to this conclusion was the finding that

> [t]he command structure of the [Yugoslav People's Army] JNA and the re-designation of a part of the JNA as the VRS, while undertaken to create the appearance of the compliance with international demands, was in fact designed to ensure that a large number of ethnic Serb armed forces were retained in Bosnia and Herzegovina.[69]

Additionally, the court found "extensive financial, logistical and other assistance" as well as an identical structure and rank system between the VJ and VRS.[70] This resulted in the conclusion that the VJ "exercised overall control over the Bosnian Serb Forces,"[71] rendering the armed conflict international in character.

In contrast to this *overall* control test, the International Court of Justice (ICJ) has focused on evidence of *effective* control. Thus, in the case of *Nicaragua v. United States*, the ICJ concluded that the U.S. support, training, and advising of the Contras was insufficient to prove that the United States exercised effective control over their activities, and therefore the United States was not engaged in an armed conflict with Nicaragua (allowing attribution of IHL violations by the Contras to the United States). Specifically, the ICJ determined that:

> All the forms of United States participation mentioned above, and even the general control by the respondent State over a force with a high degree of dependency on it, would not in themselves mean, without further evidence, that the United States directed or enforced the perpetration of the acts contrary to human rights and humanitarian law alleged by the applicant State. Such acts could well be committed by members of the contras without the control of the United States. For this conduct to give rise to legal responsibility of the United States, it would in principle have to be proved that that State had effective control of the military or paramilitary operations in the course of which the alleged violations were committed.[72]

This is clearly a more restrictive test for relying on the activities of a supported or sponsored organized armed group as evidence of an IAC. However, it does seem that, once control is considered effective, it would satisfy both tests.[73]

4.3   *Transnational armed conflicts?*

Not long after 11 September 2001, the United States invoked the armed conflict characterization to define its military actions against al Qaeda. This indicated that the United States would take a far more aggressive approach to the struggle against international terrorism. For the first time since the inception of the Geneva Convention law-triggering equation, a State asserted that it was engaged in an armed conflict of international scope with a non-State entity.[74] Designating the struggle against a transnational non-State opponent as an armed conflict seemed, at least at the military operational level, logical. U.S.-armed forces leveraged a full range of combat power to seek out and engage al Qaeda operatives, and captured terrorist operatives were to be detained without charge or trial to prevent their return to the global fight.[75] However, a legal incongruity was almost immediately exposed: because al Qaeda was not a State, the armed conflict did not trigger the full corpus of the law pursuant to Common Article 2; and, because the conflict was not confined to the territory of the United States, it did not seem to fit into the widely accepted scope of Common Article 3.[76]

This legal interpretation was central to President Bush's 7 February 2002 directive on the status and treatment of captured al Qaeda operatives.[77] The directive explicitly disavowed any U.S. IHL obligation vis-à-vis these detainees. Because of the international scope of this non-State armed conflict, neither

Common Article 2 nor Common Article 3 dictated IHL application.[78] The United States had effectively classified the struggle against transnational terrorism as an armed conflict, but one beyond the scope of any IHL humanitarian regulation.

As noted earlier, the Supreme Court in *Hamdan v. Rumsfeld* ultimately rejected this IHL interpretation by concluding that Common Article 3 applied to any armed conflict falling outside the scope of Common Article 2.[79] While many experts continue to criticize the underlying assumption that a State can engage in an armed conflict with a non-State opponent that operates transnationally, this entire sequence of events undoubtedly called into question the long-standing assumption that IHL establishes an exclusive inter-/intra-State law applicability paradigm.

4.4   *The intersection of international humanitarian law and international human rights law*

One issue of increasing significance is the relationship between IHL and international human rights law (IHRL). Unlike IHL, IHRL is a relatively new branch of international law, although human rights protection within domestic jurisdictions predated its emergence internationally. IHRL treaties were developed following World War II to impose international legal limits on the relationship between a State and individuals under the State's control. IHRL is centered on giving rights to individuals, while IHL primarily imposes obligations on States and those who wield power over others.[80] And, unlike IHL, IHRL is not dependent on some triggering event to come into force; quite simply, IHRL applies to protect individuals at all times, with limited derogations. While both branches of international law reflect the same underlying objective of balancing legitimate State authority with humanitarian protections, *how* that balance is struck is often quite different.

Since 1945, IHRL has evolved substantially to provide a wide array of protections against arbitrary State power. In some respects, IHRL provides more robust protections than IHL. Particularly, in terms of the detail provided in treaties there are also areas where IHL is more robust and protective than IHRL. Further, these bodies of law share a common language and philosophy.[81] IHL also contains human rights provisions. For example, the Fourth Geneva Convention has been called a bill of rights for an occupied population.[82] Additionally, both Article 75 of AP I and Article 4 of AP II were heavily influenced by the 1948 Universal Declaration on Human Rights and the 1966 International Covenant on Civil and Political Rights (ICCPR).

When IHRL first emerged as a distinct branch of international law, it was widely understood to place limits on the authority of a State vis-à-vis its own population. Thus, from inception, IHRL seemed to be a relevant source of law in relation to internal armed conflicts, although there was virtually no authority indicating how this law should interact with Common Article 3. In reality, this was in large measure of minimal significance, as the humane treatment obligation imposed by Common Article 3 during such armed conflicts was essentially synonymous with fundamental IHRL obligations. Thus, compliance with Common Article 3 would result in respect for IHRL, and vice versa.

This original understanding of the scope of IHRL suggested that this branch of law had virtually no role to play vis-à-vis IACs. For this category of conflict, the much more comprehensive IHL regime was often regarded as the exclusive source of international legal regulation. However, over time, the scope of IHRL evolved significantly to extend beyond territorial borders and essentially follow State armed forces where they operate, although there is a lack of consensus on how, or the degree to which that jurisdiction is established. Under this expanded theory of IHRL applicability, what matters is not the territory where the individual is located but whether State authorities exercise jurisdiction over that individual in the very pragmatic sense of asserting control over the individual. As a result, IHRL is today widely understood to apply concurrently with IHL during both NIACs and IACs.

However, there remain States—most notably the United States and Israel—that, with narrow exception, reject this interpretation of IHRL's scope of extraterritorial application and persist in the view that IHL is the primary, if not exclusive, source of international legal regulation for IACs. This position seems increasingly at odds with the great weight of legal authority. Despite this approach there was a recognition by a plurality of Justices of the U.S. Supreme Court in *Hamdan v. Rumsfeld* that Article 75 applied as a matter of customary international law to the NIAC with al Qaeda.[83] Further, the United States appears to apply the protections of human rights law on international operations as a matter of practice, if not overtly as a result of the recognition of a treaty or customary law obligation to do so.[84]

Where the substantive obligations of IHL and IHRL are relatively analogous, like the example of the humane treatment obligation cited above, conceding the concurrent application of IHL and IHRL during all armed conflicts leads to very little uncertainty. However, where these two bodies of law provide inconsistent regulatory effect, the complicated question of how to reconcile these inconsistencies arises. For example, IHL permits lethal targeting during armed conflict based solely on the determination that an individual is a member of an enemy belligerent group, whereas this *status* targeting is incompatible with IHRL's requirement to employ deadly force only as a measure of last resort based on an individualized assessment of homicidal necessity.

In its Advisory Opinion on the Use or Threat of Nuclear Weapons, the ICJ tackled this deconfliction question head on. The court first noted that, as a *lex generalis*, IHRL applies at all times, even during armed conflict. However, the court then invoked the doctrine of *lex specialis*, noting that IHL is a body of law developed to address many specific issues related to armed conflict. As a result, this *lex specialis* informs interpretation and application of the *lex generalis* when the two bodies of law touch on the same issue. To illustrate the point, the court used the example of lethal targeting during armed conflict. The court first noted that the fundamental IHRL protection against arbitrary deprivation of liberty applied at all times, even during armed conflict. However, the meaning of *arbitrary* is not uniform in all situations. The permissible scope of use of force authority in armed conflict is necessarily broader than in peacetime, and the *lex specialis* rules of IHL define this authority. Accordingly, any killing is arbitrary during armed conflict in violation of IHRL only if it violates the use of force rules of IHL.

This guidance on the operation of IHRL and IHL was expanded by the ICJ in the Wall Decision to indicate that there were three possible situations concerning the relationship between these two bodies of law: "some rights may be exclusively matters of international humanitarian law; others may be exclusively matters of human rights law; yet others may be matters of both these branches of international law."[85] Other domestic and regional tribunals have invoked the concept of complementary application of both these branches of international law to adjudicate claims arising in the context of armed conflicts.[86] Other entities, such as review commissions and human rights organs of the United Nations have done the same. All of this, coupled with ever-increasing evidence of State practice indicating official recognition of IHRL applicability during armed conflict, has resulted in a widely held view that the ICJ had it exactly right. While some States continue to resist this interpretation of international law, their position seems increasingly untenable.

However, there is also an ongoing trend to expand the role of IHRL beyond what was clearly contemplated by the ICJ. Today, many advocates assert that where IHRL provides more protective norms of State conduct, those norms should modify the more expansive authority provided by IHL. This is especially significant in the context of lethal targeting and belligerent detention, with IHRL advocates asserting that attacking armed forces owe the enemy a duty of care far beyond that demanded by IHL, for example an obligation to warn prior to launching an attack, or to capture instead of using lethal force whenever doing so is objectively feasible, or a prohibition on long-term detention of a captured enemy belligerent absent express detention authority provided by United Nations Security Council Resolution or domestic law.

How the relationship between these two branches of law will evolve is a proverbial work in progress, although it seems indisputable that it is a relationship that is here to stay. It is equally indisputable that, as the nature of armed conflict continues to devolve from the classic State versus State war, where participants and clearly identifiable and the scope of hostilities have predictable geographic bounds, the interests in protecting individuals from potentially over-broad assertions of State power under the umbrella of armed conflict authority will increase pressures to consider IHRL norms, at minimum, as a supplement to IHL.

5 Conclusion

Identifying the controlling law is an essential aspect of operational regulation and humanitarian protection. In 1949, the international community, stung by the painful experiences of World War II and the brutal civil wars that preceded that war, sought to simplify this identification process by adopting de facto tests for triggering application of the Geneva Conventions.[87] The term armed conflict was adopted to meet this necessity, indicating a situation of armed hostilities justifying the imposition of international legal regulation.[88] The existence of de facto hostilities was expected to prevent States from disavowing the constraints on hostilities at the expense of war victims.[89] Even in the realm of intra-State hostilities—what today would be called internal armed conflicts—which in the first half of the twentieth century were regarded as generally beyond the scope of international legal regulation, both State and non-State actors would be compelled to respect the most basic humanitarian limitations on their conduct.[90] This law-triggering equation subsequently evolved to apply to all sources of IHL, indicating when an armed conflict exists and when IHL applies.

This innovation did not, however, eliminate all uncertainties associated with conflict regulation. What was meant by armed conflict? Must inter-State disputes show some level of intensity or duration to trigger the law? What law applies when one State intervenes in the territory of another State without consent, not to fight that State but to fight a non-State group in that territory? Where is the line between domestic peacetime disturbance and internal armed conflict? Can a State be involved in a NIAC against a non-State transnational opponent, and if so where do IHL authorities and obligations apply? Do IHL norms developed for IACs extend to NIACs? What role, if any, should IHRL play in the regulation of armed conflicts?

These questions, and others, continue to challenge the international community to this day. However, the clarity provided by the Geneva Conventions has substantially mitigated the risks of law avoidance the drafters so obviously sought to prevent. What is less clear is whether the evolution of the law will reflect a rational balance between authority to leverage the power of war to bring an opponent into submission and the interests of humanitarian protection. Striving for such a balance is, however, ultimately necessary to fulfill the underlying purpose of the law, and will hopefully animate its continued evolution.

Notes

1 *Prosecutor v. Tadić*, Case No. IT-94-1-AR72, Decision on Defence Motion for Interlocutory Appeal on Jurisdiction, para 67 (Int'l Crim. Trib. for the former Yugoslavia, 2 October 1995). Note also that IHL still applies after cessation of hostilities, for instance in dealing with the return of prisoners of war and criminal accountability.

2 *See* Geneva Convention for the Amelioration of the Condition of the Wounded and Sick in Armed Forces in the Field, Art 2, 12 August 1949, 6 U.S.T. 3114, 75 U.N.T.S. 970; Geneva Convention for the Amelioration of the Condition of Wounded, Sick, and Shipwrecked Members of the Armed Forces at Sea, Art 2, 12 August 1949, 6 U.S.T. 3217, 75 U.N.T.S. 971; Geneva Convention Relative to the Treatment of Prisoners of War, Art 2, 12 August 1949, 6 U.S.T. 3316, 75 U.N.T.S. 972; Geneva Convention Relative to the Protection of Civilian Persons in Time of War, Art 2, 12 August 1949, 6 U.S.T. 3516, 75 U.N.T.S. 973 [hereinafter Common Article 2].

3 *Id.*

4 Commentary on the First Geneva Convention: Convention (I) for the Amelioration of the Condition of the Wounded and Sick in Armed Forces in the Field (2nd edn, 2016), paras 201–2, *available at* www.icrc.org/applic/ihl/ihl.nsf/Treaty.xsp?action= openDocument&documentId=4825657B0C7E6BF0C12563CD002D6B0B [hereinafter 2016 Commentary GWS].

5 *Id*. para 236.

6
> The quality of common Article 3 as a 'Convention in miniature' for conflicts of a non-international character was already noted during the 1949 Diplomatic Conference. Since then, the fundamental character of its provisions has been recognized as a 'minimum yardstick', binding in all armed conflicts, and as a reflection of 'elementary considerations of humanity.'
>
> *Id*. para 356

7 Geneva Convention for the Amelioration of the Condition of the Wounded and Sick in Armed Forces in the Field, Art 3, 12 August 1949, 6 U.S.T. 3114, 75 U.N.T.S. 970; Geneva Convention for the Amelioration of the Condition of Wounded, Sick, and Shipwrecked Members of the Armed Forces at Sea, Art 3, 12 August 1949, 6 U.S.T. 3217, 75 U.N.T.S. 971; Geneva Convention Relative to the Treatment of Prisoners of War, Art 3, 12 August 1949, 6 U.S.T. 3316, 75 U.N.T.S. 972; Geneva Convention Relative to the Protection of Civilian Persons in Time of War, Art 3, 12 August 1949, 6 U.S.T. 3516, 75 U.N.T.S. 973 [hereinafter Common Article 3].

8 2016 Commentary GWS, paras 518–28.

9 *See* Common Article 2.

10 *See* Int'l & Operational Law Dep't, The Judge Advocate Gen.'s Legal Ctr. & Sch., U.S. Army, *Law of Armed Conflict Deskbook*, pp. 25–34 (2004).

11 2016 Commentary GWS, paras 210–84, 414–51.

12 Stephen Lee Myers, *Serb Officer, Captured By Rebels, Held by U.S., N.Y. Times*, 17 April 1999, at A6.

13 2016 Commentary GWS, para 236.

14 *Prosecutor v. Tadić*, Case No. IT-94-1-AR72, Decision on Defence Motion for Interlocutory Appeal on Jurisdiction, para 70 (Int'l Crim. Trib. for the former Yugoslavia 2 October 1995).

15 2016 Commentary GWS, paras 357–83.

16 *Id*. para 378.

17 *Id*. paras 416–17, 861–3.

18 *Id*.

19 *See* Common Article 2.

20 *Id*.

21 *Prosecutor v. Haradinaj*, Case No. IT-04-84-T, Judgment, para 40 (Int'l Crim. Trib. for the former Yugoslavia 3 April 2008).

22 2016 Commentary GWS, paras 416–17.

23 Jean S. Pictet, Geneva Convention for the Amelioration of the Condition of the Wounded and Sick in Armed Forces in the Field: Commentary (ICRC, 1952), 35–36 [hereinafter 1952 Commentary GWS].

24 2016 Commentary GWS, paras 420–1.

25 1952 Commentary GWS, at 35–6.

26 *Prosecutor v. Tadić*, Case No. IT-94-1-AR72, Decision on Defence Motion for Interlocutory Appeal on Jurisdiction, para 70 (Int'l Crim. Trib. for the former Yugoslavia 2 October 1995).

27 *Prosecutor v. Haradinaj*, Case No. IT-04-84-T, Judgment, para 49 (Int'l Crim. Trib. for the former Yugoslavia 3 April 2008).

28 2016 Commentary GWS, paras 550–64.

29 Sylvain Vite, *Typology of Armed Conflicts in International Humanitarian Law: Legal Concepts & Actual Situations*, 91 Int'l Rev. Red Cross 69, 76 (March 2009), *available at* www.icrc.org/eng/assets/files/other/irrc-873-vite.pdf

30 *See Prosecutor v. Tadić*, Case No. IT-94-1-AR72, Decision on Defence Motion for Interlocutory Appeal on Jurisdiction, para 70 (Int'l Crim. Trib. for the former Yugoslavia 2 October 1995).

31 *Id.* paras 96–127.

32 *Id.* para 127.

33 2016 Commentary GWS, paras 220–35.

34 *Id.*

35 *See* Pierre Tristam, *The 2006 Lebanon War: Israel and Hezbollah Square Off*, About.com, *available at* http://middleeast.about.com/od/lebanon/a/me070918.htm. *See also Security Council Calls for an End to Hostilities Between Hezbollah, Israel, Unanimously Adopting Resolution 1701*, UN Security Council (11 August 2006), *available at* www.un.org/News/Press/docs/2006/sc8808.doc.htm (indication that Hezbollah and not Lebanon was responsible for the attacks).

36 *See generally* Ctr. for Law & Military Operations, The Judge Advocate Gen.'s Legal Ctr. & Sch., U.S. Army, *CLAMO Report: The Marines Have Landed at CLAMO*, Army Law, December 1998, at 37–8.

37 *See, e.g.*, Tristam, *The 2006 Lebanon War: Israel and Hezbollah Square Off*, About.com, *available at* http://middleeast.about.com/od/lebanon/a/me070918.htm

38 *See* Kenneth Watkin, *Controlling the Use of Force: A Role for Human Rights Norms in Contemporary Armed Conflict*, 98 Am. J. Int'l L. 1, 3–4 (2004) (discussing the challenge of conflict categorization related to military operations conducted against highly organized non-State groups with transnational reach). *See also* Kirby Abott, "Terrorists: Combatants, Criminals, or . . . ?," published in *The Measures of International Law: Effectiveness, Fairness, and Validity*, Proceedings of the 31st Annual Conference of the Canadian Council on International Law, Ottawa, 24–26 October 2002; Jennifer Elsea, Cong. Research Serv., Order Code RL31191, *Terrorism and the Laws of War: Trying Terrorists as War Criminals before Military Commissions*, 10–14 (2001) (analyzing whether the attacks of 11 September 2001, triggered the law of war).

39 *See* Common Article 3.

40 Gabor Rona, Legal Adviser at the ICRC's Legal Division, *When Is a War Not a War?— The Proper Role of the Law of Armed Conflict in the "Global War on Terror,"* Presentation at the "International Action to Prevent and Combat Terrorism"—Workshop on the Protection of Human Rights While Countering Terrorism, Copenhagen (16 March 2004), *available at* www.icrc.org/eng/resources/documents/statement/5xcmnj.htm

41 *See* Memorandum from George W. Bush, President, to Richard "Dick" Cheney, Vice President, *Humane Treatment of Taliban and al Qaeda Detainees*, para 2(c) (7 February 2002), *available at* www.pegc.us/archive/White_House/bush_memo_20020207_ed.pdf

42 *Id.*

43 *Hamdan v. Rumsfeld*, 548 U.S. 557 (2006).

44 *Id.* at 630.

45 *See, e.g.*, Mary Ellen O'Connell, *Defining Armed Conflict*, 13 J. Conflict & Sec. L. 393 (Winter 2008).

46 Protocol (I) Additional to the Geneva Conventions of 12 August 1949, and Relating to the Protection of Victims of International Armed Conflicts, 8 June 1977, 1125 U.N.T.S. 3 [hereinafter AP I] (entered into force 7 December 1978) (signed by the United States 12 December 1977, not transmitted to U.S. Senate, *see* S. Treaty Doc. No. 100–2 (1987)).

47 Protocol (II) Additional to the Geneva Conventions of 12 August 1949, and Relating to the Protection of Victims of Non-International Armed Conflicts 8 June 1977,

1125 U.N.T.S. 609 [hereinafter AP II] (entered into force 7 December 1978) (signed by the United States 12 December 1977, transmitted to the U.S. Senate 29 January 1987, still pending action as S. Treaty Doc. No. 100–2 (1987)).

48 *See* Introduction to the Commentary on the Additional Protocols I and II of 8 June 1977, ICRC, *available at* www.icrc.org/ihl.nsf/COM/470-750001?OpenDocument

49 AP I, Art 1(3).

50 AP I, Art 1(4).

51 Pictet et al., Commentary on the Additional Protocols of 8 June 1977 to the Geneva Conventions of 12 August 1949 (ICRC, 1987), paras 66–113 [hereinafter AP Commentary].

52 *Id*. at 47.

53 There are 172 States Parties to AP I out of 193 member States in the United Nations.

54 Ronald Reagan, Letter of Transmittal, The White House, 29 January 1987, *available at* www.loc.gov/rr/frd/Military_Law/pdf/protocol-II-100-2.pdf. *See also* Protocol Additional to the Geneva Conventions of 12 August 1949, and Relating to the Protection of Victims of International Armed Conflicts (Protocol I), 8 June 1977, ICRC, *available at* www.icrc.org/ihl.nsf/WebSign?ReadForm&id=470&ps=P (for a list of States Parties to AP I).

55 *See* Protocol Additional to the Geneva Conventions of 12 August 1949, and Relating to the Protection of Victims of International Armed Conflicts (Protocol I), 8 June 1977, ICRC, *available at* www.icrc.org/ihl.nsf/WebSign?ReadForm&id=470&ps=P

56 George Aldrich, *Prospects for United States Ratification of Additional Protocol I to the 1949 Geneva Conventions*, 85 Am. J. Int'l L. 1, 4–5 (1991); H.P. Glasser, *Agora: The US Decision Not to Ratify Protocol I to the Geneva Conventions on the Protection of War Victims*, 81 Am. J. Int'l L. 910, 916–17 (1987).

57 Christopher Greenwood, *Terrorism and Humanitarian Law—The Debate Over Additional Protocol I*, 19 Isr. Y.B. Hum. Rts 187 (1989).

58 AP Commentary, para 4447.

59 *Id*. para 4453.

60 AP II, Art 1(2).

61 Keith Suter, *An International Law of Guerrilla Warfare* 148 (1984).

62 Gary D. Solis, *The Law of Armed Conflict: International Humanitarian Law in War* 131–2 (2010).

63 Treaties And States Parties To Such Treaties, ICRC, *available at* www.icrc.org/applic/ihl/ihl.nsf/vwTreaties1949.xsp?redirect=0

64 James G. Stewart, *Towards a Single Definition of Armed Conflict in International Humanitarian Law: A Critique of Internationalized Armed Conflict*, 85 Int'l Rev. Red Cross 313, 315 (2003), *available at* www.icrc.org/Web/fre/sitefre0.nsf/htmlall/5PXJXQ/$File/irrc_850_Stewart.pdf

65 *Prosecutor v. Tadić*, Case No. IT-94-1-A, Appeals Judgment, para 80 (Int'l Crim. Trib. for the former Yugoslavia 15 July 1999) (emphasis added).

66 *Id*. para 91.

67 *Id*. para 95.

68 *Id*. para 151.

69 *Id*. para 151(i).

70 *Id*. para 151(ii).

71 *Id*. para 156.

72 *Military and Paramilitary Activities in and Against Nicar. (Nicar. v. U.S.)*, Merits, 1986 I.C.J. 14, 54–5 (27 June).

73 The different terminology, *effective* and *overall* control, may have resulted from the starting points in the two cases. The ICTY was looking at qualification of conflict for criminal accountability, whereas the ICJ was considering the State responsibility.

For more on these two tests, *see* Yoram Dinstein, *War, Aggression, and Self-Defense* 221–4 (4th edn, 2005).

74 Press Release, White House Office of the Press Sec'y, *Fact Sheet: Status of Detainees at Guantanamo* (7 February 2002), *available at* www.presidency.ucsb.edu/ws/index.php?pid=79402

75 *Detention, Treatment, and Trial of Certain Non-Citizens in the War Against Terrorism*, 66 Fed. Reg. 57, 831–6 (16 November 2001).

76 *Hamdan v. Rumsfeld*, 548 U.S. 557, 630 (2006).

77 *See* Memorandum from George W. Bush, President, to Richard "Dick" Cheney, Vice President, *Humane Treatment of Taliban and al Qaeda Detainees* (7 February 2002), *available at* www.pegc.us/archive/White_House/bush_memo_20020207_ed.pdf

78 *Id.*

79 *Hamdan v. Rumsfeld*, 548 U.S. 557 (2006).

80 René Prevost, *International Human Rights and Humanitarian Law* 116 (2002).

81 *Id.* at 55.

82 Eyal Benvenisti, *The International Law of Occupation* 9 (1993).

83 *Hamdan v. Rumsfeld*, 548 U.S. 557, 633 (2006).

84 Press Statement from Hillary Rodham Clinton, Sec'y of State, United States, *Reaffirming America's Commitment to Humane Treatment of Detainees* (7 March 2011).

85 Legal Consequences of the Constr. of a Wall in the Occupied Palestinian Territory, Advisory Opinion, 2004 I.C.J. 136, 178 (9 July).

86 *Hassan v. United Kingdom*, Eur. Ct. of Hum. Rt. (Application no. 29750/09) (16 September 2014), *available at* http://hudoc.echr.coe.int/fre#{"itemid":["001–146501"]}

87 2016 Commentary GWS, paras 197–8.

88 *Id.* paras 201–2.

89 *Id.* paras 210–16.

90 *Id.* paras 384–92.

2 Non-international armed conflict

1 Introduction

Contemporary international law has been challenged by the need to address armed conflict that occurs in a context that is not focused on State against State violence. The law impacting the State use of force has developed with a particularly inter-State focus. This is true whether considering restrictions on recourse to war or the governance of the conduct of hostilities. An armed conflict is identified traditionally through a binary categorization as being either international or non-international in character. *International armed conflict* is most frequently defined as being uniquely restricted to hostilities between States.[1] *Non-international armed conflict* (or conflict not of an international character) has, until relatively recently, been dealt with primarily occurring internal to States. Such conflicts generally pit government forces against non-State actors that are often referred to as insurgents, or terrorists, although they may also take place been two non-State organized armed groups. Armed conflict between States and non-State actors is undergoing fundamental change brought on, in part, by increasing globalization and technology enhanced operations.[2] In this regard, "the purely internal scope of application [of NIAC] did not account for combat operations launched by a state using regular armed forces against a transnational nonstate opponent outside its borders."[3] Neither did it necessarily provide for trans-border attacks by such an opponent against a State (e.g., 9/11). The twenty-first century security environment has increasingly had to deal with threats that do not necessarily fit neatly within the traditional binary categorization for armed conflict.

Of note, notwithstanding the historical focus on inter-State warfare, the predominant form of armed conflict has always involved violence between States and non-State actors. This is a form of conflict that is proportionately on the rise, when compared to the number of contemporary IACs. The ratio of internal to external conflicts is reported to have changed from 2:1 before 1945 to nearly 5:1 since then.[4] Despite the predominance of State versus non-State actor conflict, it is violence between States that has been, as a matter of treaty and customary international law, subjected to the most comprehensive regulatory regime. This has left armed conflict between States and non-State actors being subject to a less well defined IHL regime, particularly since States preferred to treat these conflicts as matters subject to domestic sovereign prerogative. This explains, in large measure, why States have been far more reluctant to allow international legal regulation to apply to this type of conflicts in comparison to conflicts with other States that are occur in a more international domain. Those challenging the government are viewed as criminals, and are often labeled as terrorists who are subject to domestic prosecution for their activity. The changing nature of the twenty-first century non-State actor threat is forcing change in the assessment of how IHL impacts NIACs. Aspects of this change have also created controversy. Emblematic of the post-9/11 disagreements among international lawyers are questions regarding how conflict with non-State actors is categorized and, in particular, when that violence crosses the threshold from activity subject exclusively to a human rights–based law enforcement regime to an armed conflict subject to the IHL framework.

This chapter explores unique aspects of contemporary violence with non-State actors and the categorization of such violence when it arises to the level of armed conflict. The first part of the chapter will consider the genesis of non-State actor conflict in just war theory, and the unique role the State plays in regulating that violence as a proper authority. This part will also consider traditional approaches toward assessing the threat posed by non-State actors such as rebels, insurgents, and belligerents. The discussion will then turn to the contemporary threat posed by transnational non-State groups. This includes Salafi jihadists who focus on creating a caliphate that does not recognize the State-based framework of international law, or the international borders and sovereignty that is a fundamental aspect of this body of law. The analysis will also extend to the question of, at what point criminal organizations, such as drug cartels, may become criminal insurgencies potentially subject to regulation under IHL.

The second part of the chapter explores the treaty and customary law framework governing armed conflict with non-State actors, focusing primarily on Common Article 3 to the 1949 Geneva Conventions, the two 1977 Protocols additional to those Conventions, and customary international law.[5] This provides a baseline for discussing the impact of the potential regulatory gaps that exists in comparison to inter-State conflict. The third part highlights the lack of consensus regarding how non-State actor conflict is categorized. As will be discussed, although not sufficiently part of the contemporary dialogue, some conflict with non-State actors can occur in the context of IAC, or at least conflict that is viewed as being international in character. In respect of NIAC, the numerous classification theories will be outlined. Discussion of such conflicts is complicated by the terminological confusion that occurs when violence with non-State actors is considered to be not of an international character, even though it can transcend national borders. The fourth part of the chapter sets out the criteria to be applied for determining when violence with non-State actors enters the realm of armed conflict. This will include an analysis of whether the criteria most widely applied to identify when an armed conflict is occurring are adequate to address contemporary security threats. Finally, the fifth part of this chapter will explore the issue of States acting in self-defense against non-State actor threats, and the challenge of one-off attacks.

2   The non-State actor threat

2.1   Internal conflict

The challenge of regulating violence involving non-State actors is directly linked to the just war roots of this body of international law. As societies developed, the authority to maintain order was concentrated in the hands of the sovereign. As described by Grotius, warfare was divided into public, private, and mixed war categories.[6] Public warfare occurred between sovereigns, private war between individuals, and mixed war involved war "made on one Side by public Authority, and on the other by mere private Persons."[7] Ultimately, this meant that there was one *proper* authority to use violence, *the State*. Inter-State conflict was to be referred to as IAC. Those hostilities are primarily governed by IHL, with a special protected status for those who fought on behalf of States. That status developed to include both combatant immunity from prosecution for killing carried out pursuant to the law governing warfare, and the right to be treated as a prisoner of war. Notably, conflict between the State and those it governs did not readily come to be regulated by international law. In this respect, for threats emanating from within the State, "[t]he sovereign retained absolute authority in their domestic dealings, and international law had no say in how such domestic affairs were to be carried out."[8]

The preference of States was to avoid any injection of international law to regulate an internal conflict involving rebels, insurgents, or other groups seeking to overthrow the existing government. In this regard, international law was not concerned with domestic conflicts, or even "a conflict between an imperial power and a colonial territory."[9] What this meant was that there was no concept of combatant, POW status, or combatant immunity in NIAC.[10] Civilian participants, even when they became members of organized armed groups and even if those groups seemed to appear and conduct themselves like a combatant group in an inter-State conflict, were treated as criminals subject to prosecution under national law. However, human rights law developed to constrain the activities of the State in respect of its citizens. In this respect, IHL and IHRL can be seen to fundamentally serve different functions, with the former regulating "the relationship between two co-equal belligerents in battle, whereas IHRL constrains the sovereign's treatment of subjects under its control."[11] State rejection of humanitarian law being applicable to internal violence has the effect of raising the profile of human rights law, both domestic and international. In practical terms it makes human rights law the default legal regime governing the regulation of internal violence.

However, even from a historical perspective this did not mean that all internal violence escaped the application of IHL. Internal violence has been categorized as rebellion, insurgency, and belligerency. *Rebellion* was viewed as "a modest, sporadic challenge by a section of the population intent on attaining control."[12] *Insurgency* referred to "a more substantial attack against the legitimate order of the State, the rebelling faction being sufficiently organised to mount a credible threat to the government."[13] Both forms of violent challenge to State authority were viewed as remaining subject to domestic law. However, *belligerency* was different. This situation occurred "when belligerents themselves behaved as if they were involved in an international conflict, or third States treated a conflict as if it was international in character (i.e. recognition of belligerency)."[14]

The nineteenth century witnessed the development of the concept of *recognition of belligerency* in situations where the violence reached such a sustained level that the customary international law of neutrality was viewed as being applicable, and the "parent State brought into effect the *jus in bello* [IHL] in its entirety between it and the rebels."[15] Recognition of belligerency is linked to significant internal conflict at the level of a civil war, and is most readily identified with the United States Civil War. However, resistance to this form of recognition that brought a special status to non-State actors was strong, and by World War II that doctrine had fallen into disuse.[16] What is clear though is that this doctrine "nevertheless represented a shift in state practice, eroding the impermeability of state sovereignty in international law." [17] This was a shift that was to manifest itself more substantively in the aftermath of World War II.

Notwithstanding a contemporary focus on transnational threats, which is discussed below, internal conflict between States and insurgent groups, so-called small wars, remain a staple of present day security challenges. One analyst has suggested that, in 2012, "[g]lobally, there are well over one hundred ongoing small irregular, asymmetric, and revolutionary wars, in which violent nonstate actors are helping, their own organizations or political patrons bring about radical change or acquire power."[18] Elsewhere it is noted that "[b]etween World War II and 2015, there were 181 insurgencies. They averaged over 12 years in duration with a median of seven years."[19] One example is the FARC, which after 52 years of conflict saw a peace agreement reached in 2016 between that organized armed group and Columbia.[20] Notwithstanding a State preference to treat such conflicts as internal matters, there frequently arises a requirement to resolve the interface between human rights law and humanitarian law (*see* Chapter 1, 4.4: *The intersection of international humanitarian law and international human rights law*). Inevitably, States will remain focused on internal violence. However, as is discussed in the next section, non-State actors are also presenting unique transnational threats to international peace and security.

2.2 *Transnational threats*

The actions of contemporary non-State actors have forced renewed consideration that international law can regulate armed conflict between States and non-State actors. Numerous non-State organized armed groups increasingly present a *transnational* threat as the result of projecting violent activities beyond the borders of one State. Even with traditional views of armed conflict there was, in reality, frequently a cross-border aspect to the conflict. Insurgents often relied on the existence of safe haven in bordering countries from which to launch attacks on the State authorities they were seeking to overthrow. It has been suggested that the existence of a safe haven is a key factor in the success of an insurgency campaign.[21] However, the calculated projection of belligerent actions well beyond the borders of one State in order to attack targets in non-adjacent States can present a different challenge than the spillover effect frequently associated with primarily internal armed conflicts.

At the dawn of the twenty-first century, the transnational nature of non-State actor threats was graphically demonstrated by the al Qaeda attacks of 9/11. The Salafi jihadist threat represents an insurgent movement that engages in trans-border terrorism, that some States have characterized as being part of an armed conflict. The violence can involve attacks on both the near and far enemy.[22] The Jihadist movement is a broad one with al Qaeda and its associated groups form-ing only one part.[23] For example, by 2015, the Islamic State had grown to 19 *Walayat* (provinces) in Syria and Iraq, and 15 elsewhere in the world.[24] The trans-border reach of Salafi jihadists is evident in their doctrine,[25] and, following a series of attacks in Europe and elsewhere, was reflected in a 2015 United Nations Security Council Resolution concerning the Islamic State and al Qaeda threat emanating from Syria.[26] Trans-border attacks, either directed or motivated by the jihadist movement have occurred in such diverse locations as Paris, Istanbul, Dhaka, Ottawa, Brussels, Berlin, Istanbul, Baghdad, and Orlando.

The most complex of these conflicts has occurred in Syria. It is fundamentally an internal conflict, with 150,000 insurgents operating by 2015 "within as many as 1,500 operationally distinct armed groups."[27] There were over 50,000 jihadists,[28] with 25,000 fighters having traveled to Syria (6,000 from Europe) to participate in the hostilities.[29] The jihadist groups included more than 20 transnationally minded jihadist factions.[30] Added to these secular and Salafi-based non-State actors are the Syrian armed forces, its paramilitary National Defence Force, Hezbollah, Iran, Kurdish non-State groups, Russia, Turkey, Jordan, Lebanon, Israel, the United States, and other Coalition States. It is a conflict that by 2017 involved inter-sectarian violence (i.e., Shia versus Sunni), inter-jihadist group conflict (i.e., the Islamic State and al Qaeda), regional disputes (e.g., Turkey/Kurdistan, Israel/Hezbollah), transnational terrorism, and inter-State rivalries.

2.3 Crime and non-State actor conflict

Transnational threats have also arisen in the form of *criminal insurgencies,*[31] in other words transnational criminal organizations that not only challenge the authority of their home State but also operate internationally. These new threats have been described as *non*-State (e.g., gangs, insurgents, warlords, drug traffickers, transnational criminal organizations, and terrorists), which "thrive in 'ungoverned or weakly governed space' between or within various host countries."[32] Transnational crime is directly linked to globalization. Drug cartels, such as those in Mexico and Columbia, feature significantly as part of this contemporary threat. In addition, various hybrid criminal organizations, such as the Red Commando in the favelas of Brazil, the Shower Posse in Jamaica, and the Mara Salvatrucha in Central America, represent postmodern networks of gangs, mafias, death squads, religious cults, and urban guerrillas.[33] The criminal activity is not limited to drugs. For example, drug trafficking organizations "have branched into other profitable crimes such as kidnapping, assassination for hire, auto theft, controlling prostitution, extortion, money-laundering, software piracy, resource theft, and human smuggling."[34]

The general approach, especially for governments dealing with these situations, has been to consider the violence associated with these criminal organizations as internal law enforcement matters, and not as armed conflicts.[35] A key factor is that the motivation of these groups is viewed as being economic rather than political.[36] They sit on the dividing line between law enforcement and armed conflict. It often meets the traditional criteria for an armed conflict in terms of group organization and levels of violence, with the remaining question being the point at which these criminal groups undermine the power of the State such that their economic motive becomes a political one as well.[37]

This is not the only way in which crime and armed conflict intersect in relation to non-State actors. Inevitably "where insurgency takes root, organized crime will be pervasive."[38] This is because both insurgency and crime "sprout from common roots: ineffective governance, systemic weakness and pathology, and a culture or tradition of clandestine activity."[39] Many insurgent groups engage in crime in order to fund their military or terrorist campaigns.[40] Whether it is Taliban involvement in drug trafficking, Hezbollah being implicated in arms smuggling, money laundering, or fraud, Iraqi groups smuggling oil, or al Shabaab engagement in charcoal smuggling and the ivory trade, insurgent groups can be directly implicated in criminal activity. They may rely on existing crime and smuggling networks to facilitate their financing efforts through the proceeds of crime.[41]

All this indicates that untangling the complex nature of internal and transnational armed violence can be challenging. The reality is that not all non-State actor violence will rise to the level of armed conflict, and, even when it does, not all violent activities will occur in the context of the armed conflict. Because of this, even when the State considers an armed conflict to exist as the result of the activities of non-State organized armed groups, State security forces will still be obligated to apply law enforcement means to deal with criminal gangs not directly involved in the hostilities. It is therefore essential that situations of law enforcement and armed conflict be distinguished from one another. As will be discussed in the context of conflict categorization, "[t]he key analytical focus in doing so has historically been to identify the line between internal civil disturbances (situations falling below the threshold of armed conflict), and internal hostilities of sufficient magnitude to require application of international legal conflict regulation."[42]

3   The legal framework

3.1   Treaty law

The end of World War II witnessed the beginning of a treaty-based application of IHL to NIACs. Common Article 3 of the 1949 Geneva Conventions extended humanitarian protection, including to detained persons and those who are *hors de combat*, in an "armed conflict not of an international character occurring in the territory of one of the High Contracting Parties." Of note, it dealt generically with "each Party to the conflict," and referred to "[p]ersons taking no active part in hostilities, including members of armed forces." As such, it applied equally to States and the non-State actors they were fighting against. However, this effort must be placed in context as it represented a more modest result in an effort sponsored by the ICRC to have the entire Geneva Conventions apply to internal conflicts.[43] Further, its scope of application was originally intended to apply to conflicts reaching the level of a civil war.[44] As will be discussed, it was to be applied by legal interpretation and, in practice, to hostilities much lower on the conflict scale. Common Article 3 also did not address the law governing the conduct of hostilities, highlighting that from the beginning of efforts to codify the IHL applicable to internal armed conflicts, the treaty law would be less comprehensive than for its inter-State counterpart. This void was to be increasingly filled through reliance on customary international law.[45]

Much of the effort of the international legal community in the post–World War II era was focused on the negotiation of international human rights treaties. However, by the late 1960s, international pressure grew to deal with the guerrilla wars that marked the Cold War and the end of the colonial period.[46] The result, as noted in Chapter 1, was development of two Protocols additional to the 1949 Geneva Conventions. Highlighting the degree to which non-State actor participation in conflict straddles the full range of violence, AP I dealt with IAC, while AP II addressed NIAC. Both Protocols represented an amalgamation of the Geneva Law (humanitarian) and the Hague Law (largely conduct of hostilities-based) streams of IHL. However, AP I reflected a more significant and direct incorporation of the conduct of hostilities norms as can be seen in its targeting provisions, including precautions in the attack.[47] In contrast, AP II refers to civilians not being the object of an attack, and that they enjoying the protection of their status "unless and for such time as they may take a direct part in hostilities."[48] It is clear from this provision that the principle of distinction applies during NIACs covered by the Protocol. However, it is important to note that AP II is today supplemented by extending the targeting rules applicable during IAC through customary international law (*see* Chapter 6: *Targeting*).[49]

AP I is noteworthy for its extension of humanitarian law to wars of national liberation (i.e., "peoples fighting against colonial domination and alien occupation and against racist regimes *in the exercise of their right of self-determination*").[50] Importantly, this form of conflict is international. This approach was counter to the traditional State reluctance to be seen to legitimize such non-State actor con- flict. It also served as a reminder that not all violence with non-State actors occurs in the context of a NIAC. The result is that, while the Protocol has been widely adopted, it has not been ratified by the United States and a number of other militarily powerful countries.[51] For States that did ratify the Protocol, that step was undoubtedly aided by the view that wars of national liberation are relics of the 1960s and 1970s, and its scope is to be narrowly interpreted.[52]

Because of its scope, AP II represents a relatively narrow injection of treaty obligations into NIAC. This is because it applies not only on the territory of a High Contracting Party, but also requires the non-State actor, described as dissident armed forces or other organized armed groups to be "under responsible command, exercise such control over a part of its territory as to enable them to carry out sustained and concerted military operations and to implement this Protocol."[53] This threshold has been equated to a civil war. However, it is important to note that the Article establishing this scope of application indicates that it does not modify Common Article 3's existing conditions of application. In other words, AP II recognized that Common Article 3 could apply to situations of armed conflict that failed to qualify for application of this new treaty. This is another indication of the historical reluctance by States to apply international law to internal conflicts, even newly created States of the post-colonial period, which were not keen to see potential adversaries given legal status. Accordingly, they supported a high threshold for application of AP II's more extensive international regulation of such conflicts.[54] The result was a text that "has a vague threshold and which does not specifically regulate guerrilla warfare, either."[55]

Notwithstanding the negative assessment, one unique aspect of AP II was its outline of a lower threshold below which armed conflict was viewed as not occurring. That Protocol did "not apply to situations of internal disturbances and tensions, such as riots, isolated and sporadic acts of violence and other acts of a similar nature."[56] This once again highlights the narrow divide that can exist between ordinary crime and armed conflict when dealing with violence involving non-State actors. This is an issue that will be seen to have considerable relevance as international law grapples with the categorization of armed conflict involving contemporary non-State security threats.

As one analyst perceptively summarized the complexity of the treaty framework regarding the regulation of guerrilla warfare in the aftermath of the creation of the two Additional Protocols:

> It may well be that we now have sliding scale of international texts, ranging from full international conflicts (Protocol I and most of the articles in the Geneva Conventions) through civil wars (Protocol II) and serious international violence (common article 3) to lower levels internal violence, such as Northern Ireland (existing UN and regional intergovernmental human rights treaties).[57]

While theoretically accurate, this description masks a less definitive reality regarding conflict regulation. The threshold between wide scale criminal violence and armed conflict can be difficult to ascertain. As has been noted, the connection between non-State actor threats and AP I has largely fallen into disuse. Many conflicts between States and insurgent groups do not rise to the level of a civil war (i.e., AP II) and, when they do, States are reluctant to admit it. Further, States may choose to treat an insurgency as criminal matter. This was evident in the United Kingdom's nearly 30-year struggle with the terrorist group the Irish Republican Army during the Northern Ireland Troubles. Notwithstanding commentators concluding that the levels of violence perpetrated by that organized group rose to the level of an insurgency,[58] the United Kingdom made a policy choice to apply human rights–based law enforcement to resolve the conflict.[59] Given the uncertainty regarding the application of this treaty-based law, and their limitations in terms of what is regulated (e.g., targeting), considerable attention is paid to customary international law and soft law to determine the regulatory framework governing NIAC.

3.2   Customary and soft law

Treaty law regulates only a portion of the issues that arise during an armed conflict between States and non-State actors. In response to this disparity between the proclivity of such armed conflicts and the limited nature of treaty regulation, in the aftermath of the Cold War efforts were made through the development of interpretive guidance, such as the 2005 International Review of the Red Cross *Customary International Humanitarian Law Study*,[60] or through judge-made law to identify the degree to which customary humanitarian law applies to internal conflicts.[61] However, the full extent to which that law governs such conflict remains uncertain. Considerable additional work has been done to fill in perceived gaps in the law through what have sometimes been described as soft law instruments, such as the ICRC Interpretive Guidance on the Notion of Direct Participation in Hostilities Under International Humanitarian Law,[62] the Commentary on the *HPCR Manual on International Law Applicable to Air and Missile Warfare*,[63] and the *Tallinn Manual on the International Law Applicable to Cyber Warfare*.[64]

States also set out their understanding of the law applicable to such conflicts in military manuals.[65] However, important differences do remain. As has been noted:

> [B]ecause certain core regulatory concepts remain applicable exclusively in the context of IAC—such as the entitlement to prisoner-of-war status and the accordant lawful combatant's privilege, and international legal rules related to obligations of neutral states—distinguishing IAC from NIAC remains an important aspect of defining operational legal obligations.[66]

Adding to the challenges that arise in determining what law applies to conflicts not of an international character is the State preference to treat such violence as criminal law matters. Further, there is frequently a connection between insurgency and crime. This ensures human rights law, both international and domestic, plays a role in terms of regulating non-State actor violence even during an armed conflict. In this respect, human rights advocates and courts have often turned to soft law instruments, such as the United Nations Basic Principles on the Use of Force and Firearms by Law Enforcement Officials[67] and the Standard Minimum Rules for the Treatment of Prisoners,[68] to determine appropriate legal standards in situations where it is not evident that IHL applies.

3.3   The role of human rights law

A unique aspect of conflict with non-State actors is that law enforcement involving an application of a human rights–based framework to govern State activity has become a defining feature of many contemporary security operations. This may arise as a matter of law or policy. For example, if the violence does not reach the level of an armed conflict the non-State actor must be dealt with under the human rights law paradigm. This means that law enforcement–type rules apply to much of the government response to the threat it confronts. Similarly, where a civilian is not taking a direct part in hostilities, he or she cannot be targeted under the conduct of hostilities provisions of IHL. Instead the civilian may remain subject to arrest and prosecution for indirect support provided to an organized armed group. Criminal gangs may proliferate within a territory because of the instability caused by an armed conflict. Responding to those gangs requires a law enforcement approach even when a conduct of hostilities framework may be used simultaneously to counter a non-State organized armed group. States may also choose, as a matter of policy, to apply a law enforcement response even when an armed conflict is in existence. This is frequently done when countering threats generated within a country. The same approach is often adopted by military commanders who understand that even when they are authorized to use armed conflict rules they are not obligated to do so. This is why military commanders may choose to apply a law enforcement approach to deal with organized armed groups even when a more expansive use of force may be legally permissible. In this respect, the use of a police primacy approach is a widely recognized part of successful counterinsurgency operations.[69]

The application of international human rights law to a NIAC is, for many States, considered obligatory as the result of extraterritorial application of international or regional human rights treaties. However, not all States accept that treaties such as the 1966 International Covenant on Civil and Political Rights apply extraterritorially.[70] Notwithstanding that approach, human rights principles (e.g., protection from murder, torture, or other cruel, inhuman, or degrading treatment or punishment or prolonged arbitrary detention) are part of customary international law. For the United States, this is reflected in Restatement of the Law: The Foreign Relations Law of the United States.[71] This interpretation of the law can be found in the U.S. Army *Operational Law Handbook*.[72] Recognizing their customary law status means that those principles have universal application regardless of whether a human rights treaty has jurisdictional limitations.

Importantly, IHL also includes a significant incorporation of human rights principles. This can be seen in Common Article 3, Article 75 of AP I, and Article 4 of AP II. Although the United States is not bound by the APs, it has indicated that out of a sense of legal obligation it would "treat the principles set forth in Article 75 as applicable to any individual it detains in an international armed conflict."[73] Further, "Additional Protocol II to the Geneva Conventions contains detailed humane treatment standards and fair trial guarantees that would apply in the context of non-international armed conflicts, such as the hostilities authorized by the 2001 AUMF."[74] And, as noted in Chapter 1, the U.S. position on AP II is even more significant because, unlike AP I, the United States has never rejected AP II. Instead, Presidents Reagan, Clinton, and Obama all requested Senate advice and consent to allow them to ratify this treaty, and indicated that the United States will apply the provisions of the treaty to any armed conflict falling within the scope of Common Article 3. This means that, even though the United States and other countries may follow a policy of applying IHL in situations where the applicable rules governing hostilities may not be clearly established at law, State armed forces must remain cognizant that not all threats will emanate from members of opposing organized armed groups.[75] There will remain an obligation to apply human rights principles as a matter of human rights law, or as part of humanitarian law when dealing with non-State actor–related violence.

4   Classifying conflict with non-State actors

A significant challenge that arises when dealing with armed conflict involving non-State actors is the lack of consensus among political leaders, government officials, diplomats, and international lawyers regarding how those hostilities should be described and categorized. This is another area of international law that in the post-9/11 period is in a considerable state of flux.[76] The discussion is complicated by the fact that simply because State armed forces are engaged in combat with a non-State actor organized armed group does not make the conflict a non-international one. Indeed, State armed forces may engage with organized armed groups under a variety of circumstances in the context of inter-State warfare, or IAC. Further, there is a significant disagreement about how to describe non-State actor conflict, or the degree to which such conflict may be geographically limited. The issues will be explored first by discussing non-State actor involvement in conflicts classified as being international in character. Next, numerous theories that have been suggested to describe conflicts that are viewed as being non-international in character will be explored. Finally, the criteria to be applied in assessing the threshold separating conflicts not of an international character from matters uniquely subject to a law enforcement will be outlined.

4.1 Non-State actors and international armed conflict

Non-State actors are frequent participants in inter-State IACs, either on their own or while operating under the control of a State. This is perhaps most evident from the post–World War II effort during the Third Geneva Convention deliberations to recognize that members of organized resistance movements could, under certain limited conditions, qualify for POW status during an IAC (*see* Chapter 3, 2.1.2: *In the aftermath of World War II*). A fundamental criterion to be met by such groups in Article 4(A)(2) was their belonging to a party to the conflict. Despite that requirement, it is clear some resistance groups operating during that conflict, such as Josip Tito's communist forces operating in Yugoslavia, did not meet that criteria.[77] However, being unlawful did not make them any less participants in the conflict. In this respect, hostilities between States and organized armed groups is particularly likely during periods of occupation where inhabitants may rise up against an invading force. That was the case for Coalition forces that entered Iraq in 2003. By 28 June 2004, at the official end of the occupation,[78] there were a significant array of non-State armed groups fighting United States and other State armed forces engaged in that conflict.[79]

As has been previously noted, non-State participation in IAC had been recognized prior to World War II under recognition of belligerency doctrine. Similarly, the 1977 AP I contemplated that a non-State national liberation movement could become a party to an IAC. While the recognition of belligerency has fallen into disuse, and the Protocol recognition of non-State actors has been narrowly interpreted, the contemplation of such participation continues to be part of the contemporary international law dialogue. For example, an armed attack against a State by a non-State actor that is sent by or is operating under the control of another State will be attributable to the controlling State. This means that the resulting armed conflict will be one between the two States involved, and not simply constitute hostilities between the State and non-State actor. This is the situation even if the violence is only between the attacked State and the non-State protagonist.

Another way in which an IAC can arise as a result of an attack by a non-State actor is if another State is viewed as harboring or controlling the organized armed group. Often discussed in the post-9/11 period as *harboring* terrorists, this theory formed the basis for the United States response against Afghanistan following the attacks carried out through means of hijacked aircraft.[80] Under this theory, Afghanistan had an obligation not to permit its territory to be used by al Qaeda to carry out attacks in New York and Washington. This approach has a legal basis in the 1980 International Court of Justice decision *Case Concerning United States Diplomatic and Consular Staff in Tehran (United States v. Iran)*. In that case it was ruled that the after-the-fact approval by Iranian officials of the militant takeover of U.S. diplomatic premises, the detention of diplomatic staff hostages, "and the decision to perpetuate them translated continuing occupation of the Embassy and detention of the hostages into acts of that State."[81]

The Israeli Supreme Court posited a different theory, whereby conflict between that State and the non-State actors on its borders constitutes a conflict that is international in character. The court noted that the law governing IAC governs violence in occupied territory, and added, "[t]his law applies in any case of an armed conflict of international character—in other words, one that *crosses the borders of the state—whether or not the place in which the armed conflict occurs is subject to belligerent occupation.*"[82] This focus on cross-border attacks by non-State groups stands in contrast to traditional interpretations of IHL that view such conflict as internal to States. However, it does accurately describe the nature of the activity carried out by organized armed groups with a State-like capacity to wage war.

The post-9/11 period has spawned another theory regarding conflict character-ization that is focused on the non-consensual entry by one State into the territory of another State in response to a threat posed by a non-State actor. Even if the action by the threatened State is not directed at the governmental structures of the territorial State, the cross-border action is viewed as being "against the territorial State."[83] This is because the State is viewed as extending to the people and territory controlled by the State. The result is the hostilities are said to be an IAC even though violence may only occur between the responding State and the non-State actor. It is a theory that appears to have been prompted by counterterrorist operations, such as the United States' use of drones outside of areas of active hostilities. In that regard, it seems to be more focused on a *jus ad bellum* goal of restricting such military action than addressing the actual hostilities between States and non-State actors.[84]

While it is acknowledged by its author that the non-consensual theory does not represent the majority view in the existing literature, it has attracted the attention of the ICRC. The 2016 ICRC Updated Commentaries on the First Geneva Convention of 1949 (2016 GWS Commentary) adopted this approach toward conflict characterization, however with a significant alteration.[85] That Commentary indicates that finding there is an inter-State conflict between the two States does "not exclude the existence of a parallel non-international armed conflict between the intervening State and the armed group."[86] In contrast, the non-consensual theory was based on an interpretation that "the conflict with the non-State group will be so bound up with the international armed conflict between the States that it will be impossible to separate the two conflicts."[87]

The ICRC adoption of this theory has attracted criticism,[88] and it is not clear what its practical effect will be in terms of the actual regulation of hostilities between the threatened State and the non-State actor. While it provides for POW status for some of the participants in the conflict, it also makes the operating environment more complex with an application of humanitarian law in simultaneous IACs and NIACs occurring within the same territory brought on by the single act of a State exercising its lawful right of self-defense. What this theory does indicate is that there is a considerable lack of consensus concerning the categorization of conflict with non-State actors even in terms of IAC. As will become evident in the next section, this lack of consensus is also demonstrated regarding how NIAC is dealt with.

4.2   *Non-State actors and non-international armed conflict*

Given the traditional association of non-State actor armed groups and NIACs, it might be thought that this area of the law would be well settled. Certainly, the traditional notion of such conflicts being internal to a State is well settled in international law, as is reflected in AP II.[89] This has been extended to accepting the concept of a *spillover* NIAC when organized armed groups operate from safe havens in adjacent States. A prime example of such a conflict is Afghanistan, where the Taliban also operates from within Pakistan.[90] However, there is also recognition that non-State actors may act transnationally from locations that are not adjacent to territories where NIACs are occurring.

Transnational threats have prompted the development of a number of legal theories by which to categorize conflict with terrorists and other organized armed groups. One basis for the idea that a NIAC does not have to occur exclusively within the territory of a specific State is reflected in the interpretation that Common Article 3 is not limited to conflicts within a State "providing that it applies to armed conflicts 'not of an international character occurring in the territory of *one* of the High Contracting Parties.'"[91] The term *extraterritorial law enforcement* has been used to describe cross-border operations by States against terrorist groups, although the governing legal framework for the conduct of those hostilities remains rooted in the notion of a spillover NIAC.[92] Immediately following the attacks of 9/11, the theory of transnational armed conflict was also developed. It was designed to address the perceived regulatory gap between interpretations of IAC occurring between States and NIAC being internal to a State.[93] This theory did not gain broad acceptance, but it is noteworthy for its focus on the means required to respond to non-State actor threats. Under this approach, the use of military forces authorized to conduct operations pursuant to IHL (most notably the authority to employ deadly force under a more permissive legal framework, and detain based on belligerent status determinations) was a critical factor in determining whether an armed conflict was in existence.[94] This is a factor that arises again regarding contemporary assessments of when the threshold is reached for NIAC (*see* Chapter 2, 4.3: *The non-international armed conflict threshold*).

The theory that perhaps best represents the struggle which has occurred in categorizing transnational non-State actor threats arose from the 2006 *Hamdan v. Rumsfeld* decision of the U.S. Supreme Court.[95] In that case the court determined that the Common Article 3 protections of the 1949 Geneva Conventions were applicable to the conflict with al Qaeda. None of the parties involved in that litigation asserted, nor did the court find, that the conflict was international within the meaning of Common Article 2. Furthermore, both Hamdan and the U.S. Government implicitly conceded that the situation was at least an armed conflict. However, the U.S. Government took the view that because it was not international in *character*, but was international in *scope*, it did not fall within the scope of Common Article 3 because that treaty provision applied only to armed conflicts internal to the State. While this interpretation of Common Article 3 may have had some historical merit, the Supreme Court rejected it, and with it the creation of a humanitarian protection gap. Rather it was held, "[t]he term 'conflict not of an international character' is used here in contradistinction to a conflict between nations."[96] It has been noted that

> the Court not only closed the regulatory gap that enabled the United States to deny CA3 [Common Article 3] protections to al Qaeda detainees [on the basis the conflict was international in scope but not in legal terms], but it contributed to what many believe is an important revision to the understanding of what qualifies as a CA3 NIAC.[97]

That is not to say that this approach has gained full acceptance. The *Hamdan* decision has been criticized on the basis that the U.S. Supreme Court "subscribed to the fiction that the cross-border worldwide 'war on terrorism' is a non-international armed conflict."[98] In addition, the use of the term *non-international armed conflict* to describe trans-border hostilities can create confusion (although it should be noted that, because the parties to the *Hamdan* litigation conceded the existence of an armed conflict, the Supreme Court confronted a binary choice: either interpret Common Article 3 as applicable, or endorse the U.S. Government interpretation that would have allowed for the existence of an armed conflict with no obligatory humanitarian rules). Similarly, describing military operations as extraterritorial law enforcement also highlights many of the terminological challenges that have arisen as lawyers struggle to categorize non-State actor conflict. Further, while championing the novel theory of non-consensual cross-border operations automatically creating an IAC, the 2016 GWS Commentary analysis of Common Article 3 is less supportive of the *Hamdan*-based approach. That Commentary suggests "the practice of States party to the Geneva Conventions in support of a global or transnational non-international armed conflicts remains isolated."[99] Notwithstanding these perspectives, the *Hamdan v. Rumsfeld* recognition of these hostilities constituting a NIAC forms the basis for a significant portion of the State action being taken to counter a spreading jihadist threat.

Other analysts take the view that the type of terrorist action that prompts State responses against non-State actors involves criminal action, and "the isolated terrorist attack, regardless of how serious its consequences, is not an armed conflict."[100] However, the reality is that although violence with non-State actors can occur in situations of IAC, and some non-State actor threats may not rise to the level of armed conflict, it is highly likely that the threat posed by organized armed groups like al Qaeda or the Islamic State will be seen as part of a NIAC. Such conflict is more prevalent than hostilities between States. For practitioners, the uncertainty and complexity of the existing legal debate has frequently led to the simple question of whether there is an armed conflict in existence. There are differences between the extent to which humanitarian law impacts the two forms of armed conflict. However, for important issues, such as targeting and the requirement that detainees be humanely treated, the governing framework is substantially the same.

4.3   The non-international armed conflict threshold

Prior to the end of the Cold War, it was not clear how the threshold for NIAC was to be established. As has been discussed, AP II set a high threshold for its application. Common Article 3 came to be viewed as having a lower, though undefined threshold that did not require the control of territory by an organized armed group.[101] The complex conflicts of the 1990s prompted a search for workable criteria upon which to determine when an armed conflict exists. In *Prosecutor v. Tadić*, the ICTY determined there were two foundational criteria for a NIAC: intensity of violence (protracted armed violence) and group organization.[102] Such criteria were also incorporated into the 1998 Rome Statute of the International Criminal Court, which indicated that certain crimes applied in "armed conflicts that take place in the territory of a State when there is *protracted armed conflict* between governmental authorities and organized armed groups or between such groups."[103] While there has been discussion about whether the reference was to an armed conflict being protracted, rather than simply protracted armed violence, there should be no difference in meaning.[104]

One of the issues that has attracted considerable discussion is the first criterion: the intensity requirement of the violence. The original *Tadić* appellate-level decision referred to "protracted armed violence,"[105] while a subsequent Trial Chamber described the violence threshold as the "intensity of violence."[106] This raises the issue of whether there must be a certain duration of hostilities before violence between States and non-State actors rises to the level of an armed conflict. Requiring such a time requirement means that, unlike violence between States, a short duration but extremely violent attack by an organized armed group would not meet the threshold of an armed conflict. On its face, this would appear to exclude one-off attacks by jihadist groups that have come to define many of the high-profile operations against States (e.g., 2012 Benghazi, 2013 Nairobi Westgate Mall, 2015 Paris).

However, there has been a move away from reliance on duration as a precondition part of the threshold requirements for an armed conflict. In this respect, intensity can be viewed as "a much broader notion of which duration only forms a part."[107] This means "violence of a relatively brief duration may still amount to a non-international armed conflict provided that other indicia suggesting intensity are present to a significant degree."[108] The 2016 GWS Commentary also recognized the limits of the duration when it noted that this criterion is better suited to an after-the-fact judicial assessment than an on-the-spot determination of the intensity of violence.[109] In this regard,

> an independent requirement of duration could, in contrast, lead to a situation of uncertainty regarding the applicability of humanitarian law during the

initial phase of fighting among those expected to respect the law, or to a belated application in situations where its regulatory force was in fact already required at an earlier moment.[110]

In taking this approach, the 2016 GWS Commentary relies on the *La Tablada Case (Abella v. Argentina)*, where

> the Inter-American Commission on Human Rights, generally applying the criteria of intensity and organization, came to the conclusion that an attack by 42 armed persons against an army barracks, leading to combat lasting about 30 hours, had crossed the threshold of a non-international armed conflict.[111]

This suggests that even one sufficiently violent attack by a non-State actor could be considered to be a NIAC.

The second criterion of group organization raises the question of what level of organization is required to indicate the violence may not simply be crime-related. The ICTY has indicated that factors such as an official command structure, headquarters, internal regulations, disciplinary procedures, control of territory, use of uniforms, modes of communication undertaking negotiations with third parties, distribution of arms, and recruiting new members should be taken into consideration.[112] However, there is a need to be careful as relying on criteria associated with State regular armed forces is too limiting. Organized armed groups can take on a traditional hierarchical command structure, a horizontal, more decentralized approach, a cellular organization, or even a *hybrid* combination of these factors. For example, Hezbollah is reported to have a hybrid structure. During its 2006 conflict with Israel it had "so-called elite or regular fighters, who number about 1,000 men and who were often given advanced weapons training; and village fighters, whose numbers are difficult to estimate because they often include local men only loosely affiliated with Hezbollah."[113]

Much also depends upon the tactics and the security environment within which the organization is operating. The organization structure may change over time. For example, Islamic State forces adopted a more conventional military organization as it began to take territory in Iraq.[114] Such an approach is entirely consistent with the jihadist embrace of the three-stage guerrilla revolutionary war strategy.[115] The adoption of a cellular structure can make a group look like a criminal gang, and may make it more susceptible to a law enforcement response. However, as has been noted, "decentralization does not mean that groups do not meet the international humanitarian law requirement of organization."[116] In this regard, as the court in *Prosecutor v. Limaj* stated, "*some degree of organisation by the parties will suffice to establish the existence of an armed conflict.*"[117]

The criteria of intensity of violence and group organization are widely viewed as constituting the starting point for a discussion regarding the existence of an armed conflict with non-State actors. However, questions remain regarding what these criteria mean in practice, and whether additional factors need to be applied.

There appears to have developed a broader, more contextual approach to assessing whether the threshold for NIAC has been reached. Such factors include consideration of the exceptionally broad range of non-State actor violence; the nature of the threat (i.e., criminal or politically motivated); the increased lethality of non-State actor violence (e.g., improvised explosive devices, suicide bombing); the need to ensure that States' security forces can adequately respond to those threats (i.e., a military or policing response); as well as the intertwined nature of insurgent conflict and criminal activities, and with it the desire to separate the latter activity from the former.

One indicia that has gained prominence is the AP II reference to it not applying to riots, disturbances, and similar criminal acts.[118] As the 2016 GWS Commentary notes,

> it is understood that Article 1(2) of Additional Protocol II, which provides that the "Protocol shall not apply to situations of internal disturbances and tensions, such as riots, isolated and sporadic acts of violence and other acts of a similar nature, as not being armed conflicts", also defines the lower threshold of common Article 3.[119]

More recently, a totality of the circumstances approach has been developed to assess whether an armed conflict is occurring.[120] This approach looks at multiple factors, including the nature of the armed group threat, and the type of State response required to defeat it. Consideration of the type of State forces required to counter non-State actor violence finds its basis in a variety of sources, including the 1958 ICRC Geneva Convention I Commentary (1958 GWS Commentary),[121] the 1997 *Tadić* decision,[122] and the 2008 *Prosecutor v. Boškoski* case.[123] As was noted in the latter decision,

> while isolated acts of terrorism may not reach the threshold of armed conflict, when there is protracted violence of this type, *especially where they require the engagement of the armed forces in hostilities,* such acts are relevant to assessing the level of intensity with regard to the existence of an armed conflict.[124]

Similarly, the 2016 GWS Commentary indicates that "the requisite degree of intensity may be met 'when hostilities are of a collective character or when the government is obliged to use military force against the insurgents, instead of mere police forces.'"[125]

In light of the growth of powerful transnational criminal organizations, another categorization criterion that is attracting attention is whether the purpose of the violence is economic or political. IHL has traditionally avoided any reference to the purpose for which violence may occur in order to maintain the equal application principle, wherein the law is seen to apply equally to all protagonists regardless of the justness of their cause.[126] However, it is also clear that armed conflict, even in its non-international form, occurs for a political purpose.[127]

In that respect, the identification of a solely economic motivation by drug cartels and other transnational criminal groups provides an important point of demarcation between criminal activity and engagement in hostilities.[128]

4.4   Non-State actors, self-defense and armed conflict

The use of force by States to thwart an attack by an organized armed group has raised some of the most interesting and challenging issues for international lawyers. A traditional view of international law is that the State right to act in self-defense was restricted to conflict between States. Given the low threshold for IAC set out in Common Article 2 of the 1949 Geneva Conventions, defensive action taken by States against other States ordinarily gives rise to such hostilities. Non-State actors might be involved, however only a coordinated and general campaign by those actors "*with obvious or easily proven complicity of the government of a state* from which they operate would constitute an 'armed attack.'"[129] This would not extend to "[s]poradic operations by armed bands."[130] As has been noted, the attribution of the non-State action to a State (e.g., exercising control) underpinned the determination the conflict was an international one.

However, the post-9/11 period has witnessed a significant shift with increasing recognition that an armed attack can be carried out by non-State actors on their own, which justifies a State response in self-defense. The right to take defensive action against non-State actors has been recognized in academic writing,[131] the 2005 Chatham House Principles of International Law on the Use of Force by States in Self-Defence,[132] and the 2010 Leiden Policy Recommendations on Counter-Terrorism and International Law.[133] Thus, attribution, or connection, to a State is no longer considered the majority view.[134] Further, it is an approach that is entirely consistent with the historical understanding of the right of self-defense outline in the *Caroline* incident, a case that involved a non-State actor.[135]

Defensive action against non-State actors raises the question of whether it is humanitarian law, or human rights law that governs the use of force. Further, for the United States there is the issue of whether an exercise of self-defense is separately governed by its own legal principles (e.g., necessity, proportionality, imminence, and immediacy) without the need to determine the existence of an armed conflict (*see* Chapter 6, 5.1: *Drones*). Much of this debate centers around how narrowly the principles in *Prosecutor v. Tadić*[136] (e.g., intensity of violence, group organization) are interpreted, and whether the additional criteria such as those found in a totality of the circumstances approach can be applied. A key practical issue is consideration of the nature of the threat, and the responses that are available to counter it. This also has a legal aspect, since human rights–based law enforcement may not be capable of underpinning the levels of force necessary to respond to the non-State actor. Such analysis can lead to greater acceptance that a one-off attack by a non-State actor could result in a NIAC.

The advantage for States in applying this threshold is that there is less of a distinction between attacks by non-State actors controlled or harbored by a State and one carried out solely by an organized armed group. There would still be a requirement to meet a conflict threshold that separates criminal action from the conduct of hostilities. It also leaves less room for a unique self-defense theory since humanitarian law would readily apply once a NIAC is determined to be in existence. Finally, determining an armed conflict is in existence would not preclude a State from choosing to respond with a human rights–based law enforcement response. Indeed, in many cases the first responders will be police forces, which by training and armament would ordinarily apply force under that legal framework.[137]

5 Conclusion

In conclusion, conflicts with and between non-State actors present particular challenges when assessing the impact of international law. States have historically resisted qualifying internal violence as armed conflicts. However, the threat of transnational terrorism in the post-9/11 period has forced change, leading to greater consideration of the application of IHL when confronting non-State actors. The requirement to consider the interface between that body of law and human rights law (international and domestic) has also arisen because of the prevalence of criminal insurgencies and transnational criminal groups that thrive in ungoverned or poorly governed territory. Resolving the application of humanitarian law inevitably leads to greater consideration of the customary IHL rules. However, it is evident that the international legal community continues to struggle with key humanitarian law concepts such as the categorization of conflicts. Conflicts with non-State actors can occur in the context of an IAC, including when a State controls or harbors the organized armed group. In terms of a NIAC, there are numerous classification theories, with the United States approach toward a conflict other than one between two States being assessed as a NIAC having a prominent place in the international dialogue.

Increased scrutiny has also been placed on the question of the threshold for NIAC. Here there has been a shift toward a totality of the circumstances approach that looks at factors, which are additional to the traditional levels and duration of violence, and degree of organization of the armed group. This includes the nature of the armed group and the type of State response (e.g., military forces) required to defeat it. What is clear is that there is a more general acceptance among international lawyers that States can act in self-defense against non-State actors under Article 51 of the United Nations Charter. With this recognition has come an acknowledgment that the duration of the violence is not as key a factor is assessing whether an armed conflict is in existence.

Notes

1 Leslie Green, *The Contemporary Law of Armed Conflict* 91 (3rd edn, 2008); Legal Consequences of The Construction of A Wall in the Occupied Palestinian Territory, Advisory Opinion, 2004 I.C.J. 136, 194 (9 July), *available at* www.icj-cij.org/docket/files/131/1671.pdf. *See also Prosecutor v. Tadić*, Case No. IT-94-1-A, Appeals Judgment, para 84 (Int'l Crim. Trib. for the former Yugoslavia 15 July 1999), *available at* www.icty.org/x/cases/tadic/acjug/en/tad-aj990715e.pdf

2 Virginia Comolli, *Boko Haram: Nigeria's Islamist Insurgency* 155 (2015) (referring to advances and information technology providing a benefit to Boko Haram "their predecessors could never have imagined").

3 Geoffrey S. Corn, "Legal Classification of Military Operations," in *U.S. Military Operations: Law Policy, and Practice* 67, 77 (Geoffrey S. Corn, Rachel E. Vanlandingham, & Shane R. Reeves eds, 2016).

4 Jack S. Levy & William R. Thompson, *Causes of War* 12 (2010).

5 Protocol (I) Additional to the Geneva Conventions of 12 August 1949, and Relating to the Protection of Victims of International Armed Conflicts, 8 June 1977, 1125 U.N.T.S. 3 [hereinafter AP I] (entered into force 7 December 1978) (signed by the United States 12 December 1977, not transmitted to U.S. Senate, *see* S. Treaty Doc. No. 100–2 (1987)); Protocol (II) Additional to the Geneva Conventions of 12 August 1949, and Relating to the Protection of Victims of Non-International Armed Conflicts, Art 6(5), 8 June 1977, 1125 U.N.T.S. 609 [hereinafter AP II] (entered into force 7 December 1978) (signed by the United States 12 December 1977, transmitted to the U.S. Senate 29 January 1987, still pending action as S. Treaty Doc. No. 100–2 (1987)).

6 Hugo Grotius, 1 *The Rights of War and Peace* 240 (2005).

7 *Id.*

8 Crawford, *The Treatment of Combatants and Insurgents under the Law of Armed Conflict* 71 (2010).

9 Green, *supra* note 1, at 66.

10 Emily Crawford, *Identifying the Enemy: Civilian Participation in Armed Conflict* 15 (2016).

11 Jens David Ohlin & Larry May, *Necessity in International Law* 121 (2016).

12 Lindsay Moir, *The Historical Development of the Application of Humanitarian Law in Non-International Armed Conflicts to 1949*, 47 Int'l & Comp L.Q. 337, 338 (1998).

13 *Id.*

14 Kenneth Watkin, *Fighting at the Legal Boundaries: Controlling the Use of Force in Contemporary Conflict* 104 (2016).

15 Moir, *supra* note 12, at 343.

16 Sandesh Sivakumaran, *The Law of Non-International Armed Conflict* 192 (2012).

17 Anthony Cullen, *The Concept of Non-International Armed Conflict in International Humanitarian Law* 23 (2010).

18 Max G. Manwaring, *The Complexity of Modern Asymmetric Warfare* 3 (2012).

19 Seth Jones, *Waging Insurgent Warfare: Lessons from the Vietcong to the Islamic State* 5 (2017).

20 "Colombia's Government Formally Ratifies Revised Farc Peace Deal," *The Guardian* (1 December 2016), *available at* www.theguardian.com/world/2016/dec/01/colombias-government-formally-ratifies-revised-farc-peace-deal

21 Abdulkader H. Sinno, *Organizations at War in Afghanistan and Beyond* 13 (2008). But *see* Jones, *supra* note 19, at 171–2 (where it is stated "the ability of insurgents to establish a sanctuary in neighbouring States does not increase insurgent probability of victory," although it is suggested that such a sanctuary can be helpful if the insurgent force cannot control territory in their home country. *See Id.* at 149).

22 Fawaz Gerges, *The Far Enemy: Why Jihad Went Global* 1 (2005) (for reference to "jihadis who have used violence against . . . their own governments (the near enemy) . . ."); *Id.* at 1 ("*The Far Enemy*, or al-Adou al-Baced, is a term used by jihadis to refer to the United States and its Western Allies.").

23 Mark E. Stout et al., *Terrorist Perspectives Project: Strategic and Operational Views of Al Qaida and Associated Movements* 19 (2008).

24 *See* Charles Lister, *The Syrian Jihad: Al-Qaeda, the Islamic State and the Evolution of an Insurgency* (2015).

25 *A Terrorist's Call to Global Jihad: Deciphering Abu Musab Al-Suri's Islamic Jihad Manifesto* 51 (Jim Lacey ed., 2008) ("Islam pays no heed to the borders the Crusaders drew up between our countries and nationalities, citizenship regimes, and pass-ports they invented."); Abu Bakr Naji, *The Management of Savagery: The Most Critical Stage Through Which the Umma Will Pass* 16 (William McCants trans., 2006), *available at* https://azelin.files.wordpress.com/2010/08/abu-bakr-naji-the-management-of-savagery-the-most-critical-stage-through-which-the-umma-will-pass.pdf ("I mean an area that is not limited to the borders (set by) the United Nations, since the mujahids move with freedom within the borders of the Yemen, the Hijaz, and Oman.")

26 S. C. Res. 2249, UN Doc. S/RES/2249 *Preamble* (20 November 2015).

27 Lister, *supra* note 24, at 2.

28 *Id.* at 385.

29 *Id.* at 386.

30 *Id.*

31 Ioan Grillo, *El Narco: Inside Mexico's Criminal Insurgency* 206 (2011).

32 Manwaring, *Gangs Pseudo-Militaries and Other Modern Mercenaries* 131 (2010).

33 Grillo, *Gangster Warlords: Drug Dollars, Killing Fields, and the New Politics of Latin America* 11 (2016).

34 S. Beittel, *Mexico's Drug Trafficking Organizations: Source and Scope of the Rising Violence*, Congressional Research Service 20 (15 April 2013), *available at* www.hsdl.org/?view&did=735457

35 Watkin, *supra* note 14, at 175–7; Crawford, *supra* note 10, at 182–9.

36 Watkin, *supra* note 14, at 177–9; Crawford, *supra* note 10, at 186–7.

37 Watkin, *supra* note 14, at 178.

38 Steven Metz, *Rethinking Insurgency*, Strategic Studies Institute, U.S. Army War College 29 (2007), *available at* www.strategicstudiesinstitute.army.mil/pubs/display.cfm?pubID=790

39 *Id.*

40 Crawford, *supra* note 10, at 190.

41 Watkin, *supra* note 14, at 169.

42 Corn, *supra* note 3, at 73.

43 Jean S. Pictet, Geneva Convention Relative to the Treatment of Prisoners of War: Commentary (ICRC, 1960), 32 [hereinafter Commentary GPW].

44 Cullen, *supra* note 17, at 60.

45 Corn, *supra* note 3, at 75.

46 *See* Keith Suter, *An International Law of Guerrilla Warfare* 43 (1984); Richard Baxter, "Humanitarian Law or Humanitarian Politics?," in *Humanizing the Laws of War* 287 (Detlev F. Vagts et al. eds, 2013) (first appearing in 16 Harv. Int'l L.J. 1 (1976)).

47 *See, e.g.*, AP I, Art 57(2)(a).

48 AP II, Art 13(3).

49 Brian Egan, *International Law, Legal Diplomacy, and the Counter-ISIL Campaign: Some Observations*, 92 Int'l L. Stud. 235, 242–3 (2016).

50 AP I, Art 1(4) (emphasis added).

51 Ronald Reagan, Letter of Transmittal, The White House, 29 January 1987, *available at* www.loc.gov/rr/frd/Military_Law/pdf/protocol-II-100-2.pdf. Other States that are not bound by AP I include India, Pakistan, Iran, Turkey, South Korea, North Korea, and Israel. *See* State Parties to the Following International Humanitarian Law

and Other Related Treaties as of 6 January 2014, ICRC, *available at* https://
ihl-databases.icrc.org/applic/ihl/ihl.nsf/vwTreatiesByCountry.xsp.

52 Theodor Meron, *The Time Has Come for the United States to Ratify Geneva Protocol
I*, 88 Am. J. Int'l L. 678, 683 (1994).

53 AP II, Art 1(1).

54 Suter, *supra* note 46, at 177.

55 *Id.* at 169.

56 AP II, Art 1(2).

57 Suter, *supra* note 46, at 173.

58 Mark Cochrane, "The Role of the Royal Ulster Constabulary in Northern Ireland,"
in *Policing Insurgencies: Cops as Counterinsurgents* 107 (C. Christine Fair & Sumit
Ganguly eds, 2014) (where the Northern Ireland conflict is referred to as an
insurgency).

59 Watkin, *supra* note 14, at 536–44.

60 *Customary International Humanitarian Law Study* (Jean-Marie Henckaerts & Louise
Doswald-Beck eds, 2005).

61 *Prosecutor v. Tadić*, Case No. IT-94-1-A, Appeals Judgment, paras 96–127 (Int'l
Crim. Trib. for the former Yugoslavia 15 July 1999), *available at* www.icty.org/
x/cases/tadic/acjug/en/tad-aj990715e.pdf

62 *See* N. Melzer, Interpretive Guidance on the Notion of Direct Participation in
Hostilities Under International Humanitarian Law (2009).

63 *See,* Program on Humanitarian Policy and Conflict Research (HPCR) at Harvard
University, Commentary on the *HPCR Manual on International Law Applicable to
Air and Missile Warfare* (2009).

64 *See* Crawford, *supra* note 10, at 211–17 (for a discussion of the utility of soft law
instruments).

65 *See, e.g.*, U.S. Dep't of Def., *Law of War Manual* (June 2015, updated December
2016) [hereinafter *DoD Law of War Manual*]; *Manual of the Law of Armed Conflict*
(UK Ministry of Defence ed., 2004); *The U.S. Army, Marine Corps, Counterinsurgency Field Manual* (2007) [hereinafter *Counterinsurgency Manual*].

66 Corn, *supra* note 3, at 75.

67 Adopted by the Eighth United Nations Congress on the Prevention of Crime and
the Treatment of Offenders, Havana, Cuba, 27 August to 7 September 1990, *available at* www.ohchr.org/EN/ProfessionalInterest/Pages/UseOfForceAndFirearms.
aspx

68 Adopted by the First United Nations Congress on the Prevention of Crime and the
Treatment of Offenders, held at Geneva in 1955, and approved by the Economic
and Social Council by its resolutions 663 C (XXIV) of 31 July 1957, and 2076
(LXII) of 13 May 1977, *available at* www.unodc.org/pdf/criminal_justice/UN_
Standard_Minimum_Rules_for_the_Treatment_of_Prisoners.pdf

69 *Counterinsurgency Manual*, paras 6–90, at 229. *See also* David H. Bayley & Robert
M. Perito, *The Police in War: Fighting Insurgency, Terrorism, and Violent Crime*
68–9 (2010).

70 Michael J. Dennis, *Application of Human Rights Treaties Extraterritorially in Times
of Armed Conflict and Military Occupation*, 99 Am. J. Int'l. L. 119 (2005). *See also*
Mary E. McLeod, Acting Legal Adviser, U.S. Department of State, Opening Statement
at the Committee Against Torture—Permanent Mission of the United States of
America to the United Nations and Other International Organizations in Geneva
(12–13 November 2014), *available at* https://geneva.usmission.gov/2014/11/
12/acting-legal-adviser-mcleod-u-s-affirms-torture-is-prohibited-at-all-times-in-all-
places/ (acknowledging a limited extraterritorial application of the Torture
Convention).

71 *Restatement of the Law Third: The Foreign Relations Law of the United States* 161–75 (1987).

72 Int'l & Operational Law Dep't, The Judge Advocate Gen.'s Legal Ctr. & Sch., U.S. Army, JA 422, *Operational Law Handbook* 48–9 (2014).

73 Report On The Legal And Policy Frameworks Guiding The United States' Use Of Military Force And Related National Security Operations, The White House 32 (December 2016), *available at* https://assets.documentcloud.org/documents/ 3232594/Read-the-Obama-administration-s-memo-outlining.pdf

74 *Id.*

75 *DoD Law of War Manual*, at 3.1.1.2. ("DoD practice also has been to adhere to certain standards in the law of war, even in situations that do not constitute 'war' or 'armed conflict,' because these law of war rules reflect standards that must be adhered to in all circumstances.").

76 Watkin, *supra* note 14, at 335–63 (for a detailed discussion of the categorization of non-State actor conflict).

77 John Shy & Thomas W. Collier, "Revolutionary War," in *Makers of Modern Strategy from Machiavelli to the Nuclear Age* 833 (Peter Paret ed., 1986) (where it is noted that Tito was fighting to take over power from the exiled regime, as well as the German-led occupiers).

78 *Al-Skeini v. The United Kingdom*, IV Eur. Ct. H. R. Rep. 99, para 19, at 118 (2011).

79 Ahmed S. Hashim, *Insurgency and Counter-Insurgency in Iraq* 138–9 (2006).

80 Christine Gray, *International Law and the Use of Force* 200 (3rd edn, 2008).

81 *Case Concerning United States Diplomatic and Consular Staff in Tehran (United States v. Iran)*, 1980 I.C.J. 1, para 74.

82 *Public Committee Against Torture in Israel v. Israel*, Israel Supreme Court [16 December 2006], 46 ILM 375, para 18, at 382 (2007) (emphasis added).

83 Dapo Akande, "Classification of Armed Conflicts: Relevant Legal Concepts," in *International Law and the Classification of Conflicts* 32, 73 (Elizabeth Wilmshurst ed., 2012).

84 *Id.* at 74 (where it is indicated the theory is based on such cross-border action representing a *wrong* under international law).

85 Commentary on the First Geneva Convention: Convention (I) for the Amelioration of the Condition of the Wounded and Sick in Armed Forces in the Field (2nd edn, 2016), *available at* www.icrc.org/applic/ihl/ihl.nsf/Treaty.xsp?action=open Document&documentId=4825657B0C7E6BF0C12563CD002D6B0B [hereinafter 2016 Commentary GWS].

86 *Id.* para 261.

87 Akande, *supra* note 83, at 77.

88 Terry Gill, *Classifying the Conflict in Syria*, 92 Int'l L. Stud. 353 (2016).

89 AP II, Art 1(1).

90 Susan Breau, Marie Aronsson, & Rachel Joyce, *Discussion Paper 2: Drone Attacks, International Law, and the Recording of Civilian Casualties or Armed Conflict*, Oxford Research Group 12 (June 2011), *available at* www.oxfordresearchgroup. org.uk/sites/default/files/ORG%20Drone%20Attacks%20and%20International%20 Law%20Report.pdf. *See also Aerial Drone Deployment on 4 October 2010 in Mir Ali/Pakistan*, 157 I.L.R. 722, 742 (2013) (where a German federal prosecutor general indicates that the Afghanistan conflict spilled over into Pakistan).

91 Liesbeth Zegveld, *The Accountability of Armed Opposition Groups in International Law* 136 (2002) (emphasis added).

92 Yoram Dinstein, *War, Aggression and Self-Defence* 273 (5th edn, 2011).

93 Corn, *Hamdan, Lebanon, and the Regulation of Hostilities: The Need to Recognize a Hybrid Category of Armed Conflict*, 40 Vand. J. Transnat'l L. 295, 341–6 (2007).

94   *Id.* at 342.
95   *Hamdan v. Rumsfeld*, 548 U.S. 557 (2006).
96   *Id.* at 1154.
97   Corn, *supra* note 3, at 79.
98   Dinstein, *The Conduct of Hostilities Under the Law of International Armed Conflict* 56 (2nd edn, 2010).
99   2016 Commentary GWS, para 482.
100 Mary Ellen O'Connell, *The Choice of Law Against Terrorism*, 4 Nat'l Sec. L. & Pol'y 343, 355 (2010).
101 Cullen, *supra* note 17, at 138 n.114. *See also* Sivakumaran, *supra* note 16, at 181.
102 *Prosecutor v. Tadić*, Case No. IT-94-1-AR72, Decision on Defence Motion for Interlocutory Appeal on Jurisdiction, para 70 (Int'l Crim. Trib. for the former Yugoslavia 2 October 1995).
103 Rome Statute of the International Criminal Court, Art 8(2)(f), 17 July 1998, 2187 U.N.T.S. 90 (emphasis added).
104 Cullen, *supra* note 17, at 177–9.
105 *Id.*
106 *Prosecutor v. Tadić*, Case No. IT-94-1-T, Opinion and Judgment, para 562 (Int'l Crim. Trib. for the former Yugoslavia 7 May 1997). *See also* Yoram Dinstein, *Non-International Armed Conflicts in International Law* 34 (2014).
107 Sivakumaran, *supra* note 16, at 168. *See also Prosecutor v. Haradinaj*, Case No. IT-04-84-T, Judgment, para 49 (Int'l Crim. Trib. for the former Yugoslavia 3 April 2008).
108 Sivakumaran, *supra* note 16, at 168.
109 2016 Commentary GWS, para 439.
110 *Id.*
111 *Id.* para 440 n. 438.
112 Sivakumaran, *supra* note 16, at 370.
113 Anthony H. Cordesman, George Sullivan, & William D. Sullivan, *Lessons of the 2006 Israeli-Hezbollah War* 80 (2007).
114 *Leaked Document Shows Makeup of an Islamic State Fighting Unit, Jerusalem Post* (6 November 2016), *available at* www.jpost.com/Middle-East/ISIS-Threat/Leaked-document-shows-makeup-of-an-Islamic-State-fighting-unit-471695
115 Michael W.S. Ryan, *Decoding Al-Qaeda's Strategy: The Deep Battle Against America* 230 (2013).
116 *Id.* at 371.
117 *Prosecutor v. Limaj*, Case No. IT-03-66-T 37, Judgment para 89 (Int'l Crim. Trib. for the former Yugoslavia 30 November 2005); Robin Geiß, *Armed Violence in Fragile States*, 91 Int'l Rev. Red Cross 127, 135–6 (2009).
118 AP II, Art 1(2).
119 2016 Commentary GWS, para 431.
120 *See Prosecutor v. Boškoski*, Case No. IT-04-82-T 90, Judgment para 257 (Int'l Crim. Trib. for the former Yugoslavia 10 July 2008) (for reference to the *totality of circumstances*); Laurie R. Blank & Geoffrey S. Corn, *Losing the Forest for the Trees: Syria, Law, and the Pragmatics of Conflict Recognition*, 46 Vand. J. Trans'l. L. 693, 731–45 (2013); Watkin, *supra* note 14, at 375–8; Corn, *supra* note 3, at 74–5.
121 Pictet, Geneva Convention for the Amelioration of the Condition of the Wounded and Sick in Armed Forces in the Field: Commentary (ICRC, 1952), para 1A(2) at 49 [hereinafter 1952 Commentary GWS].
122 *Prosecutor v. Tadić*, Case No. IT-94-1-T, Opinion and Judgment, para 562 (Int'l Crim. Trib. for the former Yugoslavia 7 May 1997).
123 *Prosecutor v. Boškoski*, Case No. IT-04-82-T, Judgment, para 90 (Int'l Crim. Trib. for the former Yugoslavia 10 July 2008) (emphasis added).

124 *Id.* para 190.

125 2016 Commentary GWS, para 431.

126 Adam Roberts, *The Equal Application of the Laws of War: A Principle Under Pressure*, 90 Int'l Rev. Red Cross 931, 932 (2008).

127 Randall Wilson, *Blue Fish in a Dark Sea: Police Intelligence in a Counterinsurgency* 15 (2013).

128 Crawford, *supra* note 10, at 185–6; Watkin, *supra* note 14, at 175–7.

129 Ian Brownlie, *International Law and the Use of Force by States* 279 (1963).

130 *Id.*

131 *See, e.g.*, Michael N. Schmitt, *Drone Attacks Under the Jus Ad Bellum and Jus In Bello: Clearing the "Fog of Law,"* 13 Y.B. Int'l L. 311, 317 (2010); Moir, *Reappraising the Resort to Force: International Law, Jus ad Bellum and the War on Terror* 54 (2010).

132 Elizabeth Wilmshurst, *Principles of International Law on the Use of Force by States in Self-Defence* Rule 6, at 11 (October 2005), Chatham House, *available at* www. chathamhouse.org/publications/papers/view/108106

133 "Leiden Policy Recommendations on Counter-Terrorism and International Law," in *Counter-Terrorism Strategies in a Fragmented International Legal Order: Meeting the Challenges*, Annex, para 38, at 715–16 (Larissa Van Den Herik & Nico Schrijver eds, 2013).

134 David Kretzmer, *The Inherent Right to Self-Defence and Proportionality in Jus Ad Bellum*, 24 Eur. J. Int'l L. 235, 273 (2013).

135 George F.G. Stanley, *Canada's Soldiers: The Military History of an Unmilitary People* 203–4 (3rd edn, 1974) (describing the *Caroline* incident).

136 *Prosecutor v. Tadić*, Case No. IT-94-1-A, Decision on The Defence Motion for Interlocutory Appeal on Jurisdiction, para 70 (Int'l Crim. Trib. for the former Yugoslavia 2 October 1995).

137 Watkin, *supra* note 14, at 592–5.

3 The status of individuals in armed conflict

1 Introduction

In 1911, it was stated that "[t]he separation of armies and peaceful inhabitants into two distinct classes is perhaps the greatest triumph of International Law."[1] In this statement there is considerable wisdom, but also the potential to mask some of the most challenging aspects of the law governing the conduct of hostilities. The categories of belligerent, or *combatant* as it is now called, and *civilian* underpin some of the fundamental aspects of humanitarian law. The separation of populations into these two categories is clearly reflected in the principle of distinction regarding who may be lawfully targeted. It forms the basis for the principle of proportionality, with its determination of excessive collateral casualties and damage arising from an attack, and affects the standards of treatment for persons falling under the power of the participants in an armed conflict. Significantly, under humanitarian law, belligerents who qualify as combatants have a right to participate in hostilities and not be prosecuted for killing an opponent, unless they commit a war crime. In this regard, combatants enjoy the *combatant immunity* from prosecution for their wartime acts that flows from their qualification for lawful status. Belligerents who do not satisfy the requirements to qualify as *combatants* in the legal sense, as well as civilians, do not enjoy this same immunity, although they have historically taken a direct part in hostilities, and continue to do so. Civilians are provided considerable protection under the law as a result of their status (*see* Chapter 4: *Dealing with civilians, wounded, and sick*). During IAC, lawful combatants also enjoy the privileges of prisoner of war status (*see* Chapter 5: *Prisoners of war and other detainees*). Prisoner of war status does not exist in respect of NIAC.

For a variety of reasons, these simple bifurcated categories of combatant and civilian have proven challenging to apply. These reasons include the complexity of modern society, including the harnessing of the resources of the modern technologically advanced State in its prosecution of total war, and the very nature of irregular warfare, which has continued to represent a dominant part of conflict even with the rise of the nation-state. Furthermore, disagreement over categorization has spawned a number of additional terms: *unlawful combatant, unprivileged belligerent,*[2] and *quasi-combatant*, in the attempt to identify unique participants in conflict. The criminalization of lawful participation in combat, and the uncertain status of those participants, has historically been reflected in terms such as bandits, rebels, marauders, insurgents, and now more often by simply referring to them as *terrorists.* The embrace of such terminology is evident in the United States, where *unprivileged enemy belligerents* are subject to criminal prosecution by military tribunal per the 2009 Military Commissions Act.[3] And adding an even further complication to this issue is that not everyone has viewed those fighting as part of a non-State organized armed group as illegal, a view which is reflected in terminology such as *freedom fighters* and *people's wars.*

Notwithstanding the challenge presented by the complexity of modern warfare, correctly identifying the status of individuals in armed conflict remains one of the most important tasks for participants and those who seek to hold them accountable for their actions. This chapter will discuss the status of individuals in armed conflict first in IAC, and then in respect of NIAC. First, this analysis will look at the historical background to the formal development of the categories of combatant and civilian. That discussion will highlight the areas where ready agreement has been forged regarding combatant and civilian status, as well as identify the gray areas where consensus has proven more elusive. It is these areas of uncertainty that continue to plague the application of the basic legal principle of the separation of combatants from civilians in the twenty-first century. The analysis will then turn to assessing lawful combatancy and its constitutive criteria in terms of codification efforts at the turn of the twentieth century, following World War II, and in the 1970s.

Second, the concept of unlawful or unprivileged belligerency and the status of unlawful participants in armed conflict will be discussed. Third, there is an assessment of civilian status and the protection that status affords. The discussion will also focus on how, and for what periods of time, civilians may lose that protection such that they can be targeted or, if captured, tried for their actions. Fourth, the categorization challenges presented by conflicts between State and non-State actors will be assessed. This discussion will center on the lack of combatant status in the legal sense of the term in NIAC, and its effect on analyzing State and non-State actor participation in such conflict. Finally, the chapter will look at various unique categories of persons protected, or provided for under IHL: child soldiers, mercenaries, and journalists.

2 International armed conflict

2.1 *Regulating combatant status*

2.1.1 *Early codification*

Identifying who qualifies as a combatant (or belligerent) or a peaceful civilian has been a key aspect of the codification of the law of war since the last half of the nineteenth century. As the 1863 U.S. Lieber Code indicated, "[s]o soon as a man is armed by a sovereign government and takes the soldier's oath of fidelity, he is a belligerent; his killing, wounding, or other warlike acts are not individual crimes or offenses."[4] While the interpretation of contemporary IHL is largely based on maintaining a separation between the law governing the recourse to war (i.e., *jus ad bellum*) and that governing the conduct of hostilities (i.e., *jus in bello*), this provision of the Lieber Code highlights that these two bodies of law are linked on the issue of combatant status. A key aspect of lawful combatant status is belonging to and fighting for a State. In other words, combatants had to be fighting for the *proper* (or *competent*) authority, one of the key principles of just war theory.[5]

The link between the State and combatant status was clearly evident in the first major effort to codify that status found in the 1907 Hague Land Warfare Regulations.[6] The Regulations provided belligerent status to armies, and also to militia and volunteer corps that fulfilled four conditions: (1) being under responsible command; (2) having a fixed distinctive emblem that is recognizable at a distance; (3) carrying arms openly; (4) and carrying out operations in accordance with the laws and customs of war.[7] However, the concepts of the *leveé en masse* and non-combatants belonging to the armed forces of a belligerent party were also recognized. Regarding the *leveé*, the inhabitants of a territory which was not occupied who spontaneously take up arms to resist invading troops without meeting all the criteria for armies, or militia and volunteer corps, were to be regarded as belligerents.[8] These participants in hostilities were required to carry arms openly and respect the laws and customs of war. The term *non-combatants* was identified along with *combatants* as the constitutive elements of the armed forces of a belligerent party, where both have the right to be treated as prisoners of war. At that time, non-combatants included medical personnel, as well as military personnel "whose function is ancillary to that of the fighting men and who do not themselves oppose the enemy arms in hand (e.g., members of the commissariat, veterinary services, clerks, orderlies, and bandsmen)."[9] Finally, civilians who historically accompanied the armed forces, "such as newspaper correspondents and reporters, sutlers and contractors," were entitled to prisoner of war status if they were in possession of a certificate from the military authorities of the army they were accompanying.[10]

The *leveé en masse* category presents an interesting example of one of the challenges presented by this body of law. While the *leveé en masse* has not been widely used since it was codified in the 1907 Regulations, the history leading up to its inclusion reflects a struggle that continued to exist among States throughout the twentieth century regarding the categorization of participation in armed conflict. There were two contrasting approaches at the time, with the Prussians, representative of dominant military powers, seeking to have all legitimate engagement in armed conflict requiring the use of regularly organized armed forces. In contrast, the less powerful "patriotic States" sought legitimacy for civilians who rose up on a less organized basis to repel an invader.[11] The compromise reached during the conference leading to the 1907 Hague Land Warfare Regulations was belligerent status for members of the *leveé* who acted prior to an occupation being established. Legitimization did not extend to those acting as insurgents against an occupying power once the invasion phase was completed. Participants in hostilities who did not meet the criteria set out in the Regulations were ultimately considered to be war criminals, or in the aftermath of World War II, unprivileged belligerents. Notwithstanding its more historic nature, this provision remains part of IHL, as is reflected in Article 4(A)(6) of the 1949 Third Geneva Convention.[12]

Importantly, the preferred linking of legitimacy with the regular armed forces of a State highlights a tension in this area of the law that extends to conflict between State and non-State actors (e.g., insurgents, terrorists), regardless of whether it occurs in the context of an IAC or NIAC. Those who do not fight for a State, conduct hostilities out of uniform, and otherwise fail to distinguish themselves from the civilian population are not qualified to claim international legal privilege to engage in hostilities and therefore are liable to be considered criminals subject to prosecution by a detaining power, hence the term *unprivileged belligerent*. This late nineteenth-century dispute between powerful and patriotic States highlights that the involvement of irregular fighters in armed conflict has, since the inception of attempts to codify IHL, proven difficult to deal with.

This difficulty is evident in two historic examples. First, the impasse leading up to the 1907 Regulations regarding the expansion of the category of combatants resulted in the now famous Martens Clause, where the president of the negotiating conference declared that the unresolved cases not dealt with would "remain under the protection and empire of the principles of international law, as they result from the usages established between civilized nations, from the laws of humanity, and the requirements of public conscience."[13] This is now viewed as a principle of broader application that would afford unprivileged belligerents some modest protection, "in which international humanitarian law could provide at least some basic protections," rather than assume "a lack of tight-fitting treaty law meant *carte blanche* freedom to act, unconstrained by any law."[14]

Second, as was evident in the immediate aftermath of the creation of the 1907 Regulations, there continued to be inconsistency regarding how States viewed persons who were not part of the regular armed forces. For example, the U.S. Rules of Land Warfare of 1914 recognized members of the *leveé en masse* as belligerents, but also uniquely viewed them as civilians who qualified for prisoner of war status.[15] This approach appears inconsistent with the foundational position that a person cannot be a lawful belligerent and a civilian at the same time.[16] In contrast, the 1914 *UK Manual of Military Law* clearly places members of the *leveé* within the category of armed forces.[17] As will be discussed, irregular participation in hostilities, and issues concerning the status of those participants, have continued to be the subject of considerable controversy right up to the present day.

One term found in the 1907 Land Warfare Regulations that has the potential to cause confusion is *non-combatant*. As has been noted, at that time, this term referred to non-combatant members of the armed forces. However, the nature of armed forces and warfare itself changed over the course of the late nineteenth and early twentieth centuries. The military logistics and support chain became more professional and integrated within the military forces as nation-states increased the size of their regular standing armies.[18] Further, the increased range of weapons systems (e.g., artillery and airplanes) extended warfare beyond the immediate interface of the opposing combatant armed forces.[19] This made much of the uniformed administrative personnel accompanying the force, who might previously have been viewed as non-combatants, now seen as lawful targets. However, medical personnel and chaplains maintained their protected status. In addition, the term *non-combatant* became commonly and increasingly associated with civilians, thereby extending the meaning of that term far beyond military forces.[20] However, while it is not uncommon to see the principle of distinction referred to in terms of separating combatants from non-combatants, and legitimate military targets from civilian ones,[21] issues related to status are primarily discussed in the terms of *combatant* and *civilian status.* Military non-combatants (medical and religious personnel) are protected under treaty and customary international law, as explained in detail in Chapter 4.

Other categorization challenges remain. As the historian John Keegan noted, it was supply and logistics that brought about a clear-cut victory in World War II.[22] However, those support functions were never fully militarized. A significant aspect of the State ability to conduct hostilities has depended upon its civilian-based industrial capability and logistics chain. This meant the status of civilians accompanying the force continued to be an important issue. Further, particularly in the post–Cold War period, there has been a growing privatization of military supply and support functions, as well as the contracting out of some security functions. This has made the questions of who is a combatant or a civilian, and whether such civilian functions amount to participation in hostilities such that they can be targeted and treated as criminals or must be protected, some of the most challenging twenty-first-century humanitarian law issues.

2.1.2   In the aftermath of World War II

Following World War II, some adjustments affecting combatant status were made to the regulatory framework in the Third Geneva Convention. The criteria found in Article 4(A)(2) of that Convention largely mirror the 1907 Hague Land Warfare Regulations; however, specific reference was also made to organized resistance movements *belonging* to a party to the conflict, even when operating in occupied territory. This provision represented an effort to acknowledge the use by the Allied Powers of such movements during that conflict.[23] Additional changes included recognition of the refusal by Germany to recognize French Free Forces, or Italians fighting them after 1943, by providing that "[m]embers of regular armed forces who profess allegiance to a government or authority not recognized by the Detaining Power" were prisoners of war.[24]

One drafting change from the 1907 Hague Land Warfare Regulations was that members of the armed forces of a party to a conflict (including its members of militia and volunteer corps) were placed in a separate sub-paragraph from the other "militia and members of volunteer corps, including organized resistance movements."[25] The paragraph dealing with these latter forces listed the criteria of being organized, under responsible command, belonging to a party to the conflict, wearing a fixed distinctive sign, carrying weapons openly and acting in compliance with the customs and law of war.[26] One issue that has arisen is whether these criteria are individual or collective in nature such that there can be a denial of prisoner of war status to all the members of an armed group.[27]

Notably, it has been suggested that the paragraph separation meant that regular armed forces members are not required to meet the criteria for combatancy set out for the other militia and volunteer corps not forming part of the armed forces of a State. If that interpretation were adopted, regular armed personnel captured out of uniform engaged in sabotage would not lose their entitlement to prisoner of war status.[28] However, as Howard Levie noted in his 1978 treatise on prisoners of war, such an interpretation would be

> unrealistic, as it would mean that the dangers inherent in serving as a spy or saboteur could be immunized merely by making the individual a member of the armed forces; and that members of the armed forces could act in a manner prohibited by other areas of the law of armed conflict and escape penalties therefor, still being entitled to prisoner-of-war status.[29]

Similarly, the 2016 *DoD Law of War Manual* indicates the loss of prisoner of war status for persons "engaged in spying, sabotage, or other hostile, secretive activities behind enemy lines" is not explicitly recognized in the Prisoner of War Convention, but "this understanding was the general understanding at the 1949 Diplomatic Conference and is reflected in other treaties, judicial decisions, military manuals, and scholarly works."[30] The more historically accurate, and widely accepted, view is that a member of the regular armed forces wearing civilian clothes who is captured while in espionage or sabotage in enemy territory is entitled to be treated the same as a civilian carrying out similar activity (i.e., an unprivileged belligerent).[31] There is no exceptional status for regular armed forces personnel.

As has been noted, in what appeared to be a significant addition, *organized resistance movements* were included within other *militias and volunteer corps* eligible for prisoner of war status, provided they met the same criteria for combatancy.[32] Having provided support to, and made significant use of, resistance groups in Axis-occupied territory, there was considerable pressure on the Allied powers to recognize that fact in the post-War changes to humanitarian law. However, it has been widely recognized that it would be extremely difficult for resistance movements to meet the listed criteria for combatancy, except for the most exceptional of conditions. The unrealistic nature of the provisions prompted one commentator to note "[i]f memory be short, so is gratitude."[33] What the setting of such high standards for participants in irregular warfare did reflect was the continuing tension between powerful military and more patriotic States regarding who qualified as combatant, and therefore who was eligible for prisoner of war status. The resistance toward recognizing irregular participation in hostilities remained dominant.

One area where there was a significant expansion on the 1907 Hague Land Warfare Regulations was in the area of civilians providing support to the armed forces. The civilian non-combatants entitled to prisoner of war status are identified in Article 4(A)(4) of the Third Geneva Convention as "persons who accompany the armed forces without actually being members thereof." Specific examples of those civilians are "civilian members of military aircraft crews, war correspondents, supply contractors, members of labour units or of services responsible for the welfare of the armed forces." These civilians have to receive authorization from the armed forces they accompany, in the form of an identity card provided to "them for that purpose." Separately, in Article 4(A)(5), "[m]embers of crews, including masters, pilots and apprentices, of the merchant marine and the crews of civil aircraft of the Parties to the conflict, who do not benefit by more favourable treatment under any other provisions of international law" are also provided prisoner of war status.

A key component of these 1949 Geneva Convention provisions is civilians being granted prisoner of war status if captured while accompanying the armed forces. Historically, the activities performed by those civilians have been connected to supply, logistics, and support functions (*see* Chapter 3, 2.1.1: *Early codification*). An important issue in terms of their status is whether those civilians may act in a manner that causes them to lose their protected status. In particular, could they be targeted, and possibly be denied prisoner of war status upon capture? This has always proven to be a difficult issue for international law. One historic example is the crews of merchant vessels, who were viewed as being entitled to defend their ships but not engage in offensive combat operations. In contrast, merchant men sailing as part of a convoy were seen as taking part in hostilities.[34]

Given the integral nature of support activities related to the conduct of hostilities, it may be inevitable, particularly at the tactical level, that some civilians may be viewed as taking a direct part in hostilities while carrying out their assigned duties. This could include while delivering supplies to the frontlines, or loading ordnance on aircraft. In this regard, much will depend upon the scope of the interpretation of the term *take a direct part in hostilities*. Adding to the potential misidentification of civilian activity, there is nothing to prohibit the arming of civilians for their personal self-defense.[35] However, if civilians are authorized by their State to perform the type of support-type functions traditionally recognized under IHL, they remain entitled to prisoner of war status, even if their activities are interpreted to be taking a direct part in hostilities, for example being civilian members of military aircraft crew. When these civilians take a direct part in hostilities they lose the protection provided to civilians to the extent that they may be targeted. What they do not lose is their entitlement to prisoner of war status.

However, including civilians within the definition of POW cannot be interpreted as a broad permission to utilize civilians to perform functions traditionally reserved for combatants, most notably functions that amount to direct participation in hostilities, for example manning gun positions, patrolling, conducting ambushes, or carrying out acts of sabotage. Accordingly, any civilian authorized to accompany the force who directly participates in hostilities in these capacities, whether pursuant to the orders of military superiors or on his or her own initiative, accepts the risk of being denied POW status if captured. Their pre-capture conduct is inconsistent with civilian POW status, and will more likely be classified as an unprivileged belligerent. The grant of POW status to civilians accompanying the force was premised on the expectation that these individuals, while performing support functions important to the force (hence justifying their detention for the duration of hostilities), were in fact civilians, and not combatants.

This issue is particularly important in respect of the State employment of paramilitary units controlled by civilian intelligence agencies, or private security contractors. While engaged in a combat role those persons would not be performing a support function that falls within the traditional employment of civilians accompanying the force found in Articles 4(A)(4) and (5) of the Geneva Conventions. Similar to the issue of regular armed forces having to meet all the criteria for combatant status, the status of persons accompanying the armed forces cannot be used to circumvent the requirements of lawful combatancy, and with it prisoner of war status.[36] Civilian contractors engaged in espionage or sabotage missions would not meet the prisoner of war criteria.[37] These civilians could be viewed as unprivileged belligerents subject to prosecution by an opposing detaining power.

The 1949 Geneva Conventions also entered new territory in extending international humanitarian treaty law to internal armed conflicts. Common Article 3 to the 1949 Geneva Conventions outlined minimum humanitarian protections applicable to "[p]ersons taking no active part in hostilities, including members of the armed forces who have laid down their arms and those placed hors de combat by sickness, wounds, detention, or any other cause." However, it did not address the status of the participants to the conflict other than to state its application "shall not affect the legal status of the Parties to the conflict."[38] (*see* Chapter 2: *Non-international armed conflict*). Again, there was, and remains an extreme reluctance by States to extend any form of legitimacy to insurgents, rebels, and others challenging their authority.

2.1.3 Additional Protocol I

In the immediate post–World War II era, there was little State interest in further developing the law of war. Instead, this period witnessed greater concentration being placed on the development of human rights treaties. However, the significant number of guerrilla wars with the end of the colonial era during that period meant that humanitarian law could not be neglected for long. This ultimately led to the development of two 1977 Protocols additional to the 1949 Geneva Conventions. As explained in Chapter 1, AP I dealt with IACs,[39] while AP II applied to civil wars or significant armed conflicts within States.[40] But, as also explained in Chapter 1, AP I expanded the definition of IAC to what had to that point been considered NIAC so long as the non-State group was "fighting against colonial domination and alien occupation and against racist regimes in the exercise of their right of self-determination."[41] By doing so, the treaty opened the door for members of such groups to claim lawful combatant status, which is one reason the treaty remains controversial to this day—although 90 percent of States are party to it. The United States was and remains a principal opponent of this expansion, based on the concern was that it would extend legitimacy to terrorist organizations as international actors.[42] In many respects, this debate relates to a historical situation unique to the breakup of the colonial empires and the Cold War. However, it also reflects the continuing dominant military State concern over legitimizing members of non-State (i.e., irregular) armed groups participating in hostilities.

Notwithstanding AP I, the criteria for attaining combatant status have remained largely those set out in the 1949 Geneva Conventions. In this respect, it must be noted that AP I only supplements the 1949 Conventions.[43] This can be seen in the distinction that is made between lawful combatants and civilians being based on the former being one of the categories of persons referred to in Article 4(A)(1), (2), (3), and (6) of the Third Geneva Convention, as well as Article 43 of AP I.[44] The Protocol does provide greater clarity in terms of stating that all members of armed forces, other than medical personnel and chaplains are "combatants, that is to say, *they have the right to participate directly in hostilities.*"[45] This reference to direct participation in hostilities reflects the broader scope of the Protocol, since it encompasses both conduct of hostilities (Hague Law) and the protection of victims of armed conflict (Geneva Law). Direct participation in hostilities is a fundamental aspect of targeting, which is a key in determining when civilians forfeit their presumptive protection from attack. The Protocol effectively narrows military non-combatants to medical personnel and chaplains, thereby recognizing that both fighters and support personnel who are part of the armed forces are combatants. Further, AP I recognizes the principle of combatant immunity in stating that combatants have a right to participate in hostilities. In other words, they cannot be tried for such participation, including killing their enemies, unless they commit a war crime or act in a manner inconsistent with their privileged status (e.g., conduct sabotage out of uniform, or spy). In contrast, the Third Geneva Convention had previously simply recognized prisoner of war status, from which combatancy was inferred (in part because, as explained above, the criteria for prisoner of war qualification mirrored the Hague Regulations, which referenced the "laws, rights, and duties of war"). In effect, AP I finally aligned the relationship between belligerent qualification for prisoner of war status upon capture and the international legal privilege to participate in hostilities, which essentially means a *combatant* is synonymous with being a *privileged belligerent*.

One innovative aspect of this combatant definition was that, in some limited circumstances, Article 44(3) of AP I removes the requirement that a combatant wear a fixed distinctive sign recognizable at a distance, and prescribes a limited requirement for combatants to carry their arms openly. The Protocol first reinforces the principle of distinction by obliging combatants to distinguish themselves from the civilian population while engaged in an attack, or in a military operation preparatory to an attack.[46] However, it also goes on to recognize that there are situations during armed conflict where "owing to the nature of the hostilities an armed combatant cannot so distinguish himself"; he retains combatant status provided he carries armed openly during an attack, or while engaged in a deployment prior to an attack.[47] Article 44(4) of AP I provides that persons who do not meet these relaxed requirements for combatancy forfeit their right to prisoner of war status, but must be given equivalent protection.[48] The Protocol is also careful to note that these relaxed requirements are "not intended to change the generally accepted practice of States with respect to the wearing of the uniform by combatants assigned to the regular, uniformed armed forces of the Party to the conflict."[49] While clearly intended to reinforce the practice of wearing uniforms, it also provides recognition of the long-standing practice of using special forces and other units to clandestinely provide support to armed groups in occupied territory (e.g., Jedburgh teams in World War II).[50]

This relaxed criterion for attaining combatant status has proven to be particularly controversial. The United States specifically objected to this provision because it "would endanger civilians among whom terrorists and other irregulars attempt to conceal themselves."[51] Notably, a number of States have indicated that it would only apply to conflicts involving wars of national liberation and occupied territory.[52] In reality, the circumstances in which this provision would apply are for a couple of reasons quite limited. First, the non-State armed group would have to operate on behalf of a State or national liberation movement. Second, given the unique historical basis for wars of national liberation, it is highly unlikely such a conflict would now occur. However, what is clear is that the traditional resistance toward relaxing the uniform, or at least the distinguishing sign criterion for combatancy, continues to have a powerful influence on the development of humanitarian law.

AP I also made specific reference to "a paramilitary or armed law enforcement agency" being incorporated into the armed forces. The opposing parties to the conflict have to be notified of that incorporation.[53] The ICRC AP I Commentary makes specific reference to this provision referring to law enforcement, with the terms *paramilitary* and *armed* taking into account the different ways that States may organize their internal security forces.[54] The use of police forces during armed conflict is a complex subject, particularly in the context of an occupying force. Under humanitarian law, an occupying power is required to maintain public order and safety[55] and the orderly government of the territory.[56] This inevitably means policing the territory, which can be carried out by indigenous police forces, the police and military forces of the occupying power, or a combination of all three.[57] Both ordinary police and those incorporated into the armed forces may end up fighting insurgents.

The reliance on local police forces to maintain order during occupation can be controversial, particularly since they can be put in opposition to organized resistance movements and others who are fellow nationals. Local police forces cannot be forced to participate in operations opposing legitimate belligerent acts, but can be required to maintain law and order.[58] As has been noted, the reality is that few resistance movements operating in occupied territory will meet the requirements of the Third Geneva Convention. As the ICRC Commentary for the Fourth Geneva Convention notes, the "Occupying Power is entitled to require the local police to take part in tracing and punishing hostile acts committed" by illegitimate participants in the conflict.[59] In any event, police forces are often the subject of attack by armed groups because they are located in the community, and an insurgent goal is frequently to establish that the occupying power is not capable of governing. In addition, armed groups regularly engage in criminal activity. This means that police forces, both local and foreign, may have to confront insurgents. Private military contractors may also be employed to provide local security. This includes non-governmental organizations, the political staff of the occupying power, etc. Employment on security related tasks dealing with crime and instability would not necessarily make those civilian contractors unlawful participants in hostilities, even if they are attacked by terrorists or members of an organized armed group.

2.2   Unlawful or unprivileged belligerents

The theoretical approach of dividing populations into two categories, lawful combatants and civilians, has never represented the reality of armed conflict. Otherwise lawful combatants may engage in combat, but in a fashion that causes them to lose their protected status. Similarly, some civilians may take a direct part in hostilities. Members of armed groups that fail to qualify for lawful or privileged belligerent status, or individuals who participate in warfare without legitimate authority have long been a fixture on the battlefield. The group nature of such participation is reflected in the Fourth Geneva Convention recognition of organized resistance movements.[60] It can also be seen in a NIAC context in the consistent reference to parties to the armed conflict, indicating a contest between organized armed groups, and in AP II's reference to organized armed groups operating under a responsible command and controlling territory.[61]

Under the 1949 Geneva Conventions, resistance movements that do not qualify for prisoner of war and therefore legitimate status would still be participating in an IAC. This raises the theoretical question of whether these participants are illegitimate combatants, or civilians who lose the protection of their status. One challenge for international law is that there is no official category for these illegitimate participants in conflict. By the mid-twentieth century, they were referred to in case law as unlawful combatants or unlawful belligerents.[62] An important issue is whether illegitimate participation in armed conflict is a criminal act, and if so, does it constitute a war crime. If not fighting for a State in terms of belonging to its armed forces and meeting the criteria for combatancy, unlawful combatants have historically been subject to detention, prosecution, and sometimes the death penalty.[63] Not infrequently, they have been dealt with improperly by the capturing State, including being tortured and murdered.[64] Up until World War II, unlawful belligerents were viewed as war criminals under international law. In *Ex Parte Quirin*, the Supreme Court of the United States listed German saboteurs who entered the United States in uniform, but who changed into civilian dress in order to carry out their mission, along with spies, as "familiar examples of belligerents who are generally deemed not to be entitled to the status of prisoners of war, but to be *offenders against the law of war* subject to trial and punishment by military tribunals."[65]

However, the widespread support for resistance movements by the Allied Powers during World War II had an impact on how such unlawful belligerence was viewed. In the *Hostages Case*, German personnel were put on trial regarding their treatment of members of the resistance, and for the killing of hostages.[66] Like the *Quirin* decision, the military tribunal equated the activities of resistance members to spying. However, the tribunal also found that a person

> may act lawfully for his country and at the same time be a war criminal to the enemy, so guerrillas may render great service to their country and, in the event of success, become heroes even, still they remain war criminals in the eyes of the enemy and may be treated as such.[67]

This decision made a distinction between how participation in indirect or irregular warfare was perceived by the parties to the conflict. Similar to the negotiations for the 1907 Hague Land Warfare Regulations, there was a struggle between viewing that participation as being patriotic or a crime.

Following World War II, a future judge of the International Court of Justice, Richard Baxter, wrote the seminal article on unprivileged belligerency. He suggested the term *unprivileged belligerent* to describe the status of spies, guerillas, and saboteurs.[68] After reviewing the lack of consensus during the 1907 Hague Land Warfare Regulation deliberations, and the extensive use of guerrilla forces by the Allied Powers, he noted that "[o]nly a rigid formalism could lead to the characterization of the resistance conduct against Germany, Italy, and Japan as a violation of international law."[69] He also noted that the *Quirin* case involved violations of the U.S. Articles of War, and as such "it would appear that these provisions of municipal law afforded a surer grounds for their punishment that did the offence of 'unlawful belligerency' under international law."[70]

As a result, the individuals involved simply lost the protection they might otherwise have under international law as the result of qualifying as *privileged* belligerents with the accordant international legal immunity from criminal sanction pursuant to the domestic laws of a detaining State. Accordingly, rather than unlawful belligerency, their actions constituted an unprivileged belligerency.[71] Unprivileged belligerents have been defined as:

> [P]ersons who are not entitled to treatment either as peaceful civilians or as prisoners of war by reason of the fact that they have engaged in hostile conduct without meeting the qualifications established by Article 4 of the Geneva Prisoners of War Convention of 1949.[72]

These unprivileged belligerents—combatants in the pragmatic but not legal sense, regardless of whether they are civilians or part of State armed forces, are treated the same. They may be tried under the domestic law of the capturing State for any pre-capture conduct that violated that law, and under international law remain liable for any war crimes they commit (e.g., killing civilians, pillaging, refusing to give quarter).[73]

As is reflected in the 2004 *UK Manual of the Law of Armed Conflict*, the term *unprivileged belligerent* continues to be used.[74] It has been generally accepted that the employment of unprivileged belligerents is not a war crime, although a capturing State may prosecute these belligerents under any applicable domestic law.[75] Notwithstanding this approach, the United States has resurrected the idea that captured enemy unprivileged belligerents should be treated as war criminals before its post-9/11 military commissions.[76] In can be argued this approach is consistent with the 1941 *Quirin* decision; however, it also reflects a traditional dominant military power attitude toward illegitimate participation in armed conflict.

Complicating the issue of whether unprivileged belligerency constitutes a war crime contrary to international law is the 2006 determination by the U.S. Supreme Court in *Hamdan v. Rumsfeld* that the conflict with al Qaeda is not of an international character.[77] As will be discussed, it is legally impossible for a member of a non-State group to qualify as either a prisoner of war or a combatant (privileged belligerent) in such conflicts, and traditionally insurgent or rebel forces have been viewed as criminals that are subject to prosecution under domestic law. War crimes are limited to breaches of IHL. However, as explained in detail in Chapter 8, there is no doubt that these individuals, even if unprivileged, must be treated humanely if captured. Both treaty and customary international law impose this obligation, which is based on human rights norms incorporated into humanitarian law and human rights law.[78]

2.3 Civilians

The twentieth century experienced a rising percentage of civilian deaths over military ones resulting from armed conflict.[79] The expanding scope of military operations (e.g., unrestricted submarine warfare, strategic bombing), the techno-logical reach of modern weapons systems, genocide, and the abuse of civilians under the control of occupying powers all contributed to the elevated dangers posed to civilians. The strategic bombing campaigns of World War II provide one example of how some civilian activity became intertwined with notions of participation in hostilities. For example, arguments had been made prior to the conflict that civilian factory workers could be considered to be quasi-combatants.[80] That is no longer the case. Ultimately, strategic bombing was aimed "not at the forces in the field, but at the war-willingness and productive capacity of the society behind them."[81]

The 1949 Fourth Geneva Convention provides clear evidence of the post-War reinforcement by the international community of the protection associated with civilian status. This treaty—the first exclusively dedicated to the protection of civilians—expanded upon the provisions of the 1907 Hague Land Warfare Regulations.[82] It was a direct result of the abuse and murder of civilians in occupied territory. This treaty imposes on an occupying power a range of obligations toward the population under its control, including ensuring family honor and rights, as well as the dignity and lives of the occupied population. Religious practices and convictions must be respected. Private property cannot be confiscated. Nor can the property of municipalities, even if State-owned, where it is dedicated to religion, charity, education, or the arts and sciences.[83] As has been discussed regarding unprivileged belligerency, the occupying power is responsible for maintaining law and order, and as a result can become directly involved in countering resistance movements and their supporters. This includes interning, detaining, and possibly trying civilian participants in conflict. Further, the taking of hostages is prohibited.[84]

The post–World War II focus on protecting civilians as victims of conflict was extended in AP I to hostilities related provisions. Chapter 6 explains these so-called targeting rules in detail, but at this point what is critical to understand is that all of these rules necessitated a workable definition of civilian, as these were the individuals subject to the protective effect of these rules. Civilians are protected from being made the object of attack, meaning being deliberately attacked, "unless and for such time as they take a *direct part in hostilities.*"[85] Civilians were not to be considered quasi-combatants. However, they do remain at risk of being lawfully collaterally killed or injured as long as a belligerent applies certain precautions in carrying out an attack against a lawful military objective.[86] To implement this fundamental equation of civilian protection from the effects of attacks, the Protocol refers to the principle of distinction;[87] the obligation to protect the civilian population and individual civilians against the dangers arising from military operations;[88] prohibitions against directly attacking civilians[89] or civilian objects;[90] a prohibition against terrorizing the civilian population;[91] and rules governing targeting that are focused on minimizing or avoiding collateral civilian casualties and damage.[92]

It should be noted, though, that, while AP I indicates that there are two definite categories of persons, lawful combatants and civilians, that Protocol also reflects the more complex history of combatant status and unprivileged belligerency. For example, reference is made in Article 44(3) to "*[a]ny person* who has taken part in hostilities" when setting out the protection available to those who do not qualify for prisoner of war status.[93] It can even be argued there are five categories of people referred to in the Protocol: (1) lawful combatants; (2) otherwise lawful combatants failing to meet even its relax distinction requirements; (3) members of organized armed groups who do not qualify for lawful combatant criteria; (4) civilians who take a direct part in hostilities; and (5) and protected civilians. The second, third, and fourth references could be considered to be unprivileged belligerents. Notwithstanding this lingering complexity, it must be stressed that civilians have a protected status, even if that protection is not absolute.

Identifying when civilians take a direct part in hostilities has been one of the most controversial areas of IHL in the post-9/11 period. The phrase itself—*direct part in hostilities*—found in the 1977 Additional Protocols, was 25 years old by the time it attracted the attention of the international legal community. This attention was brought about by the controversy surrounding the early use of drone strikes in Yemen, the Occupied Territories, and Iraq.[94] The concept of direct participation in hostilities provides the basis for targeting participants in armed conflict. In 2009 ICRC published its study, Interpretive Guidance on the Notion of Direct Participation in Hostilities Under International Humanitarian Law, which sought to explain the meaning of that phrase.[95] That document is noteworthy for its recognition that members of an organized armed group, as well as individual civilians who take a direct part in hostilities may be targeted. The result is a general consensus, albeit not a unanimous one,[96] that persons can be targeted on the basis of membership in an organized armed group,[97] in other words based on their status. Subsequent disagreements over how membership in those armed groups is to be determined have often masked the importance of this point. The ICRC Interpretive Guidance has contributed to a better understanding of this area of the law; however, a number of its provisions remain controversial, and are the subject of considerable ongoing discussion and disagreement (*see* Chapter 6, 3: *Targeting persons*).[98]

What is important to note is that civilians who take a direct part in hostilities would be considered to be unprivileged belligerents by virtue of their having, in the words of Richard Baxter, "engaged in hostile conduct without meeting the qualifications established by Article 4 of the Geneva Prisoners of War Convention of 1949."[99] Direct participation in hostilities is a narrow term linked to the membership in an organized armed group (i.e., continuous involvement in acts or preparations amounting to direct participation in hostilities) or to individual civilians performing the type of hostile activity associated with members of armed forces. The scope for civilian support is potentially much broader than direct participation, as civilians can provide indirect support for an organized resistance movement, insurgents, etc. Civilians who provide support to a resistance movement in occupied territory may be liable to internment or assigned residence for imperative reasons of security, as contemplated under the Fourth Geneva Convention. However, such indirect support does not mean they can be targeted as they would not be taking a direct part in hostilities.

3   Non-international armed conflict

A distinguishing feature of NIAC is the lack of a lawful combatant and, with it, prisoner of war status. On one level, this is surprising given the wide range of conflict involving non-State actors, and the potential for some conflicts to take on the attributes of inter-State warfare. Non-State conflict (between a State and a non-State actor or between two non-State actors) can be exceptionally complex. It can range from low-level terrorist violence involving groups with a cellular structure to conventionally organized, uniformed, and armed protagonists.

Combat between State and non-State actors can look like and be as violent as its international counterpart. Further, such conflict has always been the predominant form of warfare.[100]

However, the reason for the lack of recognition of a lawful combatant status in armed conflict with non-State actors is firmly rooted in history and just war theory.[101] As society developed, the authority to use violence was concentrated first in the hands of the sovereign and then in the State. It is the State that has the lawful authority to maintain internal order. A modern reflection of that authority is found in AP II, which states that nothing in that document affects "the sovereignty of a State or the responsibility of the government, by all legitimate means, to maintain or re-establish law and order in the State."[102] In the same manner as unprivileged belligerents in IAC, those challenging the authority of the State by force of arms (e.g., rebels, insurgent) are viewed as criminals subject to prosecution under domestic law, and potentially for war crimes under international law.

Common Article 3 to the 1949 Geneva Conventions was the first significant international codification of protections under humanitarian law regarding NIAC. A minimum set of protections are provided to "*[p]ersons* taking no active part in hostilities" who are placed *hors de combat* by sickness, wounds, detention, or another other cause. The generic *persons* encompasses members of the military and other security forces, civilians and unprivileged belligerents. Reference is also made generically to "members of armed forces," which would include insurgents and other organized armed groups. However, it is also clearly stated that these provisions "shall not affect the legal status of the Parties to the conflict."[103] The term *active part in hostilities* has come to be viewed as being synonymous with *direct part in hostilities*.[104] The potential for a broader incorporation of the Geneva Law into internal conflict is provided for as well by means of special agreements.[105]

The 1977 AP II, which, as explained in Chapter 1 included a scope of applicability provision that indicates it applies only when a non-State group, among other things, controls territory. In essence, this treaty, which supplements Common Article 3, is applicable to civil war–type conflicts and refers to "armed forces, and dissident armed forces or other organized armed groups."[106] This suggests a group status for non-State participants in armed conflict that has become the basis for targeting non-State actors owing to their membership in an organized armed group. What is clear is that detained or arrested unlawful participants in NIAC are required to be provided humane treatment, with provisions of AP II reflecting the same human rights principles found in AP I.[107] Since captured non-State belligerents are likely to be prosecuted under domestic criminal law, the rights provided for in international and domestic human rights law are applicable as well.

What does remain key is the protection afforded to civilians. AP II requires the protection of the civilian population and individual civilians from the dangers arising from military operations; civilians not being made the objects of an attack, or subjected to violence for the primary purpose of spreading terror, starvation;

civilians being protected from attacks causing the release of dangerous forces (e.g., dams, dykes, and nuclear generating stations); the protection of cultural and religious objects that constitute the cultural or spiritual heritage of peoples; or being displaced, "unless the security of the civilians involved or imperative military reasons so demand."[108] As in IAC, civilians are protected "unless and for such time as they take a direct part in hostilities."[109] Again, while the majority of States (86 percent) are bound by these provisions, a number of major powers are not (although, in the case of the United States, a number of official presidential statements have asserted a commitment to applying the treaty to any conflict falling within the scope of Common Article 3). However, the general requirement to protect civilian population is also part of customary international law.[110] This can also be seen in the customary "proportionality" rules governing targeting, which mirror those found in AP I.[111]

With there being no lawful combatant status similar to IAC, the question arises as to what the status is for government participants in NIAC, and whether they enjoy any form of combatant immunity. The answer is found in both the lingering effect of the just war–based proper authority principle, and State practice. While those who fight against a lawful government are viewed as criminals, members of the State security services presumptively act under lawful authority, for example under the domestic law of their own State. This privileged status can extend to service internationally when fighting insurgents in other States, whether acting at the invitation of the territorial government or under a United Nations mandate or when exercising the right of State self-defense. However, the security forces do remain liable to prosecution under both domestic law (either their own, or the State they are operating in as applicable), and for any war crimes that are committed.[112]

Notably, the law applicable to NIAC does not set out rules for membership in State security forces. That status would be established by domestic legal provisions of the county involved. Military, paramilitary, and police forces may engage in hostilities and enjoy a form of combatant immunity, although any perfidious conduct such as feigning civilian status would be contrary to international law. For example, the 1998 Rome Statute of the International Criminal Court prohibits "[k]illing or wounding treacherously a combatant adversary."[113]

One significant example of State practice that confirms this notion of combatant immunity for State armed forces engaged in such conflicts is the NIAC-related operations in Afghanistan. In that conflict, for over 15 years up to 50 countries have engaged in hostilities against the Taliban, al Qaeda, and now the Islamic State. Members of those State security forces are not liable for prosecution for their actions carried out during those combat operations so long as those actions comply with IHL.

4   Miscellaneous categories

In addition to individuals who fall into the categories of combatancy, unprivileged belligerency, and civilian, there are other persons found on the battlefield for whom special humanitarian law provisions apply. These include child soldiers, mercenaries, and journalists.

4.1 *Child soldiers*

The use of children as combatants is contrary to IHL and human rights law. Both Additional Protocols to the 1949 Geneva Conventions require the parties to a conflict to take feasible measures so that children do not participate in hostilities.[114] A similar provision is found in the Convention on the Rights of the Child.[115] Parties to armed conflicts must refrain from recruiting children into the armed forces.[116] The minimum age regarding participation and recruitment is 15 years.[117] This is also viewed as customary international law.[118] It is also a crime under the 1998 Rome Statute to use children to actively participate in hostilities during both IAC and NIAC.[119] It must be noted that the Optional Protocol to the Convention of the Rights of the Child raises the bar on compulsory recruitment from 15 to 18 years. However, it remains possible to have voluntary recruitment under the age of 18 years.[120] It does remain a tragic aspect of warfare that children are subject to being targeted while taking a direct part in hostilities.

4.2 *Mercenaries*

Mercenaries have been an enduring part of warfare. Although often shunned as guns for hire and as murderers, their involvement in conflict remains a reality. During the 1960s, a number of mercenaries engaged in indiscriminate killings while operating in Africa.[121] Further, other mercenary forces were associated with the attempted overthrow of governments.[122] In 1969, involvement in mercenary activity was declared a criminal act by the UN General Assembly resolution, although the resolution did not have force of law.[123] Although controversial, perceptions began to change with mercenary companies like Executive Outcomes becoming involved in the 1990s in helping to defeat an insurgency in Angola, and in stabilizing Sierra Leone.[124] Eventually, the expanded use of private military companies in Iraq and Afghanistan during the post-9/11 period, often performing traditional military functions, have raised questions whether mercenaries and other private actors have become an indispensable part of contemporary operations.

Under IHL, mercenaries do not qualify as combatants and therefore may not claim lawful combatant privilege. They have no right to be a combatant, or a prisoner of war. This makes them civilians who, upon capture, are liable to be treated as unprivileged belligerents subject to trial under the domestic law of the capturing State. AP I identifies a mercenary as any person who is specially recruited to fight in an armed conflict, actually takes part in hostilities, is motivated for private gain at rates substantially above the belligerent's own armed forces (a criterion that lacks clear definition), is not a national or resident of the territory of a party to the conflict, is not a member of its armed forces, and is not sent by another State on official duty as a member of its armed forces.[125] The definition would not include foreign volunteer forces such as the Gurkhas serving in the British or Indian armies, the French Foreign Legion, or volunteers joining the Israel Defense Forces.[126] There is also the 1989 International Convention against the Recruitment, Use, Financing and Training of Mercenaries,[127] which does not require the mercenary to take part in hostilities and extends to situations outside of armed conflict involving "concerted acts of violence."[128] However, the Convention has not attracted widespread support.[129]

During IAC, a distinction has to be made between persons qualifying as civilians accompanying the armed forces eligible for prisoner of war status (*see* Chapter 5: *Prisoners of war and other detainees*) and those who might be considered mercenaries. The ability to make that distinction is enhanced by the requirement for accompanying civilians to have a State-issued identity card.[130] Given the technical nature of prisoner of war status under the Third Geneva Convention, as well as the unique requirements of the mercenary definition (e.g., persons not nationals of the belligerent party), there very well could be persons engaged in hostilities who are unprivileged belligerents but not mercenaries at law. Overall, States have been reluctant in the post-9/11 period to condemn the use of private military contractors even if they may qualify as mercenaries. Whether such individuals are motivated by money alone, specially recruited for a conflict, or take a direct part in hostilities are often hotly debated questions, but ones that have evaded anything close to consensus.[131]

Indeed, post-9/11, the conflicts in Afghanistan and Iraq saw a large increase in the use of private military contractors and security companies by the United States and coalition partners alike. Military contractors in particular were seen to be taking an active role in hostilities, which on a number of occasions resulted in harm to civilians—the killing of 17 civilians and wounding of 14 others at Nisour Square in Bagdad, by Blackwater employees in September 2006, being one of the worst instances. In 2006, the ICRC and the Swiss Government launched an intergovernmental initiative to clarify that under existing international law private contractors do not operate in a legal vacuum.[132] Their status is to be determined on a case-by-case basis under IHL, with particular regard to the nature and circumstances of their functions. If they are deemed to be civilians, private contractors may not be the object of attack, unless and for such time as they directly participate in hostilities.

4.3 Journalists

Journalists are civilians who are entitled to the protection associated with that status. One type of journalist, the war correspondent, is recognized in the Third Geneva Convention as a person accompanying the armed forces. Consistent with that status, war correspondents shall be provided with an identity card reflecting their authorization to accompany the force, thereby qualifying as prisoners of war if captured.[133] AP I indicates more generally that journalists engaged in dangerous professional missions in areas of conflict are civilians. Journalists are protected provided they take no action adversely affecting their status as civilians.[134] The Protocol also provides for an identity card attesting to the status of a journalist to be issued by the State of which that person is a national "or in whose territory he resides or in which the news medium employing him is located." Practicing journalism is not considered to be taking a direct part in hostilities,[135] although relaying target coordinates for the specific purpose of facilitating a strike could be considered as such.[136] Practicing journalism is a war zone is an inherently dangerous activity that can expose journalists to considerable risk.[137]

5 Conclusion

The separation of armed forces and the civilian population has proven to be a fundamental, indeed foundational, principle of IHL. However, it is also one that has been demonstrated to be very challenging to implement. This has arisen, in part, from the complexity of modern warfare, but also because the legal status of participants in warfare is intimately associated with belonging to the armed forces of a State. Those who do not fight on behalf of a State do not have the status of lawful combatants. It is also clear that, notwithstanding efforts by the international community to encourage participants to seek legitimacy, and with it combatant immunity and prisoner of war status, unprivileged belligerents continue to engage in hostilities. What has changed is a move by the international community to see those belligerents less as war criminals and more as persons who have breached the domestic law of the capturing States.

International law has sought to extend legal recognition to some organized armed groups through their inclusion as legitimate combatants in AP I. That recognition occurred in the 1970s at a time when States were increasingly confronted with threats from non-State actors. However, resistance to such recognition by some States has remained. This area of the law is further complicated by the use of civilian contractors to support contemporary military operations, and the increased occurrence of NIAC since World War II.

Yet, despite the complexity of contemporary conflict, there remains a need to ensure civilians, and the civilian population are protected from the violence of armed conflict. While civilians may lose the protection of their status by taking a direct part in hostilities, it continues to be a requirement that they otherwise must be spared the dangers arising from military operations. It is that requirement that offers the most important protection for civilians.

Notes

1 James Malony Spaight, *War Rights on Land* 37 (1911).
2 Richard R. Baxter, "So-Called 'Unprivileged Belligerency': Spies, Guerrillas, and Saboteurs," in *Humanizing the Laws of War: Selected Writings of Richard Baxter* 37, 42 (Detlev F. Vagts et al. eds, 2013).
3 Military Commission Act of 2009, Pub. L. No. 111–84, Section 948(a)(7), 123 Stat. 2190 (codified at 10 U.S.C 47A (2006).

4   General Order No. 100, Instructions for the Government of Armies of the United States in the Field (24 April 1863), reprinted in *The War of the Rebellion: A Compilation of the Official Records of the Union and Confederate Armies* (Lieber Code), Series III, vol. 3, Art 57 (GPO 1899) [hereinafter Lieber Code].

5   James Turner Johnson, *Morality and Contemporary Warfare* 27–38 (1999) (The principle of *jus ad bellum* consists of seven principles on how to justify resorting to war: war must have a just cause, competent authority, the right intention, a reasonable hope of success, and overall proportionality of good over harm, be a last resort, and have the goal of peace).

6   Convention (IV) Respecting the Laws and Customs of War on Land and its annex: Regulations concerning the Laws and Customs of War on Land, 18 October 1907, 36 Stat. 2277, 3 Martens Nouveau Recueil (ser. 3) 461 [hereinafter 1907 Hague IV Regulations].

7   *Id.* Art 1.

8   *Id.* Art 2.

9   Spaight, *supra* note 1, at 58.

10   1907 Hague IV Regulations, Art 13. *See also* Lieber Code, Art 50.

11   Geoffrey Wawro, *The Franco-Prussian War: The German Conquest of France in 1870–1871*, 257–60 (2003) (Outlining that the Prussians had encountered the *leveé en masse* during the 1870 Franco-Prussian War, and had dealt with captured members of the *leveé* very harshly).

12   Geneva Convention Relative to the Treatment of Prisoners of War, Art 4(A)(6), 12 August 1949, 6 U.S.T. 3316, 75 U.N.T.S. 972 [hereinafter GPW].

13   Ministry of Foreign Affairs, The International Peace Conference 548 (1907).

14   Jeffry Kahn, *"Protection and Empire": The Martens Clause, State Sovereignty, and Individual Rights*, Va. J. Int'l. L. 1, 5 (2016). *See* Protocol (I) Additional to the Geneva Conventions of 12 August 1949, and Relating to the Protection of Victims of International Armed Conflicts, Art 1(2), 8 June 1977, 1125 U.N.T.S. 3 [hereinafter AP I] (entered into force 7 December 1978) (signed by the United States 12 December 1977, not transmitted to U.S. Senate, *see* S. Treaty Doc. No. 100–2 (1987)).

15   *Rules of Land Warfare of 1914*, War Department, Art 47(d) (1917).

16   *Id.* Art 29.

17   *Manual of Military Law*, War Office, para 20(iii) (1916).

18   Martin Van Creveld, *The Rise and Decline of the State* 249 (1999) (indicating that "modern death and destruction" would never have been possible without the State, its ministry of defense, and "its regular, uniformed, bureaucratically managed armed forces").

19   Lester Nurick, *The Distinction Between Combatant and Noncombatant in the Law of War*, 39 Am.J. Int'l.L. 680, 683–5, 689–96 (1945).

20   *Manual of the Law of Armed Conflict* paras 4.1–4.2.3 (UK Ministry of Defence ed., 2004) [hereinafter *UK LOAC Manual*].

21   *Id.* para 2.5.1.

22   John Keegan, *A History of Warfare* 313 (1994).

23   GPW, Art 4(A)(2).

24   Jean S. Pictet, Geneva Convention Relative to the Treatment of Prisoners of War: Commentary (ICRC, 1960), 61 [hereinafter Commentary GPW].

25   *See* GPW, Art 4(A)(1)-(2) (Article 1 of the 1907 Hague IV Regulations only made reference to armies, and militia and volunteer corps. 1907 Hague IV Regulations, Art 1).

26   GPW, Art 4(A)(2).

27   *See* G.I.A.D. Draper, *The Status of Combatants and the Question of Guerrilla War-fare*, 45 Brit. Y. B. Int'l L. 173–4 (1971); Kenneth Watkin, *Warriors Without*

Rights? Combatants, Unprivileged Belligerents, and the Struggle over Legitimacy 2 Occasional Paper Series 34–7 (Program on Humanitarian Policy and Conflict Research Harvard University, Winter 2005), *available at* http://reliefweb.int/sites/relief web.int/files/resources/52332277E2871AF7C125704C0037CF99-hpcr-gen-09may.pdf (where it is suggested all six have group attributes while: wearing the distinctive sign, carrying weapons and compliance with the law also must be performed by combatants on an individual basis).

28 W. Hays Parks, *Special Forces' Wear of Non-Standard Uniforms*, Chic. J. Int'l. L. 493, 508–11 (2003).

29 Howard S. Levie, *Prisoners of War in International Armed Conflict*, 59 Int'l. L. Stud. 37 (1978).

30 U.S. Dep't of Def., *Law of War Manual* 4.17.5 (June 2015, updated May 2016) [hereinafter *DoD Law of War Manual*].

31 Levie, *supra* note 29, at 37.

32 GPW, Art 4(A)(2).

33 G.I.A.D. Draper, "The Legal Classification of Belligerent Individuals," in *Reflections on Law and Armed Conflict* 101 (Michael A. Meyer & Hilaire McCoubrey eds, 1998).

34 Leslie Green, *The Contemporary Law of Armed Conflict* 194 (3rd edn, 2008).

35 Yoram Dinstein, *The Conduct of Hostilities Under the Law of International Armed Conflict* 122 (2nd edn, 2010).

36 *See* Levie, *supra* note 29, at 37 (where it is suggested there can be no special status for regular armed forces personnel regarding meeting the prisoner of war criteria because to do so would immunize a spy or saboteur, and permit members of armed forces to act contrary to the laws of war).

37 *See* Simon Chase & Ralph Pezzullo, *Zero Footprint: The True Story of a Private Military Contractor's Covert Assignments in Syria, Libya, and the World's Most Dangerous Places* 70–124 (2016) (for an account of private contractors being used to search for Osama bin Laden in 2004. At this time, the United States viewed the conflict as an international one).

38 *See, e.g.*, GPW, Art 3.

39 *See generally* AP I.

40 Protocol (II) Additional to the Geneva Conventions of 12 August 1949, and Relating to the Protection of Victims of Non-International Armed Conflicts, 8 June 1977, 1125 U.N.T.S. 609 [hereinafter AP II] (entered into force 7 December 1978) (signed by the United States 12 December 1977, transmitted to the U.S. Senate 29 January 1987, still pending action as S. Treaty Doc. No. 100–2 (1987)).

41 AP I, Art 1(4).

42 Ronald Reagan, Letter of Transmittal, The White House, 29 January 1987, *available at* www.loc.gov/rr/frd/Military_Law/pdf/protocol-II-100-2.pdf

43 AP I, Art 1(3).

44 *Id.* Art 50(1).

45 *Id.* Art 43(2) (emphasis added).

46 *Id.* Art 44(3).

47 *Id.*

48 *Id.* Art 44(4).

49 *Id.* Art 44(7).

50 *See* Colin Beavan, *Operation Jedburgh: D-Day and America's First Shadow War* 109–11 (2006).

51 Ronald Reagan, Letter of Transmittal, The White House, 29 January 1987, *available at* www.loc.gov/rr/frd/Military_Law/pdf/protocol-II-100-2.pdf

52 *See* Watkin, *supra* note 27, at 59.

53 AP I, Art 43(3).

54   Pictet et al., Commentary on the Additional Protocols of 8 June 1977 to the Geneva Conventions of 12 August 1949 (ICRC, 1987), para 1682. *See also* Grant Wardlaw, *Political Terrorism: Theory, Tactics, and Counter-Measures* 97–100 (2nd edn, 1990) (for a discussion of third-force paramilitary police units).
55   1907 Hague IV Regulations, Art 43.
56   Geneva Convention Relative to the Protection of Civilian Persons in Time of War, Art 64, 12 August 1949, 6 U.S.T. 3516, 75 U.N.T.S. 973 [hereinafter GC].
57   *See, e.g.*, Gerhard von Glahn, *The Occupation of Enemy Territory* 136 (157).
58   Dinstein, *The International Law of Belligerent Occupation* 60 (2009).
59   Pictet, Geneva Convention Relative to the Protection of Civilian Persons in Time of War: Commentary (ICRC, 1958), 307 [hereinafter Commentary GC].
60   GPW, Art 4(A)(2).
61   AP II, Art 1(2).
62   *See Ex Parte Quirin*, 317 U.S. 1, 35 (1942) (which makes reference to both unlawful combatants and unlawful belligerents); *The Hostage Case*, 11 Trials of War Criminals (T.W.C.) 757, 1224 (where members of resistance movements were referred to as not being lawful belligerents, or unlawful combatants).
63   Lester Nurick & Roger W. Barrett, *Legality of Guerrilla Forces Under the Laws of War*, 40 Am. J. Int'l. L. 563, 572–9 (1940).
64   M.R.D. Foot, SOE: *The Special Operations Executive 1940–1946*, at 308–9 (1999).
65   *Ex Parte Quirin*, 317 U.S. 1, 31 (1942) (emphasis added).
66   *The Hostage Case*, 11 Trials of War Criminals (T.W.C.) 1224.
67   *Id*. at 1245.
68   Baxter, *supra* note 2, at 40.
69   *Id*. at 48.
70   *Id*. at 53.
71   *Id*. at 55.
72   *Id*. at 42.
73   *Id*. at 57.
74   *UK LOAC Manual*, para 11.4.
75   Dinstein, *supra* note 35, at 35–9; Green, *supra* note 34, at 176.
76   Military Commission Act of 2009, Pub. L. No. 111–84, Section 948(a)(7), 123 Stat. 2190 (codified at 10 U.S.C 47A (2006)) (for the definition of *unprivileged enemy belligerent*).
77   *See Hamdan v. Rumsfeld*, 548 U.S. 557 (2006).
78   *See, e.g.*, GC, Arts 65–78; AP I, Art 75; AP II, Art 4.
79   Valerie Epps, *Civilian Casualties in Modern Warfare: The Death of the Collateral Damage Rule*, 41 Ga. J. Int'l & Comp. L. 307, 319–29 (2013).
80   Spaight, *Air Power and War Rights* Ch. X, 244–58 (3rd edn, 1947).
81   Richard Overy, "The Second World War," in *The Oxford History of Modern War* 138, 149 (2005).
82   1907 Hague IV Regulations, Arts 43–56.
83   Green, *supra* note 34, at 288.
84   Dinstein, *supra* note 35, at 261.
85   *Id*. Art 51(3) (emphasis added).
86   *Id*. Art 57(2).
87   AP I, Art 48.
88   *Id*. Art 51(1).
89   *Id*. Art 51(2).
90   *Id*. Art 52(1).
91   *Id*. Art 51(2).
92   *Id*. Art 57(2)(ii).
93   *Id*. Art 45(3) (emphasis added).

94 Watkin, *Opportunity Lost: Organized Armed Groups and the ICRC "Direct Participation in Hostilities" Interpretive Guidance*, 42 N.Y.U. J. Int'l L. & Pol. 641, 642 (2010).

95 *See generally* N. Melzer, Interpretive Guidance on the Notion of Direct Participation in Hostilities Under International Humanitarian Law (2009) [hereinafter DPH Interpretive Guidance].

96 Report of the Special Rapporteur on extrajudicial, summary or arbitrary executions, Philip Alston, UN Doc. A/HRC/14/24/ Add. 6 (28 May 2010), 57–69, at 19–21, *available at* www2.ohchr.org/english/bodies/hrcouncil/docs/14session/A.HRC.14.24.Add6.pdf

97 DPH Interpretive Guidance, at 34.

98 *See, e.g.*, M. N. Schmitt, *Deconstructing Direct Participation in Hostilities*, 42 N.Y.U. J. Int'l L. & Pol. 697 (2010); B. Boothby, *"And For Such Time As": The Time Dimension to Direct Participation in Hostilities*, 42 N.Y.U. J. Int'l L. & Pol. 741 (2010); Parks, *Part IX of the ICRC "Direct Participation in Hostilities" Study: No Mandate, No Expertise, and Legally Incorrect*, 42 N.Y.U. J. Int'l L. & Pol. 769 (2010); Watkin, *supra* note 94; Melzer, *Keeping the Balance Between Military Necessity and Humanity: A Response to Four Critiques of the ICRC's Interpretive Guidance on the Notion of Direct Participation in Hostilities*, 42 N.Y.U. J. Int'l L. & Pol. 831 (2010).

99 Baxter, *supra* note 2, at 42.

100 Jack S. Levy & William R. Thompson, *Causes of War* 12 (2010).

101 Hugo Grotius, *The Rights of War and Peace* 240 (2005) (for reference to public, private, and mixed war).

102 AP II, Art 3.

103 GC, Art 3(2).

104 Commentary on the First Geneva Convention: Convention (I) for the Amelioration of the Condition of the Wounded and Sick in Armed Forces in the Field, Art 3, para 525 (2nd edn, 2016) [hereinafter Commentary on the First Geneva Convention, 2016], *available at* https://ihl-databases.icrc.org/applic/ihl/ihl.nsf/Comment.xsp?action=openDocument&documentId=59F6CDFA490736C1C1257F7D004BA0EC. Commentary on the First Geneva Convention: Convention (I) for the Amelioration of the Condition of the Wounded and Sick in Armed Forces in the Field (2nd edn, 2016), para 525, *available at* www.icrc.org/applic/ihl/ihl.nsf/Treaty.xsp?action=openDocument&documentId=4825657B0C7E6BF0C12563CD002D6B0B [hereinafter 2016 Commentary GWS].

105 GC, Art 3(2).

106 AP II, Art 1(1).

107 *Id*. Arts 4–6.

108 *Id*. Arts 13–16.

109 *Id*. Art 13(3).

110 *Customary International Humanitarian Law* 5–8 (Jean-Marie Henckaerts & Louise Doswald-Beck eds, 2005).

111 *Id*. at 48–9; Brian Egan, *International Law, Legal Diplomacy, and the Counter-ISIL Campaign: Some Observations*, 92 Int'l. L. Stud. 235, 242–3 (2016).

112 Ian Henderson, *Civilian Intelligence Agencies and the Use of Armed Drones*, 13 Y.B. Int'l Hum. L. 133. 149–50 (2010); Kenneth Anderson, "Readings: Civilian Intelligence Agencies and the Use of Armed Drones by Ian Henderson," *Lawfare* (27 June 2014), *available at* www.lawfareblog.com/readings-civilian-intelligence-agencies-and-use-armed-drones-ian-henderson

113 Rome Statute of the International Criminal Court, 17 July 1998, Art 8(2)(d)(ix), 2187 U.N.T.S. 90 [hereinafter Rome Statute].

114 AP I, Art 77(2); AP II, Art 4(3)(2).

115 Convention on the Rights of the Child, 1577 U.N.T.S. 3, Art 38(2) [hereinafter CRC].
116 AP I, Art 77(2); AP II, Art 4(3)(2); CRC, Art 38(2).
117 CRC, Art 38(2).
118 Dinstein, *supra* note 35, at 158.
119 Rome Statute, Art 8(2)(b)(xxvi), (e)(vii).
120 Dinstein, *supra* note 35, at 158–9.
121 Al J. Venter, *Mercenaries: Putting the World to Right with Hired Guns* 13–15 (2014).
122 *Id.*
123 *See* General Assembly Resolution 2548 (XXIV), para 7 (11 December 1969); Green, *supra* note 34, at 139.
124 Venter, *supra* note 121, at 15–26.
125 AP I, Art 47.
126 Green, *supra* note 34, at 138.
127 *See generally* International Convention Against the Recruitment, Use, Financing and Training of Mercenaries, 4 December 1989, 2163 U.N.T.S. 75.
128 *Id.* Art 3(1).
129 International Convention against the Recruitment, Use, Financing and Training of Mercenaries, 4 December 1989, ICRC, *available at* https://ihl-databases.icrc.org/ihl/INTRO/530 (where it is noted there are 34 States Parties and nine signatories).
130 GPW, Art 4(A)(5).
131 Dinstein, *supra* note 35, at 57–8.
132 The initiative led to the adoption in September 2008 of the Montreux Document on pertinent international legal obligations and good practices for States related to operations of private military and security companies during armed conflict. It has been signed by more than 50 States to date. *See* Schweizerische Eidgenossenschaft Federal Department of Foreign Affairs, Participating States of the Montreux Document, *available at* www.eda.admin.ch/eda/en/home/foreign-policy/international-law/international-humanitarian-law/private-military-security-companies/participating-states.html.
133 *Id.*
134 AP I, Art 79.
135 *DoD Law of War Manual*, 4.21.2.
136 *Id.* at 4.22.2.1.
137 AP I, Art 79(3).

4 Dealing with civilians, wounded, and sick

1 Introduction

Mitigating the risks of unnecessary suffering in armed conflict is the core objective of IHL. To implement this objective, IHL includes rules that protect two groups of individuals especially vulnerable to the consequences of war—the wounded and sick, and civilians. In the case of armed conflict, it will often be the armed forces and armed groups engaged in the conflict that are in the best position to mitigate this suffering inflicted on these victims of war. This innately human-itarian objective is indelibly linked to the modern characterization of international *humanitarian* law.

The very origins of the Geneva tradition—the tradition of humanitarian protection that evolved into and from the Geneva Conventions—sprung from a movement motivated by a book titled *A Memory of Solferino*.[1] The book, written by Swiss businessman Henry Dunant, detailed his firsthand observations of the suffering endured by the unattended wounded on the Solferino battlefield. The ensuing international outrage over his solemn observations led to the Red Cross movement, and ultimately the 1864 Geneva Convention for the Amelioration of the Suffering of the Wounded in Armies in the Field,[2] the seed from which four 1949 Geneva Conventions blossomed.[3] To this day, sparing the wounded soldier from the condition of being injured and stranded on the field of battle, and especially facilitating efforts of military medical personnel to collect and care for casualties of all sides to the conflict, serves as a touchstone for assessing commitment to IHL. Indeed, few IHL violations are considered more indicative of illegitimacy in warfare than attacking persons or places exclusively engaged in this humanitarian endeavor and displaying the protective symbols of the Geneva Conventions.

Civilians, of course, also suffer the terrible consequences of war. But the protection of civilians developed more slowly than the protection of the military wounded and sick. This might seem counterintuitive, as today civilians are almost always the first victims of hostilities. But extensive risk to the civilian population is a relatively new reality of war. In 1864, when the First Geneva Convention was adopted, wars were generally confined to limited geographic areas, normally removed from civilian population centers (although civilians were often victimized by the general destruction left in the wake of hostilities).[4] However, as the nature and capability of military weaponry evolved (both in range and effect), the dangers to civilians grew exponentially, with an accordant need to address civilian protection through humanitarian law.

The lessons from World War II led to a determined effort to enhance humanitarian protection for civilians, but in a specific context. Civilians suffered extensively during that conflict as the result of combat operations. However, the post-War legal developments did not focus on protecting civilians from the immense risk associated with proximity to combat. Instead, the States that assembled in 1947 to revise the Geneva Conventions focused on the terrible and widespread suffering inflicted upon civilians under enemy military occupation. The outcome of this effort was, *inter alia*, a treaty devoted specifically to protecting civilians—the 1949 Geneva Convention Relative to the Protection of Civilian Persons in Time of War (GC).[5] This new treaty focused heavily on enhancing protection for civilians under the authority of an enemy State, either as the result of enemy occupation or being stranded in enemy territory during an IAC.[6] This post–World War II, occupation-based focus resulted in a now-puzzling omission—almost nothing in the new *Civilians'* Convention addressed mitigating civilian risk resulting from the conduct of hostilities, for example imposing limits on when, where, and how armed forces may attack enemy targets in close proximity to civilians and civilian property. This vital aspect of civilian protection was not comprehensively addressed in an IHL treaty until the revision effort that commenced in 1975, and culminated in 1977 with the two Additional Protocols to the Geneva Conventions (*see* Chapter 1, 3: *The impact of the 1977 Additional Protocols*).

This chapter will provide an overview of IHL applicable to two broad categories of war victims: civilians and the wounded and sick. It will begin by explaining how IHL endeavors to shield civilians from the risks associated with being under the control of, and at the mercy of, an enemy armed force. It will then shift to the even more comprehensive mosaic of rules that are intended to maximize the opportunity to mitigate the impact of armed conflict on those who become casualties—the wounded and sick in the field and at sea.

2 Protecting civilians

There is perhaps no image of war more evocative of the need for humanitarian protection than that of an innocent civilian suffering the consequences of hostilities. If there has been one unquestioned achievement in IHL, it has been the universal rejection of the notion of *total war*, a concept in which the civilian population of the enemy State is proverbial fair game. Today, the protection of the civilians and civilian property is at the very core of IHL.

Acknowledging this protective objective of IHL is, however, much easier than explaining the complex web of rules and principles developed to achieve this objective. This is not only because the evolution of IHL has steadily increased emphasis on civilian protection but also because of the wide spectrum of situations during armed conflict that place civilians at risk. Accordingly, when seeking to understand what might best be understood as IHL's overall civilian protection regime—what one expert characterized as civilian protection law (CPL)[7]—it is useful to consider the multiple, law-based functional areas: first, protection from the harmful effects of hostilities, often referred to as *targeting* law; second, special protections for especially vulnerable civilians, like the elderly or children; third, protections for civilians who find themselves under the civil or military authority of an enemy State; and, finally, protection of civilian property from unlawful interference, such as pillage or unjustified destruction. Each of these areas of risk and the law that functions to protect against these risks will be discussed below. First, however, it is necessary to understand the subject of protection—who qualifies as a *civilian* within the meaning of IHL.

2.1   Who is a civilian?

Chapters 3 and 5 explain how the term *civilian* is defined in IHL. Essentially, during an IAC, a civilian is any individual who does not qualify as a combatant or a retained person (military medical personnel and chaplains) upon capture.[8] During a NIAC, almost everyone other than State security forces are considered civilians, although by becoming members of the non-State organized armed group the civilian will usually be treated as an unlawful participant in the conflict.

2.2   Protection from the effects of attack

One of the most important consequences of civilian status is that it triggers a presumptive protection against being made the object of attack pursuant to the principle of distinction. However, as explained in Chapter 6, this does not mean that civilians are immune from unintended harm. In fact, this does not even mean that civilians are immune from known harm—a risk addressed through the targeting principle of proportionality. Furthermore, the direct participation in hostilities rule explained in Chapter 3 indicates that IHL is not illogical: the protection civilians enjoy from deliberate attack is forfeited or suspended for such time that a civilian directly participates in hostilities.

2.3   Protecting civilians from maltreatment: the humane treatment obligation

The risk to civilians produced by armed conflict is not limited to the harmful effects of attack but also includes the risk of maltreatment by armed forces who have control over areas where they are encountered. Such maltreatment, whether related to an IAC or NIAC, is incompatible with the most basic protection provided by IHL—the obligation to ensure civilians are treated humanely at all times. This humane treatment obligation is enumerated in a variety of IHL provisions, most notably Common Article 3 to the four Geneva Conventions,[9] Article 4 of AP II, and Article 75 of AP I.[10] However, while perhaps originally a purely treaty-based obligation, today it is almost universally considered an obligation imposed by customary international law. Thus, all civilians benefit from the humane treatment shield of protection, best understood as a baseline protection, what the International Court of Justice characterized as the minimum yardstick of humanitarian protection during armed conflict.[11]

Humane treatment is obviously an essential obligation, shielding civilians from many forms of maltreatment unfortunately associated with past (and probably future) armed conflicts. Humane treatment also is the foundation upon which IHL further provides a host of additional protections in both IAC and NIAC. However, because these additional protections are more robust in terms of being articulated in humanitarian treaty law in IAC than in NIAC, it remains important to distinguish the condition of civilians in these two types of armed conflicts. The *existence* of an armed conflict and the *nature* of that conflict are respectively essential in determining whether or not to even look to IHL for protections. As a result, such protections may be found in IHRL. If the situation is indeed an existing armed conflict, then it becomes important to assess the type of conflict and the varied protections that IHL provides to civilians in conflicts of that nature.

2.4   Building on humane treatment: the spectrum of civilian protection

When an armed conflict does not yet exist (for example, when social order is only disrupted by civil disturbances), IHRL protects individuals from, *inter alia*, cruel, inhumane, and degrading treatment at the hands of the State and its agents (*see* Chapter 1, 4.4: *The intersection of international humanitarian law and international human rights law*). But the content of that body of law and its associated terminology are beyond the scope of this chapter. What is significant for purposes of this discussion is that where an armed conflict exists IHL comes into force, which will result in applicability of civilian protection rules in addition to the international human rights obligations that function to protect civilians from abusive treatment during times of peace and armed conflict. But, while every civilian is protected by IHL during an armed conflict, not all civilians are protected to the same extent. It is therefore useful to think of the civilian protection regime as a series of benefit packages. All civilians receive *a* benefit package, but some benefit packages are more comprehensive than others.

2.4.1   Civilian protection in non-international armed conflicts

During a NIAC, Common Article 3 represents the primary benefit package provided by IHL.[12] As noted above, Common Article 3 mandates that any person not actively participating in hostilities be treated humanely at all times. Unless a civilian is directly participating in hostilities, he or she benefits from this protection. Common Article 3 enumerates actions that are especially incompatible with this obligation, although it also emphasizes that this list is not exclusive. Specifically, Common Article 3 provides that:

> In the case of armed conflict not of an international character occurring in the territory of one of the High Contracting Parties, each Party to the conflict shall be bound to apply, as a minimum, the following provisions:
>
> 1) Persons taking no active part in the hostilities, including members of armed forces who have laid down their arms and those placed *hors de combat* by sickness, wounds, detention, or any other cause, shall in all circumstances be treated humanely, without any adverse distinction founded on race, colour, religion or faith, sex, birth or wealth, or any other similar criteria.
>
>   To this end, the following acts are and shall remain prohibited at any time and in any place whatsoever with respect to the above-mentioned persons:
>   a) violence to life and person, in particular murder of all kinds, mutilation, cruel treatment and torture;
>   b) taking of hostages;
>   c) outrages upon personal dignity, in particular humiliating and degrading treatment;
>   d) the passing of sentences and the carrying out of executions without previous judgment pronounced by a regularly constituted court affording all the judicial guarantees which are recognized as indispensable by civilized peoples.
> 2) The wounded and sick shall be collected and cared for.[13]

It should be somewhat self-evident that this list is indicative of the types of abuses to civilians and other individuals rendered *hors de combat* (out of action) that the drafters of Common Article 3 were both familiar with and sought to prevent in future conflicts. But it is also important to recognize that these are just examples of acts or omissions that were easily identified as cruel and inhumane. Beyond this list, what else is prohibited? The simple answer is anything that is inhumane, but the harder question is how is this assessed? As the 2016 ICRC Commentary associated with Common Article 3 notes,

> [i]n accordance with the ordinary meaning of the word "humane", what is called for is treatment that is "compassionate or benevolent" towards the persons protected under common Article 3. . . . Persons protected under common Article 3 must never be treated as less than fellow human beings and their inherent human dignity must be upheld and protected.[14]

This might seem equally simplistic, but in situations of armed conflict—and especially in NIACs, which tend to tear societies apart—dehumanization of opponents and the civilians they are associated with by opposing armed forces and armed groups is a common reality. Humane treatment requires these participants in hostilities to essentially treat all civilians as they would demand the civilians associated with their cause be treated.

Where applicable, AP II supplements this "package of protection" by adding some proverbial flesh to the bones of Common Article 3. Not all States are bound by AP II as a matter of treaty obligation, but the humane treatment provisions of that treaty are widely considered obligatory as a matter of customary international law. The United States appears to agree with this proposition, as both Presidents Reagan and Clinton indicated that the United States would apply AP II to any armed conflict falling within the scope of Common Article 3, and they, along with President Obama, sought Senate advice and consent for AP II in order to ratify the treaty.[15] These additional protections include: respect for religious beliefs and practices; a prohibition against terrorism directed against civilians; more robust protections for individuals subjected to detention; and protections for individuals subjected to penal sanction associated with the armed conflict.[16]

2.4.2   *Civilian protection in international armed conflicts*

All other civilian protection packages in the remainder of this discussion as a matter of convention are applicable only during IAC. The two primary sources of these humanitarian law–based protections are the 1949 Geneva Convention Relative to the Protection of Civilian Persons in Time of War (GC),[17] which directly provides rights and protections to civilians, and AP I,[18] which provides indirect or derivative benefits to civilians by limiting what the military may permissibly target or attack and the manner by which they do so.

Just like civilians in NIAC, all civilians in IAC are protected by the humane treatment obligation. Interestingly, though, the source of this protection during IAC is more complicated than the source applicable to NIACs—Common Article 3. When the GC emerged in 1949 from the conference to revise the then-existing 1929 Geneva Conventions, it did not include a broad, Common Article 3–type provision applicable to IACs. Instead, several specific Articles in the GC protected civilians from maltreatment, but these Articles applied in different contexts. For example, Article 4 protects civilians when they are effectively stranded in the territory of an enemy State, as well as those civilians under the authority of an enemy occupying force.[19]

The GC also included a range of protections for all civilians, no matter where they were located or what their nationality. Specifically, Part II of the GC provides what the treaty characterizes as general protections for all civilians impacted by IACs.[20] Part II provisions, however, are framed in terms of encouraging belligerent parties to a conflict to *endeavor* to implement measures to mitigate civilian risk. For example, Articles 14 and 15 encourage parties to agree upon the establishment of neutralized and/or hospital zones so that civilians can be assembled and shielded from hostilities.[21] Article 23 obligates parties to take measures to facilitate civilian access to consignments of medical supplies, food, and clothing.[22] As a result of this expansive, individualized-article approach to civilian protection, most civilians are in fact included within the scope of a humane treatment obligation, but not as the result of a direct and comprehensive rule analogous to Common Article 3.

Still, there was always the possibility that a civilian might fall outside the scope of one of these specific Articles included in the GC. For example, some civilians fail to qualify for protection of Article 4 during occupation because they are nationals of a co-belligerent of the occupying power. Another example involves civilians considered mercenaries, who are therefore denied status and protection by both the GPW and GC.[23] This possibility, coupled with the recognition that the general protections provided by the GC left too many gaps in civilian protection law, led the drafters of AP I—the treaty that supplements the Geneva Convention regulation of IACs—to include a number of Articles intended to enhance civilian protections. The most significant of these is Article 75, which is best understood as the Common Article 3 for IAC.[24] Article 75 establishes that any individual who fails to qualify for more beneficial treatment under the Geneva Conventions or the AP I (for example, the co-belligerent civilian or the mercenary) must be treated humanely.[25] And, just like Common Article 3, AP I's Article 75 specifically enumerates prohibited activities that contravene the humane treatment obligation.[26]

It is true that not all States are bound to AP I. But it is increasingly difficult to sustain the assertion that the humane treatment obligations enumerated in Article 75 can be ignored, even by non-treaty States. As a result, the treaty basis for the humane treatment of civilians during IAC may ultimately be a question of form over substance, as there is widespread consensus that customary international law imposes the Article 75 obligation vis-à-vis any civilian in *any* armed conflict.[27] Thus, even for States that are not bound to AP I, such as the United States, the substantive obligation reflected in this treaty provision should be assumed to apply at all times.

2.4.2.1   PROTECTING ESPECIALLY VULNERABLE CIVILIANS

IHL recognizes that some civilians are in need of special protections—civilians who are especially vulnerable to the effects of IAC. Protection for these civilians necessitates an enhanced protection package. To accomplish this, the GC provides a range of additional protections for these vulnerable civilians: the wounded, sick, aged, children under the age of 15, expectant mothers, and mothers of children under the age of seven.[28] In terms of enhanced protection, the GC includes the following rules applicable to these civilians:

- Calling for parties to a conflict to agree to remove the "wounded, sick infirm, and aged persons, children and maternity cases . . . from besieged or encircled areas."[29]
- Requiring that "civilian hospitals organized to give care to the wounded and sick, the infirm and maternity cases, may in no circumstances be the object

of attack, but shall at all times be respected and protected by the Parties to the conflict."[30]

- Ensuring that "children under fifteen, who are orphaned or are separated from their families as a result of the war, are not left to their own resources, and that their maintenance, the exercise of their religion and their education are facilitated in all circumstances."[31]

Importantly, these provisions, found in Part II of the GC, "cover the whole of the populations of the countries in conflict, without any adverse distinction based, in particular, on race, nationality, religion or political opinion, and are intended to alleviate the sufferings caused by war."[32] This may seem only logical, but because other protections provided by the GC turn on question such as nationality and location it is an important emphasis that parties to an armed conflict should always endeavor to make special efforts to protect the especially vulnerable from the adverse consequences of the conflict.

2.4.2.2 PROTECTED PERSONS: THE MAXIMUM SHIELD OF PROTECTION

As discussed earlier, because the GC was developed in the aftermath of World War II, the bulk of its protective provisions are directed toward civilians under enemy control—an obvious response to the countless abuses of civilians who found themselves in such a situation during that war. Thus, the GC's maximum benefit package applies to what the treaty defines as *protected persons*—a term that should not be confused as suggesting that other civilians are not protected by IHL, but instead that some civilians are provided more protections than others.

According to the GC, protected persons are civilians "who, at a given moment and in any manner whatsoever, find themselves, in case of a conflict or occupation, in the hands of a party to the conflict or Occupying Power of which they are not nationals."[33] Thus, the GC seeks to ensure maximum protection for civilians who find themselves at the mercy of the authorities of an enemy State.

Because of this very clear protective focus,

> [n]ationals of a neutral State who find themselves in the territory of a belligerent State, and nationals of co-belligerent State, shall not be regarded as protected persons while the State of which they are nationals has normal diplomatic representation in the State in whose hands they are.[34]

Additionally, because the status is limited to civilians, individuals falling within the protective scope of one of the other Geneva Conventions, such as prisoners of war and the wounded and sick, "shall not be considered as protected persons" falling within the scope of the GC.[35]

The experience of World War II may explain why the GC links maximum treaty protection to nationality of the civilian vis-à-vis the party to the conflict under whose control the civilian falls. However, this civilian protection formula is not without controversy. Since 1949, many IACs have exposed the reality that civilians may be victimized not only when under the control of an enemy armed force but also when subjected to arbitrary or abusive actions by their own armed forces or co-belligerent forces. In practice, a nationality-based test for applicability of important civilian protection rules seems increasingly at odds with IHL's core humanitarian objective. Nonetheless, the GC's definition of protected person remains controlling as a matter of treaty law. The significance of this definition encompasses both the protections it triggers and the criminal consequences for violating these obligations, as only violations directed against protected persons qualify as grave breaches triggering Article 147's prosecute or extradite obligation[36] (*see* Chapter 11: *International justice and compliance*).

While, as noted above, all civilians are protected against inhumane treatment, protected persons benefit from a much more comprehensive civilian protection regime. Included among the many GC protections applicable to protected persons are Articles providing the following:

- "[R]espect for their persons, their honour, their family rights, their religious convictions and practices and their manners and customs";[37]
- "Women shall be especially protected against any attack on their honour, in particular against rape, enforced prostitution, or any form of indecent assault";[38]
- Access to the ICRC, the respective National Red Cross/Crescent/Lion/Sun (and now also the Red Crystal), as well as any organization that might assist them;[39]
- "No physical or moral coercion shall be exercised against [them], in particular to obtain information";[40] and
- No collective punishment.[41]

These basic protections provide a foundation for more extensive protections, the applicability of which turns on whether the civilian is stranded in enemy territory or is subjected to enemy belligerent occupation. The GC also provides for appointment of a *protecting power* to oversee compliance with the treaty[42]— in a sense a substitute for diplomatic protection normally unavailable once conflict breaks out and diplomatic relations are severed. Unfortunately, parties to a conflict have rarely agreed on the neutral State that will serve as a protecting power as is required by the GC. As a result, representatives of the ICRC normally perform the functions of the protecting power, a role explicitly authorized in Article 5 of AP I.[43]

Civilians stranded in the national territory of an enemy are protected from arbitrary treatment by enemy authorities. Additionally, these civilians receive the following protections:

- Entitlement to leave the territory, and, where that request is denied, to have the refusal reconsidered by an appropriate court or administrative board;[44]

- Entitlement to receive relief supplies;[45]
- Right to, "if their state of health so requires, receive medical attention and hospital treatment to the same extent as the nationals of the State concerned";[46]
- Opportunity to find employment equal to that enjoyed by nationals of the state concerned;[47]
- Right to only be compelled to work to the same extent as nationals of the state concerned.[48]

A more common predicament for civilians is that they find themselves at the mercy of an enemy authority as a result of the occupation of their own national territory. While IHL occupation obligations are not the focus of this chapter, occupation essentially involves the displacement of national authority by enemy armed forces and the assertion of firm control over enemy territory by those armed forces. At this point, the invading or occupying military commander assumes governing authority over the territory, including the obligation to maintain public order. The GC substantially expanded the law that protects civilians when they find themselves under such enemy military authority.

Most civilians in occupied territory fall within the scope of the protected person definition, which includes not only nationals of the occupied State but also civilians of neutral nationality. Only nationals of the occupying power and its co-belligerents are excluded from the protected person category during occupation (based on the assumption that these civilians are in no way deprived of the protections of their own governments as the result of the occupation). Part III of the GC provides an extensive array of rules related to the treatment of civilians who qualify as protected persons as the result of an occupation, and relations between them and the occupying power. Some of the more significant of these rules are:

- Protected persons who are *not* nationals of the occupied territory may leave;[49]
- Reprisals (violations of IHL intended to compel an enemy or occupied civilians to cease violating their obligations) are prohibited;[50]
- Individual or mass forcible transfers or deportations are prohibited;[51]
- Civilians may not be compelled to serve in the occupying power's armed forces, or to engage in labor essential to the defense of those forces;[52]
- Civilian property may not be destroyed absent imperative military necessity;
- Deprivation of liberty is authorized only based on individual conduct and is subject to extensive treaty regulation.

Like civilians protected while in enemy territory, a protecting power should monitor compliance with the GC in order to "safeguard the interests of the Parties of the conflict."[53] This can entail a range of functions, including visiting internment camps and assessing living conditions; monitoring penal prosecutions; and lending assistance in case of disagreement with respect to treaty obligations.[54]

3 Protecting civilian property

Armed conflict will obviously endanger not only civilians but also civilian property. While IHL's targeting regime functions to mitigate risks to civilian property resulting from the conduct of hostilities (*see* Chapter 6: *Targeting*), there will be many situations where civilian property will be subjected to risk, not as the result of the destructive effects of combat but instead from interference with the property by armed forces or other belligerent operatives.

As a general proposition, any interference with or destruction of civilian property must be justified by military necessity. The UK's *Joint Service Manual of the Law of Armed Conflict* explains this basic necessity requirement, providing:

> It may be permissible to destroy a house in order to clear a field of fire or because it is being used as an enemy military observation or sniper post. It would not be permissible to burn down a house simply to prevent its being inhabited by persons of a different ethnic group or religious persuasion.[55]

Similarly, there may be a legitimate military necessity to destroy "crops, food-stuffs, and water sources," including to deny their use by the enemy, but not to an extent that starvation of the civilian population is likely to result.[56] Indeed, AP I expressly prohibits the use of starvation of the civilian population as a method of warfare.[57]

In certain specific contexts, IHL imposes a heightened necessity standard to justify destroying or seizing civilian property. First, in occupied territory, the GC establishes a general prohibition against "[a]ny destruction . . . of real estate or personal property belonging individually or collectively to private persons."[58] This prohibition is not, however, absolute. Instead, it is qualified by a caveat, "except, unless such destruction is rendered absolutely necessary by military operations."[59] This *absolute* qualifier to military necessity suggests that destruction is permissible only as a genuine measure of last resort. Such necessity may arise, for example, when an enemy is retreating from occupied territory and utilizing scorched earth tactics to impede enemy pursuit. In one significant post–World War II war crimes trial, the tribunal concluded this tactic was justified because the defendant, German General Lothar Rendulic, reasonably believed it was the only viable tactic to slow down the advance of his Soviet pursuers (though, interestingly, AP I adopts a more restrictive rule, imposing an absolute prohibition against scorched earth tactics in occupied territory but permitting such tactics on the territory of that of the party employing the tactic).[60]

In many cases, armed forces may seek to seize or confiscate civilian property instead of destroying it. Like destruction, any taking must be justified by military necessity. Pillaging, looting, or stealing private property, however, is absolutely prohibited. *Confiscation*, which is the permanent deprivation of private property, is also prohibited unless the owner is provided fair compensation.[61] In contrast, temporary deprivation of civilian property, known as seizure, is permitted by IHL. *Seizure* is therefore distinguished from confiscation because of its temporary nature, but is permissible only if the property is susceptible for military use.[62] It is hardly possible to list all property potentially subject to seizure, as the tactical and operational situation will dictate such decisions. However, so long as the property can be utilized to support military operations, and temporary seizure is necessary, the property will qualify for seizure. Any property seized must, however, be returned to the owner when it is no longer needed, and compensation for the loss of use or damage to the property must be provided. U.S. military practice is to provide a receipt to the owner at the time of seizure; or, if this is not possible (for example, if the owner cannot be identified), make a record of the seizure for future compensation purposes.[63]

It is lawful and common for armed forces to seize real property during military operations, as such property and associated structures will often be needed to support or facilitate military activities.[64] This can present many challenges, not the least of which is accurate identification of ownership, especially in less developed areas where land records are minimal to non-existent. Nonetheless, IHL requires good faith efforts to identify owners, restore property when use is no longer necessary, and provide fair compensation for the use and/or damage to the property.

During belligerent occupation, the occupying forces may also requisition civilian property.[65] *Requisition* differs from seizure in a number of important ways. First, requisitioning involves the taking of private property necessary for the maintenance of the occupying armed forces. Thus, property is not normally requisitioned because it is needed to support a certain military operation (for example, a vehicle needed to transport ammunition to friendly forces) but instead to supply the occupying armed forces with resources for sustainment. Items normally subject to requisition include: fuel, food, clothing, building materials, machinery, tools, vehicles, furnishings for quarters, and space to billet or lodge troops.[66] Second, requisition is subject to additional constraints, most notably, a requirement that the requisitions "shall be in proportion to the resources of the country"[67] Third, requisition may only be authorized by the local military commander.[68] However, like seizure, compensation is required for requisitioned property, although unlike seizure payment at the time of requisition is the norm.[69]

4   Protecting the wounded and sick

Armed conflict, by its very definition, will almost inevitably result in the infliction of injury and death. While the use of force is justified by military necessity and the specific targeting rules that implement this principle (*see* Chapter 6: *Targeting*), international law has long recognized that once an opponent is incapacitated as the result of wounds or sickness—a condition known in IHL as *hors de combat* (out of the fight)[70]—the necessity for attacking the individual terminates. In other words, the law permits the use of highly lethal combat power against all members of the enemy armed group, *but* that authority terminates once an individual member of the group is rendered *hors de combat* by wounds or sickness (or capture).

At this point, the individual, who a moment earlier was a participant in hostilities, is considered a victim of war. In order to mitigate the suffering of such individuals, parties to the conflict are bound by a carefully reasoned mosaic of rules that function to respond to the plight the wounded and sick. These rules are most easily understood by focusing on three aspects of ameliorating the suffering of the wounded and sick: first, the protection extended to the actual casualty; second, the protection extended to the individuals engaged in the process of searching for, collecting, and treating the casualty; and, third, the protection extended to the equipment and facilities used by these individuals. While there are other aspects of implementing the objective of mitigating the suffering of the wounded and sick, this three-pronged focus will maximize understanding of this regulatory mosaic.

There is, of course, one additional complexity in implementing this protective regime—the impact of conflict classification. As a matter of treaty obligation, most of the rules related to the protection of the wounded and sick, and the wounded, sick, and shipwrecked at sea, apply only during IAC. However, in practice, most of these rules are routinely extended to NIAC, certainly by most armed forces committed to IHL compliance. Furthermore, the law applicable to NIAC—specifically Common Article 3 of the four Geneva Conventions and, in more limited circumstances, AP II—include more general obligations related to the wounded and sick. It is therefore logical to first address the law applicable to IAC, as these rules will often be extended, at least as a matter of policy, to NIACs. A discussion of the law expressly applicable to NIAC will then follow.

4.1 Protecting the wounded and sick in international armed conflicts

The 1949 Geneva Convention for the Amelioration of the Condition of the Wounded and Sick in Armed Forces in the Field (GWS) establishes a comprehensive regime for the protection of the wounded and sick and respect for the deceased.[71] The overarching purpose of the GWS is to facilitate the prompt collection of and effective care for the wounded and sick. The treaty establishes basic obligations, defines special protections for the wounded and sick as well as those exclusively engaged in their collection and care, and provides special protected status for equipment and facilities devoted to this mission. The GWS explicitly defines those individuals protected by the treaty in Article 13.[72] Any individual falling within the scope of this definition is a *protected person*, meaning that they qualify for the protections provided by the treaty.[73] As with the GC and civilians, this status is also critical for purposes of war crimes accountability, as the GWS defines a *grave breach*—the most serious violations of the treaty triggering the obligation on treaty parties to bring those responsible for such violations to justice—as certain violations directed against a protected person.

The GWS protects wounded and sick members of the armed forces and other associated forces who have fallen into enemy hands.[74] Obligations imposed by the GWS apply to "the Party to the conflict in whose power they may be," which means the nation whose armed forces take control of the wounded or sick enemy.[75] The GWS also defines who qualifies for protection as the result of being wounded or sick, limiting this category of treaty beneficiaries to individuals who would, if captured, qualify as prisoners of war pursuant to the GPW. What this means in practice is that the GWS's protections apply almost exclusively to members of armed forces and associated units and personnel, like militia groups, volunteer units, and civilians working for and in support of the armed forces.[76] In contrast, civilians generally do not fall within the scope of the GWS.

AP I adopted a much broader definition of *wounded and sick* to expand the protection of war victims. AP I reinforced many of the protections established by the GWS, but unlike the GWS, it did not restrict protections to members of the armed forces and associated units and personnel.[77] Instead, civilians are expressly included within the scope of AP I's wounded and sick definition,[78] as well as other individuals the treaty defines as *hors de combat*. Overall, AP I reflects an attempt to address the needs of the wounded and sick more pragmatically, with far less emphasis on limited categories of military wounded and sick.[79] As noted earlier, unlike the GWS, some States (such as India, Iran, Israel, North Korea, Pakistan, and the United States) are not parties to AP I. Nonetheless, AP I's expansive and pragmatic definition of wounded and sick—a definition driven by need and not status—is consistent with contemporary military practice. Indeed, for professional armed forces it is unlikely that distinctions related to casualty collection and medical care are made based on the status of the casualty, but instead on the urgency of the medical needs.

Furthermore, even for those limited number of States that are not bound by AP I, wounded and sick civilians still benefit from a variety of IHL and IHRL obligations, most notably the customary international law humane treatment obligation. Nonetheless, it is important to distinguish between the source and scope of obligations related to the wounded and sick. In many cases, the GWS imposes obligations that are more robust than those applicable to civilians. And, in situations where the medical needs of civilians are beyond the responsive capability of the armed forces, the treaty obligations imposed by the GWS may result in prioritization of collection, care, and treatment of military wounded and sick.

Accordingly, what might best be described as medical rules of engagement are frequently implemented as an aspect of medical support to military operations.[80] These are command directives indicating how and when military resources will be devoted to the care of civilian wounded and sick. Common aspects of these directives include: drawing a distinction between acute and chronic health issues (limiting intervention only to acute issues); authorizing essential care when necessary to save life, limb, or sight; sharing expertise and providing expert assistance in support of the efforts of civilian health care capabilities; and coordinating the collective efforts of military and non-government organizations with the shared mission of enhancing civilian health care capacity. Even when not considered legally obligatory, intervening in extreme cases, where failing to do so will result in loss of life, limb, or sight, will almost always be an authorized action. However, emphasizing assistance to local and non-governmental efforts to adequately provide for the civilian community is essential to husband military resources and capabilities so that they are available to meet the primary demand to which they are intended to respond—military casualties.

4.1.1 Handling the wounded and sick

The GWS imposes two foundational obligations upon parties into whose hands the wounded and sick fall—an obligation to *respect* and an obligation to *protect*.[81] The respect obligation is one of inaction—do no harm.[82] The protect obligation is one of action—come to the aid of the wounded and sick, regardless of whose side they fought for in the conflict.[83] These obligations are broad, as originally explained in the 1952 Commentary to the GWS, which provides that it is

> unlawful for an enemy to attack, kill, ill-treat or in any way harm a fallen and unarmed soldier, while at the same time . . . the enemy [has] an obligation to come to his aid and give him such care as his condition require[s].[84]

This latter obligation is most notably implemented by efforts to search for, discover, collect, and evacuate the wounded and sick. Once collected, the obligation also extends to ensuring they are cared for and defending them from harm or victimization.[85]

The fundamental obligation to care for the wounded and sick is a non-discriminatory, purely humanitarian obligation. Equality of care is obligatory pursuant to Article 12, which mandates that order of care must be based solely on considerations of medical necessity and feasibility—a process called triage.[86] It is therefore prohibited to prioritize treatment of friendly wounded soldiers over wounded enemy soldiers based on the soldiers' nationality. Thus, it is the nature of the wound or illness, and not the nationality of the patient, that dictates treatment priorities.[87] This equality of treatment rule is obviously vital to the mitigation of the suffering for all casualties. In addition, individuals who fall under the protection of the GWS may never be subjected to reprisal (a prohibited act as a measure to compel an enemy to cease its violations of IHL). This prohibition extends not only to casualties but also to personnel, facilities, and equipment exclusively devoted to the care of the wounded and sick.[88]

Article 12 of the GWS is perhaps the most important Article in the treaty, as it establishes the requirements of care, and defines the standard as one of humane treatment. As the 2016 Commentary notes:

> The gist of the prohibition of adverse distinction is not to prevent one's own soldiers from receiving the best possible medical care, but to ensure that enemy soldiers receive the kind of care required by their medical condition and that the standard of care that enemy soldiers receive is not lowered in order to make personnel and other resources available for the treatment of one's own forces.[89]

Wounded and sick must be provided with necessary medical care and shielded from the adverse effects of the environment, infection and contagious disease, and ongoing military operations.[90] In fact, the obligation to care for and protect the wounded and sick even includes a prohibition against abandoning such casualties without medical assistance. According to the GWS, if the wounded and sick must be abandoned to the enemy, the abandoning force is obligated to leave with them medical personnel and equipment essential for their care (however, the presence of personnel left behind does not in any way release the adverse party from its duty to provide additional assistance to the abandoned casualties once they come under the control of that party).[91]

Political and military considerations can play no role in determining priority of care; the determination must be made based on medical necessity and how best to allocate available medical supplies and services.[92] For example, pursuant to triage, a party could provide the highest level of medical assets to those members of the enemy wounded and sick with significant injuries that might benefit from treatment and survive, while those who suffered mortal wounds and will die regardless of treatment may justifiably be given lesser priority. While no adverse distinctions may be established in providing care, *favorable* distinctions may be made by taking certain attributes into account, such as age or pregnancy. Perhaps most importantly, medical personnel must make all decisions regarding priority based on their expert knowledge and medical ethics.[93]

4.1.2   Casualties

It is virtually inevitable that combatants will be killed and wounded during armed conflict. In order to mitigate the suffering of the wounded, and to reduce the number of combatants who die from their wounds, the GWS obligates all parties to a conflict to "take all possible measures to search for and collect" the wounded and sick.[94] This obligation also extends to the dead, a measure obviously essential to mitigate the risk of disease.[95] When searching for, collecting, and evacuating the wounded, sick, and deceased, no distinction may be made based on whose side in the conflict the victim fought.[96]

This obligation is not, however, absolute. Instead, it is reasonably qualified— military personnel are not obligated to engage in those efforts when doing so will subject them to unnecessary risk.[97] But, in order to facilitate collection and mitigate risks, the GWS encourages hostile forces to enter into suspension of fire agreements to facilitate casualty collection. In practice, such agreements are rare. The GWS seems to recognize this and further advocates for the negotiation of local arrangements—ceasefires arranged by local commanders.[98] Still, it is more likely that search and collection efforts will take place during ongoing hostilities. In these circumstances, commanders must make case-by-case judgments that balance the risk of exposing friendly personnel to enemy fire with the reward of collecting battlefield casualties.

When the wounded and sick are collected, a broad range of obligations arise, which will be addressed in more detail below. Obligations also extend to the handling of collected dead, to include examination for the purpose of confirmation of death and identity (as far as circumstances permit).[99] Indeed, establishing the identity of both the dead and the wounded recovered from the battlefield is vital to providing notice of captivity and condition and, more subtly, to ensure accountability for their post-recovery treatment. Accordingly, once collected, parties to the conflict must retain the following information regarding the wounded, sick, and the dead: name, nationality, identification number, any particulars shown on the identity card or disk, date of birth, date and place of capture or death, and particulars concerning wounds, illness, or cause of death.[100]

This information must be transmitted to an entity called the Information Bureau as soon as possible. This entity, established pursuant to the GPW,[101] essentially functions as a clearing house for information related to captured armed forces and associated personnel. This information is then transmitted from the detaining power to the Central Prisoners of War Agency,[102] which ultimately transmits the information to captives' country of origin. The Information Bureau also exchanges information about deceased captives between the parties, the goal being the free flow of information concerning the wounded, sick, or dead between parties to a conflict and, ultimately, to the individual's next of kin.

The GWS also calls for the examination of the dead, followed by burial or cremation.[103] Burial must be by honorable interment, preferably with individual graves (although mass graves are permitted when necessary for health or operational reasons) and should follow "the rites of the religion to which [the deceased] belonged";[104] graves should be grouped by nationality if possible, and must be marked and maintained so that they might be found.[105] Cremation should only occur for hygienic or religious reasons.[106] Records of internment should be maintained and ashes preserved. The exchange of grave locations and information regarding the occupants of the graves should occur as "soon as circumstances permit, and at latest at the end of hostilities."[107]

There may be times when the number of casualties and deceased overwhelm military collection capabilities. It is therefore important that the GC provides for a military request for civilian assistance to collect and care for the wounded and sick.[108] Such assistance must be voluntary; however, there is no restriction on a commander taking advantage of spontaneous civilian contribution in support of the collection and care efforts.[109] Because the GWS contemplates civilian participation in the collection and care for the wounded and sick, Article 18 requires that civilians respect the wounded and sick as would the military.[110] If civilians do contribute to these efforts, the military authority should provide support by extending protection to these civilians and, where feasible, facilities, supplies, and equipment.[111] However, commanders may not consider the efforts of civilians as relieving them of their primary respect and protect obligations.[112]

4.1.3 *The distinctive emblem: the symbol of special protection*

Mitigating the suffering of the wounded and sick often depends on the efforts of personnel engaged in the search for, evacuation, and treatment of casualties. Unless these personnel and resources are themselves protected from enemy attack, their efficacy will be substantially degraded. Protection from enemy attack is therefore essential, which in turn requires that all parties to a conflict are able to identify personnel, equipment, and facilities exclusively engaged in these humanitarian tasks. Unless opposing armed forces are confident that these assets are both inoffensive and devoted to a medical humanitarian mission, the goals of the GWS will be jeopardized.

The Red Cross and the Red Crescent are perhaps the most ubiquitous symbols of humanitarian action known throughout the world. Today, the humanitarian ethos represented by these symbols—along with its Red Crystal analogue—transcend protection of just the wounded and sick, and represent a much broader ethos of humanitarian action. However, it is the suffering of the wounded and sick stranded on the battlefield that was the genesis for these symbols and what they represent. Each functions as a shield of protection—protection provided by the GWS (or, in the case of the Red Crystal, the relatively new AP III).[113]

Because these symbols function as shields against deliberate attack, their use must be carefully regulated. Accordingly, the GWS and the Additional Protocols define conditions that must be satisfied before these protection emblems may be used. Furthermore, because improper use of these emblems compromises the message of exclusive humanitarian function they are intended to convey, improper use is not only prohibited but considered one of the most serious IHL violations.

Article 38 of the GWS describes the several recognized emblems that mark a person, transport, or facility as medical in nature.[114] The primary distinctive emblem is the Red Cross; however, there are additional authorized exceptions, including: the Red Crescent (used predominantly in Muslim nations), the Red Lion and Sun (formerly used by Persia/Iran, which now uses the Red Crescent), and the Red Crystal.[115] The Red Shield (the six-pointed hexagram) or Star of David has been traditionally used by Israel, and, while never officially recognized, it has been respected during armed conflict.[116] AP III, which entered into force in 2005, provides for the use of the Star of David within the Red Crystal, and the associated Commentary indicates that "the red shield of David is the only other emblem which qualifies for inclusion in the third Protocol emblem."[117] Importantly, only competent military authority may authorize use of these emblems.[118]

Personnel, facilities, and transport must display one of these distinctive emblems in order to signal to the belligerents that they are protected from deliberate attack.[119] Compliance with this display aspect of protection is routine in all armed conflicts today, although violations of the protection indicated by such display remain unfortunately all too common. Medical and religious personnel must wear one of the distinctive emblems on their left arm[120] and must also carry an identity disk and an identity card that also bear the distinctive emblem.[121] These latter identification requirements indicate entitlement to special status if captured: unlike combatants, medical and religious personnel are considered retained persons. This means that they may be detained by a capturing enemy only for so long as their services are required to aid their fellow captives, and that they must be permitted to perform their humanitarian function.[122]

Use of the protective emblem on facilities or equipment is not mandated by IHL. However, because not displaying emblems makes it difficult—if not impossible—for an enemy to recognize the medical function of a potential military target, it increases the risk of deliberate attack. Nonetheless, there may be times when operational considerations lead commanders to conclude that assuming this risk is necessary. For example, the U.S. Army *Field Manual on Medical Evacuation in a Theater of Operations* notes that camouflaging medical facilities is authorized "if the failure to camouflage endangers or compromises tactical operations."[123]

4.1.4 Personnel aiding the wounded and sick

Pursuant to the GWS, only personnel *exclusively engaged* in the collection, evacuation, and care for the wounded and sick may wear the protective emblem.[124] These individuals are normally members of the armed forces. However, because they must be exclusively engaged in humanitarian functions, they are considered non-combatant members. As noted in Chapter 3, these military personnel are not considered combatants.

This special military status, and the confidence in the protection it affords, is central to advancing the humanitarian goals of the GWS. Indeed, it would make no sense to cloak the wounded and sick with a proverbial blanket of protection without allocating accordant protections to those responsible for their collection and care. Accordingly, the GWS provides personnel exclusively engaged in the search for, collection, and care of the wounded and sick (to include chaplains and members of national relief organizations) with substantial protection. Auxiliary medical personnel receive a lessened degree of protection and different treatment rules if captured. The notion of being exclusively engaged in humanitarian functions is central to understanding this special status.[125] IHL, through the GWS and relevant Additional Protocol provisions, encourages parties to an armed conflict to field personnel, units, equipment, and facilities devoted exclusively to the amelioration of the suffering of the wounded and sick. The special status and protections granted to such personnel, transport, and facilities—even when they are members of an armed force—serves the interests of all parties to the conflict, as such personnel will act to protect all casualties pursuant to medical considerations and not based on whose side they are associated.

Because these personnel (with the exception of members of national relief societies) are part of their armed forces, they wear uniforms and will often also carry weapons. Carrying a weapon does not disqualify them from their special status and protection. However, they may not use their weapons to participate in hostilities, but instead for the sole purpose of defending themselves and the wounded and sick under their care from unlawful violence. Because medical personnel and facilities are supposed to be permitted to continue their medical functions if captured by an enemy, there is no justification to resist such capture. Only when there is indication that an enemy will refuse to comply with the law requiring respect and protection for the wounded, sick, and medical personnel and facilities may those associated with medical units use force in response.

If medical facilities are guarded by combat units, they are authorized to use force only to defend the facility from unlawful attack.[126]

Because the permissible use of weapons is so limited, medical personnel may be armed only with light weapons.[127] While the GWS does not define what falls within this category of armaments, the 2016 GWS Commentary provides some insight, indicating that:

> [A]ll medical and religious personnel of the armed forces can be equipped with light individual weapons without losing their protection. It is the sole remit of the national authorities to decide whether or not such personnel are entitled to be armed. If it is decided at the domestic level to authorize (or compel) medical and religious personnel to carry permitted types of weapons, the mere fact of their being so armed cannot be considered an "act harmful to the enemy outside their humanitarian duties". The weapons in question, however, can only be used for two specific purposes: for the persons' "own defence" or for the defence of the "wounded and sick in their charge". Thus, even when the use of the weapons is defensive in nature, they may not be used for the defence of other persons, let alone for the defence of military objectives. . . . Further, such personnel may not take up arms on their own initiative, for example for offensive purposes, or in a defensive military operation in which the "defensive" element would go beyond the bounds of the two permitted purposes.[128]

Members of the armed forces exclusively engaged in humanitarian activities, along with personnel working for voluntary aid societies (such as national Red Cross or Red Crescent societies), may be captured by an opposing armed force. When this occurs, the GWS affords such personnel a special status, designating them as *retained personnel*.[129] Retained personnel are afforded all the protections provided to prisoners of war pursuant to the GPW. However, unlike prisoners of war, they are not subject to internment for the duration of hostilities. Instead, they may be retained only they may "be retained insofar as the state of health, the spiritual needs, and the number of [enemy prisoners of war] require."[130] Furthermore, retained persons may not be required to perform any work other than the regular medical or religious duties they perform under their own governmental authority. U.S. Army detention policy illustrates how this obligation is implemented:

> *b.* Enemy personnel who fall within any of the following categories, are eligible to be certified as RP:
>
> (1) Medical personnel who are members of the medical service of their armed forces.
> (2) Medical personnel who are exclusively engaged in:
>   (*a*) The search for or the collection, transport, or treatment of the wounded or sick.
>   (*b*) The prevention of disease.

(c) Staffs exclusively engaged in administering medical units and establishments.

(3) Chaplains.

(4) The staff of the National Red Cross, Red Crescent, and other voluntary aid organizations. These organizations must be duly recognized and authorized by their governments. The staff of these organizations may be employed on the same duties as persons in (2) above, if such organizations are subject to military laws and regulations.[131]

When retention is not indispensable for the health and spiritual needs of these captives, the GWS requires repatriation of retained persons.[132] Selection of personnel for repatriation should be based on a chronological, first in/first out approach, barring health-related concerns.[133] The same U.S. Army detention policy illustrates how this first in/first out process is implemented, establishing a minimum retained persons (RP) to POW ratio and requiring repatriation of RPs once POW numbers fall below the retention ratio.[134]

Some armed forces utilize *auxiliary medical personnel* to contribute to the collection and care of the wounded and sick. These are military personnel trained in medical specialties, such as hospital orderlies or auxiliary stretcher-bearers.[135] Typically, auxiliaries are combatant members of the armed forces who perform these medical duties only as the need arises.[136] When acting in a medical capacity, they are entitled to the same respect and protection accorded to those meeting the qualification requirements of Article 24.[137] Auxiliary personnel must wear an armlet displaying a distinctive emblem in miniature, but only while carrying out medical duties, and their identification cards "should specify what special training they have received, the temporary character of the duties ... engaged upon, and their authority for wearing the armlet."[138]

It is important to note that, while auxiliary medical personnel are protected while engaged in their medical support function, they *are not* considered retained persons upon capture but are instead prisoners of war.[139] Accordingly, the treatment of auxiliaries depends on the function they are providing at any given time, meaning that they can effectively move back and forth between combatant and non-combatant roles. Because of the potential confusion as to the status of an individual moving back and forth between these roles, some States, like the United States, do not classify auxiliaries.[140]

4.1.5 *Medical units, establishments, and transportation*

Protecting the wounded and sick and those who care for them necessitates analogous protection for their transport and treatment facilities, which is also addressed by the GWS.[141]

4.1.6 *Facilities and vehicles*

Pursuant to Article 19, fixed and mobile facilities established for medical use and marked with one of the distinctive emblems are protected from attack,[142] unless their use is inconsistent with their exclusive medical function (this protection also extends to hospital ships covered by the Geneva Convention (Second) for the Amelioration of the Condition of Wounded, Sick, and Shipwrecked Members of the Armed Forces at Sea (GWS-Sea)).[143]

To maximize this protection, the GWS encourages the placement of medical units away from potential military targets whenever feasible.[144] This, coupled with restrictions on the permissible use of force to defend such facilities, will inevitably create a risk of capture by the enemy. If this occurs, medical units and personnel must be permitted to continue caring for the wounded and sick.[145] The protection against attacking medical units is not absolute, but is forfeited if they commit acts harmful to the enemy that are inconsistent with being exclusively engaged in their humanitarian mission.[146] However, unlike any other potential targets, the GWS requires what is in effect a cease and desist warning as a precondition to actually launching an attack on such a facility, and allows attack only if the warning remains unheeded after a reasonable amount of time.[147]

Some activities may seem harmful to the enemy in a general sense but do not qualify as activity that forfeits protection. The GWS specifically indicates that the following shall not result in a loss of protection: (1) that personnel of the medical unit are armed and use their arms in their own defense or in the defense of the wounded and sick under their care; (2) that the facility is protected by a picket, sentries, or an escort; (3) that small arms and ammunition taken from the wounded and sick and not yet handed over to the proper service are found in the unit; (4) that personnel and material of veterinary services are found in the unit without forming an integral part of the unit; or (5) that the humanitarian activities of the medical unit or its personnel extend to caring for civilian wounded and sick.[148]

Captured medical units may be retained by the enemy but may be used only to care for wounded and sick.[149] Urgent military necessity will allow fixed facilities to be repurposed for other functions, but the capturing force must ensure the continued care of any wounded and sick in the facility before converting it to another use.[150] It is also critical to distinguish captured medical supplies from other supplies captured from an enemy. Unlike the normal booty of war, under no circumstances may medical material and stores be intentionally destroyed.[151] If they cannot be used by the capturing force, they must be abandoned intact.

Vehicles may be employed for medical duties either permanently or temporarily. When used exclusively for medical purposes and properly marked with the protective emblem, they must be respected and protected in the same manner as mobile medical units.[152] Any vehicle may be used in such a capacity, even if not specifically designed or equipped as an ambulance. However, a vehicle temporarily employed as a medical vehicle will be protected only if it displays a protective emblem while engaged in the medical mission. This is a common practice, done to maximize casualty evacuation capability, and will often involve the use of supply transports to backhaul casualties.[153]

Accordingly, it is common to use vehicles for a non-medical mission when traveling in one direction and for a medical evacuation mission when traveling in the other direction. There is no prohibition against such practices, nor against marking the vehicle with the protective emblem while exclusively engaged in casualty evacuation. However, the emblem must be removed whenever the vehicle is not exclusively engaged in the medical function. Failing to do so will erode confidence in the protective effect of the emblem and invite attack on properly marked vehicles.

If an enemy captures medical vehicles, they may, like the fixed medical facility, be repurposed, but the enemy must ensure the care of any wounded and sick in the vehicle, and treat any medical personnel as retained persons.[154] The capturing force must also remove any distinctive medical emblems prior to utilizing the vehicle for a non-medical purpose.[155]

In some situations, for example where the enemy disregards its IHL obligations, or when marking a transport with the protective emblem might compromise tactical surprise of a group of vehicles, the commander may conclude that a marking may actually increase exposure to attack. There may also be situations where the exigencies demand the use of unmarked vehicles to transport casualties without the opportunity to mark them, or the use of vehicles not exclusively engaged in casualty evacuation to transport casualties.[156] In all these situations, using vehicles without a protective emblem to transport the wounded and sick is permissible. A party to the conflict may use whatever assets that are available to transport casualties. However, it is important to note that whenever transport equipment is not marked with a protective emblem it is in danger of being seen as a lawful target by the enemy, even if it is transporting the wounded and sick.

4.1.7 Medical aircraft

Many armed forces use aircraft devoted exclusively to casualty evacuation. These aircraft, whether planes, helicopters, or, perhaps in the not-so-distant future, remotely piloted aircraft (drones), are protected like ground medical transports so long as they are "aircraft exclusively employed for the removal of wounded and sick and for the transport of medical personnel and equipment."[157] Like vehicles, aircraft may be permanently or temporarily employed for medical purposes, and ordinary aircraft may be converted to medical use. Although less common, medical aircraft may also be converted to other use, but it is imperative that any protective emblems are then removed.[158] To remain protected during a relief mission, an aircraft must be used exclusively for medical purposes.[159]

As a general proposition, any aircraft bearing the protective emblem should be considered protected from deliberate attack. However, the extent of actual legal protection for aircraft is more complex, based on what the somewhat arcane provisions of the 1949 GWS. During that period of time, the primary consideration focused on fixed-wing medical aircraft. Because of the limited capability of anti-aircraft weaponry to positively identify friend from foe, the GWS established a protection regime based on the belligerent parties entering into overflight agreements. The GWS provides that, absent such agreements, medical aircraft fly at their own risk.[160] Accordingly, the GWS imposes the respect obligation only when medical aircraft fly at "the altitude, route and time of the aircraft's flight over enemy territory [specified]."[161]

The GWS also addressed concerns that a party to a conflict might misuse aircraft marked with the protective emblem. To that end, the GWS provides a mechanism whereby a suspicious party may summon the aircraft to land for inspection.[162] Upon receiving such a summons, even from an enemy, the medical aircraft is obligated to obey.[163] If the aircraft is engaged in a proper medical function, it should be allowed to continue; if it is not, the enemy will then take appropriate action to detain the occupants and confiscate the aircraft as booty. In the event of an involuntary landing in enemy territory, the personnel aboard the aircraft and any wounded and sick aboard are POWs or RPs, depending on their status.[164] The capturing party retains the obligation to care for any wounded and sick aboard the aircraft.[165]

As indicated above, medical aircraft, even when properly marked, assume risk if they overfly enemy territory without prior agreement on permissible routes, heights, and times.[166] If the aircraft must overfly neutral territory, notice should be provided to the neutral power, and the aircraft must obey all commands to land.[167] Neutrals bear an obligation to prevent use of their territory by belligerents, and therefore may consider it necessary to prevent such use, even by medical aircraft, without prior agreement. Technically, neutral overflight should not occur without prior agreement between the neutral and *all* belligerent parties establishing routes, heights, and times.[168] If any wounded and sick disembark into a neutral's territory—whether the result of heeding a warning to land or landing in neutral territory owing to aircraft disability or distress—the neutral must detain the wounded and sick in a manner preventing them from taking part in the operation of war.[169]

These agreement rules were almost never utilized following adoption of the GWS in 1949. This fact, coupled with the substantial increase in the use of helicopters for casualty collection and transport, led to efforts to update these aircraft protection regime in AP I. In an effort to exploit friend-or-foe air defense identification technology, AP I added optional signals identifying medical aircraft that could quickly and easily be identified by air defense target acquisition.[170] AP I also created three new *overflight regimes* for medical aircraft. Article 25 of AP I covers land controlled by friendly forces and does not require agreement by the parties to the conflict for use of such airspace by friendly medical aircraft.[171] However, agreement with or notice to an enemy party is encouraged, particularly if the flight plan brings medical aircraft into range of enemy air defense systems.[172] Article 26 addresses medical aircraft in contact zones, defined as "any area on land where the forward elements of the opposing forces are in contact with each other, especially where they are exposed to direct fire from the ground."[173] When flying in such areas, aircraft safety will be maximized by an agreement between the parties; if no agreement is exists, the aircraft flies at its own risk.[174] Article 27 covers territory controlled by an enemy, and requires a prior agreements to ensure protection of medical flights.[175] If the aircraft flies over such territory without an agreement, Article 27 includes procedures to facilitate identification of the aircraft and verification of its humanitarian mission. Most importantly, even without an agreement, Article 27 imposes as "warning and compliance" obligation before attack on an aircraft identified as bearing a protective emblem is permitted.[176] In sum, though overflight of enemy territory clearly involves substantial risks, *ideally*, properly marked aircraft will nonetheless be respected.

It is obvious that medical aircraft assume great risk even when operating under AP I's expanded protection regime. This was not lost on the drafters of what is known as the *HPCR Air and Missile Warfare Manual*, a non-binding yet highly authoritative interpretation of laws related to air and missile operations during armed conflicts.[177] The *Air and Missile Warfare Manual* sought to clarify the application of many of the rules related to medical aircraft, and to propose a uniform approach to medical aircraft protection applicable in any type of armed conflict.[178]

Like AP I, the *Air and Missile Warfare Manual* indicates that it is not the presence of the protective emblem that establishes the protection of the medical aircraft, but instead the humanitarian function being performed—the protected emblem merely facilitates identification.[179] Therefore, the vital rule derived from this clarification is that protection is derived from status, and medical aircraft are protected even if they do not bear a distinctive emblem, so long as they can still be identified as such (for example, as the result of communication between the aircraft and the enemy).

The *Air and Missile Warfare Manual* confirms that, when flying over contact zones or enemy-controlled territory, prior express consent by the enemy is necessary to *maximize* protection for medical aircraft.[180] If a medical aircraft deviates from the terms of an agreement or enters an area not covered by an agreement owing to either navigational error or emergency, it must immediately attempt to identify itself and comply with any order given by enemy air traffic control. Once identified as such, the medical aircraft cannot be attacked unless it fails to comply with orders given to it (i.e., orders to divert course or land) after a sufficient period of time to comply has elapsed.[181]

The enemy always has the right to demand medical aircraft land for inspection.[182] If the aircraft is in fact engaged in activities consistent with its medical status, it must be allowed to continue with its flight.[183] However, where the aircraft "engaged in activities inconsistent with its medical status, or if it has flown without or in breach of a prior agreement," the enemy may seize the aircraft and treat anyone aboard in compliance with IHL obligations.[184]

The *Air and Missile Warfare Manual*, which was influenced substantially by post-GWS and AP I State practice, notes that medical aircraft may be equipped with deflective defenses such as flares or chaff.[185] Furthermore, like medical personnel, medical aircraft may be equipped with light weapons for defense against unlawful attack.[186] However, heavy weapons such as machine guns (which could be used either offensively or defensively) could either cause complete forfeiture of protection or, at the least, erode the effect of the protective emblem.[187] In fact, the *Air and Missile Warfare Manual* draws a distinction between military-operated medical aircraft (engaged exclusively in the transport of the wounded and sick) and military aircraft on missions to search-and-rescue combatants—the latter being normal military aircraft that should not be marked with the protective emblem and are subject to attack.[188] Of course, any aircraft may be equipped with crew served or heavy weapons while engaged in casualty search and identification, but doing so necessitates removal of the protective emblem.

4.2   *Protecting the wounded and sick in non-international armed conflicts*

Almost all the rules addressed above apply, as a matter of treaty obligation, only during IACs. Common Article 3 is the only Article included in the four 1949 Geneva Conventions applicable to NIACs. Common Article 3 imposes a broad humane treatment obligation applicable to any individual rendered *hors de combat*—not actively participating in hostilities. This category includes anyone incapacitated by "sickness, wounds, detention, or any other cause."[189] Common Article 3 protections "have been recognized by the ICJ as an emanation of 'elementary considerations of humanity' constituting 'a minimum yardstick' applicable to all armed conflicts."[190] Common Article 3 also prohibits any adverse distinction affecting treatment of such individuals based on race, religion, sex, wealth, or nationality.[191] Broadly speaking, this Article requires that the wounded and sick be respected and protected, and expressly requires that they be collected and cared for.[192]

Still, as it relates to the protection of the wounded and sick, Common Article 3 is relatively meager compared to rules that apply during IACs. This disparity is mitigated to a certain extent by the applicability of many of these IAC rules to the NIAC context by operation of customary international law.[193] Furthermore, AP II sought to narrow this gap, expanding the rules related to the protection of the wounded and sick in NIAC. Nonetheless, AP II's regulatory regime is still less comprehensive than that applicable to IAC, but nonetheless it is an important advancement in humanitarian protections.

AP II explicitly extends several core rules established for the regulation of IAC to NIAC. These include the obligation to respect and protect all wounded and sick; the equality of treatment rule; the obligation to respect and protect medical and religious personnel; the protection of medical transport equipment and medical facilities; the prohibition of attacking a medical facility being misused without first issuing a warning; and the protective effect of the distinctive emblem.[194] Finally, the treaty expressly acknowledges the role of relief organizations in aiding the wounded and sick.[195]

AP II also establishes several additional safeguards for medical personnel deemed especially important because of the non-international nature of the armed conflict. Perhaps most importantly, AP II prohibits any criminal or other sanction for medical personnel because they perform their medical duties, regardless of the beneficiary (shielding such personnel from criminal prosecution by the State for activities in support of internal dissident forces).[196] Furthermore, such personnel may not be compelled to perform acts contrary to the rules of medical ethics, nor may they be prevented from performing acts required by rules of medical ethics.[197] Finally, medical personnel may not be penalized for refusing to give information concerning any of the wounded and sick under their care, even when such information is considered essential to the internal security of the State.[198]

5   Conclusion

Protection of the wounded and sick is a critically important component of humanitarian protections during armed conflicts. The history of warfare is replete with examples of the willingness of belligerents to come to the aid of their suffering comrades *and* enemies. The GWS establishes rules to facilitate this humanitarian action, rules that are among the most widely known and respected, and deeply woven into the fabric of IHL. Indeed, attacking personnel, facilities, or equipment marked with the emblems of special protection established by IHL would legitimately be considered *malum in se*, leaving virtually no room for doubt about the illegality of such attacks even for the most inexperienced soldier. The core of these protections applies today in all armed conflicts, and in many ways these protections establish a baseline, with parties often striving to enhance the protections for wounded and sick beyond that strictly required by the law.

It is therefore essential that military planners contemplate the scope of the obligations related to the wounded and sick, plan accordingly, and ensure personnel are properly trained and resourced to meet these obligations. Like so many other areas of the law, compliance will often become more challenging as operational situations mature. For the soldier on the front line, it is axiomatic that individuals marked with the Red Cross or similar protective emblem must not be subjected to attack. But issues related to collection, evacuation, interment, record keeping, equality of care, location of facilities, air evacuation, and dual use of equipment present far more complex issues. Commanders and medical officers will therefore invariably turn to legal advisors to assist them in resolving these issues. Competence in the law that guides resolution is therefore essential to a State legal advisor, for few IHL violations will be more corrosive to the credibility of the operation than those that compromise the protections of the wounded and sick.

Notes

1   *See generally* Henry Dunant, *A Memory in Solferino* (1862), *available at* www.icrc. org/en/publication/0361-memory-solferino

2   *See* Geneva Convention for the Amelioration of the Condition of the Wounded in Armies in the Field, 22 August 1864, 22 Stat. 940.

3   *See* Geneva Convention for the Amelioration of the Condition of the Wounded and Sick in Armed Forces in the Field, 12 August 1949, 6 U.S.T. 3114, 75 U.N.T.S. 970 *and* Geneva Convention for the Amelioration of the Condition of Wounded, Sick, and Shipwrecked Members of the Armed Forces at Sea, 12 August 1949, 6 U.S.T. 3217, 75 U.N.T.S. 971 *and* Geneva Convention Relative to the Treatment

of Prisoners of War, 12 August 1949, 6 U.S.T. 3316, 75 U.N.T.S. 972 *and* Geneva Convention Relative to the Protection of Civilian Persons in Time of War, 12 August 1949, 6 U.S.T. 3516, 75 U.N.T.S. 973 [collectively, hereinafter Geneva Conventions] (which are presently the only treaties universally ratified by all nations).

4 For example, the historic and decisive 1815 Battle of Waterloo was an engagement involving over 200,000 men, and it took place over an area of just four square miles. Simon Worrall, "How the Battle of Waterloo Changed the World," *Nat'l Geographic* (16 June 2015), *available at* http://news.nationalgeographic.com/2015/06/150616-waterloo-napoleon-wellington-history-world-ngbooktalk/

5 *See* Geneva Convention Relative to the Protection of Civilian Persons in Time of War, 12 August 1949, 6 U.S.T. 3516, 75 U.N.T.S. 973 [hereinafter GC].

6 The GC *enhanced* as opposed to *created*, because the 1907 Hague Convention IV included minimal protections related to belligerent occupation. *See generally* Convention (IV) respecting the Laws and Customs of War on Land and its annex: Regulations concerning the Laws and Customs of War on Land, 18 October 1907, 36 Stat. 2277 [hereinafter 1907 Hague IV Regulations].

7 *See* Major Richard M. Whitaker, *Civilian Protection Law in Military Operations: An Essay*, Army Lawyer 3, 7 (November 1996), *available at* www.jagcnet.army.mil/DOCLIBS/ARMYLAWYER.NSF/c82df279f9445da185256e5b005244ee/0c286c1d66f4fa7f85256e5b0054f7e9/$FILE/TAL%2027–50–288%2019961101.pdf (for more discussion on CPL).

8 Protocol (I) Additional to the Geneva Conventions of 12 August 1949, and Relating to the Protection of Victims of International Armed Conflicts, Art 50, 8 June 1977, 1125 U.N.T.S. 3 [hereinafter AP I] (entered into force 7 December 1978) (signed by the United States 12 December 1977, not transmitted to U.S. Senate, *see* S. Treaty Doc. No. 100–2 (1987)).

9 *See* Geneva Convention for the Amelioration of the Condition of the Wounded and Sick in Armed Forces in the Field, 12 August 1949, Art 3, 6 U.S.T. 3114, 75 U.N.T.S. 970; Geneva Convention for the Amelioration of the Condition of Wounded, Sick, and Shipwrecked Members of the Armed Forces at Sea, 12 August 1949, Art 3, 6 U.S.T. 3217, 75 U.N.T.S. 971; Geneva Convention Relative to the Treatment of Prisoners of War, 12 August 1949, Art 3, 6 U.S.T. 3316, 75 U.N.T.S. 972; Geneva Convention Relative to the Protection of Civilian Persons in Time of War, 12 August 1949, Art 3, 6 U.S.T. 3516, 75 U.N.T.S. 973 [hereinafter Common Article 3].

10 *See* AP I, Art 75.

11 *Military and Paramilitary Activities in and Against Nicar. (Nicar. v. U.S.)*, 1986 I.C.J. 14, 114 (27 June).

12 AP II, which applies in some NIACs, does provide some additional protections beyond those of Common Article 3. But these protections are nowhere near as robust as those provided through the GC, and derivatively through AP I.

13 Common Article 3.

14 Commentary on the First Geneva Convention: Convention (I) for the Amelioration of the Condition of the Wounded and Sick in Armed Forces in the Field (2nd edn, 2016), paras 556–7, *available at* www.icrc.org/applic/ihl/ihl.nsf/Treaty.xsp?action=openDocument&documentId=4825657B0C7E6BF0C12563CD002D6B0B [hereinafter 2016 Commentary GWS].

15 *See* Ronald Reagan, Letter of Transmittal, The White House, 29 January 1987, *available at* www.loc.gov/rr/frd/Military_Law/pdf/protocol-II-100-2.pdf; William J. Clinton, Letter of Transmittal, The White House, 6 January 1999, *available at* www.loc.gov/rr/frd/Military_Law/pdf/GC-message-from-pres-1999.pdf; Press Release, The White House, *Fact Sheet: New Actions on Guantanamo and Detainee*

Policy (7 March 2011), *available at* www.whitehouse.gov/the-press-office/2011/03/07/fact-sheet-new-actions-guant-namo-and-detainee-policy

16   *See generally* Protocol (II) Additional to the Geneva Conventions of 12 August 1949, and Relating to the Protection of Victims of Non-International Armed Conflicts 8 June 1977, 1125 U.N.T.S. 609 [hereinafter AP II] (entered into force 7 December 1978) (signed by the United States 12 December 1977, transmitted to the U.S. Senate 29 January 1987, still pending action as S. Treaty Doc. No. 100–2 (1987)).

17   *See generally* GC.

18   *See generally* AP I.

19   *See* GC, Art 4.

20   *See Id.* pt. II (Part II, titled "General Protection of Populations Against Certain Consequences of War," begins at Article 13 and carries through Article 26).

21   *Id.* Arts 14–15.

22   *Id.* Art 23.

23   *Id.* Art 4.

24   *See* Jean S. Pictet et al., Commentary on the Additional Protocols of 8 June 1977 to the Geneva Conventions of 12 August 1949 (Int'l Comm. of the Red Cross, 1987), para 3007 [hereinafter AP Commentary].

25   *Id.*

26   *Id.*

27   *See* AP I, Art 75.

28   *See* GC, pt. II.

29   *Id.* Art 17.

30   *Id.* Art 18.

31   *Id.* Art 24.

32   *Id.* Art 13.

33   *Id.* Art 4.

34   *Id.*

35   *Id.*

36   Article 147 of the GC defines the following acts, if committed against protected persons, as grave breaches:

> wilful killing, torture or inhuman treatment, including biological experiments, wilfully causing great suffering or serious injury to body or health, unlawful deportation or transfer or unlawful confinement of a protected person, compelling a protected person to serve in the forces of a hostile Power, or wilfully depriving a protected person of the rights of fair and regular trial prescribed in the present Convention, taking of hostages and extensive destruction and appropriation of property, not justified by military necessity and carried out unlawfully and wantonly.
>
> *Id.* Art 147

37   *Id.* Art 27.

38   *Id.*

39   *Id.* Art 30.

40   *Id.* Art 31.

41   *Id.* Art 33.

42   *Id.* Art 9.

43   According to the ICRC, there have been five conflicts in which protecting powers were designated. 2016 Commentary GWS, para 1115.

44   GC, Art 35.

45   *Id.* Art 38(1).

46   *Id.* Art 38(2).

47   *Id.* Art 39.
48   *Id.* Art 40.
49   *Id.* Art 48.
50   *Id.* Art 33.
51   *Id.* Art 49. Although individual or mass forcible transfers or deportations are prohibited, an occupying power "may undertake total or partial evacuation of a given area if the security of the population or imperative military reasons so demand." *Id.*
52   *Id.* Art 51.
53   *Id.* Art 9.
54   Canada, Department of National Defence, *Joint Doctrine Manual* B-GJ-005–104/FP-021, *Law of Armed Conflict at the Operational and Tactical Levels* (13 August 2001), para 1004.
55   *Manual of the Law of Armed* Conflict para 15.17.12 (UK Ministry of Defence ed., 2004) [hereinafter *UK LOAC Manual*].
56   *Id.* para 5.19.
57   AP I, Art 54(1).
58   GC, Art 53.
59   *Id.*
60   *See The Hostage Case*, 11 Trials of War Criminals (T.W.C.) 1295–6.
61   1907 Hague IV Regulations, Arts 45–6.
62   *See* U.S. Dep't of Def., *Law of War Manual* 5.17 (June 2015, update December 2016) [hereinafter *DoD Law of War Manual*].
63   *Id.* at 5.17.5.1.
64   *See* 1907 Hague IV Regulations, Art 53.
65   *See Id.* Art 52.
66   *DoD Law of War Manual*, 11.18.7.2.
67   1907 Hague IV Regulations, Art 52.
68   *Id. See also DoD Law of War Manual*, 11.18.7.1.
69   *Id. See also DoD Law of War Manual*, 11.18.7.3.
70   Article 41 of AP I defines those considered *hors de combat*:

> A person is "hors de combat" if:
>
> (a) he is in the power of an adverse Party;
> (b) he clearly expresses an intention to surrender; or
> (c) he has been rendered unconscious or is otherwise incapacitated by wounds or sickness, and therefore is incapable of defending himself;
>
> provided that in any of these cases he abstains from any hostile act and does not attempt to escape.
>
> AP I, Art 41(2)

> However, the ICRC does not agree that *wounded and sick* and *hors de combat* are analogous terms. Specifically, the 2016 GWS Commentary notes that:
>
> It has been suggested that Article 12 only pertains to those persons whose medical condition is of such severity that they are physically incapable of continuing to fight. Such an interpretation is too limiting. A definition which refers only to physically incapacitating medical conditions would equate being wounded or sick with being *hors de combat*, which does not provide an all-encompassing definition of "wounded or sick" for the purposes of Article 12. While a narrow reading may arguably enhance legal certainty on the battlefield, it would not address all of the cases Article 12 is designed to cover. In particular, it would exclude all those who are wounded or sick, whether severely or not, but who are not (yet) incapacitated by their medical condition. Furthermore, it would *de facto* reduce the obligation

to care for the wounded and sick to an obligation of first aid. After all, if being wounded or sick required an incapacitating medical condition, the legal status of being "wounded or sick" and the obligations that hinge on it would cease as soon as the medical condition is no longer incapacitating—including when a person is in the power of his or her own armed forces. At such a point, and given that being wounded or sick is typically a transitory status, a person may, however, still require medical care. Thus, globally for Article 12, any medical condition requiring care, no matter the severity, suffices to trigger the application of the article. In a combat situation, however, the fact that a combatant is wounded or sick must be visible or have some outward manifestation such that an opposing combatant is able to be aware of it.

2016 GWS Commentary, para 1344

71 Geneva Convention for the Amelioration of the Condition of the Wounded and Sick in Armed Forces in the Field, 12 August 1949, 6 U.S.T. 3114, 75 U.N.T.S. 970 [hereinafter GWS].
72 *Id.* Art 13.
73 *Id.*
74 In addition to defining protections bestowed on protected persons, the GWS also creates an absolute prohibition preventing protected persons from voluntarily relinquishing any of the protections bestowed upon them. *See* GWS, Art 7.
75 GWS, Art 12.
76 *Id.* Art 5.
77 *See, e.g.,* AP I, Art 17 (discussing the role of the civilian population in caring for the wounded and sick, and ensuring that civilians will not be punished for doing so).
78 *See Id.*
79 AP I explicitly lists medical personnel and chaplains, who are members of the armed forces as non-combatants. AP I, Art 43(2).
80 *Cf.* U.S. Dep't of Army, *Field Manual 8–10–6, Medical Evacuation in a Theater of Operations: Tactics, Techniques, and Procedures* (14 April 2000) [hereinafter FM 8–10–6]. While FM 8–10–6 provides for comprehensive procedures in medical evacuation scenarios, it notes that "[t]he patient's medical condition is the overriding factor in determining the evacuation." *Id.* para 4–1(2).
81 GWS, Art 12. Article 12 states, specifically, that "[m]embers of the armed forces and other persons mentioned in the following Article who are wounded or sick, shall be respected and protected in all circumstances."
82 There are many instances, even in modern history, of violations of the respect and protect principles. For example, North Vietnamese personnel shot wounded Americans on the Ia Drang Valley battlefield in November 1965. *See* Int'l & Operational Law Dep't, The Judge Advocate Gen.'s Legal Ctr. & Sch., U.S. Army, *JA 423 Law of War Handbook* pt. IX.A(1)(a)(1) (2005), *available at* http:// military.laws.com/law-war-handbook-2005 [hereinafter *2005 Law of War Handbook*].
83 *See, e.g., Id.* pt. IX.A(1)(a)(2) ("An excellent example of this concept occurred in the Falklands when a British soldier came upon a gravely wounded Argentine whose brains were leaking into his helmet. The British soldier scooped the extruded material back into the soldier's skull and evacuated him. The Argentine survived.").
84 Pictet, Geneva Convention for the Amelioration of the Condition of the Wounded and Sick in Armed Forces in the Field: Commentary (ICRC, 1952), 135 [hereinafter 1952 Commentary GWS].
85 Armed forces field manuals have generally adopted the definitions of GWS Commentary in defining their obligations. *See UK LOAC Manual*, para 7.3.1 ("The duty of respect means that the wounded and sick are not to be made the target of attack. The duty of protection imposes positive duties to assist them.").

86 Triage principles are designed to "provide the greatest medical assets to those with significant injuries who may benefit from treatment, while those wounded who will die no matter what and those whose injuries are not serious are given lesser priority." *2005 Law of War Handbook*, pt. IX.D(1)(a). *See also* GWS, Art 12 (stating "[o]nly urgent medical reasons will authorize priority in the order of treatment to be administered.").

87 *See* GWS, Art 12.

88 *Id*. Art 46

89 2016 GWS Commentary, para 1396.

90 *Id*. paras 1369–96, 1419–20. A primary reason for these prohibitions arises out of practices during World War II, such as those of "the German[s] . . . at their main aircrew interrogation center [where] [t]hey frequently delayed medical treatment until after interrogation. [The Germans also] seal[ed] off Russian PW camps once typhus or tuberculosis was discovered." *2005 Law of War Handbook*, pt. IX.D(5)(a). Under Article 46, these practices are now expressly forbidden.

91 GWS, Art 12. The requirement to leave medical personnel and equipment with abandoned wounded and sick is qualified by military necessity considerations. *See Id*.

92 For example, during the Falklands War, scholars note that "the quality of medical care provided by the British to the wounded, without distinction between British and Argentinean, was remarkable. More than 300 major surgeries were performed, and 100 of these were on Argentinean soldiers." *Id*. pt. IX.D(1)(d).

93 *See* AP I, Art 10.

94 GWS, Art 15.

95 *Id*. (". . . and to search for the dead and prevent their being despoiled.").

96 *See Id*. Arts 12, 15.

97 As military operations may render the search obligation impractical, the drafters left the decision of when to search up to the commander's discretion. 2016 GWS Commentary, para 1487. *See also 2005 Law of War Handbook*, pt. IX.F(1)(2) ("By way of example, US policy during Operation DESERT STORM was not to search for casualties in Iraqi tanks or armored personnel carriers because of concern about unexploded ordnance.").

98 GWS, Art 15.

99 *Id*. Art 17.

100 *Id*. Art 16.

101 The GPW states that "[u]pon the outbreak of a conflict and in all cases of occupation, each of the Parties to the conflict shall institute an official Information Bureau for prisoners of war who are in its power." GPW, Art 122. A party must give its Information Bureau certain information relating to identification, transfer, and health of POWs in order for the Bureau to pass that information on to the party to whom the POW depends and his or her next of kin. *See Id*.

102 GWS, Art 16. Defined in the GPW, the Central Prisoners of War Information Agency "shall be created in a neutral country" and its function is to

> collect all the information it may obtain through official or private channels respecting prisoners of war, and to transmit it as rapidly as possible to the country of origin of the prisoners of war or to the Power on which they depend.
>
> GPW, Art 123

103 GWS, Art 17.

104 *Id*. (The United States' disposal of Osama bin Laden's body at sea caused a rather interesting debate as to whether his burial was conducted in accordance with IHL).

105 *Id*. In addition, half of the double identity disk, or the identity disk itself if it is a single disk, should remain on the body. *Id*.

106 *Id.*
107 *Id.* While individual burial is preferred, the military necessity exception permits mass graves if circumstances exist to necessitate it. *See* Pictet, Geneva Convention Relative to the Treatment of Prisoners of War: Commentary (ICRC, 1960), 177. Additionally, the individual inhumation or cremation was considered important because "the idea of a common grave conflicts with the sentiment of respect for the dead, in addition to making any subsequent exhumation impossible or very difficult." *Id.*
108 GWS, Art 18.
109 *Id.*
110 *Id.*
111 *Id.*
112 *See Id. See also* 2016 GWS Commentary, para 1762.
113 Protocol (III) Additional to the Geneva Conventions of 12 August 1949, and Relating to the Adoption of an Additional Distinctive Emblem, 8 December 2005, Art 2, 2404 U.N.T.S. 1 [hereinafter AP III].
114 GWS, Art 38.
115 2016 GWS Commentary, paras 2531–6 (explaining the origin of the Red Cross symbol and discussing the reasons why Turkey (and formerly the Ottoman Empire before formal adoption of the Red Crescent in 1929) refused to use the Red Cross, and instead adopted the Red Crescent, and Persia's desire to use the Red Lion).
116 *See* Jean-François Quéguiner, Commentary on the Protocol Additional to the Geneva Conventions of 12 August 1949, and relating to the Adoption of an Additional Distinctive Emblem (Protocol III) (ICRC, 2007), 191. [hereinafter AP III Commentary].
117 AP III, Art 3; AP III Commentary, at 191.
118 GWS, Art 39. The Commentary notes that "[i]t is at the military commander's discretion to determine when the emblem will not be displayed on protected objects entitled to respect under the Geneva Conventions and their Additional Protocols." 2016 GWS Commentary, para 2565.
119 GWS, Arts 38–44.
120 *Id.* Art 40.
121 *Id.* Arts 16, 40.
122 *Id.* Art 28.
123 *See* FM 8–10–6, app. A–1–2.
124 GWS, Art 44.
125 *See* 2016 GWS Commentary, paras 1977–81 (providing a more detailed discussion on the "exclusive nature of the assignment").
126 *See* FM 8–10–6, app. A–4 (further providing the lawful parameters (and U.S. approach) of medical personnel's right to self-defense and the defense of their patients).
127 2016 GWS Commentary, para 2005.
128 *Id.*
129 GWS, Art 26. During either peacetime or upon the commencement of hostilities, all parties to the conflict must notify each other of which societies it has authorized to render assistance to the medical service of its armed forces. *Id.*
130 *Id.*
131 U.S. Dep't of Army, Army Regulation 190–8: *Enemy Prisoners of War, Retained Personnel, Civilian Internees and Other Detainees* Section 3–15(b) (1 October 1997) [hereinafter AR 190–8].
132 *See* GWS, Art 30. Parties may enter into agreements determining the percentage of personnel to be retained in proportion to the number of POWs. *Id.* Art 31.

133 GWS, Art 31. *See also* 2016 GWS Commentary, paras 2264–8 ("priority for return may be granted to wounded or sick medical or religious personnel over able-bodied personnel who may have been captured earlier").

134 AR 190–8, Section 3–15(k).

135 GWS, Art 25.

136 *Id.*

137 *Id.*

138 *Id.* Art 41.

139 GWS, Art 29 (however, they "shall be employed on their medical duties in so far as the need arises").

140 *DoD Law of War Manual*, 4.13.1 (the United States has instead opted to employ military medical and religious personnel).

141 *See* GWS, Art 35.

142 "'[F]ixed' can be understood as attached or positioned securely, and 'establishments' as something 'set up on a firm or permanent basis'. Because buildings such as hospitals are immovable, they would undoubtedly fall within this category." 2016 GWS Commentary, para 1775.

143 GWS, Arts 19, 21. *See also* Geneva Convention for the Amelioration of the Condition of Wounded, Sick, and Shipwrecked Members of the Armed Forces at Sea, 12 August 1949, 6 U.S.T. 3217, 75 U.N.T.S. 971.

144 GWS, Art 19.

145 *Id.*

146 *Id.* Art 21. "Examples of such use include firing at the enemy for reasons other than individual self-defence, installing a firing position in a medical post, the use of a hospital as a shelter for able-bodied combatants, as an arms or ammunition dump, or as a military observation post, or the placing of a medical unit in proximity to a military objective with the intention of shielding it from the enemy's military operations." 2016 GWS Commentary, para 1842.

147 GWS, Art 21.

148 *Id.* Art 22.

149 *Id.* Art 28.

150 *Id.* Art 33.

151 *Id.*

152 *Id.* Art 35.

153 G.I.A.D. Draper, *The Red Cross Conventions of 1949*, at 87 (1958).

154 *See* GWS, Art 35.

155 *See Id.*

156 One tactical situation wherein a commander may order his or her medics not to wear the distinctive emblem is when the enemy makes a practice of *not* respecting the GWS's provisions protecting medical personnel, and instead actually targets them. For example, during the Vietnam conflict,

> US soldiers claimed that the NVA and Vietcong targeted medical personnel because of their importance in maintaining morale. They'd shoot medics even if they were giving care. Consequently[,] medics often avoided wearing armbands[,] which acted as bulls-eyes. There were even reports that the Vietcong paid an incentive for killing medics.
>
> 2005 *Law of War Handbook*, pt. X.A(1)(a)

In such circumstances, a commander might strongly consider ordering his or her medical personnel not to wear a distinctive emblem.

157 GWS, Art 36.

158 2016 GWS Commentary, para 2465.

159 *See Id.* para 2449.

160 *See Id*. paras 2466–8.

161 *See Id*. para 2567.

162 GWS, Art 36.

163 *Id*.

164 *Id*.

165 *Id*.

166 *See Id*.

167 *Id*. Art 37.

168 *Id*.

169 *Id*.

170 *See generally* AP I, Art 18.

171 *Id*. Art 25.

172 *See Id*.

173 *Id*.

174 *Id*. Art 29. Agreements must state the proposed number of medical aircraft, their flight plans, means of identification, and shall be understood to mean that every flight will be carried out in compliance with the restrictions on operations of medical aircraft from Article 28. *Id*.

175 *Id*. Art 27(1).

176 *Id*.

177 *See generally* Program on Humanitarian Policy and Conflict Research (HPCR) at Harvard University, *Manual on International Law Applicable to Air and Missile Warfare* iii–iv (2009) [hereinafter *HPCR Air and Missile Warfare Manual*].

178 The Commentary to each *HPCR Air and Missile Warfare Manual* Rule clarifies whether or not that particular Rule applies to IAC or NIAC. *See generally* Program on Humanitarian Policy and Conflict Research (HPCR) at Harvard University, Commentary on the *HPCR Manual on International Law Applicable to Air and Missile Warfare* iii–iv (2009) [hereinafter *HPCR Air and Missile Warfare Manual* Commentary].

179 *Id*. r. 76(d).

180 *Id*. rr. 78–9. The Commentary notes that the *HPCR Air and Missile Warfare Manual*'s requirement to strictly follow all conditions for consent is a wider prohibition than AP I's requirement that a medical aircraft will be protected so long as it does not engage in acts harmful to the enemy. *Id*. r. 79 cmt. 3.

181 *Id*. r. 80 cmt. 2.

182 *HPCR Air and Missile Warfare Manual*, r. 80.

183 *Id*.

184 *Id*. r. 80(c). The occupants are entitled to treatment as POWs and/or RPs, whichever is applicable, and the detaining party assumes responsibility for providing medical care to any wounded and sick aboard the aircraft. *HPCR Air and Missile Warfare Manual* Commentary, r. 80(c) cmt. 3. The Commentary notes that if the detaining party is unable to care for wounded and sick onboard the aircraft, it may have to allow the aircraft to continue on its flight. *Id*.

185 *HPCR Air and Missile Warfare Manual* Commentary, r. 82.

186 *Id*.

187 *Id*. r. 82 cmts. 1, 5.

188 *HPCR Air and Missile Warfare Manual*, r. 86. Military aircraft on search-and-rescue missions are deemed to be engaged in combat activities. *See HPCR Air and Missile Warfare Manual* Commentary, r. 86(a) cmts. 1–2. Civilian aircraft engaged in such activities are generally protected in the same manner as other civilian aircraft, and do not gain the specific manner of medical aircraft. *Id*. cmt. 3.

189 Common Article 3.

190 *Handbook of International Humanitarian Law* 620 (Dieter Fleck & Michael Bothe eds, 2008) (citing *Military and Paramilitary Activities in and Against Nicar. (Nicar. v. U.S.)*, 1986 I.C.J. 14, 112, 114 (27 June)).
191 *Id.*
192 Common Article 3.
193 *Customary International Humanitarian Law Study* (Jean-Marie Henckaerts & Louise Doswald-Beck eds, 2005).
194 *See generally* AP II.
195 *Id.* Art 18.
196 *Id.* Art 10(1).
197 *Id.* Art 10(2).
198 *Id.* Art 10(4).

5 Prisoners of war and other detainees

1 Introduction

Imagine you are commanding a military unit engaged in an armed conflict against the armed forces of another State in that State's territory. Your forces engage enemy forces and report to you that they have captured dozens of enemy military personnel. Mixed in with the group of captives are a group of medics—members of the enemy armed forces wearing the red cross and armed only with side arms (pistols). Your subordinate commander also reports that, while transporting this group of capture personnel to the friendly rear area for detention, a group of local civilians attempted to block the road, and some started throwing rocks at the trucks in the convoy. Military police escorting the convoy detained about a dozen of these civilians, who are among the captives being brought to a processing facility in your area of operations. Shortly after this report, you learn from your assistant commander of a request by a representative of the ICRC to visit the processing and detention camp your military police have set up and to meet with the captives currently being transported.

The status and treatment of captured and detained personnel is one of the most important, and at times complex issues addressed by IHL. While one of the four Geneva Conventions is devoted exclusively to these issues as they relate to prisoners of war (the Geneva Convention Relative to the Treatment of Prisoners of War),[1] and another of the Conventions focuses extensively on these issues as they relate to civilian detainees (the Geneva Convention for the Treatment of Civilians),[2] much uncertainty persists to this day. This uncertainty is most significant in relation to NIACs, but it also impacts IACs when the captured opponent does not fit neatly into one of the several categories expressly recognized by the Conventions.

This chapter provides an overview of what might be best characterized as *detention law*. It will begin by explaining the concept of *prisoner of war*, how that status is defined and assessed, and the basic protections that flow from prisoner of war designation. The chapter will then address the unique status and treatment of non-combatant members of the armed forces—medical and religious personnel. Detention of civilians assessed as representing a threat to friendly forces will then be explained. The chapter will close by outlining the status and treatment of captives in NIACs.

2 Prisoners of war

Armed conflicts will almost always result in the capture of members of opposition belligerent groups. When the public sees images of captured enemy fighters, it instinctively assumes they are prisoners of war (or POWs). However, the truth is that many detainees are not in fact POWs; indeed, it is increasingly infrequent owing to the nature of the conflicts that dominate the contemporary threat environment. Nonetheless, POW status is a logical start point for understanding detention law, as it is highly developed and reflects the principal international law regulatory focus for captured personnel.

Not every captured enemy fighter or belligerent captive qualifies as a POW, and some individuals who are not belligerents will qualify for POW status. Article 4 of the 1949 Geneva Convention Relative to the Treatment of Prisoners of War (GPW) establish the universally accepted POW qualification requirements, stating:

> A. Prisoners of war, in the sense of the present Convention, are persons belonging to one of the following categories, who have fallen into the power of the enemy:
>
> (1) Members of the armed forces of a Party to the conflict, as well as members of militias or volunteer corps forming part of such armed forces.
>
> (2) Members of other militias and members of other volunteer corps, including those of organized resistance movements, belonging to a Party to the conflict and operating in or outside their own territory, even if this territory is occupied, provided that such militias or volunteer corps, including such organized resistance movements, fulfil the following conditions:
>
> (a) that of being commanded by a person responsible for his subordinates;
>
> (b) that of having a fixed distinctive sign recognizable at a distance;
>
> (c) that of carrying arms openly;
>
> (d) that of conducting their operations in accordance with the laws and customs of war.
>
> (3) Members of regular armed forces who profess allegiance to a government or an authority not recognized by the Detaining Power.
>
> (4) Persons who accompany the armed forces without actually being members thereof, such as civilian members of military aircraft crews, war correspondents, supply contractors, members of labour units or of services responsible for the welfare of the armed forces, provided that they have received authorization from the armed forces which they accompany, who shall provide them for that purpose with an identity card similar to the annexed model.
>
> (5) Members of crews, including masters, pilots and apprentices, of the merchant marine and the crews of civil aircraft of the Parties to the conflict, who do not benefit by more favourable treatment under any other provisions of international law.

(6) Inhabitants of a non-occupied territory, who on the approach of the enemy spontaneously take up arms to resist the invading forces, without having had time to form themselves into regular armed units, provided they carry arms openly and respect the laws and customs of war.

B. The following shall likewise be treated as prisoners of war under the present Convention:

(1) Persons belonging, or having belonged, to the armed forces of the occupied country, if the occupying Power considers it necessary by reason of such allegiance to intern them, even though it has originally liberated them while hostilities were going on outside the territory it occupies, in particular where such persons have made an unsuccessful attempt to rejoin the armed forces to which they belong and which are engaged in combat, or where they fail to comply with a summons made to them with a view to internment.

(2) The persons belonging to one of the categories enumerated in the present Article, who have been received by neutral or non-belligerent Powers on their territory and whom these Powers are required to intern under international law, without prejudice to any more favourable treatment which these Powers may choose to give and with the exception of Articles 8, 10, 15, 30, fifth paragraph, 58–67, 92, 126 and, where diplomatic relations exist between the Parties to the conflict and the neutral or non-belligerent Power concerned, those Articles concerning the Protecting Power. Where such diplomatic relations exist, the Parties to a conflict on whom these persons depend shall be allowed to perform towards them the functions of a Protecting Power as provided in the present Convention, without prejudice to the functions which these Parties normally exercise in conformity with diplomatic and consular usage and treaties.

C. This Article shall in no way affect the status of medical personnel and chaplains as provided for in Article 33 of the present Convention.[3]

The 1977 AP I, which supplements the GPW, expanded the categories of individuals who qualify for POW status upon capture. However, as explained in more detail below, unlike the GPW definition, the AP I expansion is not a universally accepted supplement.[4] A useful methodology to apply these provisions is to apply a two-part test when assessing status: is the individual captured in the *right type of conflict*? And if so, does the individual qualify as the *right type of person*?

As a threshold matter, POW status is applicable only in the IAC context, because Article 4 of the GPW and the associated AP I provisions do not come into force during NIAC. This means that no matter how "regular" a non-State fighter may appear during a NIAC (i.e. wearing a uniform and part of what appears to be a regular military unit), he or she simply cannot qualify for POW status. Thus, IACs are the exclusive right type of conflict for purposes of POW status.

As noted above, Article 4 of the GPW establishes what captured personnel qualify as POWs. The essential POW qualification requirement is, accordingly, not that an individual is a fighter or belligerent but instead that the individual is a member of State armed forces, or otherwise associated with those armed forces. Members of the regular armed forces and militia or volunteer groups incorporated into the regular armed forces are logically the first category of captives who qualify for POW status.[5] What constitutes *regular armed forces* is a matter for the State to define. However, for irregular forces associated with the regular armed forces, Article 4(A)(2) imposes four conditions that must be satisfied: carrying arms openly, wearing a fixed distinctive emblem recognizable at a distance, operating under responsible command, and conducting operations in accordance with the laws and customs of war.[6] Article 4(A)(2) also covers resistance fighters who continue their struggle after their territory is occupied. Like associated militia, these individuals must also comply with the four express qualification criteria. All such irregular forces must *belong* to a party to the conflict. While the GPW does not define what this means, they must, at a minimum, be conducting their operations in a common cause with the party to the conflict they claim to be associated with.

As noted in Chapter 3, there is some controversy over whether the absence of analogous conditions applicable to members of the regular armed forces indicates that they forfeit POW status if they fail to satisfy these conditions. Although the most widely held view is that regular armed forces must comply with these criteria, some experts believe that POW status afforded to members of the regular armed forces pursuant to Article 4(A)(1) is not qualified by an implicit requirement that such forces satisfy these four conditions.

Chapter 3 also explained why the GPW included other categories of captives within the definition of prisoner of war. Article 4(A)(3) was included in the 1949 revision of the 1929 GPW to address the status of regular armed forces fighting on behalf of government not recognized by the detaining power, such as the governments in exile fighting against the Axis in World War II.[7] To address this problem, the 1949 GPW included such armed forces within the scope of POW qualification.[8] The U.S. invasion of Afghanistan resurrected the significance of this provision of Article 4, because the United States did not recognize the Taliban as the legitimate government of Afghanistan. However, Taliban armed forces were nonetheless denied POW status based on the U.S. interpretation of the GPW that generated substantial criticism. That interpretation concluded that the four POW qualification conditions expressly included in Article 4(A)(2) applied implicitly to members of the regular armed forces falling within Article 4(A)(1), which meant that because the Taliban armed forces routinely violated the laws and customs of war, they were conclusively disqualified for POW status.

Article 4(A)(4) and (5) extend POW status to certain civilians who *accompany* or *support* the armed forces so long as they are properly authorized by the armed forces to do so (sub-paragraph (4) covers civilians who accompany the armed forces in the field; sub-paragraph (5) covers civilian crew members of merchant vessels and military aircraft[9]). It may seem odd that civilians would qualify as POWs. However, this provision is a practical response to the quite common practice of military reliance on civilians to support armed forces, not only during peacetime but also during armed conflicts. Because civilians are presumptively protected from internment—which is allowed only for imperative reasons of security—it is logical that, when captured, a civilian who was working alongside enemy forces and providing important support to those forces would be detained for the duration of hostilities. It is also logical to provide the same rights and conditions of detention for such individuals as apply to the armed forces they are captured alongside. But it is important not to equate civilian POW qualification with combatant status. As the GPW indicates, these are civilians who, while accompanying or working alongside the armed forces, are *not* members thereof.[10] Accordingly, while the definition of combatant included in AP I incorporates by reference individuals who qualify as POW pursuant to Article 4(A)(1), (2), (3), and (6), it expressly excludes those who qualify as POWs pursuant to sub-paragraphs (4) and (5) from that definition.[11]

Article 4(A)(6) addresses the final category of individuals who qualify as POWs: members of a what is known historically as a *leveé en masse*.[12] These are residents of an area invaded by an enemy who spontaneously rise up to resist. So long as these individuals carry arms openly and comply with the laws and customs of war, they qualify as POWs upon capture. However, it is important to distinguish members of a *leveé en masse* from isolated acts of violence by local civilians: only if the uprising is general in nature will it be treated as falling within the scope of Article 4(A)(6).[13] Civilians who engage in acts of violence without being part of such a general response will not qualify as POWs and risk being subject to criminal sanction for their conduct.

This enumeration of POW qualification remained exclusive until 1977, when AP I came into force. One of the most contested provisions of this treaty expanded the definition of POW to include any person who qualified as a combatant within the meaning of the Protocol. Article 43 of the Protocol defines combatant to include:

1. The armed forces of a Party to a conflict consist of all organized armed forces, groups and units which are under a command responsible to that Party for the conduct of its subordinates, even if that Party is represented by a government or an authority not recognized by an adverse Party. Such armed forces shall be subject to an internal disciplinary system which, *inter alia*, shall enforce compliance with the rules of international law applicable in armed conflict.

2. Members of the armed forces of a Party to a conflict (other than medical personnel and chaplains covered by Article 33 of the Third Convention) are combatants, that is to say, they have the right to participate directly in hostilities.

3.   Whenever a Party to a conflict incorporates a paramilitary or armed law enforcement agency into its armed forces it shall so notify the other Parties to the conflict.[14]

Article 44 then indicates that any individual who qualifies as a combatant is a POW (although AP I explicitly excludes mercenaries and spies from POW status).[15] This may seem somewhat unremarkable, as the definition of combatant mirrors POW qualification established pursuant to Article 4(A)(1), (2), (3), and (6). However, Article 44 then indicates that a combatant qualifies as a POW so long as:

3.   In order to promote the protection of the civilian population from the effects of hostilities, combatants are obliged to distinguish themselves from the civilian population while they are engaged in an attack or in a military operation preparatory to an attack. Recognizing, however, that there are situations in armed conflicts where, owing to the nature of the hostilities an armed combatant cannot so distinguish himself, he shall retain his status as a combatant, provided that, in such situations, he carries his arms openly:
       (a) During each military engagement, and
       (b) During such time as he is visible to the adversary while he is engaged in a military deployment preceding the launching of an attack in which he is to participate.
       Acts which comply with the requirements of this paragraph shall not be considered as perfidious within the meaning of Article 37, paragraph 1 (c).[16]

Chapter 3 explained why this was considered by the United States and several other States to be an unjustified and unacceptable dilution of the historic requirement that combatants distinguish themselves from the civilian population *at all times*.[17] This concern was exacerbated by the fact that the relaxation of the distinction obligation applied only to *irregular* armed forces, and *not* to members of the regular armed forces they fight. Specifically, Article 44 provides that, "[t]his Article is not intended to change the generally accepted practice of States with respect to the wearing of the uniform by combatants assigned to the regular, uniformed armed units of a Party to the conflict."[18] This seems an overt concession of tolerating disparate obligations between parties to an IAC, a disparity the United States and other States considered fundamentally inconsistent with the laws and customs of war.

When coupled with the expanded definition of IAC resulting from AP I's war of national liberation provision in Article 1, the combined result was seen as incentivizing terrorist activities and illicit warfare in many armed conflicts.[19] This was a primary reason why the United States rejected AP I, and led other States to include reservations to these provisions as part of the ratification process.[20]

Nonetheless, for States that ratified AP I without reservation, these provisions expand the list of individuals who qualify as POWs.

2.1 *And who decides?*

In most situations, there will be little difficulty in assessing which captives qualify as POWs. Because qualification is limited to IAC, most captives will qualify as POWs because they are members of the regular armed forces. But it is also common for questions to arise as to the qualification of a given captive or group of captives. For example, routed enemy troops may abandon their uniforms and equipment in an effort to avoid capture and detention. Or, as has been more common in recent conflicts, captives may actually seek POW status in order to avoid being detained in a less favorable status (which will be explained in more detail below). Article 5 of the GPW addresses the procedure to be followed when a detaining power is uncertain as to the status of a captive, specifically:

> The present Convention shall apply to the persons referred to in Article 4 from the time they fall into the power of the enemy and until their final release and repatriation.
>
> Should any doubt arise as to whether persons, having committed a belligerent act and having fallen into the hands of the enemy, belong to any of the categories enumerated in Article 4, such persons shall enjoy the protection of the present Convention until such time as their status has been determined by a competent tribunal.[21]

There are several important aspects of Article 5. First, it only requires a tribunal when the detaining power is in doubt as to whether a captive qualifies as a POW. This suggests that it is up to the detaining power to decide whether doubt exists. This became controversial in 2002, when President George W. Bush issued a blanket determination that there was no doubt that captured Taliban fighters *did not* qualify as POWs pursuant to Article 4(A)(1) (because the Taliban did not comply with the four criteria expressly included in Article 4(A)(2) and considered implicitly applicable to members of the regular armed forces).[22] While it is likely that the drafters of the GPW contemplated a case-by-case assessment of doubt at the tactical level, nothing in the text of the provision precluded the approach taken by the United States. Parties to AP I, however, are bound to a different methodology, because Article 45 provides for Article 5 treatment and requires an Article 5 tribunal not only when the detaining power considers there to be doubt as to the qualification of a captive, but also when the captives asserts a right to POW status.[23]

Second, Article 5 requires treatment according to the GPW until doubt as to a captive's status is resolved. In other words, captives of uncertain status benefit from a presumption that they *will* qualify as POWs, rebutted only after an Article 5 tribunal determines they do not qualify. Third, Article 5 does not indicate the composition of, or procedures for the tribunal. While the associated Commentary suggests that the tribunal should be composed of at least three officers, it is clear that States retain substantial flexibility in implementing the Article 5 obligation. U.S. practice is to utilize three officers: normally one military police officer, one intelligence officer, and one JAG officer (military lawyer).[24] The captive is not represented and the hearing is not adversarial, although the captive is permitted to utilize a prisoner representative (another POW) to assist during the hearing. Finally, it is important to note that the exclusive function of the Article 5 tribunal is to answer one question: does the captive qualify as a POW? If so, the status is confirmed; if not, the captive will normally be treated as a civilian (although, as explained below, the United States may conclude that the captive is an unprivileged belligerent subject to POW-type detention without POW status).

2.2   Retained persons

Some members of the armed forces will qualify not as POWs, but as retained persons (RPs). This status is provided to non-combatant members of the armed forces: military medical and religious personnel. While the term *non-combatant* is routinely used as a synonym for civilian, it actually covers these members of a State's regular armed forces. To qualify as a non-combatant member of the armed forces, an individual must be *exclusively* engaged in the search for, collection of, and care of the wounded and sick. When such individuals are captured, their status will normally be indicated by a special category on their identification card, and/or the fact that they wear the distinctive protective emblem and carry only small arms. These individuals, when detained, are afforded all the rights and protections applicable to POWs. However, unlike POWs, their detention is strictly necessity-based: they may be detained only if their services are required to address the needs of the POW population. If they are not needed for this purpose, they must be repatriated immediately (U.S. military regulations establish POW to RP ratios to facilitate the process of repatriation or retention). Furthermore, they must be permitted to continue to engage in their humanitarian functions in accordance with the principles of the Geneva Convention for the Amelioration of the Condition of the Wounded and Sick in Armed Forces in the Field (GWS) and/or the Geneva Convention for the Amelioration of the Condition of Wounded, Sick, and Shipwrecked Members of the Armed Forces at Sea (GWS-Sea) while retained by an enemy.[25]

2.3   Civilians

As explained in Chapter 3, establishing who is a *civilian* is essential for assessing who is safeguarded by rules of humanitarian law, such as the protection from deliberate attack. To that end, AP I provided the first treaty definition of civilian— any person who does not qualify as a combatant (or a non-combatant member of the armed forces).[26] Civilians are not only protected from deliberate attack (unless they take a direct part in hostilities) but also protected from unjustified deprivations of liberty. This protection is not, however, absolute. The Geneva Convention Relative to the Protection of Civilian Persons in Time of War (GC) provides for the internment of civilians when necessitated by imperative considerations of security.[27] Accordingly, civilians assessed as representing a threat to the security of military forces in an area of operations may be administratively detained.

Detention of civilians is fundamentally different from POW detention in a number of ways. First, unlike POWs, who are detained based on a determination of a status that falls within the POW definition, civilian detention is exclusively conduct-based. This means that the detention is justified only when the civilian engages in specific conduct that indicates that he or she is a security threat (whereas a POW is detained based on status with no consideration of whether he or she poses an actual threat to the detaining force). Second, because civilian detention is conduct-based, a hearing is always required to consider the justification for detention. While there is some similarity between this Article 78 hearing and an Article 5 tribunal in that neither is adversarial or governed by criminal-type rules of evidence or procedure, the objective of each hearing is fundamentally different: the Article 5 tribunal determines a captive status; the Article 78 hearing determines whether a civilian poses a threat to the force. Third, civilian detention is purely necessity-based, which means it must terminate when the civilian is no longer considered a threat to the detaining force. In contrast, POW detention is considered presumptively necessary for the duration of hostilities, and therefore is authorized for that duration. Fourth, in order to periodically revalidate the necessity for civilian detention, the reason for detention must be reviewed every six months.

2.4 Unprivileged belligerents

Chapter 3 explains the importance and controversy related to the status of captured enemy personnel who fail to qualify for POW status. There is no consensus view on whether such individuals should be detained as civilians who represent an imperative threat to the security of the detaining armed forces or as unprivileged belligerents subject to POW-type detention even though they do not qualify as POWs—the approach adopted by the United States.[28]

The GPW does not include such captives within the definition of POW, and nothing in the Geneva Conventions explicitly provides for an unprivileged belligerent designation. Nor does AP I, although the Commentary to Article 75 of AP I, which indicates that the humane treatment obligation also applies to, "any person who has taken part in hostilities, who is not entitled to prisoner-of-war status and who does not benefit from more favourable treatment in accordance with the fourth Convention,"[29] seems to be an acknowledgment that some individuals may be detained as the result of their belligerent activity but fail to qualify as either POWs or civilians for purpose of status. The unprivileged belligerent designation is based on the conclusion that treating a member of an organized enemy belligerent group as a civilian, even considering such a civilian is subject to security detention, is incongruous. For the United States and other proponents of this category of captives, once an individual becomes a member of such a belligerent group, he or she should not be presumptively protected from detention but instead should be presumed a continuing threat for the duration of hostilities subject to detention no differently from any other POW.

The complexities that arise as the result of characterizing captives as unprivileged belligerents are exacerbated by the fact that there are no treaty provisions that define how to assess this status, or the rights and obligations of such detainees. This has led to incorporation by analogy to many of the provisions applicable to both POWs and civilian security detainees. The most notable example of this law-by-analogy solution to the absence of any express treaty provisions applicable to such detainees was the creation by the United States of the Combatant Status Review Tribunal (CSRT).[30] This was an Article 5–type review tribunal that assessed the status of all detainees brought by the United States to Guantanamo Bay, Cuba. These review tribunals applied a definition of *unlawful combatant* (later changed to *unprivileged belligerent*) created unilaterally by the United States. A similar procedure was later created for detainees held by the United States in Parwan, Afghanistan.[31] Like the United States, Israel also designates such captives as unprivileged belligerents, although an Israeli domestic law both defines this type of detainee and provides the procedures applicable to detention decisions.[32] Considering the increasingly common confrontation between State armed forces and irregular enemies, it is unlikely that the controversy surrounding the proper characterization of such fighters will dissipate in the foreseeable future.

3   Detainee treatment

No matter what category some captives fall into, once detained by a military force issues related to their treatment become the central focus of the law. The obligations applicable to each category vary in terms of scope and substance, and many of these obligations are beyond the scope of this chapter. It is therefore useful to address fundamental aspects of detainee treatment that apply to all categories, and then address some of the most important aspects of treatment unique to each category.

3.1   Location and duration of detention

One of the most important rights accorded to all detainees is the right of repatriation once the necessity for detention terminates.[33] As noted above, for POWs this necessity is presumed to continue for the duration of hostilities. Accordingly, POWs must be repatriated promptly upon the termination of hostilities, and failure to do so may constitute a war crime. Note that the repatriation obligation arises when *hostilities* terminate, and *not* when the armed conflict is terminated by some formal arrangement such as a peace agreement. It is also possible that a POW may be repatriated prior to termination of hostilities pursuant to specific provisions of the GPW that address extraordinary humanitarian situations, such as terminal illness. Repatriation of RPs is, as explained above, based on a determination that they are no longer needed to care for the POW population, although in practice this means they will normally be detained until the end of hostilities. POWs and RPs may be detained in the territory where they were captured or in some other territory.

Civilians subject to security detention must be released when the conduct-based necessity for the detention terminates. Accordingly, there is no fixed event that requires their release. In some cases, a civilian national of an enemy belligerent State will be in the territory of the detaining State, in which case detention is permitted in that State. However, if a civilian is captured or apprehended in his or her own national territory, and subsequently subjected to security detention, it is prohibited to remove the civilian from that territory.

Because of an absence of treaty rules applicable to unprivileged belligerents, rules related to duration and location of detention are unclear. It would therefore seem that, as a minimum, they should benefit from the same repatriation rule applicable to POWs, requiring repatriation at the end of hostilities. This was the original U.S. position when it began detaining Taliban and al Qaeda captives designated as unprivileged belligerents. However, the United States subsequently implemented a hybrid approach to these detainees, mixing elements of POW and civilian security detention. Like POWs, these individuals are subject to detention based on a status determination. However, like civilian security detainees, the justification for detention is reviewed on an annual basis, and detainees are released based on a determination that they no longer pose a threat of returning to hostilities. It also seems that the United States' approach is that, like POWs, unprivileged belligerents may be detained in the territory where they were captured, or at some other location outside that territory.[34]

3.2 *Criminal liability*

Another important benefit accorded to POWs is what is commonly called *combatant immunity*—they are immune from criminal sanction for their *lawful* belligerent conduct. In other words, a POW may not be prosecuted by the detaining power for the violent actions committed prior to capture, so long as his or her conduct complied with IHL. This benefit is based on the rule that combatants are vested with international legal privilege to participate in hostilities, and therefore may not be subjected to criminal sanction for doing so. However, because this privilege applies only to combatants, it does not extend to civilians who qualify for POW status. Because these are civilians who accompany the armed forces without being members thereof, they are not considered combatants and cannot assert combatant immunity. This means that, if such a civilian directly participates in hostilities prior to capture, the detaining power may prosecute the captive for violation of its law resulting from that participation (for example, murder or attempted murder of the person attacked by the civilian).

Combatant immunity is obviously an important protection for combatants, or lawful belligerents, but it is not absolute or unlimited. The immunity afforded to these individuals extends only to conduct that complies with IHL. When a combatant engages in conduct that violates IHL (for example, murdering a POW) or is beyond the scope of the legitimate combatant function (for example, raping a civilian), the combatant may be subjected to criminal sanction by the detaining power, his or her own State, or in some instances an international criminal tribunal. Nor is combatant immunity applicable to any offense against the law of the detaining power committed prior to the armed conflict. For example, General Manuel Noriega, the commander of the Panamanian Defense Forces and de facto leader of Panama, qualified as a POW because he was captured in the context of the IAC between the United States and Panama resulting from the 1989 U.S. invasion, but he was also tried and convicted for violation of U.S. federal criminal long-arm statutes related to narcotics trafficking.[35]

In contrast, there is no analogous immunity for individuals who do not qualify as combatants/lawful belligerents. If these individuals directly participate in hostilities, they have no protection from an assertion of criminal jurisdiction by a detaining power for acts and/or omissions that violate the laws of that State. This includes members of organized belligerents groups who do not qualify for POW status, whether characterized as civilians or unprivileged belligerents. In fact, the ability to subject such belligerents to criminal sanction for their participation in hostilities likely influenced the U.S. decision to adopt the unlawful combatant/unprivileged belligerent designation for Taliban and al Qaeda captives in the early phases of the military response to the September 11 terrorist attacks.

Once subject to detention, both POWs and RPs become subject to the domestic criminal jurisdiction of the detaining power. The GPW indicates that non-criminal disciplinary measures should be utilized to deal with POW/RP misconduct whenever possible.[36] However, the GPW also allows for criminal prosecution of POWs/RPs for serious acts of misconduct.[37] To protect the fundamental rights of any POW/RP subjected to criminal prosecution, the detaining power must use the same tribunal it would use to prosecute its own nationals and afford the same procedural protections. Capital punishment is not prohibited, but there are certain GPW obligations that must be respected prior to carrying out such a penalty.

Whether civilians detained for imperative security in their own national territory are also subject to the criminal jurisdiction of the detaining power will depend on whether that State's criminal law extends to such individuals. However, during periods of occupation, the occupying/detaining power will be authorized to apply local criminal law to civilians in the occupied territory, either through local courts that continue to function during the occupation or through the use of detaining power military tribunals. Any detainee designated an unprivileged belligerent would also, in theory, be subject to same scope of criminal jurisdiction applicable to civilian security detainees. Both civilians and unprivileged belligerents would also be subject to criminal prosecution for any war crimes committed prior to capture.

3.3 Fundamental protections

All detainees are beneficiaries of IHL rules that provide for fundamental protections during detention, although the extent of these protections will depend on the status of the detainee. Generally, POWs, RPs, and civilian security detainees will be afforded the most extensive protection package because obligations related to their treatment are enumerated in the respective Geneva Conventions. In contrast, because unprivileged belligerents are not defined by these Conventions, there protections are less well defined. Nonetheless, many of the most fundamental protections provided by the Conventions will also apply to detainees who do not fall within the protection of these treaties by operation of customary international law, and for States bound to AP I, by operation of Article 75 of that treaty. A detailed recitation of the many protective provisions of the Conventions and Protocols is beyond the scope of this chapter, which will instead highlight several core or fundamental rules of protection.

First, no detainee falls outside the protection of the law, which means that all detainees must be respected and protected. *Respect* indicates an obligation to refrain from any intentional infliction of harm on the detainee; *protect* indicates an obligation to take affirmative measures to shield the detainee from harm. In short, all detainees must be treated humanely, which means as any other human being would hope to be treated if detained by an opponent. The most basic manifestation of this two-pronged protection obligation is reflected in Article 75 of AP I, titled "Fundamental Guarantees."[38] This Article was included in AP I to specifically address the plight of any detainee who falls outside the more favorable treatment provisions of one of the four Geneva Conventions.[39] In practice, the most significant group of detainees protected by Article 75 are those designated by a detaining power as unprivileged belligerents, as this characterization removes them from the protection of both the GPW and the GC. While not all States are bound by AP I, this fundamental protection Article is universally considered a reflection of customary international law. Even the assertion by the United States that Article 75 was not binding as a matter of customary international law was reversed when President Obama revised many of his predecessor's detention policies.[40]

The *respect* prong of humane treatment includes categorical prohibition against murder; torture; cruel, inhuman, and degrading treatment; and collective punishment.[41] When the detainee qualifies as a POW, RP, or is a civilian falling within the protective scope of the GC, violating any of these obligations will qualify as a *grave breach*, the most serious category of war crime (*see* Chapter 12: *War crimes and accountability*). Importantly, there is no necessity-type justification or override for deviating from these categorical prohibitions. This means that coercion is never permitted against a detainee, even to obtain what a commander may assess as vital information. To this end, the GPW includes a specific provision that prohibits coercion of any type against a POW, and another provision that indicates that, when questioned, a POW is required to provide only name, rank, and military identification number.[42] Even if a POW refuses to provide this information, it does not justify coercive measures. Instead, the POW will be simply be assumed to be a soldier of the lowest rank.

Even if a detainee does not qualify for status in one of these categories, subjecting the detainee to this type of abuse is considered a violation of international law that triggers individual criminal responsibility. In short, this type of maltreatment or abuse of any detainee is fundamentally inconsistent with international law and has been the basis for numerous prosecutions, both by a detaining power's own domestic military or civilian courts and by international criminal tribunals.

Respect for a detainee's religious beliefs almost certainly also falls within this scope of this obligation, which includes facilitating the exercise of faith, for example by providing access to holy books. Respect for religious faith also includes good faith efforts to provide detainees with meals that comply with their religious beliefs, such as kosher or halal rations. The *protect* prong of humane treatment includes the following obligation: promptly evacuate detainees from dangerous areas; provide detainees with essential nutrition, hydration, medical care, shelter from the elements, and clothing; segregate men from women; and facilitate prompt access to representatives of the ICRC.

During the outset of detainee operations, it is common for commanders to seek guidance on the amount of required rations, the quality of shelter and clothing they must provide detainees, and the extent of the medical care required. Of course, prior planning for detainee operations mitigates the significance of such questions because many will be addressed in operational plans, which in turn drives logistics preparations. However, it is not always possible to anticipate with precision the extent of a detainee population, or the needs of detainees. At a minimum, detainees should be provided with resources at a level analogous to friendly forces. In other words, if command is low on rations, the allocation per detainee should at least match that allocated to a commander's own forces. A similar approach to shelter is logical: if friendly forces are living in tents, that is the minimum that should be provided to detainees. As for medical care, the GWS requires equality of treatment for friendly and enemy casualties alike, which means that friendly forces may not be prioritized over detainees.[43] During the initial phase of detention, treatment of acute conditions will obviously be the priority, but, as conditions permit, treatment of chronic conditions will also be required. Most importantly, when commanders responsible for detention operations are constrained by resource limitations, they should constantly endeavor to improve the situation for detainees in order to achieve full compliance with Convention obligations.

These basic humanitarian protections also apply to POWs, RPs, and civilian security detainees. Specific Articles of the respective Geneva Conventions applicable to each of these categories of detainees enumerate these humanitarian obligations. Each Convention also provides other important protections for detainees qualifying for a status that places them within the protective scope of a given Convention.

One of the most important of these specific obligations is the requirement that the detaining power provide notice that an individual has in fact been captured and is in the detaining power's custody.[44] This notice is provided through a well-established mechanism whereby the detaining power informs the ICRC of the identity of detainees. Normally, the ICRC then provides notice to the detainee's national authorities. This is a crucial humanitarian protection for a number of reasons. First, it facilitates ICRC access to the detainee in order to assess the detainee's treatment and condition, which often contributes to dialogue between the detaining power and the ICRC that results in improved conditions for all detainees. Second, it means that the detaining power will eventually have to account for the whereabouts and well-being of detainees. In other words, this notice of the existence of detention will often enhance the conditions of detention because the detaining power knows that at some point the detainee must be released, or that the death of the detainee must be explained. History has shown time and again that, even when detained by an authority that routinely violates its humanitarian obligations, most detainees survive the ordeal and are not subjected to execution or murder. While it is impossible to establish an absolute correlation between notice of detention, and a limit to how far a detaining power is willing to go in abusing detainees, it seems logical that this notice plays some role in a limit to that abuse.

Closely related to the notice obligation are treaty rules that allow the detainee to communicate through correspondence.[45] The detaining power is authorized to place certain security-based limitations on such communication, for example by censoring POW correspondence or, in the case of a civilian detained because of espionage related activities, cutting off correspondence altogether. The humanitarian purpose of facilitating such communication is relatively obvious: the psychological well-being of detainees is ultimately enhanced when they are permitted to communicate with family and others in their home country. Correspondence by mail is facilitated by the ICRC, as it is rare that normal mail communications continue between States engaged in armed conflict. While this is not a common practice today because of the rarity of long-term inter-State armed conflicts, in prior conflicts this was a very common practice facilitated by well-established mechanisms between detaining powers, the ICRC, and national Red Cross or Red Crescent societies. One issue that will almost certainly arise in future conflicts is whether a detaining power should, or perhaps must, allow the use of electronic mail as a substitute for traditional mail.

A detaining power may require POWs, RPs, and civilian internees to work.[46] However, there are a number of limitations on the type of work they may be required to perform, and additional rules related to work conditions and compensation. As noted above, RPs may be required to work while retained, but must be permitted to perform duties related to their humanitarian mission. In contrast, the only limitation on the type of work that may be required of a POW is that they may not perform tasks to contribute to the enemy war effort, for example building fortifications or military runways. Assisting in constructing the facilities in a POW detention camp would, however, be permissible. Historically, POW labor has been used extensively by detaining powers in agriculture, industry, and other activities, although this is less common in contemporary armed conflicts. POW officers cannot be required to work, but may do so voluntarily. If the detaining power requires or allows POWs to work, they must be compensated in accordance with the provisions of the applicable Geneva Convention, and the detaining power must ensure compliance with health and safety regulations applicable to that type of work.

In contrast, civilian internees may not be required to work, but may do so voluntarily (however, medical personnel may be required to perform their humanitarian functions).[47] Like POWs, they may not be employed in tasks that directly support the enemy war effort, and if they consent to employment, they must be compensated fairly, and the detaining power must ensure implementation of all relevant national health and safety measures. Any civilian who consents to work may cease working after a six-week period.

3.4   Protections related to escape

POWs may be under the control of the detaining power, but their duty as soldiers is to seek any opportunity to return to their own forces. These escape efforts will rarely be successful. However, by requiring the enemy to devote resources to escape prevention, or the recapture of POWs who do escape from a detention facility, the POW is fulfilling his or her duty to contribute to the war effort. The GPW anticipates these escape efforts and provides a number of protections applicable to POWs who engage in such efforts, whether successful or unsuccessful. The detaining power may use force to thwart an escape effort, although the GPW indicates that use of deadly force must be treated as an extreme measure and must be preceded by a warning.[48]

Escape efforts will frequently involve a range of activities that violate the laws of the detaining power. For example, a POW may resort to violence against a camp guard to effectuate an escape, break into private homes to evade discovery and recapture, and steal food and other items needed during the evasion effort. If the POW is recaptured prior to returning to his or her own forces—in other words, if the escape is unsuccessful—the GPW allows the detaining power to use only disciplinary measures, not criminal prosecution, as a punishment tool.[49] This restriction on punishment extends not only to the POW who attempted the escape but to any other POW who assisted in that effort. In contrast, if the escape effort is successful, meaning the POW returns either to his or her own forces or national territory, but is later recaptured, the GPW prohibits any punishment, whether disciplinary or criminal, for offenses committed during the escape.[50] If the POW reaches the territory of a neutral State, that State is obligated to prevent his or her return to his or her own State or armed forces. The GPW indicates that the neutral State must allow the escaped POW to remain at liberty, but may impose an assigned residence as a control measure.

3.5 *Oversight and the protecting power*

All four of the Geneva Conventions include provisions that indicate the drafters recognized that some oversight of Convention implementation would enhance detaining power compliance with Convention obligations. Obviously, individuals detained by the authorities of a State in conflict with their State will not be able to rely on diplomats to intervene when their rights are not respected, as diplomatic relations are normally the first casualty of inter-State conflicts. Accordingly, each of the four Geneva Conventions provides for the appointment of a *protecting power*, ideally a neutral State, which will oversee compliance with the Conventions.[51] The mechanism for selecting a protecting power requires both parties to the armed conflict to agree the neutral State. This has almost never occurred, and as a result the ICRC is normally the entity that will perform the functions of a protecting power (*see* Chapter 11, 5.1: *A compliance gap*). In fact, AP I includes a provision vesting the ICRC with this role whenever the parties to an armed conflict are unable to agree upon a neutral State to act as the protecting power.[52]

In a sense, the protecting power or the ICRC fills the diplomatic vacuum created by the armed conflict, ensuring that an entity other than the detaining power plays some role in overseeing compliance with the Conventions (and customary international law obligations). However, this is not a true diplomatic protection substitute, because the scope of the oversight role extends only to compliance with the Conventions, Protocols, and customary international law related to detention. Nor does the protecting power or ICRC have any authority to compel any action or change of policy by the detaining power. Nonetheless, the right of access to detention facilities, to meet privately with detainees, and the ability to facilitate the provision of aid supplies for detainees all contribute to the effectiveness of this compliance enhancement mechanism. Furthermore, the impact of findings of non-compliance with international legal obligations and recommendations on changes to policies and practices to improve compliance should not be underestimated. While interactions between the detaining power and the protecting power or ICRC are almost always confidential, the ICRC is especially adept at persuading detaining powers to implement practical and feasible measures to enhance the plight of detainees.

The situation for detainees who do not qualify for protection under one of the Geneva Conventions is, as noted above, less defined. Because the entire notion of the unprivileged belligerent as a status distinct from civilian security internee remains highly controversial, the extent of protections applicable to such detainees remains uncertain because of an absence of specific treaty provisions providing for such protections. However, it is beyond dispute that *if* a detainee is designated as an unprivileged belligerent he or she must be treated humanely. This obligation includes many of the most fundamental protections afforded to POWs, RPs, and civilian internees. While discussion of humane treatment tends to focus on protection from physical and psychological abuse, the obligation almost certainly includes providing notice to the ICRC or some other appropriate authority that an individual is detained, and allowing ICRC access to detainees. The primary example of unprivileged belligerent detention in the context of an IAC was the U.S. detention of Taliban captives during the initial stages of the armed conflict with Afghanistan. Although the United States initially resisted allowing ICRC access to the detention facility at Guantanamo Bay, Cuba, it quickly reversed course, and the ICRC has played a consistent role in reviewing detention conditions and recommending improvements.

4 Detention in non-international armed conflicts

During NIACs, it is almost inevitable that State security forces will detain civilians considered a threat to security and/or civilians who are considered unprivileged belligerents by virtue of their membership in an organized non-State armed group. However, because IHL treaties provide only cursory treatment of NIAC detention, there is much more legal uncertainty related to this context of detention. This uncertainty has spurred significant efforts by both States and organizations, such as the ICRC, to identify both customary international law rules applicable to NIAC detention and best practices that States and non-State armed groups should follow to ensure respect for fundamental humanitarian principles.[53] This effort has yielded some consensus on basic procedural requirements. These sources provide an increasingly accepted baseline of rules related to the treatment of detainees, although the legal authority for detention itself remains a source of significant uncertainty (*see* Chapter 11, 5.2: *A new compliance mechanism?*).

4.1 The need and authority to detain

Detaining captured members of enemy belligerent groups during any armed conflict is operationally logical; no military commander would understand the logic in a requirement to release the fighters that form the forces of his or her enemy once they have been incapacitated by capture. The GPW recognizes this necessity in the context of IACs, and expressly provides the necessary authority to intern POWs until the termination of hostilities. Civilians, in contrast, are as noted above presumptively immune from military detention. However, when a civilian engages in activities that threaten the security of a commander's forces, it is equally logical that some restriction on that civilian may be justified, which may include detention. The GC recognizes this necessity and also provides express internment authority for such civilians in the context of an IAC.[54]

Operationally, there is no logical reason why these same necessities would not extend to NIACs when State security forces capture members of organized enemy armed groups and civilians whose conduct indicates they represent a threat to the security of a commander's forces. However, unlike the IAC context, neither the Geneva Conventions nor AP II—the treaty adopted to supplement the very limited Geneva Convention treatment of NIACs—provide express detention authority. As a result, States that have implemented detention operations in NIACs have relied on a number of theories to justify their actions as consistent with international law. Three of these theories will be outlined below.

An important threshold question, however, is *who* is being detained in NIAC? When a State engages in an armed conflict with an organized armed non-State group, is it a contest between regular armed forces and civilians who are engaged in conduct that threatens the security of the State? Or is it a contest between two belligerent groups, one formed under the authority of the State and acting with the legal sanction of the State, the other formed without any legal authority and therefore acting with no legal privilege?

4.2 Sources of authority

The starting point for understanding NIAC detention is the law applicable to NIAC. As noted in Chapter 1, unlike the extensive treaty regime applicable to IACs, only a small number of treaty provisions apply to NIACs. The first of these provisions is Common Article 3 of the four Geneva Conventions. Common Article 3 is limited in the sense that it is only one Article, but not in the sense of its importance. This first treaty foray into the NIAC domain was profoundly significant, for it mandated the humane treatment of any individual not actively participating in hostilities, to include those rendered *hors de combat* (out of action) as the result of wounds, sickness, *or capture*.[55] Common Article 3 then enumerated a non-exclusive list of especially significant aspects of this humane treatment obligation, including a categorical prohibition against murder, summary execution, group punishment, torture, and cruel, inhuman, or degrading treatment.[56]

The 1977 AP II evolved from an effort to substantially supplement NIAC treaty law. This treaty adds flesh to the proverbial bones of Common Article 3, focused almost exclusively on the humanitarian treatment of those negatively impacted by NIACs. However, the treaty also includes several provisions regulating the use of force during NIACs in order to mitigate risk to the civilian population. Article 5 of AP II specifically addresses "Persons Whose Liberty has been Restricted" and provides:

1. In addition to the provisions of Article 4, the following provisions shall be respected as a minimum with regard to persons deprived of their liberty for reasons related to the armed conflict, whether they are interned or detained:
    (a) the wounded and the sick shall be treated in accordance with Article 7;
    (b) the persons referred to in this paragraph shall, to the same extent as the local civilian population, be provided with food and drinking water and be afforded safeguards as regards health and hygiene and protection against the rigours of the climate and the dangers of the armed conflict;

    (c) they shall be allowed to receive individual or collective relief;

    (d) they shall be allowed to practise their religion and, if requested and appropriate, to receive spiritual assistance from persons, such as chaplains, performing religious functions;

    (e) they shall, if made to work, have the benefit of working conditions and safeguards similar to those enjoyed by the local civilian population.

2.   Those who are responsible for the internment or detention of the persons referred to in paragraph 1 shall also, within the limits of their capabilities, respect the following provisions relating to such persons:

    (a) except when men and women of a family are accommodated together, women shall be held in quarters separated from those of men and shall be under the immediate supervision of women;

    (b) they shall be allowed to send and receive letters and cards, the number of which may be limited by competent authority if it deems necessary;

    (c) places of internment and detention shall not be located close to the combat zone. The persons referred to in paragraph 1 shall be evacuated when the places where they are interned or detained become particularly exposed to danger arising out of the armed conflict, if their evacuation can be carried out under adequate conditions of safety;

    (d) they shall have the benefit of medical examinations;

    (e) their physical or mental health and integrity shall not be endangered by any unjustified act or omission. Accordingly, it is prohibited to subject the persons described in this Article to any medical procedure which is not indicated by the state of health of the person concerned, and which is not consistent with the generally accepted medical standards applied to free persons under similar medical circumstances.

3.   Persons who are not covered by paragraph 1 but whose liberty has been restricted in any way whatsoever for reasons related to the armed conflict shall be treated humanely in accordance with Article 4 and with paragraphs 1 a), c) and d), and 2 b) of this Article.

4.   If it is decided to release persons deprived of their liberty, necessary measures to ensure their safety shall be taken by those so deciding.[57]

Although AP II significantly expanded the treaty regulation of NIACs, its scope of application may at times be more limited than Common Article 3. Common Article 3 applies to any armed conflict not of an international character. Accordingly, so long as a situation qualifies as an armed conflict, and it is not an armed conflict between two or more States, Common Article 3 is applicable. In contrast, Article 1 of AP II, which defines when the treaty applies, provides that it applies to armed conflicts that take place in the territory of a High Contracting Party between its armed forces and dissident armed forces or other organized armed groups which, *under responsible command, exercise such control over a part of its territory as to enable them to carry out sustained and concerted military operations and to implement this Protocol.*[58]

The italicized requirements indicate that there may be NIACs that fall within the scope of Common Article 3 that do not fall within the scope of AP II.

Some States considered this inclusion of a two-tier NIAC applicability equation inconsistent with the humanitarian objectives of AP II. For example, when President Reagan submitted AP II to the Senate for advice and consent, he indicated that the United States did not agree with Article 1 and would therefore apply AP II to any armed conflict falling within the scope of Common Article 3.[59] Although the United States has yet to ratify AP II, both President Clinton and President Obama expressed similar support for AP II.[60]

4.3 Customary incident of any armed conflict?

One theory to legally justify NIAC detention is that the capture and detention of enemy belligerent forces for the duration of hostilities is a fundamental and necessary incident of waging war recognized by customary international law. This theory depends on two underlying assumptions: first, that members of non-State organized armed groups engaged in NIACs are unprivileged belligerents for purposes of attack and detention authority; second, customary international law includes not only obligations related to the treatment of such detainees, but also an implicit affirmative authority to detain. Both of these assumptions are controversial.

Some States interpret Common Article 3 as an implicit recognition that customary international law authorizes parties to a NIAC to not only capture, but also detain opponents. Why else would the Article address the treatment of individuals who are captured and detained? However, it is clear that no such authority is expressly provided by Common Article 3. Accordingly, other States and many experts reject the notion that Common Article 3 provides an implicit source, or even recognition of detention authority. According to this view, Common Article 3 is purely humanitarian, recognizing that detention may occur, but agnostic on whether it is legally authorized. At best, the drafters of Common Article 3 anticipated that insurgents and rebel fighters would be detained pursuant to the domestic legal authority of the State engaged in the NIAC, and exclusively focused on the treatment of such detainees, not the legal basis for the detention.

This issue generated two disparate and important judicial interpretations of detention authority. In 2004, in *Hamdi v. Rumsfeld*, the U.S. Supreme Court considered a challenge by a U.S. citizen to his detention based on an executive branch determination that he was an unlawful enemy combatant.[61] A key component of Hamdi's argument was that his detention without charge or trial violated due process because it was without legal authority. This required the court to address a key question: what is the authority to detain an enemy combatant during armed conflict? The court focused on the 2001 statutory Authorization for the Use of Military Force enacted by Congress in response to the September 11 terrorist attacks, which authorized the president to use "all necessary and appropriate force" in response to the attacks. This necessitated analysis of whether detention of captured enemy personnel fall within the scope of this statutory authorization. Relying on a World War II precedent that involved the detention and military trial of captured German saboteurs, a majority of members of the court concluded that the capture and detention of enemy combatants was a necessary incident of waging war and therefore fell within the scope of the statutory authority granted by Congress to the president.[62] Accordingly, that statute, as informed by the laws and customs of war, provided substantive legal authority for Hamdi's detention.

Concededly, this opinion reflects only the U.S. interpretation that the principle of military necessity authorizes the detention of enemy belligerents, whether privileged (POWs) or unprivileged (members of non-State organized armed groups). However, its broader significance is that it reflects the detention authority consequence of characterizing civilians who become members of organized armed groups as unprivileged belligerents. This is also reflected in the following excerpt from the U.S. *DoD Law of War Manual*:

> The authority to detain is often understood as an incident to more general authorities because detention is fundamental to waging war or conducting other military operations (e.g., noncombatant evacuation operations, peace-keeping operations). Detention operations may be militarily necessary to achieve the object of those operations. In addition, the right to use force in self-defense during such operations includes at least a limited right to detain for security reasons. In fact, it may be inhumane to conduct military operations without some provision for those who are detained incident to the operations (e.g., being prepared to conduct detention operations, and provision for transfer of captured persons to coalition partners who are conducting humane detention operations).[63]

A contrasting view of unprivileged belligerent detention authority was relied on in the initial court of appeals decision in the UK case of *Serdar Mohammed v. Ministry of Defence*. Mohammed was an Afghan national detained by UK armed forces in Afghanistan based on the determination following his capture that he was a member of the Taliban insurgent forces. He subsequently sued the UK government alleging his detention violated the UK international human rights obligation prohibiting arbitrary deprivation of liberty. Mohammed's theory was that his detention was without legal authority because there was no statute or treaty that authorized detention of unprivileged belligerents in NIAC. The UK government responded with two primary arguments. First, it asserted the same theory relied on by the *Hamdi* Court to conclude Hamdi's detention was legally authorized: that the customary IHL principle of military necessity provided sufficient detention authority. Second, it asserted that by providing for the protection of detainees during NIAC, Common Article 3 implicitly authorized unprivileged belligerent detention.

The initial court of appeals opinion in this case rejected both these arguments and ruled in Mohammed's favor. The court concluded that invoking Common Article 3 as a source of detention authority fundamentally distorted its purpose, which was purely humanitarian.64 According to the court, all Common Article 3 indicates is that the drafters anticipated detention of non-state belligerents *would* be legally authorized by states engaged in armed conflict with such groups. The court also rejected the military necessity argument, concluding that while military necessity may authorize the initiate *capture* of an enemy belligerent during a NIAC, it does not follow that his or her subsequent detention is also authorized by this customary IHL principle. Instead, the court concluded that detention beyond that associated with the initial capture necessitated positive legal authority: either a statute authorizing detention, or a treaty provision provides express detention authority. Because Mohammed's detention could not be based on any such source of express legal authority, it was arbitrary and therefore violated his human rights. An appeals court subsequently upheld the decision, prompting the UK Defence Secretary Michael Fallon to declare the finding fundamentally flawed with no legal basis.

The UK Supreme Court subsequently reversed this decision, but on different grounds. Specifically, the Court concluded that the detention was authorized pursuant to resolutions adopted by the United Nations Security Council. Interestingly, regarding the authority to detain there was an indication that while a significant number of states, including the United Kingdom, did not recognize a customary law basis for such action, it is a rule that might eventually reach that stage. What the Court's treatment of the authority to detain issue, including reference to the *Hamdi* decision and an ICRC recognition that detention is a reality of armed conflict, does highlight is that the 'positivist' approach taken by the appeals court is far from universally endorsed.

Because it is unlikely that a treaty will be adopted to squarely address this vexing issue, different States will continue to march to different legal drums on this issue. Those like the United Kingdom that can no longer rely on customary IHL as a source of unprivileged detention authority will be compelled to either adopt wartime detention statutes or turn detainees over to host nation authorities when they provide support to beleaguered governments fighting non-State enemies. This latter approach raises its own potential dilemmas, notably when the capturing force has reason to believe that if turned over to host nation authorities, the captive will be subjected to human rights violations. How such a conflict between the limits on detention authority and human rights obligations will be resolved in the future is unclear. For those like the United States, customary IHL may provide a wider range of detention options, as there will be no perceived obligation to turn captured enemy fighters over to host nation authorities.

4.4   *Non-international armed conflict detention and humanitarian protection*

While controversy exists as to the status of captured non-State belligerent operatives, and the source of authority for detaining such captives, detention is an undeniable reality of NIACs. Beneath the level of status and authority is, therefore, the critical issue of detainee treatment. Like POWs, detention of such captives raises important humanitarian considerations, because, like their privileged belligerent/POW counterparts, their detention is justified purely as a preventive measure to keep them from returning to hostilities and not by punitive considerations. However, unlike their POW counterparts, the humanitarian obligations that extend to such detainees are much more general. This has resulted in substantial efforts by States engaged in detention operations, and humanitarian organizations devoted to enhancing the protection of detainees, to propose measures to add flesh to the bones of IHL rules applicable to NIAC detention. These efforts have focused on two principal issues: procedures for assessing a captive's status, and the rights that should be afforded to detainees during their detention.

4.5   *Detention review process*

Nothing in Common Article 3 or AP II requires implementation of review procedures to validate the justification for detention during NIAC. This may be explained by the fact that, prior to the response to the terror attacks of 11 September 2001, it was generally assumed that NIAC was synonymous with internal armed conflict. As a result, these treaty provisions may have been framed by an expectation that States engaged in NIACs would enact domestic legislation to authorize detention, and include in that legislation procedures for detention.

Whatever the explanation, this absence of a treaty-imposed detention review requirement and accordant procedures has led to disparate approaches to this issue. However, there seems to be increasing consensus among States and humanitarian law experts that the same type of minimal process is required to validate detention during NIAC that was implemented by the United States for alleged unprivileged belligerent members of the Taliban. This is best reflected in the work of what known as the Copenhagen Process, an effort to identify best practices for detention operations across the spectrum of conflict.[65]

As noted above, U.S. detention process evolved substantially in response to the decision in *Hamdi v. Rumsfeld*. This practice also suggests an increasing consensus that all armed conflict detention necessitates some minimal procedural review mechanism. The CSRT, initially implemented only at the detention facility in Guantanamo, served as the model for similar procedures implemented by the United States at its detention facility in Afghanistan.[66] This process was utilized to review the status and validate the justification for unprivileged belligerent detentions during that long lasting NIAC. In fact, similar procedures were implemented even prior to 11 September 2001, during non-conflict military operations other than war in Kosovo. Israel has adopted a similar approach to belligerent detention in NIAC.[67] All of this points to the same conclusion— procedures to ensure that detainees are provided notice for the basis of detention, and a meaningful opportunity to contest their detention before a neutral decision-maker, seem to be justifiably considered essential elements of the humane treatment of detainees.

The permissible duration of detention during NIAC is an equally complex question. U.S. practice has been to adopt a hybrid approach for unprivileged belligerents: detain them based on the determination of this status, but conduct annual reviews to assess whether necessity for detention continues to exist (a review process derived from civilian security internment rules). Perhaps the most logical way to approach this issue is to view belligerent status determination as triggering a presumptive authority to detain for the duration of the NIAC hostilities. However, because NIACs tend to last far longer than IACs, this presumption should be periodically assessed, with release justified when the detaining power concludes that there is little to no risk that a detainee will return to hostilities if released. This is the current approach used by the United States.

4.6 Detainee treatment

Fundamentally, NIAC detention, like all other armed conflict justified detention, must be understood as preventive and non-punitive. Accordingly, conditions of detention during NIAC must comply with the humane treatment obligation of Common Article 3 and, at least as a matter of customary international law, the more defined obligations of Article 4 of AP II. As a practical matter, almost all of the basic rights and protections afforded to POWs should be extended to NIAC detainees. First and foremost, all detainees must be respected and protected, as explained above. More specifically, humane treatment should be understood to include, at a minimum: removal from the area of immediate combat; provision of essential food, hydration, shelter, and medical care; accommodation of religious preferences; communication with the ICRC or other impartial relief organization; access to humanitarian aid; and opportunity to communicate with the outside world (subject to security oversight).

Unfortunately, reality often fails to align with these minimal expectations. Nonetheless, those responsible for conducting detention operations must be cognizant of these obligations, and that how detainees are treated during armed conflict is often indicative of the overall commitment, or lack thereof, to humanitarian obligations. Detention is almost always a necessary aspect of conducting operations during NIAC, and these rules must form the foundation of any legitimate and humane detention program.

5 Conclusion

Detention of captured enemy personnel and civilians who pose a genuine threat to the security of an armed force is, as the U.S. Supreme Court noted in *Hamdi v. Rumsfeld*, "a fundamental incident of waging war."[68] But how detainees are treated is also one of the most important indicators of respect for IHL. For some detainees, like POWs, the law provides a comprehensive framework for ensuring fair and humane treatment. For others, like those designated as unprivileged belligerents—whether in IACs or NIACs—the law is less defined. Nonetheless, humane treatment is a uniform foundation that must guide the planning and implementation of all detention operations. This increasingly means procedures and standards that seem almost identical to those applicable to POWs. However, issues like combatant immunity, duration of detention, and the role of courts in reviewing detention remain subject to rules that are in substantial flux and constantly evolving. Ultimately, however, when soldiers are trained to treat those at their mercy as fellow human beings, and not as the objects of revenge or animus, humanity will be well served.

Notes

1 Geneva Convention Relative to the Treatment of Prisoners of War, 12 August 1949, 6 U.S.T. 3316, 75 U.N.T.S. 972 [hereinafter GPW].
2 Geneva Convention Relative to the Protection of Civilian Persons in Time of War, 12 August 1949, 6 U.S.T. 3516, 75 U.N.T.S. 973 [hereinafter GC].
3 GPW, Art 4.
4 Protocol (I) Additional to the Geneva Conventions of 12 August 1949, and Relating to the Protection of Victims of International Armed Conflicts, 8 June 1977, 1125 U.N.T.S. 3 [hereinafter AP I] (entered into force 7 December 1978) (signed by the United States 12 December 1977, not transmitted to U.S. Senate, *see* S. Treaty Doc. No. 100–2 (1987)).
5 GPW, Art 4(A)(1).
6 *Id*. Art 4(A)(2).
7 Id. Art 4(A)(3); Jean S. Pictet, Geneva Convention Relative to the Treatment of Prisoners of War: Commentary (ICRC, 1960), 61–4 [hereinafter Commentary GPW]. By the end of 1940, almost all the nations of Europe had been defeated by Nazi Germany—some governments formally surrendering (like France); others fled to function in exile. Armed forces from many of these nations chose to continue to resist Germany by allying with the Allied Powers. When these forces were captured—in some cases even by the armed forces of their own nation that complied with surrender terms—they were often denied POW status because the Germans and Axis forces did not consider them to be legitimately fighting on behalf of a State Party.
8 Commentary GPW, 61–4.
9 GPW, Art 4(A)(4)-(5).
10 *Id*. Art 4(A)(4).
11 AP I, Art 43.
12 GPW, 1, Art 4(A)(6).
13 Commentary GPW, 67–8.
14 AP I, Art 43.
15 *Id*. Art 44(1).
16 *Id*. Art 44(3).
17 Ronald Reagan, Letter of Transmittal, The White House, 29 January 1987, *available at* www.loc.gov/rr/frd/Military_Law/pdf/protocol-II-100-2.pdf:

> Protocol I is fundamentally and irreconcilably flawed. It contains provisions that would undermine humanitarian law and endanger civilians in war. . . . Another

provision would grant combatant status to irregular forces even if they do not satisfy the traditional requirements to distinguish themselves from the civilian population and otherwise comply with the laws of war. This would endanger civilians among whom terrorists and other irregulars attempt to conceal themselves. These problems are so fundamental in character that they cannot be remedied through reservations, and I therefore have decided not to submit the Protocol to the Senate in any form, and I would invite an expression of the sense of the Senate that it shares this view.

18 AP I, Art 44(7).
19 *Id.* Art 1.
20 Ronald Reagan, Letter of Transmittal, The White House, 29 January 1987, *available at* www.loc.gov/rr/frd/Military_Law/pdf/protocol-II-100-2.pdf:

> Protocol I is fundamentally and irreconcilably flawed. It contains provisions that would undermine humanitarian law and endanger civilians in war. One of its provisions, for example, would automatically treat as an international conflict any so-called "war of national liberation." Whether such wars are international or non-international should turn exclusively on objective reality, not on one's view of the moral qualities of each conflict. To rest on such subjective distinctions based on a war's alleged purposes would politicize humanitarian law and eliminate the distinction between international and non-international conflicts. It would give special status to "wars of national liberation," an ill-defined concept expressed in vague, subjective, politicized terminology.

21 GPW, Art 5.
22 Memorandum from George W. Bush, President, to Richard "Dick" Cheney, Vice President, *Humane Treatment of Taliban and al Qaeda Detainees* (7 February 2002), *available at* www.pegc.us/archive/White_House/bush_memo_20020207_ed.pdf
23 AP I, Art 45.
24 U.S. Dep't of Army, Army Regulation 190-8: Enemy Prisoners of War, Retained Personnel, Civilian Internees and Other Detainees 2 (1 October 1997).
25 Geneva Convention for the Amelioration of the Condition of the Wounded and Sick in Armed Forces in the Field, 12 August 1949, 6 U.S.T. 3114, 75 U.N.T.S. 970 [hereinafter GWS]; Geneva Convention for the Amelioration of the Condition of Wounded, Sick, and Shipwrecked Members of the Armed Forces at Sea, 12 August 1949, 6 U.S.T. 3217, 75 U.N.T.S. 971 [hereinafter GWS-Sea].
26 AP I, Art 50.
27 *See* GC.
28 U.S. Dep't of Def., *Law of War Manual* 4.3 (June 2015, updated December 2016) [hereinafter *DoD Law of War Manual*].
29 AP Commentary, para 3031.
30 *See, e.g.,* Paul Wolfowitz, Deputy Secretary of Defense, Order Establishing Combatant Status Review Tribunal, 7 July 2004, as amended 2006 (establishing an administrative process to review the detention of foreign nationals held as enemy combatants at Guantanamo Bay, Cuba).
31 *See* Jeff Bovarnick, *Detainee Review Boards in Afghanistan: From Strategic Liability to Legitimacy,* Army Law, June 2012, at 9, 12–20.
32 *See* Dvir Saar & Ben Wahlhaus, *Preventive Detention for National Security Purposes— the Israeli Experience,* JNSLP (forthcoming).
33 GPW, Arts 118–19.
34 *DoD Law of War Manual,* 4.19.
35 *United States v. Noriega,* 808 F. Supp. 791, 794–6 (S.D. Fla. 1992).
36 GPW, Art 83.
37 *See Id.* Ch. III.

38 AP I, Art 75.
39 Pictet et al., Commentary on the Additional Protocols of 8 June 1977 to the Geneva Conventions of 12 August 1949 (ICRC, 1987), para 3001.
40 Exec. Order No. 13,567, 76 Fed. Reg. 47 (7 March 2011); Press Release, White House Office of the Press Sec'y, *Fact Sheet: New Actions on Guantanamo and Detainee Policy* (7 March 2011), *available at* www.whitehouse.gov/the-press-office/2011/03/07/fact-sheet-new-actions-guant-namo-and-detainee-policy ("The U.S. Government will therefore choose out of a sense of legal obligation to treat the principles set forth in Article 75 as applicable to any individual it detains in an international armed conflict").
41 AP I, Art 75.
42 GPW, Art 17.
43 GWS, Art 12.
44 GPW, Arts 69–70.
45 *See Id.* Art 71.
46 *See Id.* Arts 49–57.
47 GC, Art 95.
48 GPW, Art 42.
49 *Id.* Art 92.
50 *Id.* Art 91.
51 GWS, Art 8; GWS-Sea, Art 8; GPW, Art 8; GC, Art 9.
52 AP I, Art 5.
53 *See* ICRC, *Strengthening Legal Protection for Victims of Armed Conflicts*, report prepared by the ICRC for the 31st Int'l Conf. of the Red Cross and Red Crescent in Geneva, Switzerland (October 2011); *Strengthening IHL Protecting Persons Deprived of Their Liberty in Relation to Armed Conflict*, ICRC (1 April 2017), *available at* https://ihl-databases.icrc.org/applic/ihl/ihl.nsf/vwTreatiesByCountry.xsp. Resolution 1 of the 31st International Conference of the Red Cross and Red Crescent prompted numerous consolations between the ICRC, States, and experts, and ultimately led to Resolution 1 of the 32nd Conference. This Resolution recommended a State-led, ICRC-supported effort toward the production of concrete, implementable, and non-legally binding outcomes aimed at strengthening IHL protections for persons deprived of their liberty owing to NIAC. Despite strong State engagement and a formal meeting attended by over 90 States, no consensus resolution was ultimately adopted. Still, consultation between States, experts, and the ICRC is ongoing, and the formal meeting of States and experts highlighted a number of key issues covered in this section.
54 GC, Art 78.
55 GWS, Art 3; GWS-Sea, Art 3; GPW, Art 3; GC, Art 3 (Article 3 common to all four of the 1949 Geneva Conventions).
56 *Id.*
57 Protocol (II) Additional to the Geneva Conventions of 12 August 1949, and Relating to the Protection of Victims of Non-International Armed Conflicts, Art 5, 8 June 1977, 1125 U.N.T.S. 609 [hereinafter AP II] (entered into force 7 December 1978) (signed by the United States 12 December 1977, transmitted to the U.S. Senate 29 January 1987, still pending action as S. Treaty Doc. No. 100–2 (1987)).
58 *Id.* Art 1 (emphasis added).
59 Ronald Reagan, Letter of Transmittal, The White House, 29 January 1987, *available at* www.loc.gov/rr/frd/Military_Law/pdf/protocol-II-100-2.pdf
60 William J. Clinton, Letter of Transmittal, The White House, 6 January 1999, *available at* www.loc.gov/rr/frd/Military_Law/pdf/GC-message-from-pres-1999.pdf; Press Release, White House Office of the Press Sec'y, *Fact Sheet: New Actions on Guantanamo*

and Detainee Policy (7 March 2011), *available at* www.whitehouse.gov/the-press-office/2011/03/07/fact-sheet-new-actions-guant-namo-and-detainee-policy

61 *See* 542 U.S. 507 (2004).

62 *Id.* at 521.

63 *DoD Law of War Manual*, 8.1.3.1.

64 *See Al-Waheed v. Ministry of Defence; Muhammed v. Ministry of Defence*, paras 12–16, 272–5, [2017] UKSC 2 (Eng.).

65 *The Copenhagen Process: Principles and Guidelines* (18–19 October 2012), *available at* http://um.dk/en/~/media/UM/English-site/Documents/Politics-and-diplomacy/Copenhagen%20Process%20Principles%20and%20Guidlines.pdf (for example, consider Principle 5: "Detaining authorities should develop and implement standard operating procedures and other relevant guidance regarding the handling of detainees.").

66 *See* Bovarnick, *Detainee Review Boards in Afghanistan: From Strategic Liability to Legitimacy*, Army Law, June 2012, at 9. *See also* Bovarnick, "Detention Operations at the Tactical and Operational Level," in Geoffrey S. Corn et al., *U.S. Military Operations: Law, Policy, and Practice* 307–40 (2016).

67 *See* Saar & Wahlhaus, *Preventive Detention for National Security Purposes—the Israeli Experience*, JNSLP (forthcoming).

68 542 U.S. 507, 521 (2004).

6 Targeting

1 Introduction

Bellum, the Latin word for war, finds its root in the old word *duellum*. This in turn was based on Cicero's definition that war was a contending by force.[1] It is the use of force that is at the heart of the analysis of the law of targeting. The potential for tremendous death and destruction to be caused by the use of military force, particularly among the civilian population, has resulted in targeting law taking on a particular importance. The attention paid to targeting is elevated not only in terms of potential criminal liability, but also in the public discourse regarding the scope and morality of warfare. It has been defined as follows:

> [T]argeting is a broad process encompassing, planning and execution, including the consideration of prospective targets of attack, the accumulation of information to determine whether the attack of a particular object, person, or group of persons will meet military, legal, and other requirements, the determination which weapon and method should be used to prosecute the target, the carrying out of attacks, including those decided upon at short notice and with minimal opportunity for planning, and other associated activities.[2]

As is highlighted in this definition, targeting is a broad concept that will be dealt with in this chapter in six parts. Notably, it is a process that "involves not only the selection of targets, but also the exercise of judgment including the consideration of operational factors in order to bring about a desired result."[3]

Following this introduction, the second part will provide an outline of the main treaty and customary law applicable to targeting. The third part will focus on the targeting of people. The analysis will expand on concepts introduced in Chapter 3 by exploring in greater detail the idea of direct participation in hostilities, and what this means for civilians who engage in hostilities, either as individuals or members of an organized armed group. The fourth part will look at the targeting of objects, with emphasis being placed on the criteria that make what are ordinarily civilian objects targetable as military objectives, and will then explore the application of the targeting precautions and the concept of excessive collateral casualties, or damage. The assessment of the collateral effects is often referred to as the proportionality test. This analysis looks not only at the treaty-based rules but also canvasses some of the judicial treatment of this subject. Finally, the fifth part will deal with miscellaneous issues associated with the use of force and targeting involving the use of drones, rules of engagement, and investigations.

2　The law of targeting

The genesis of targeting law can be traced back to the mid-nineteenth-century efforts to limit the effects of war brought on by the increasing destructive power of States.[4] Given the importance IHL places on mitigating the risk to non-combatants resulting from conflict, it should come as no surprise that the principle of distinction—which allows attacks only when directed at lawful targets—has always been a fundamental tenet of the law of targeting. As was first reflected in the 1863 Lieber Code, there has been, over the course of the past 150 years, a requirement to direct military force at the opposing military forces.[5] The clearest expression of the law governing targeting can be found in the 1977 AP I.[6]

AP I refers to the principle of distinction[7] and the obligation to protect the civilian population and individual civilians against the dangers arising from military operations (*see* Chapter 3: *The status of individuals in armed conflict*).[8] Specific protection is provided to civilians. Article 51(2) states:

> The civilian population as such, as well as individual civilians, shall not be the object of attack. Acts or threats of violence the primary purpose of which is to spread terror among the civilian population are prohibited.

Further, "[a]ttacks against the civilian population or civilians by way of reprisals are prohibited."[9] If an attack is carried out indiscriminately, the attacker violates IHL.[10]

Similarly, Article 52(1) indicates that "[c]ivilian objects shall not be the object of attack or of reprisals." Importantly, Article 52(2) states that "[a]ttacks shall be limited strictly to military objectives,"[11] with such objectives being either persons, or objects.[12] A military object is defined as follows:

> In so far as objects are concerned, military objectives are limited to those objects which by their nature, location, purpose or use make an effective contribution to military action and whose total or partial destruction, capture or neutralization, in the circumstances ruling at the time, offers a definite military advantage.[13]

The most obvious military objects are military equipment, barracks, and weapons of war. However, as will be discussed, any object by its *nature, location, purpose,* or *use* may become a lawful military objective subject to attack.

In cases of doubt, a "person shall be considered to be a civilian";[14] while, for objects, if there is doubt that an object normally dedicated to civilian purposes "is being used to make an effective contribution to military action, it shall be presumed not to be so used."[15] Examples of objects dedicated to civilian purposes are "a place of worship, a house or other dwelling or a school."[16] However, the test for targeting is *not any doubt*, or a *reasonable doubt*. Rather, it is one of a having a *reasonable belief* (also called an *honest belief*) that the target was a lawful military objective. The test of reasonable belief when using force is the same whether considered under IHL,[17] or IHRL.[18]

As Article 57(1) sets out, "[i]n the conduct of military operations, constant care shall be taken to spare the civilian population, civilians and civilian objects." AP I also codifies the historical ust ar doctrine of *double effect*. Under that theory, it is permissible to carry out an act with evil consequences if four conditions are met: the act must good in itself or at least indifferent; the direct effect has to be morally acceptable; "the intention of the actor is a good one and the evil effect is not one of the ends or a means to an end; and the 'good effect' is sufficiently good to compensate for any evil outcome."[19] In the Protocol, this theory is reflected in the precautions outlined in Article 57(2)(iii):

2. With respect to attacks, the following precautions shall be taken:
    (*a*) those who plan or decide upon an attack shall:
    (i)   do everything feasible to verify that the objectives to be attacked are neither civilians nor civilian objects and are not subject to special protection but are military objectives within the meaning of paragraph 2 of Article 52 and that it is not prohibited by the provisions of this Protocol to attack them;
    (ii) take all feasible precautions in the choice of means and methods of attack with a view to avoiding, and in any event to minimizing, incidental loss or civilian life, injury to civilians and damage to civilian objects;
    (iii) refrain from deciding to launch any attack which may be expected to cause incidental loss of civilian life, injury to civilians, damage to civilian objects, or a combination thereof, which would be excessive in relation to the concrete and direct military advantage anticipated;

Article 57 also requires that an attack be canceled or suspended if it becomes apparent the objective is not a military one, or that there will be excessive collateral effects.[20] There is also a requirement, unless the circumstances do not permit, to give effective advance warning of attacks that may affect the civilian population.[21] Further, Article 58 of AP I requires that, to the maximum extent feasible, civilians and civilian objects under their control be removed from the vicinity of military operations; military objectives not be located within or near densely populated areas; and other necessary precautions be taken to protect civilians and civilian objects from the dangers of military operations.

The question remains regarding the extent to which the rules governing targeting set out in AP I apply to States not bound by that treaty, and what rules apply during NIACs. The answer lies in the customary law status of these targeting rules. For example, the ICTY determined in *Prosecutor v. Kupreškić* that there was a customary international law requirement in both IAC and NIAC to verify a target was a military objective, and that "attacks, even when they are directed against legitimate military targets, are unlawful if conducted using indiscriminate means or methods of warfare, or in such a way as to cause indiscriminate damage to civilians."[22] Further, "[t]hese principles have to some extent been spelled out in Articles 57 and 58 of the First Additional Protocol of 1977."[23] The customary status of these rules for the United States, which is not bound by the Additional Protocols, was confirmed by Brian Egan, the U.S. Department of State Legal Advisor. In a 2016 presentation made to the American Society of International Law, he outlined principles governing targeting during NIACs that reflected those found in AP I.[24]

3   Targeting persons

It is completely logical that IHL makes a distinction between targeting people and objects. In this respect, the law reflects the importance that is placed on the right to life even in times of armed conflict. As was stated in the *Prosecutor v. Delalic* appeal decision, humanitarian law and human rights law "share a common 'core' of fundamental standards which are applicable at all times, in all circumstances and to all parties, and from which no derogation is permitted."[25] What is different between humanitarian and human rights law is the focus on status-based targeting. Humanitarian law permits the killing of members of opposing forces because of their status as a member of a group, be it in the armed forces of a State or an organized armed group fighting on behalf of a non-State actor or a State. In contrast, human rights law individualizes the targeting decision. That is not to say that all targeting during armed conflict is status-based. Individual civilians may also be targeted "for such time as they take a direct part in hostilities."[26]

The key phrase for targeting persons is their taking "a direct part in hostilities." Members of the armed forces have a right to "participate directly in hostilities,"[27] while civilians lose the protection associated with their status "unless and for such time" as they take such a part (*see* Chapter 3, 2.1.3: *Additional Protocol I*).[28] Accordingly, civilians are *presumptively*, although not *conclusively*, protected from deliberate attack. That presumptive protection is forfeited when they take a direct part in hostilities. Such participation can be status-related because they are members of an organized armed group, or separately based on a civilian's individual acts. This can occur regardless of whether such participation occurs on behalf of a State or a non-State actor. While membership in an organized armed group is thought of most often in terms of non-State actors (e.g., Hezbollah, the Islamic State, FARC), it might also extend to the State employment of paramilitary units that may not meet the requirements of lawful combatancy. Individual contractors and civilians accompanying the armed forces may also end up taking a direct part in hostilities. Similarly, non-State actors may periodically use civilians on an individual basis to carry out a variety of activities that directly support hostilities (e.g., intelligence gathering, logistics functions) and which are traditionally viewed as directly participating in hostilities.

The issue of who might constitute a lawful target under the direct participation in hostilities test was first substantively dealt with by the Israeli Supreme Court in a 2006 decision, which is now widely referred to as the *Targeted Killing Case*.[29] This case provided judicial recognition of the concept that a civilian is targetable as long as that person performs the *function* of a combatant.[30] The function performed determined the directness of the participation in hostilities. Examples of identified combatant functions included the gathering of intelligence;

> a person who transports unlawful combatants to or from the place where the hostilities are taking place; [and] a person who operates weapons which unlawful combatants use, or supervises their operation, or provides service to them, be the distance from the battlefield as it may.[31]

However, direct participation was not seen to include selling food and medicine, providing general strategic analysis, or general logistical support and monetary aid. For example, it would not include workers in an armaments factory.[32]

Subsequently, the ICRC issued own its Interpretive Guidance on the Notion of Direct Participation in Hostilities under International Humanitarian Law,[33] which solidified a general, if not unanimous, consensus that members of an organized armed group may be targeted based on their membership status.[34] A further helpful aspect of the Interpretive Guidance is the identification of three cumulative requirements for direct participation in hostilities: (1) a threshold of harm; (2) a direct causal link between the act carried out and the harm likely to result; and (3) a belligerent nexus such that the acts are likely to inflict the harm, and specifically designed to do so in support of a party to an armed conflict and to the detriment of another.[35] The ICRC study also adopted a number of new concepts in an effort to limit the size of the group against which targeting could be carried out. These included the notion of a *continuous combat function*, a *revolving door* of protection for periodic participants, and a *one causal step* limitation for determining when an act results in harm.[36]

Of particular note in the view of the ICRC, continuous combat function did not include "recruiters, trainers, financiers and propagandists" or persons "purchasing, smuggling, manufacturing and maintaining of weapons and other equipment outside specific military operations or to the collection of intelligence other than of a tactical nature."[37] Similarly, persons charged with the assembly and storing of an improvised explosive device (IED) in a workshop, or the purchase or smuggling of its components, were not seen as direct participants in hostilities.[38] While some of these functions would also not meet the combat function test under the *Targeted Killing Case*, the Interpretive Guidance would also exclude certain logistics functions that are frequently viewed as being integral to the conduct of military operations. For example, al Qaeda doctrine provides for a logistics element of two to four individuals, operating as part of small independent units operating in urban spaces, "to supply everything that the other units need in terms of weapons, tools, equipment, documents, safe houses, vehicles, etc."[39] The Interpretive Guidance has received some support on this issue. It has though been criticized because of these restrictive criteria used to determine membership, as well as for its introduction of rights-based law enforcement norms into interpretations of humanitarian law under defined operational situations. This latter approach promotes consideration of capture before killing an enemy.[40]

In contrast, it has been suggested that a number of States have a shared sense that "combat support and combat service support functions if performed for a regularly constituted armed force and carrying arms openly, exercising command over the group or one of its units, or conducting planning related to the conduct of hostilities" provide a more useful basis upon which to determine membership in an organized armed group.[41] Targeting would extend to persons carrying out certain logistics functions.[42] The approach adopted by the United States reflects this broader and reciprocal notion of direct participation in hostilities, including "whether the individual performs functions for the benefit of the group that are analogous to those traditionally performed by members of State militaries that are liable to attack."[43] As has been suggested, "this is an unresolved area of the law that is playing itself out on the modern battlefield."[44]

The criteria that are applied to determine what constitutes direct participation in hostilities is critical in terms of potential legal liability, as that term can form the basis for allegations of unlawful killing under international law by members both of State armed forces and organized armed groups.[45] However, it is important to recall that, even if unprivileged belligerents only kill persons taking a direct part in hostilities (in other words, the act of killing is consistent with IHL), they remain liable to prosecution for that act under the laws of a capturing State. Since the unprivileged belligerent directly participates in hostilities, he or she becomes a lawful object of attack pursuant to IHL. This means a member of State armed forces would be immune from criminal sanction for attacking such an individual, by either operation of combatant immunity (during an IAC) or State immunity (during a NIAC).

4 Targeting objects

4.1 Military objects

Objects that qualify as military objectives form a much broader category than people. The narrower justification for targeting people, including civilians who take a direct part in hostilities, reflects the importance that international law places on the right to life even in the context of armed conflict. As has been noted, the definition of military objects set out in Article 52(2) of AP I is recognized as reflecting customary international law. For an object to be become a military objective, it must contribute effectively to military action, and its destruction, capture, or neutralization must offer a definite military advantage in the circumstances ruling at the time of the attack decision.[46] There continues to be ongoing debate about the breadth of the various criteria set out in Article 52(2): an object's nature, location, purpose, or use; the scope of military action; and what constitutes a military advantage.

One area of disagreement is whether Article 52(2) is too abstract, while the development of lists of target types "is liable to cause confusion or to result in apparent arbitrariness."[47] A practical way identified to approach the issue of lists is to provide commanders a "composite definition—combining an abstract statement with a non-exhaustive catalogue of concrete illustration."[48] Another area of ongoing discussion about what constitutes a military objective arises as a result of different visions as to whether there must be a direct link to the conduct of hostilities (a tactical approach) or whether attacks can be directed on State infrastructure supporting its military capacity (a strategic approach). This latter approach includes a broader set of targets such as communication lines, war production facilities, oil and petroleum facilities, command and control, and potentially economic activity.

The different approaches can be seen in the interpretation of the *nature* of a military object. The Commentary on the *HPCR Manual on International Law Applicable to Air and Missile Warfare* indicates that nature depends upon having "an inherent characteristic or attribute with contributes to military action."[49] The experts drafting that *Air and Missile Warfare Manual* Commentary agreed in Rule 22(a) that "military aircraft (including military UAV/UCAVs); military vehicles (other than medical transport); missiles and other weapons; military equipment; military fortifications, facilities and depots; warships; ministries of defence and armaments factories" were by nature military objects.[50] However, there was disagreement regarding "factories, lines and means of communications (such as airfields, railway lines, roads, bridges and tunnels); energy producing facilities; oil storage depots; transmission facilities and equipment."[51]

Some experts looked to the criteria of use, purpose, or location to determine whether they were objects subject to attack.[52] The *location* criterion "includes objects which 'have no military function but which, by virtue of their location, make an effective contribution to military action.'"[53] For example, these could include areas of land, or bridges. However, the targeting of bridges has prompted a wide range of views. One approach is that "[a] bridge as a rule, would qualify as a military objective."[54] An alternate view is they can only be targeted when actually being used for military purposes.[55] The *purpose* criterion relates to intended future use, while *use* is connected to its present function.[56] In the *Air and Missile Warfare Manual* Commentary the differing approaches to the nature test were resolved by viewing the objects listed in Rule 22(a) as always constituting military objectives,[57] while those set out in Rule 23 were "objects which become military objectives by nature only in light of the circumstances ruling at the time."[58]

As has been noted, underpinning much of the analysis of targeting objects are competing approaches to interpreting the law governing targeting: the tactical and strategic. An example of the strategic perspective is found in the 1995 *San Remo Manual on International Law Applicable to Armed Conflicts at Sea*, where it is indicated that military objectives "do not require a *direct* connection with combat operations."[59] One expansive interpretation of the by-nature criterion suggests that "[i]ndustrial plants (even when privately owned) engaged in the manufacture of arms, munitions, military supplies and essential parts for military vehicles, vessels and aircraft" can be military objectives. Further, "[a]ll in all, very few industrial plants can be regarded as strictly civilian by nature and therefore immune from attack."[60] Narrow or broad interpretations will also be seen to be integral to the discussion of military action and military advantage. However, in either case, the criteria applied to persons assessed as direct participants in hostilities results in a much narrower set of potential targets than for military objects under Article 52(2). It must be noted that the result is that in humanitarian law terms people's lives, including those serving for State security forces, are generally privileged over objects.

4.2 *Military action and war sustaining*

One of the tests that must be satisfied is that the object "must contribute effectively to military action."[61] The term *military action* relates to a military engagement.[62] However, as has been noted (*see* Chapter 6, 4.1: *Military objects*), the object itself can have an indirect impact on that action. The question remains as to how broadly or narrowly to interpret what is meant by military action. This is an issue that has become the subject of some controversy due to a U.S. approach that replaces the term *military action*, found in AP I, with the phrase "war fighting or war sustaining capability." Found in numerous U.S. military doctrine manuals, it is also referred to in the Military Commissions Act of 2009.[63] *War fighting* is viewed as meaning the same thing as military action. The term *war sustaining* has its roots in the United States Civil War, with the Union destroying the South's raw cotton on the basis that proceeds of its sale were used to fund the war.

Owing to its broad scope, war sustaining has been criticized as too easily justifying indiscriminate attacks because of the general economic support they gave to the enemy.[64] As is evident in the recognition of naval and air blockades, economic warfare can be a lawful method of degrading the enemy capacity to make war. However, the war-sustaining approach provides a much broader range of targets than might ordinarily be targeted even during a strategic air campaign. It is not that a factory produces something that is used to support military action (e.g., oil, gas, armaments). Rather, it is the financial proceeds from the sale of the industrial output that is said to make the factory a valid target, regardless of what is physically produced or its link to military action. This issue gained some prominence in 2009 regarding the targeting of the drug production and trafficking infrastructure relied on by the Taliban in Afghanistan,[65] and again in 2014 and 2016 in respect of generalized targeting of Islamic State oil production facilities and attacks on money storage depots.[66] It has been suggested that one interpretation of military action is that it is always broad enough to encompass war-sustaining activity.[67] However, as is reflected in the *San Remo Manual*, reliance on war-sustaining criteria has consistently been rejected by most international legal experts.[68] The casual linkage between the object and the military war effort is too indirect.[69]

4.3 Military advantage

A second test to be met in determining if an object is a military objective is whether its "total or partial destruction, capture or neutralization, in the circumstances ruling, at the time offers a *definite military advantage*."[70] The term *military advantage* is also found in the test for assessing whether there has been excessive collateral civilian casualties or damage.[71] In that context, reference is made to a "*concrete and direct military advantage*." This does raise the issue of whether military advantage is to be interpreted the same way in both situations. The AP I Commentary suggests that, for Article 57(2)(iii), "the words 'concrete and direct' impose stricter conditions on the attacker than those implied by the criteria defining military objectives in Article 52."[72] However, another interpretation of the military objective provision suggests that the modifiers are similar as "[t]he thrust is that of 'a concrete and perceptible advantage rather than a hypothetical and speculative one.'"[73]

The lack of clarity concerning these terms is further compounded by there being no historical record of why they were used.[74] In any event, the terms *concrete*, *direct*, and *definite* all seem to support a simpler goal of avoiding speculative or hypothetical claims of military advantage to be gained from an attack, that a commander must have some objective basis to justify the military objective determination. In addition, the most significant modifier is that the advantage must be a military one. From a practical perspective, it can be argued that having two different assessments of military advantage within a single targeting decision process, first for identifying a military object and then for assessing the collateral effects of an attack, introduces an unnecessary and unworkable level of complexity. The targeting rules are meant to be universally applied by individual soldiers as well as for a strategic air campaign. Many targeting decisions leave little time to make the sort of nuanced assessments of military advantage this bifurcated assessment of military advantage might require. Accordingly, a unified meaning is better aligned with the realities of combat operations.

The term military advantage also raises the issue of the scope of potential targets. When dealing with military advantage in the context of Article 57(2)(iii), the AP I Commentary states "[a] military advantage can only consist in ground gained and in annihilating or weakening the enemy armed forces."[75] This tactical level view can be contrasted with States such as Canada, the United Kingdom, the Netherlands, Germany, France, and Italy, which entered Reservations or Declarations for Article 57 indicating that "the military advantage anticipated from an attack is intended to refer to the advantage anticipated from the attack considered *as a whole* and not from isolated or particular parts of the attack." This broader approach suggests a strategic approach, which from a State perspective is more reflective of how wars are fought.

4.4 Targeting precautions

4.4.1 General

AP I, Article 57(2), imposes an obligation on both commanders and planners to implement certain precautionary measures to avoid, or mitigate civilian risk whenever an attack will subject civilians and/or civilian property to such risk. The measures are divided into three parts: distinguishing between civilians, civilian objects, and military objectives; the avoidance or minimization of civilian casualties, or damage; and a proportionality assessment weighing military advantage against collateral civilian effects. It is this latter aspect of the precautions that has proven to be particularly controversial. In terms of distinction, everything *feasible* must be done to verify objectives being attacked are not civilians, or civilian objects, but rather are military objectives. Feasible is also used to describe the second precaution, concerning avoiding or minimizing civilian casualties and damage. A number of States have indicated that "the word 'feasible' means that which is practicable or practically possible, taking into account all circumstances ruling at the time, including humanitarian and military considerations."[76] States have also indicated that those

> planning, deciding upon or executing attacks have to reach decisions on the basis on their assessment of the information reasonably available to them at the relevant time and that such decisions cannot be judged on the basis of information which has subsequently come to light.[77]

It has been noted that "Article 57 recognizes that targeting is undertaken by applying a process in which there is a sequence of activities starting with the planning, progressing to the decision to attack, and culminating in the attack itself."[78] In this sequence, the importance of the second precautionary measure found in Article 57(2)(a)(ii) to "take all feasible precautions in the choice and methods of attack with a view to avoiding, and in any event minimizing, incidental loss of civilian life, injury to civilians and damage to civilian objects" is often overlooked owing to controversy surrounding the outcome of the proportionality test. The latter test focuses on outcomes: the death or injury of uninvolved civilians or the destruction of civilian property. However, it is through the application of the *avoid and minimize* precaution that collateral effects are most likely to be limited and proportionate results attained. Where there are a number of feasible attack options that offer the same or similar military advantage, this precaution forces military personnel to consider and weigh the effects of these options and select the option that poses the lowest predictable civilian risk. The process requires consideration of less destructive means and an assessment of alternative operational and tactical methods. The result of that process "will often involve more objective considerations than application of the proportionality obligation; precautions involve a series of concrete steps in a coherent targeting process that can be applied in a systematic manner."[79] One advantage of emphasizing these type of civilian risk mitigation precautions is that they are consistent with the tactical instincts of commanders, who routinely consider multiple attack options and select the option that produces the greatest probability of achieving the desired effect.

4.4.2 Excessive collateral casualties and damage

It is the *proportionality* assessment that continues to attract the most controversy concerning the use of force during armed conflict. But one aspect of this rule should not be controversial: unlike its IHRL counterpart, the targeting proportionality rule *does not* protect the intended object of attack from *excessive* uses of force. Instead, it protects the proximate civilians and civilian property from the *incidental or collateral* effects of the attack on the lawful target. Accordingly, where a commander reasonably assesses that an attack on a lawful target will create no risk to civilians or civilian property, there is no obligation to consider the IHL proportionality rule. However, the circumstances in which that might occur are quite limited.

Application of the proportionality rule can be challenging. One challenge is that the use of the term *proportionality* can be misleading since the legal test is one of excessive collateral civilian casualties, or damage in relation to the concrete and direct military advantage to be gained. The Rome Statute indicates that a criminal violation of the rule requires the collateral effects to be clearly excessive, thereby highlighting that a simple balancing of the results is not what was intended by the drafters of these treaties.[80] An enduring challenge is that this precaution requires that the military advantage of an attack be weighed against the value of human life, or civilian property. It has been noted that "since the quantities being measured, civilian losses and military advantage, are dissimilar, it is not possible to establish any reasonably exact proportionality equation between them."[81] Expressed another way, the assessment of proportionality is "likely to require the awkward balancing of apples and oranges."[82]

The rules governing targeting have been subjected to relatively little judicial assessment. A landmark decision is the 2006 *Targeted Killing Case*. In that case, the Israeli High Court of Justice noted that the proportionality assessment is a "values-based test" focused on "a balancing between conflicting values and interests," where "the benefit stemming from the attainment of the proper military objective is proportionate to the damage caused to innocent civilians harmed by it."[83] This case also introduced the concept of a *zone of proportionality.*

> Proportionality is not a standard of precision. At times there are a number of ways to fulfill its conditions. A zone of proportionality is created. It is the borders of that zone that the Court guards. The decision within the borders is the executive branch's decision. That is its margin of appreciation.[84]

However, establishing the boundaries of this proportionality zone still requires a difficult value-based assessment of when civilian collateral casualties or damage is justified.

One approach for reconciling the different value judgements associated with targeting has been to rely on scientific-based criteria to concretize the process and maximize the quality of the information considered by the commander when making a proportionality assessment. This can be seen in the use of computer programs and the collateral damage methodology applied by the United States to assist in assessing the collateral effects of targeting. Such programs often allow the commander to consider carefully developed collateral damage assessments prior to authorizing an attack.[85] Another approach is the imposition of permissible collateral damage thresholds for different levels of command. For example, a brigade commander will be restricted from authorizing any attack where the anticipated civilian casualties exceed a pre-established casualty threshold. It is important to recognize that neither the collateral damage assessment methodology nor the casualty threshold approach is a substitute for the ultimate proportionality determination. Instead, they are best understood as precautionary measures implemented to *enhance the quality* of that ultimate decision: in the case of collateral damage assessments by providing the best available civilian risk information; in the case of the casualty threshold approach by elevating the proportionality decision to higher levels of command with greater operational perspective and more attack options. Ultimately, even when such measures are integrated into the attack decision making process, the proportionality judgment remains highly contextual and dependent on the commander's judgment.

The science of targeting also heavily influenced the approach taken by ICTY when considering the lawfulness of the use of artillery in the *Gotovina* case.[86] However, in overturning a conviction, the appeal court criticized trial reliance on the impact analysis of artillery strikes. The lower court was said to have erred in using a 200-meter range of error[87] to determine that artillery shells fired in civilian-inhabited areas were evidence of indiscriminate attacks.[88] The appellate court also noted the decision "was not based on a concrete assessment of comparative military advantage, and did not make any findings on resulting damages or casualties."[89] In this respect, a scientific approach can help decision-makers, and those holding them accountable, apply the targeting process. However, it cannot change its fundamental nature as a values-based decision.

One issue to be considered is the effects of an attack, which can be categorized as cumulative, cascading, or collateral.[90] This can be particularly relevant to a strategic air campaign where military objectives being struck have an indirect impact on military action. At the same time, the effects are also felt, to varying degrees, by the civilian population. As was noted by the ICTY in the *Kupreškić* case,

> in case of repeated attacks, all or most of them falling within the grey area between indisputable legality and unlawfulness, it might be warranted to conclude that the cumulative effect of such acts entails that they may not be in keeping with international law.[91]

A key issue is one of foreseeability. The broader negative effect on civilian population caused by the destruction of a bridge was reflected in the ICTY *Prlić* judgment.[92] The challenge for any court will be attempting to determine the lawfulness of the effects of air campaigns such as the 1999 Kosovo conflict, which involved 38,004 sorties by NATO, including 10,484 strike sorties. This included the use of over 23,000 bombs and missiles.[93] It is not individual strikes that ordinarily cause substantial effects, but rather it is the impact of multiple strikes that must be considered.

The proportionality assessment will also be affected by the nature of the conflict. The proportionality assessment may be impacted by the time available to make a proportionality assessment; or whether the operations are occurring in open terrain, an urban environment, at sea or in the air. It is likely that an inter-State conflict involving countries attacking the industrial infrastructure supporting the war effort will involve an elevated number of attacks. The targets are very likely to be located within civilian areas. This will result in an increased potential for collateral civilian casualties and death. In contrast, if the conflict involves a counterinsurgency against a non-State actor, there are likely to be a more limited number of these types of strategic targets. Further, while an insurgency/counterinsurgency can involve conventional style conflict, the most significant operational challenge normally arises from members of an insurgent organization hiding and operating among the people. While this also means collateral civilian casualties and damage can result, there is also a clear military advantage in avoiding civilian casualties since the conflict with the insurgent group is ultimately about a war for the people—the very civilians who will be suffering the adverse effects of the targeting.[94]

Alienating the civilian population by causing collateral casualties—even when such casualties are assessed as not being excessive and therefore lawful—can lead to a loss of their support and, ultimately, a strengthening of the insurgent group. Tactical effects can include reduced cooperation from the local population in terms of the provision of intelligence, and an increase in successful attacks by an insurgent group, including the use of improvised explosive devices. In the post-9/11 period, there have been numerous conflicts where States have taken significant steps to avoid collateral civilian casualties, even if they may have been legally permissible, owing to the military advantage it provides both tactically and strategically.[95] It must be noted that the nature of warfare is such that the humanitarian law framework will never take on the attributes of a human rights law–based system, which generally limits the acceptance of collateral casualties and protects the intended object of State violence. However, when the humanitarian law precautions are applied, the zone of proportionality—which encompasses the justifiable collateral effects—may be significantly narrowed in a counterinsurgency context. This is because the military advantage against which the effects on the civilian population are assessed is focused on limiting the collateral impact of an attack.

However, this reduced level of justifiable collateral effects will not apply to all situations. As was demonstrated in Fallujah in 2004,[96] in Ramadi in 2016,[97] and again in Mosul in 2017,[98] the fighting during a counterinsurgency can still occur with an intensity approximating conventional conflict. The potential for increased collateral impact may be particularly evident during hostilities in an urban environment. The result is that the legal justifiable collateral casualties and damage will be dependent on the type of conflict, and remain context-dependent.

5 Miscellaneous issues

5.1 Drones

One aspect of targeting that has generated significant controversy during the post-9/11 period has been the use of remotely piloted vehicles, or "drones," to target members of insurgent/terrorist groups. Indeed, the use of drones has become a ubiquitous aspect of contemporary operations. In terms of targeting, it must be stressed that drones are not subject to special rules. They are bound as a matter of treaty and customary law by the same targeting precautions applicable to all uses of force. They are widely used by States and, with the proliferation of technology, increasingly by non-State actors. Drones have a much wider role than as aerial strike platforms, which will likely continue to increase. Owing to their impressive intelligence, surveillance, and reconnaissance capabilities, they are frequently employed as part of the targeting process to identify targets, which are subsequently attacked by other means such as artillery or aircraft assigned to close air support duties.

Part of the challenge is that drones have been used in a context that is viewed as occurring outside of an area of active hostilities. In the United States, this has led to efforts to have special rules or oversight applied, including by judicial or legislative bodies.[99] This effort was addressed in part through the development of a national drone and counterterrorism policy,[100] as is reflected in documents such as the Obama era Presidential Policy Guidance on Procedures for Approving Direct Action Against Terrorist Targets Located Outside the United States and Areas of Active Hostilities.[101] However, it has been noted that "the complaint is really about *jus ad bellum* [law governing the recourse to war] necessity, not *jus in bello* [humanitarian law] necessity."[102] In other words, expanding the conflict under the authority to act in self-defense rather than a law of war issue. The policy response also embraces other areas of law than IHL. They extend to the law governing State self-defense, IHRL, and domestic U.S. law. This includes applying human rights law principles as a matter of policy to restrain State action (e.g., consider capture before killing), and even suggests an authority to conduct drone strikes outside the context of an armed conflict. What the use of drones does not do is change the requirement at law that targeting carried out with drones must, at a minimum, comply with IHL when it is carried out in the context of an armed conflict.

5.2 Rules of engagement

Rules of engagement (ROE) is a subject that is frequently discussed in the context of targeting. It is important to note that ROE are not law. As is set out for

U.S. forces, ROE are "[d]irectives issued by competent military authority that delineate the circumstances and limitations under which U.S. forces will initiate and/or continue combat engagement with other forces encountered."[103] The law, both international and domestic, helps frame the circumstances and limitations regarding when force can be used.

The result is that the targeting precautions and other provisions found in IHL play a key role in providing the overall framework within which ROE regarding the use of force are developed. However, ROE may contain a number of operational and policy limitations that constrain the use of force more than is required by international law. In addition, where military forces are tasked with law enforcement duties, both during and external to an armed conflict, the ROE authority to use force will be based on international and/or domestic human rights principles, rather than conduct of hostilities-based rules.

5.3 Investigations

Targeting also raises questions as to when an investigation is required by law. Unlike in a human rights law–based framework, where any death results in an investigation,[104] IHL does not require the investigation of every death, including civilian deaths, that occurs during armed conflict. An investigation would be required where there is a reasonable suspicion that a civilian or civilian object was intentionally targeted, or where there was excessive collateral injury, death, or destruction. For example, the 1998 Rome Statute prohibits the

> intentional launching of an attack in the knowledge that such attack will cause incidental loss of life or injury to civilians . . . which would be clearly excessive in relation to the concrete and direct overall military advantage anticipated.[105]

Initially, a fact-finding investigation may be ordered by a military commander to determine if a criminal or administrative investigation is required.[106] Investigations may also be ordered for policy reasons independent of there being a legal obligation to do so. Further, administrative or operational investigations may be directed for a variety of operational and policy reasons. This could include inquiring why a weapons system did not perform as expected or hit an unintended target, why established procedures were not followed, or where a pattern of misconduct emerges.[107]

6 Conclusion

The development of a body of humanitarian law governing targeting is directly linked to the growth of the destructive power of States. This effort culminated in the development of the targeting provisions of AP I, which have increasingly been the subject of analysis in the complex security environment of the post-9/11 period. Central to limiting the effects of warfare are the targeting precautions. Those precautions have increasingly come to be recognized as reflecting customary international law applicable in IAC and NIAC. These measures are divided into three parts: distinguishing between civilians, civilian objects, and military objectives (including persons and objects); the avoidance or minimization of civilian casualties or damage; and a required proportionality assessment involving the weighing of military advantage against the collateral effect against civilians. Ultimately, IHL requires that constant care be taken to spare the civilian population, civilians, and civilian objects.

Notes

1   Hugo Grotius, *De Jure Belli Ac Pacis Libri Tres* 33 (Francis W. Kelsey trans., 1925).
2   William Boothby, *The Law of Targeting* 4 (2012).
3   Kenneth Watkin, *Targeting in Air Warfare*, 44 Isr. Y.B. on Hum. Rts 1, 17 (2014).
4   Watkin, *Fighting at the Legal Boundaries: Controlling the Use of Force in Contemporary Conflict* 37–42 (2016).
5   Boothby, *supra* note 2, at 13–29 (for a history of the law of targeting).
6   Protocol (I) Additional to the Geneva Conventions of 12 August 1949, and Relating to the Protection of Victims of International Armed Conflicts, 8 June 1977, 1125 U.N.T.S. 3 [hereinafter AP I] (entered into force 7 December 1978) (signed by the United States 12 December 1977, not transmitted to U.S. Senate, *see* S. Treaty Doc. No. 100–2 (1987)).
7   AP I, Art 48.
8   *Id*. Art 51(1).
9   *Id*. Art 51(6).
10 Geoffrey S. Corn et al., *The Law of Armed Conflict: An Operational Approach* 168 (2012). *See also* AP I, Art 51(4).
11 AP I, Art 52(2).
12 *Id*. (the broader nature of military objectives is reflected in the wording that "In so far as objects are concerned, military objectives are limited to those objects . . .").
13 *Id*.
14 *Id*. Art 50(1).
15 *Id*. Art 52(3).
16 *Id*.
17 *Prosecutor v. Galić*, Case No. IT-98-29-T, Judgment and Opinion, paras 50, 51, 55 (Int'l Crim. Trib. for the former Yugoslavia 5 December 2003), *available at* www.icty.org/x/cases/galic/tjug/en/gal-tj031205e.pdf
18 *Da Silva v. United Kingdom*, App. No. 5878/08, 314 Eur. Ct. H.R. paras 248–56 (2016), *available at* http://hudoc.echr.coe.int/eng?i=001-161975; *McCann v. United Kingdom*, App. No. 18984/91, 324 Eur. Ct. H.R. (ser. A) at 31, para 200 (1995), *available at* http://hudoc.echr.coe.int/eng?i=001-57943
19 Watkin, *Assessing Proportionality: Moral Complexity and Legal Rules*, 8 Y.B. Int'l Hum. L. 1, 26 (2005). *See also* Michael Walzer, *Just and Unjust Wars* 151–4 (1977).
20 AP I, Art 57(2)(b).
21 *Id*. Art 57(2)(c).
22 *Prosecutor v. Kupreškić*, Case No. IT-95-16-T, Judgment, para 524 (Int'l Crim. Trib. for the former Yugoslavia 14 January 2000), *available at* www.icty.org/x/cases/kupreskic/tjug/en/kup-tj000114e.pdf; *Customary International Humanitarian Law Study* 56 (Jean-Marie Henckaerts & Louise Doswald-Beck eds, 2005).

23 *Prosecutor v. Kupreškić*, Case No. IT-95-16-T, Judgment, para 524 (Int'l Crim. Trib. for the former Yugoslavia 14 January 2000), *available at* www.icty.org/x/cases/kupreskic/tjug/en/kup-tj000114e.pdf

24 Brian Egan, *International Law, Legal Diplomacy, and the Counter-ISIL Campaign: Some Observations*, 92 Int'l L. Stud. 235, 242–3 (2016).

25 *Prosecutor v. Delalic*, Case No. IT-96-21-A, Appeals Judgment, para 149 (Int'l Crim. Trib. for the former Yugoslavia 20 February 2001).

26 AP I, Art 50(3); Protocol (II) Additional to the Geneva Conventions of 12 August 1949, and Relating to the Protection of Victims of Non-International Armed Conflicts, Art 13(3), 8 June 1977, 1125 U.N.T.S. 609 [hereinafter AP II] (entered into force 7 December 1978) (signed by the United States 12 December 1977, transmitted to the U.S. Senate 29 January 1987, still pending action as S Treaty Doc. No. 100–2 (1987)).

27 AP I, Art 43 (medical personnel and chaplains covered by GPW Article 33 do not have such a right).

28 AP I, Art 50(3); AP II, Art 13(3).

29 *Public Committee Against Torture in Israel v. Israel*, Israel Supreme Court [16 December 2006], 46 ILM 375, para 40, at 393–4 (2007).

30 *See also* Watkin, *Controlling the Use of Force: A Role for Human Rights Norms in Contemporary Armed Conflict*, 98 Am. J. Int'l L. 1, 17 (2004).

31 *Public Committee Against Torture in Israel v. Israel*, Israel Supreme Court [16 December 2006], 46 ILM 375, para 40, at 393–4 (2007).

32 *Id.* para 35, at 392.

33 N. Melzer, Interpretive Guidance on the Notion of Direct Participation in Hostilities Under International Humanitarian Law (2009) [hereinafter DPH Interpretive Guidance]. *See also* Jamie A. Williamson, *Challenges of Twenty-First Century Conflicts: A Look at Direct Participation in Hostilities*, 20 Duke J. Comp. & Int'l L. 457 (2010).

34 Report of the Special Rapporteur on Extrajudicial, Summary or Arbitrary Executions, Philip Alston, UN Doc. A/HRC/14/24/Add.6 (28 May 2010), para 65, at 19–21, *available at* www2.ohchr.org/english/bodies/hrcouncil/docs/14session/A.HRC.14.24.Add6.pdf (for criticism of the *status*-based targeting resulting from the ICRC study).

35 DPH Interpretive Guidance, at 46.

36 *Id.* at 27–35, 53, 70–1.

37 *Id.* at 34–5.

38 *Id.* at 54.

39 Norman Cigar, *Al-Qa'ida's Doctrine for Insurgency* 123 (2009).

40 *Id.* at 77–82. For critiques of the *DPH Interpretative Guidance*, and a reply by its main author, *see* Michael N Schmitt, *Deconstructing Direct Participation in Hostilities*, 42 N.Y.U.J. Int'l L. & Pol. 697 (2010); Boothby, *"And for Such Time as"*: *The Time Dimension to Direct Participation in Hostilities*, 42 N.Y.U.J. Int'l L. & Pol. 741 (2010); Watkin, *Opportunity Lost: Organized Armed Groups and the ICRC "Direct Participation in Hostilities" Interpretive Guidance*, 42 N.Y.U. J. Int'l L. & Pol. 641, 642 (2010); W. Hays Parks, *Part IX of the ICRC "Direct Participation in Hostilities" Study: No Mandate, No Expertise, and Legally Incorrect*, 42 N.Y.U. J. Int'l L. & Pol. 769 (2010). *See also* Melzer, *Keeping the Balance Between Military Necessity and Humanity: A Response to Four Critiques of the ICRC's Interpretive Guidance on the Notion of Direct Participation in Hostilities*, 42 N.Y.U.J. Int'l L. & Pol. 831 (2010).

41 Stephen Pomper, *Toward a Limited Consensus on the Loss of Civilian Immunity in Non-International Armed Conflict: Making Progress through Practice*, 88 Int'l Leg. Stud. 181, 189 (2012).

42 Boothby, *supra* note 2, at 157–8; Watkin, *supra* note 40, at 691.

43 Egan, *supra* note 24, at 243. *See also* Summary of Information Regarding U.S. Counterterrorism Strikes Outside Areas of Active Hostilities, Office of the Dir. of Nat'l Intelligence (1 July 2016), *available at* www.dni.gov/index.php/newsroom/ reports-and-publications/214-reports-publications-2016/1392-summary-of-information-regarding-u-s-counterterrorism-strikes-outside-areas-of-active-hostilities

44 Corn et al., *supra* note 10, at 172.

45 *See* Rome Statute of the International Criminal Court, Art 8(2)(b)(i), (e)(i), 17 July 1998, 2187 U.N.T.S. 90.

46 Boothby, *supra* note 2, at 100.

47 *Id.* at 102.

48 Yoram Dinstein, *The Conduct of Hostilities Under the Law of International Armed Conflict* 91 (2nd edn, 2010).

49 Commentary on the *HPCR Manual on International Law Applicable to Air and Missile Warfare*, Program on Humanitarian Policy and Conflict Research at Harvard University, r. 22(a), (2010) [hereinafter *HPCR Air and Missile Warfare Manual* Commentary].

50 *Id.* r. 22(a).

51 *Id.* r. 23.

52 *Id.*

53 Boothby, *supra* note 2, at 103 (quoting Jean S. Pictet et al., Commentary on the Additional Protocols of 8 June 1977 to the Geneva Conventions of 12 August 1949 (ICRC, 1987), para 2201 [hereinafter AP Commentary]).

54 Dinstein, *supra* note 48, at 102.

55 Paolo Benvenuti, *The ICTY Prosecutor and the Review of the NATO Bombing Campaign Against the Federal Republic of Yugoslavia*, 12 Eur. J. Int'l. L. 503, 516 (2001).

56 *Id.*

57 But *see* Boothby, *supra* note 2, at 103 (where it is argued the two prongs of the test must still be applied (i.e., contribute to military action, and offer a definite military advantage)).

58 *HPCR Air and Missile Warfare Manual* Commentary, r. 23.

59 *San Remo Manual on International Law Applicable to Armed Conflicts at Sea*, para 40.11, at 117 (Louise Doswald-Beck ed., 1995) [hereinafter *San Remo Manual*].

60 Dinstein, *supra* note 48, at 104.

61 Boothby, *supra* note 2, at 100.

62 *Oxford Dictionary*, online, 4.1, *available at* https://en.oxforddictionaries.com/ definition/action (*action* as it pertains to *armed conflict*). *See also San Remo Manual*, para 40.12, at 117 (where *military action* is equated to *war fighting*).

63 Military Commissions Act of 2009, 10 U.S.C. 47A (2012) at Section 950 p(a)(1):

> The term "military objective" means combatants and those objects during hostilities which, by their nature, location, purpose, or use, effectively contribute to *the war-fighting or war-sustaining capability* of an opposing force and whose total or partial destruction, capture, or neutralization would constitute a definite military advantage to the attacker under the circumstances at the time of an attack (emphasis added).

64 Doswald-Beck, *The San Remo Manual on International Law Applicable to Armed Conflicts at Sea*, 89 Am. J. Int'l L. 192, 199 (1995).

65 Schmitt, *Targeting Narcoinsurgents in Afghanistan: The Limits of International Humanitarian Law*, 12 Y. B. Int'l. L. 1, 6 (2009); Report To The Senate Comm. On Foreign Relations, 111th Cong., 1st Sess., Afghanistan's Narco War: Breaking The Link Between Drug Traffickers And Insurgents 16 (2009).

66 *See* Watkin, *Reflections on Targeting: Looking in the Mirror, Just Security* (2016), *available at* www.justsecurity.org/31513/reflections-targeting-mirror/

67   Ryan Goodman, *The Obama Administration: Targeting "War-Sustaining" Objects in Non-International Armed Conflict*, 110 Am. J. Int'l L. 663 (2016).

68   *San Remo Manual*, para 40.12, at 117.

69   Boothby, *supra* note 2, at 106.

70   AP I, Art 52(2) (emphasis added).

71   AP I, Art 57(2)(iii) (emphasis added).

72   AP Commentary, at 685.

73   Dinstein, *supra* note 48, at 93.

74   AP Commentary, at 637.

75   AP Commentary, at 685.

76   *Customary International Humanitarian Law Study* 70 n.16 (Jean-Marie Henckaerts & Louise Doswald-Beck eds, 2005).

77   *Id*. at 71 n.20, 50 n.33.

78   Boothby, *supra* note 2, at 120.

79   Corn, *War, Law, and the Oft Overlooked Value of Process as a Precautionary Measure*, 42 Pepperdine L. Rev. 419, 424 (2015).

80   Rome Statute of the International Criminal Court, Art 8(2)(b)(iv), 17 July 1998, 2187 U.N.T.S. 90.

81   William Fenrick, *The Rule of Proportionality and Protocol I in Conventional Warfare*, 98 Mil. L. Rev. 91, 102 (1982).

82   Thomas M. Franck, *On Proportionality of Countermeasures in International Law*, 102 Am. J. Int'l L. 715, 729 (2008).

83   *Public Committee Against Torture in Israel v. Israel*, Israel Supreme Court [16 December 2006], 46 ILM 375, para 45, at 395–6.

84   *Id*. para 58, at 400.

85   George S. McNeal, *Targeted Killing and Accountability*, 102 Geo. L.J. 681, 740–5 (2014); Neta Crawford, *Accountability for Killing* 350–1 (2013).

86   *Prosecutor v. Gotovina*, Case No. IT-06-90-A, Appeal Chamber (Int'l Crim. Trib. for the former Yugoslavia, 16 November 2012), *available at* www.icty.org/x/cases/gotovina/acjug/en/121116_judgement.pdf

87   *Id*. para 57.

88   *Id*. para 64.

89   *Id*. para 82.

90   Schmitt, *Effects-Based Operations and the Law of Aerial Warfare*, 5 Wash. Glob. Stud. L. Rev. 274, 275–6 (2006).

91   *Prosecutor v. Kupreškić*, Case No. IT-95-16-T, Trial Chamber, para 526 (Int'l Crim. Trib. for the former Yugoslavia 14 January 2000).

92   *Prosecutor v. Prlić*, Case No. IT-04-74-T, Trial Chamber, paras 1364–6 (Int'l Crim. Trib. for the former Yugoslavia 29 May 2013). But *see* Judgment Summary, ICTY (29 May 2013), *available at* www.icty.org/x/cases/prlic/tjug/en/130529_summary_en.pdf (stating "although the Bridge was used by the ABiH and thus constituted a legitimate military target for the HVO, its destruction caused disproportionate damage to the Muslim civilian population of Mostar," the decision itself only made a factual finding). *See also* Rogier Bartels, *Prlić et al.: The Destruction of the Old Bridge of Mostar and Proportionality*, EJIL: Talk (31 July 2013), *available at* www.ejiltalk.org/prlic-et-al-the-destruction-of-the-old-bridge-of-mostar-and-proportionality/

93   Fenrick, *Targeting and Proportionality during the NATO Bombing Campaign Against Yugoslavia*, 12 Eur. J. Int'l.L. 489, 489 (2001).

94   Robert Thompson, *Defeating Communist Insurgency* 51 (1966).

95   Letter from Peter Olson, Legal Advisor, NATO/OTAN, to Judge P. Kirsch, Chair, International Comm'n of Inquiry on Libya, UN, *OLA (2012)006*, 3 (23 January

2012), *available at* www.nato.int/nato_static/assets/pdf/pdf_2012_05/20120514_120514-NATO_1st_ICIL_response.pdf

96   Bing West, *No True Glory: A Frontline Account of the Battle of Fallujah* 315–16 (2005).

97   Susannah George, Desmond Butler, & Maya Alleruzzo, *Iraq Routed IS from Ramadi at a High Cost: A City Destroyed*, Associated Press (5 May 2016), *available at* http://bigstory.ap.org/article/627a3057be2544d68aa75897e299a162/iraq-routed-ramadi-high-cost-city-destroyed

98   *How the Battle for Mosul Unfolded*, BBC News (10 July 2017), *available at* www.bbc.com/news/world-middle-east-37702442.

99   Chris Woods, *Sudden Justice: America's Secret Drone Wars* 281–4 (2015).

100 *Obama's Speech on Drone Policy*, N.Y. *Times*, 23 May 2013, *available at* www.nytimes.com/2013/05/24/us/politics/transcript-of-obamas-speech-on-drone-policy.html

101 Procedures for Approving Direct Action Against Terrorist Targets Located Outside the United States and Areas of Active Hostilities, The White House (22 May 2013), *available at* www.aclu.org/sites/default/files/field_document/presidential_policy_guidance.pdf

102 Jens David Ohlin & Larry May, *Necessity in International Law* 240 (2016).

103 *Department of Defense Dictionary of Military and Associated Terms* 205 (15 October 2016), *available at* www.dtic.mil/doctrine/new_pubs/dictionary.pdf

104 *McKerr v. United Kingdom*, 2001-III Eur. Ct. H. R., 475, 517, para 111.

105 Rome Statute of the International Criminal Court, Art 8(2)(b)(iv), 17 July 1998, 2187 U.N.T.S. 90.

106 Schmitt, *Investigating Violations of International Law in Armed Conflict*, 2 Harv. Nat'l Sec. J. 31, 63 (2011).

107 Watkin, *Use of Force during Occupation: Law Enforcement and Conduct of Hostilities*, 94 Int'l Rev. Red Cross 267, 296–8 (2012).

7 Weapons, means, and methods

1 Introduction

As Carl von Clausewitz famously noted, "[w]ar is thus an act of force to compel our enemy to do our will."[1] While warfare is conducted by means of a direct or indirect application of force, this ultimately involves the use of, or threat of, the use of weapons. Given the integral role that weapons play regarding the use of force and the tremendous levels of violence associated with warfare, it is essential they are subject to legal regulation. It is a fundamental rule of IHL that the right "to choose methods or means of warfare are not unlimited."[2] In this context "the words 'methods and means' include weapons in the widest sense, as well as the way in which they are used."[3] In this respect, it is "prohibited to employ weapons, projectiles and material and methods of warfare of a nature to cause superfluous injury or unnecessary suffering."[4] Further, such methods and means are prohibited that "are intended, or may be expected, to cause widespread, long-term and severe damage to the natural environment."[5]

This chapter discusses the law governing methods and means of warfare, with a focus on regulating weapons. The first part briefly outlines the development of the treaty law, and identifies the role performed by customary international law regarding the employment of weapons of war. The next part assesses the governing principles prohibiting superfluous injury and unnecessary suffering; the use of indiscriminate weapons; the protection of the environment; and the obligation introduced in Article 36 of AP I to review the study, development, acquisition, or adoption of new weapons. The third part considers the legality of weapons and weapons systems, such as expanding bullets; mines, booby-traps and improvised explosive devices; cluster munitions; poison, chemical, bacteriological, and nuclear weapons, as well as the use of riot control agents; cyber weapons; autonomous weapons; and nanotechnology. Finally, the fourth part looks at tactics such as perfidy and treacherous conduct, and introduces the kill or capture debate that has arisen in the post-9/11 security environment.

2 Weapons and the law

The regulation of methods and means of warfare is outlined in both treaty and customary law. Treaty-based rules are commonly traced back to the 1868

St. Petersburg Declaration Renouncing the Use, in Time of War, of Explosive Projectiles under 400 Grams Weight.[6] The regulation of weapons has had a difficult history as States have embraced technological advances in warfare. It has been noted that there were efforts made at regulating or prohibiting weapons and weapons systems following World War I (i.e., military aircraft, submarines, machineguns, chemical and bacterial weapons, incendiary weapons).[7] However, "[e]ach endeavor proved either unsuccessful or of limited success, either because each weapon or weapon system had proven military value and/or due to government and popular skepticism of arms control agreements."[8]

Between 1899 and 1974, the law regarding weapons focused on a very general prohibition found in Article 23(e) of the 1907 Hague Land Warfare Regulations regarding the employment of arms, projectiles, or material calculated to cause unnecessary suffering,[9] or superfluous injury.[10] It has been noted that "[t]he legality of weapons and munitions of war was a lacuna ripe for exploration and, perhaps, development."[11] However, it was not until the Vietnam War period that issues such as small-caliber weapons, napalm (a mixture of a gelling agent and either gasoline (petrol) or a similar fuel that blankets an area and burns intensely), cluster munitions (bombs or rockets that release hundreds of small grenade type sub-munitions to blanket an entire area), flechettes (rockets filled with hundreds of small steel darts used as an anti-personnel weapon), high-explosive munitions, and plastic fragmenting munitions prompted greater scrutiny in the process leading up to the adoption of the Additional Protocols.[12] AP I represented a significant modern foray into regulating methods and means of warfare. It reaffirmed the prohibition against the use of weapons calculated to cause unnecessary suffering, and expanded the prohibition to include weapons of a nature to cause superfluous injury or unnecessary suffering,[13] as well as prohibiting widespread, long-term and significant damage to the natural environment.[14] Notably it also introduced an obligation to determine whether the employment of weapons would in some or all circumstances be prohibited under international law.[15]

Since the mid-1970s, there have been numerous treaties developed to prohibit or regulate specific weapons, such as the 1976 Environmental Modification Convention,[16] the 1980 Convention on Prohibitions or Restrictions on the Use of Certain Conventional Weapons Which May Be Deemed to Be Excessively Injurious or to Have Indiscriminate Effects,[17] the 1993 Convention on the Prohibition of the Development, Production, Stockpiling and Use of Chemical Weapons and on Their Destruction,[18] the 1997 Convention on the Prohibition of the Use, Stockpiling, Production and Transfer of Anti-Personnel Mines and on Their Destruction (i.e., anti-personnel land mines),[19] the Rome Statute of the International Criminal Court 1998,[20] and the 2008 Convention on Cluster Munitions.[21] The regulation of weapons may also be addressed by other instruments such as joint State declarations, military manuals, and soft law studies (*see* Chapter 2, 3.2: *Customary and soft law*). Such documents include the ICRC *Customary International Humanitarian Law Study*[22] or the 1999 Secretary-

General's Bulletin: Observance by United Nations Forces of International Humanitarian Law.[23] Customary international law, with its focus on the prohibition against inflicting unnecessary suffering, remains an important part of weapons regulation. In this respect, "the unnecessary suffering principle applies the philosophy underlying the Martens Clause to weapons design by indicating that, even where there is no specific prohibition or restriction applicable to a weapon, broader principles must be complied with."[24]

William Boothby, a leading and highly respected expert on the law of weapons, has indicated that "[i]mportant parts of the treaty law of weaponry applicable to international armed conflict ... apply to States also during NIACs."[25] In addition, "[c]ustomary principles, and certain customary rules such as the prohibitions of chemical and biological weapons, will bind them."[26] The *ICRC Customary Humanitarian Law Study* is a valuable resource for assessing the customary law rules applicable in NIAC. This collective body of law is created by, and applicable primarily to States, although some rules may also bind non-State armed groups. Whether the treaty law, or customary rules derived from State practice and treaty language, bind non-State actors will usually depend on the treaty language.[27]

Of interest, there is no similar international law framework regulating or prohibiting the use of certain weapons for domestic law enforcement.[28] Thus, the common use of hollow point bullets (i.e., expanding bullets) or CS gas (i.e., riot control agents) that are lawful during law enforcement operations can at times appear at odds with more stringent humanitarian law restrictions that prohibit those same weapons in the context of armed conflicts. Questions can arise regarding the employment of these less lethal force options during NIACs, non-combatant evacuations, or humanitarian relief operations where State security forces may be required to confront civilians and maintain order. However, the issues are not unique to NIAC and low-level international operations. They may be particularly evident when military forces are required to maintain law and order when acting as an occupying power. Whether such police-type weapons and tactics may be authorized during policing operations in the broader context of an armed conflict is an especially complicated question likely to continue to generate different opinions.

3   The employment of weapons

3.1   *General*

Weapons are an integral part of warfare. *Weapon* has been defined as:

> [A] device, system, munition, implement, substance, object, or piece of equipment that is used, that is intended to be use, or that is designed for use to apply the offensive capability, usually causing injury or damage to an adverse party to an armed conflict.[29]

While a weapon is associated with an offensive capability, this does not mean its employment does not extend to defensive operations. As is suggested in the definition of *attack* in AP I, weapons may be used to inflict "acts of violence against an adversary, whether in offence or defence."[30]

In practical terms, weapons can range from knives, clubs, and arrows to high-explosive ordinance, nuclear devices, chemical and bacteriological ordnance, and even computer systems used to carry out cyber attacks. Even the most ubiquitous of implements such as machetes, screwdrivers, and hammers can be turned into a weapon, as was demonstrated during the 1994 Rwandan genocide.[31] Cyber warfare highlights the diversity and breadth of what can constitute a weapon. As indicated in the *Tallinn Manual on the International Law Applicable to Cyber Warfare*,[32] cyber weapons are:

> means of warfare that are by design, use, or intended use capable of causing either (i) injury to, or death of, persons; or (ii) damage to, or destruction of objects, that is, causing the consequences required for qualification of a cyber operation as an attack.[33]

In this respect, the computer system would qualify as a weapon system, or means of warfare.[34] Nonetheless, in terms of legal regulation, the focus is primarily on systems developed and fielded for the purpose of functioning as a weapon system.

3.2   *Superfluous injury and unnecessary suffering*

A key principle in assessing the legality of any weapon is whether it causes superfluous injury and unnecessary suffering. The principle that such weapons violate international law was first articulated in the Preamble of the 1868 St. Petersburg Declaration, which indicated that "the only legitimate object which States should endeavour to accomplish during war is to weaken the military forces of the enemy." In this respect, "it is sufficient to disable the greatest possible number of men," and that "object would be exceeding by the employment of arms which uselessly aggravate the sufferings of disabled men, or render their death inevitable." In its more contemporary form, this principle is set out in Article 35(2) of AP I as follows:

> It is prohibited to employ weapons, projectiles and material and methods of warfare of a nature to cause superfluous injury or unnecessary suffering.

The terms *superfluous injury* and *unnecessary suffering* are "purposed to encrust both the measurable objective (mostly physical injury) and subjective—psychological suffering and pain."[35] However, collectively these terms are used in an objective sense, "so that the measurement is not that of the victim but indicates there should be no resort to measures which entail suffering beyond that necessary for achieving the purpose of the attack."[36]

Accordingly, a key issue subject to constant assessment is whether the weapon, projectiles, and material and methods of warfare are of a nature to cause superfluous injury and unnecessary suffering. Article 23(e) of the 1907 Hague Land Warfare Regulations prohibited such means of warfare only when infliction of such suffering was *calculated*, which appeared to place greater emphasis on the intention rather than the nature of the weapon.[37] In contrast, AP I prohibits any means or method of warfare *of a nature to cause* such suffering, a broader standard that does not focus on the intent of the weapon, and extends to tactics. States not bound by AP I, most notably the United States, reject this broader standard and consider the calculation element essential for assessing legal compliance.

Under either standard, the issue arises whether legal assessment turns on the effects of a weapon, as opposed to the intended design or normal use of a weapon. Subsequent analysis persuasively indicates that the clearer expression of State practice is found in the idea of the intended effect of the use of a weapon rather than simply its effects.[38] The nature of the weapon refers to what happens when it is used. In other words, "the consequences that will inevitably follow from the employment of the weapon, being the consequences which will usually have been intended when the weapon was being developed."[39] Accordingly, effects resulting from unintended uses, or uses that deviate from doctrinal employment parameters, are not normally considered when assessing the weapons legality.

Superfluous injury and unnecessary suffering are comparative and not absolute concepts. The "only logical comparator is the purpose for which the weapon is being employed."[40]

> [The] legitimacy of the weapon . . . must be determined by comparing "the nature and scale of the generic military advantage to be anticipated from the weapon in the application for which it is designed to be used" with "the pattern of injury and suffering associated with the normal intended use of the weapon."[41]

The injunction "hangs on a determination whether injury/suffering is avoidable or unavoidable."[42] Weapons are only prescribed if they cause "injury or suffering that can be avoided, given the military constraints of the situation."[43]

Another question that inevitably arises is how the injury and suffering on the one hand and the anticipated military advantage on the other are compared.[44] A proportionality standard is commonly suggested, as is reflected in the ICRC *Customary Humanitarian Law Study:*

> Many States point out that the rule requires that a balance be struck between military necessity, on the one hand, and the expected injury or suffering inflicted on a person, on the other hand, and that excessive injury or suffering, i.e. that *which is out of proportion to the military advantage sought*, therefore violates the rule.[45]

The UK's *Manual of The Law of Armed Conflict* states:

> In deciding the legality of use of a specific weapon, therefore, it is necessary to assess:
>
> a.   its effects in battle;
> b.   the military task it is required to perform; and
> c.   the proportionality between factors (a) and (b).[46]

The use of a proportionality framework has been criticized by a number of analysts.[47] A problem arises if a weapon-legality proportionality test is interpreted as requiring a finely tuned balancing of military advantage and the potential injury and suffering related to the use of the weapon. Such an application would require the same methodology used to assess the collateral impact of targeting,[48] or a methodology analogous to a human rights–based law enforcement use of force.[49] There is, however, no unitary proportionality rule in international law. Instead, proportionality is used under international law in a wide variety of contexts.[50] In relation to weapons legality, proportionality has a different meaning. The "threshold for superfluous injury remains high,"[51] and "[c]omparisons may be made with the effectiveness of existing [lawful] weapons that are required for the same purpose."[52] The principle does not preclude using lethal weapons, including those leaving no chance of survival such as fuel air explosives,[53] or applying overwhelming force against an opponent because of their enemy status.[54] Instead, in this context, a weapon would be considered to produce a disproportionate effect only when it inflicted injury or suffering well beyond any justifiable military necessity, for example a projectile that, having disabled the enemy, was deliberately designed to then cause an infectious disease or elude extraction by normal surgical procedure.

The prohibition on causing unnecessary suffering and superfluous injury is a rule of customary international law applicable to IAC and NIAC.[55] One articulation of that customary rule found in the ICRC *Customary Law Study* has been criticized because it favors an effects-based assessment.[56] In this context, it has been suggested that "the relevant weapons law issue is whether the weapon inevitably breaches the principle in all designed or intended applications, not whether it is capable of use in a way that would breach the principle."[57] Thus, while the prohibition may apply to all armed conflicts, debates persist on exactly what the obligation requires.

3.3   Indiscriminate weapons

Consistent with it being a foundational principle of IHL, the second main rule governing the legality of weapons is discrimination. As was stated in the Advisory Opinion on the Legality of the Threat or Use of Nuclear Weapons:

> States must never make civilians the object of attack and must consequently never use weapons that are incapable of distinguishing between civilian and military targets.[58]

The main treaty prohibition against indiscriminate attacks is set out in Article 51(4) of AP I as follows:

> 4.   Indiscriminate attacks are prohibited. Indiscriminate attacks are:
>   (a) those which are not directed at a specific military objective;
>   (b) those which employ a method or means of combat which cannot be directed at a specific military objective; or
>   (c) those which employ a method or means of combat the effects of which cannot be limited as required by this Protocol;
>   and consequently, in each such case, are of a nature to strike military objectives and civilians or civilian objects without distinction.

Reflecting concerns over methods of warfare such as the area bombing practiced in World War II,[59] AP I identifies an attack that "treats a single military objective a number of clearly separated and distinct military objectives" located in an urban or "other area containing a similar concentration of civilians or civilian objects" as being indiscriminate.[60] Such attacks, often called carpet bombing, may be conducted with otherwise lawful weapons (although such an attack would be permissible in areas with no risk to civilians (for example carpet bombing enemy positions in a remote area)). However, launching an attack with a weapon that cannot be adequately directed at a military objective is also considered indiscriminate. A historical example of such an indiscriminate weapon is the V-2 rocket used by Nazi Germany during the final months of World War II.[61] A contemporary example is the rockets fired by Hamas at Israel during their 2014 conflict.[62] In each example, the rockets could not be directed against a particular military objective, meaning that it was the weapon itself that rendered the attack indiscriminate. In terms of weapons law, "it is clear that weapons must be capable of direction at individual military objectives and that this requirement must be understood in the context of the attack."[63] It should be noted, however, that emphasis is placed on the military objectives being clearly separated and distinct. Ultimately, it is "a question of fact and of technical design whether a particular weapon is capable of being directed at specific military objectives in this sense."[64]

AP I also includes within the definition of prohibited indiscriminate attack any attack that violates the proportionality test (i.e., an attack expected to cause incidental civilian casualties and damage that is excessive in relation to the concrete and direct military advantage anticipated).[65] However, as William Boothby notes, "this proportionality rule has no direct applicability to the legitimacy of a weapon" since it relates to an attack carried out at a particular time rather than the characteristics of the weapon itself.[66]

3.4   Environmental protection

The protection of the environment is addressed in the 1976 Environmental Modification Convention, or ENMOD, which prohibits the engagement in

" 'military or any other hostile use of environmental modification techniques having widespread, long-lasting, or severe effects' for the purposes of destroying, damaging or injuring the enemy."[67] The ENMOD Convention was negotiated at a time when "[t]he USA's widespread use of various methods of forest and crop destruction in Vietnam had been much criticized."[68] It addresses the use of "so-called 'environmental modification techniques as military instruments, i.e. the calculated abuse of the environmental damage for offensive purposes."[69] Examples would include manipulating the environment to cause earthquakes or torrential rains. This treaty has been largely successful in foreclosing the development of weapon systems capable of such manipulation.

Another prohibition regarding the use of weapons and the environment is set out in AP I, Article 35(3) which states:

> It is prohibited to employment methods or means of warfare which are intended, or may be expected, to cause widespread, long-term and severe damage to the natural environment.

Article 55 (1) of the same Protocol states:

> Care shall be taken in warfare to protect the natural environment against widespread, long-term and severe damage. This protection includes a prohibition of the use of methods or means of warfare which are intended or may be expected to cause such damage to the natural environment and thereby to prejudice the health or survival of the population.

The environment is dealt with in two different provisions because "Art. 55 deals with the protection of the civilian population while Art. 35 deals with the prohibition of unnecessary injury and has a wider scope, including transnational damage."[70] These provisions go much farther than the ENMOD, "covering not only the intentional infliction of damage to the environment in the course of warfare (as in the ENMOD Convention), but also purely unintentional and incidental damage."[71] In addition, the Protocol provisions are focused on damage to the environment, while "the manipulation of the forces of the environment as weapons" was the central concern of the ENMOD Convention.[72]

Nonetheless, it is important to note that "really severe environmental damage is required for the rule to be broken. Only if the survival or health of the population, as opposed to individual members of it, is prejudiced will the treaty threshold have been reached."[73] These rules also impose cumulative requirements: damage falls within the prohibition only if it affects "large areas *and* lasts for a long period *and also* causes severe damage to the natural environment."[74] This would not occur within the usual types of collateral damage "caused by large military operations in the course of conventional warfare."[75] The example of the burning of Kuwaiti oil wells and opening of oil valves in 1991 highlights the high threshold of these provisions. While there was clearly an impact on the atmosphere, which impacted agriculture and local civilians, "it has been suggested that in the event, owing to factors not controlled by Iraq, the long-term environmental consequences were not as bad as had seemed likely."[76]

The ICRC *Customary Humanitarian Law Study* identifies various rules dealing with the protection of the environment. These rules apply general principles to the conduct of hostilities[77] and the application of methods and means being employed with due regard to the protection of the environment,[78] and set out a basic restatement of Article 35(1) of AP I.[79] However, these rules have been critiqued as "the current position at customary law is somewhat less advanced than the ICRC *Study* would indicate."[80] For example, a number of nuclear powers have consistently rejected the application of AP I to nuclear weapons.[81] In addition, the *Nuclear Weapons Case* indicated that the powerful constraints found in Articles 35(3) and 55 of the Protocol only applied to the States having subscribed to these provisions.[82] The United States' views may reflect those of other States not party to the Protocol: these provisions are overly broad and ambiguous, and do not reflect of customary law.[83] Instead, the United States takes the view that the environment, as civilian property, is subject to proportionality assessments no different from any other civilian property.

3.5   *Weapons reviews*

Article 36 of AP I imposes an obligation on States to determine whether the employment of a new weapon, means, or method of warfare would, in some or all circumstances, be prohibited by the Protocol or by any other rule of international law applicable to that State. This obligation arises in respect of the study, development, acquisition, or adoption such weapons, means, or methods of warfare.[84] In respect of "States that are not party to AP I, the implied obligation . . . applies specifically to the acquisition or use of new weapons and means of warfare."[85] These reviews reflect a State commitment to the rule of law, provides assurance to military commanders that the weapons are legal, and offers "an instant resource for responding to questions that may arise as to the legality of a particular weapon or its ammunition."[86]

There is no obligation for reviews to be conducting in any particular manner,[87] or that such reviews be disclosed publicly.[88] As a result, the nature of weapons development makes it difficult to ascertain that an Article 36 review has been conducted. While "[t]here is a tangible need for and objective—and impartial—inspection of weapons development programmes by an impartial body . . . no such modality exists at the present time."[89] Boothby has suggested that the following five criteria should form the basis for weapons reviews:

(a) Whether the weapon is of a nature to cause superfluous injury or unnecessary suffering in its normal or intended circumstances of use;
(b) Whether the weapon is intended or likely to cause widespread, long-term, and severe damage to the natural environment;
(c) Whether the weapon is indiscriminate by nature;

(d) The existence of specific rules (treaty or customary) that prohibit or restrict the use of a weapon; and

(e) The existence of likely future developments in international humanitarian law that may be expected to affect the weapon being reviewed.[90]

If a weapon is assessed as legal and subsequently fielded, the employment of the weapon "in a manner consistent with the law of war is a battlefield commander's responsibility."[91]

4 Specific weapons

4.1 Expanding bullets

A weapon that attracted early codification efforts is the expanding bullet. There was a prohibition identified in the 1899 Hague Declaration against bullets that expand or flatten easily in the human body.[92] This prohibition applies to bullets whose hard envelope—or metal jacket—does not entirely cover the core or is pierced with incisions, as well as any other bullet that expands or flattens easily.[93] In respect of IAC, the1998 Rome Statute bans the use of bullets that "expand or flatten easily in the human body, such as bullets with a hard envelope which does not entirely cover the core or is pierced with incisions."[94] It is important to note that this does not include bullets that move through the body after entry causing substantial internal damage.

In 2010, the 1998 Rome Statute was amended to include such bullets as a war crime in NIAC.[95] The ICRC *Customary Humanitarian Law Study* states that "[t]he use of bullets which expand or flatten easily in the human body is prohibited."[96] In contrast, the United States takes the view that customary law does not prohibit bullets that expand or flatten easily, unless they also cause unnecessary suffering or superfluous injury.[97] This interpretation finds support in the preambular paragraph to the 1998 Rome Statute, which states that "the crime is committed only if the perpetrator employs the bullets to uselessly aggravate suffering or the wounding effect upon the target of such bullets, as reflected in customary international law."[98]

A number of States use expanding bullets, such as hollow point or frangible ammunition, for domestic law enforcement operations. Such ammunition is often preferred for operations such as hostage rescue and the resolution of aircraft hijackings because of there is less likelihood of over-penetration, or ricochets that could cause collateral casualties.[99] This may present a challenge for contemporary commanders, as both IAC and NIAC can involve military forces carrying out law enforcement and counterterrorism functions. For example, an occupying power during an IAC is required "to fulfill its obligations . . . to *maintain the orderly government of the territory*."[100] Similarly, NIACs are fundamentally about a struggle for governance. Success in those conflicts frequently requires the privileging of a police primacy approach.[101] As a result, military forces can become involved in hostage rescue, and other law enforcement–type operations where the use of expanding bullets could offer greater protection for the civilian population.[102] A convincing argument can be made that such ammunition could be justified in those circumstances in the same way as riot control agents (*see* Chapter 7, 4.4.2: *Chemical weapons*).[103] In this respect, the U.S. interpretation of the prohibition would allow for such use. Indeed, "the U.S. armed forces have used expanding bullets in various counterterrorism and hostage rescue operations, some of which have been conducted in the context of armed conflict."[104] However, questions remain how widely this approach is accepted by the international community, and under what circumstances expanding bullets might be used on policing duties during armed conflict.

4.2   Mines, booby-traps, and improvised explosive devices

4.2.1   Anti-personnel mines

The use of explosive devices such as mines, booby-traps and improvised explosive devices (IEDs) have long been a part of warfare. As has been noted, "[a]ll modern insurgencies including aspects of the Spanish Civil War in Europe and T.E. Lawrence's Middle East campaigns, have included as part of their central strategy the use of explosives and mines by guerrillas to disrupt mechanized transport and supply lines."[105] In the later twentieth century, concern developed regarding the impact of the use of landmines on the civilian population and, in particular, their persistent presence following the termination of a conflict. This issue, coupled with concerns over other weapons, led to the adoption of the Convention on Certain Conventional Weapons, or CCW. This treaty created a framework for adopting supplemental protocols to prohibit or regulate specific weapon systems, to include a mechanism for periodic meetings of States Parties. It is important to note that the Additional Protocols to the CCW are not connected with the 1977 Additional Protocols I and II to the Geneva Conventions.

From 1980 onward, three treaties (the Protocol on Prohibitions or Restrictions on the Use of Mines, Booby-traps and Other Devices, Protocol II 1980;[106] the Amended Protocol on Prohibitions or Restrictions on the Use of Mines, Booby-Traps and Other Devices, Amended Protocol II, 1996;[107] and the Convention on the Prohibition of the Use, Stockpiling, Production and Transfer of Anti-Personnel Mines and on Their Destruction, 1997[108]) were developed pursuant to the CCW to ban, or regulate the use of landmines, booby-traps, and other explosive devices.[109] The use of some naval mines is regulated by the 1907 Hague Convention (VIII) Relative to the Laying of Automatic Submarine Contact Mines,[110] which although dated also reflects customary international law.[111] Those principles "provide norms regulating the area where naval mines—whether antiquated or sophisticated—may be employed."[112]

In respect of land warfare, a *mine* has been defined as "any munition placed under, on or near the ground or other surface area and designed to be detonated or exploded by the presence, proximity or contact of a person or vehicle."[113]

A mine can be anti-personnel or anti-vehicle, with the former involving a mine that can be "exploded by the presence, proximity or contact of a person and that will incapacitate injure or kill one, or more persons."[114] Contrary to popular misconception, mines are not always emplaced by hand. Instead, mines may be delivered by artillery, missile, rocket, or mortar or dropped from an aircraft.[115] Owing to the varied practice of States, and a lack of universal acceptance of the treaty law, it is not possible to state that the treaty provisions reflect customary law.[116] However, the ICRC *Customary Humanitarian Law Study* asserts that certain customary rules regarding the use of landmines are recognized by States. Those rules are: "[w]hen landmines are used, particular care must be taken to minimise their indiscriminate effects";[117] "[a] party to the conflict using landmines must record their placement, as far as possible";[118] and "[a]t the end of active hostilities, a party to the conflict which has used landmines must remove or otherwise render them harmless to civilians, or facilitate their removal."[119] These rules reflect established military doctrine for some States. However, at least one respected analyst has suggested that the Amended Protocol II provisions have not attained customary law status since "AP II has yet to achieve universality or anything like it and a number of States of military significance have yet to ratify."[120]

The 1997 Ottawa Convention represented "the first time in over a century in which a major, traditional weapons system has been banned outright and not simply regulated in its use, by a treaty that has broad participation by States."[121] The Convention required States Parties "to never use anti-personnel mines, nor to 'develop, produce, otherwise acquire, stockpile, retain or transfer' them; 'destroy mines in their stockpiles within four years'; and 'clear mined areas in their territory within 10 years.'"[122] Further, States Parties are required to never in any circumstances "assist, encourage or induce, in any way, anyone to engage in any activity prohibited to a State Party under this Convention."[123] This prompted some States to clarify that it would not be illegal to participate in joint operations with another country that uses landmines.[124] This would arguably extend to assuming responsibility for an area of operations previously controlled by a coalition partner not bound to the treaty who had employed anti-personnel landmines. Further, command-detonated anti-personnel mines (e.g., the Claymore mine)—meaning explosive devices that are detonated by an individual exercising control over the mine and not by weight or contact—remain lawful.

One of the challenges in this area of weapons law is that the succession of instruments has produced "a complicated legal regime under which it is not easy to identify which rules apply to any particular State."[125] Some States have ratified various of the CCW Protocols, or the Convention, with an additional complication that States frequently enter reservations and their own statements of interpretation. This is especially the case vis-à-vis anti-personnel landmines. In 2006, when agreement was not possible regarding mines other than anti-personnel mines, a multi-State declaration was made at the Third CCW Review Conference; however, the undertakings regarding their use did not legally bind the declaring States.[126] While States Parties to the Ottawa Convention have completely renounced even the production of anti-personnel landmines, some States, most notably the United States, rejected the treaty because of the concern that a complete ban would deprive military commanders of an important capability used to shape the battlefield. The United States was also particularly concerned that land mines were necessary to defend South Korea from attacks by North Korea. Nonetheless, those non-party States may still be bound by Protocol II to the CCW, which imposes important restrictions on the use of anti-personnel landmines. As a result, "establishing a particular State's obligations requires careful consideration of customary rules, of the treaties it has accepted, and of its Stated basis for doing so."[127] For example, the United States is not a signatory to the Ottawa Convention, but in 2013 "announced policy changes that align U.S. anti-personnel landmine policy outside the Korean Peninsula with the key requirements of the Ottawa Convention."[128]

4.2.2   Booby-traps

A *booby-trap* is defined in 1996 Amended Protocol II as "any device or material which is designed, constructed, or adapted to kill or injure, and which functions unexpectedly when a person disturbs or approaches an apparently harmless object or performs an apparently safe act."[129] Protocols to the CCW prohibit the manufacture of booby-traps in the form of harmless portable objects, and their attachment or association with specific items such as internationally protected emblems; children's toys and other objects relating to children; food and drink, except in military locations; objects of a religious nature; works of art, monuments, or places of worship; and animals and their carcasses.[130]

Booby-traps are not allowed to be used directly or indiscriminately against civilians, and their use is restricted "in any city, town, village or other area containing a civilian concentration—where combat between ground forces is not taking place or does not appear imminent—unless they are placed in close vicinity to a military objective" or protective measures are taken such as posting sentries or warning signs.[131] Booby-traps are not a banned weapon, and as such are not "deemed to contravene the principle of unnecessary suffering."[132] The ICRC *Customary Humanitarian Law Study* sets out a customary rule that "[t]he use of booby-traps which are in any way attached to or associated with objects or persons entitled to special protection under international humanitarian law or with objects that are likely to attract civilians is prohibited."[133]

4.2.3   Improvised explosive devices

The protection against explosive devices in the treaty law extends not only to mines and booby-traps but also *other devices*. As is set out in the 1996 Amended Protocol II to the CCW:

> "Other devices" means manually-emplaced munitions and devices including improvised explosive devices designed to kill, injure or damage and which

are actuated manually, by remote control or automatically after a lapse of time.[134]

This specific reference to *improvised explosive devices* reflects the degree to which by the late twentieth century these weapons were recognized as an increasing threat on the modern battlefield. Insurgents have been particularly drawn to their use, and by 2003 the Iraq War was referred to as the war of the roadside bomb.[135] The head of the U.S. Joint IED Defeat Organization indicated that between January 2011 and September 2012 "there [were] more than 10,000 global IED events occurring in 112 countries that were executed by more than 40 regional and transnational threat networks."[136]

The prohibitions and restrictions applicable to booby-traps are essentially also applicable to improvised explosive devices. The purpose of these provisions is "to try to protect the civilian population and individual civilians as far as possible from coming into contact with these devices" and "to prohibit the treacherous and perfidious use of such devices."[137] As with booby-traps, improvised explosive devices do not fall necessarily within the prohibition on the use of weapons causing unnecessary suffering and superfluous injury. Unfortunately, IEDs are regularly used by insurgent groups in an indiscriminate manner.

4.3   Cluster munitions

The 2008 Dublin Convention on Cluster Munitions[138] treaty is largely patterned after the 1997 Ottawa Convention on landmines. Cluster munitions are defined as "a conventional munition that is designed to disperse or release explosive submunitions each weighing less than 20 kilograms, and includes those explosive submunitions."[139] Cluster munitions have been used by "the Soviet Union and Germany during World War II, by the United States during the Vietnam War in Laos and during Operation Desert Storm in Iraq, by the Sudanese government in Equatoria, and by Russia in Chechnya."[140] They were also used by the United States during its bombing campaign in Afghanistan following the 9/11 attacks.[141]

The main focus of the 2008 Cluster Munitions Convention is on "the relatively high rate of failed, unexploded and abandoned cluster munitions which can easily be spread over a vast area, thus potentially affecting civilians, even as ERW [explosive remnants of war]."[142] This was particularly the case where the submunitions were not self-destructing, or self-deactivating. The danger to the civilian population led to concerns that these weapons were inherently indiscriminate.[143] While by November 2017 there were 102 States Parties and 17 signatories to the CCW,[144] the United States is not a party to this Convention, nor does it view it as an emerging norm of customary law. Instead, the United States believes any regulation of this weapon should be pursued through the CCW mechanism, the same approach it took to anti-personnel landmines. In 2008, a U.S. policy was implemented indicating that its armed forces would, "after 2018, only employ cluster munitions containing submunitions that, after arming, do not result in more than 1% unexploded ordnance (UXO) across the range of intended operational environments."[145] Unlike the 1997 Ottawa Convention, the 2008 Cluster Munitions Convention, expressly indicates that "States Parties, their military personnel or nationals, may engage in military cooperation and operations with States not party to this Convention that might engage in activities prohibited to a State Party."[146] This was compromise language that helped gain the support of NATO countries, and which directly countered efforts by advocates "to deny interoperability of forces, in the hopes that such provisions would convince those not party to the treaty to abandon cluster munitions."[147]

4.4   Poison, chemical, bacteriological, and nuclear weapons

4.4.1   Poison weapons

The ban against the use of poison weapons can be traced back to ancient Greece, and finds a treaty basis in Article 23(a) of the 1907 Hague Land Warfare Regulations.[148] This ban relates to the poisoning of drinking water and food, as well as the use of poisoned weapons or spears.[149] It is "violation of the laws or customs of war, carrying individual criminal responsibility, in Article 3(a) of the ICTY Statute of 1993."[150]

4.4.2   Chemical weapons

Prohibitions relating to the use of chemical weapons in IAC can be found in the 1899 Hague Declaration 2 Concerning Asphyxiating Gases,[151] the 1925 Geneva Gas Protocol,[152] the 1993 Chemical Weapons Convention (CWC), and the 1998 Rome Statute.[153] Further, "the prohibition on the use of chemical weapons is a rule of customary law, and therefore binds all States including those not party to the CWC."[154] The 1993 Chemical Weapons Convention is applicable to NIACs, prohibits the production, use, or stockpiling of chemical weapons, and importantly includes an inspection and verification regime. And, unlike the 1925 Geneva Gas Protocol, it did not allow States Parties to enter reservations to the treaty, which foreclosed the ability of States to reserve the right to make *retaliatory* use of chemical weapons. Further, the ICRC *Customary Humanitarian Law Study*[155] and the ICTY decision *Prosecutor v. Tadić* indicates that the customary law prohibition on the use of chemical weapons extends to such conflicts as well.[156]

The prohibition against chemical weapons has been clearly demonstrated by State protests when allegations have arisen regarding its use. This can be seen in 1988, when it was alleged that Saddam Hussein used chemical weapons against the civilian population in Iraq,[157] and again in August 2013, when the Assad regime was reported to have used them in Syria.[158] This later incident is not the only occasion their use has been alleged in contemporary conflict. The jihadist terrorist organization the Islamic State is claimed in 2016 to have used "chemical weapons, including chlorine and sulfur mustard agents, at least 52 times on the battlefield in Syria and Iraq since it swept to power in 2014."[159]

However, as with expanding bullets, the use of chemicals is not completely prohibited. Importantly, there is a significant exception regarding chemical agents. Their use is not prohibited for "[l]aw enforcement including domestic riot control purposes," although riot control agents cannot be used as a method of warfare.[160] Law enforcement is a broader concept than riot control and could extend to the use of pepper spray. Further chemical incapacitants can include malodorants and calmatives, with the Russian use of fentanyl gas during the 2002 Moscow theater siege representing use of the latter type of chemical.[161] Canadian doctrine permits the use of CS gas or pepper spray for crowd control purposes.[162] The U.S. position is that the use of riot control agents is not prohibited when it is used in defensive military modes to save lives, such as using of riot control agents to control rioting POWs; to avoid civilians being used to mask or screen attacks; rescue missions of downed aircrews and passengers, and escaping prisoners in remotely isolated areas; and "outside the zone of immediate combat to protect convoys from civil disturbances, terrorists, and paramilitary organizations."[163] Such use does, however, require very high level approval. However, concern has been expressed that some of the contemplated uses under the U.S. doctrine against enemy combatants (e.g., aircrew rescue missions or dispersing human shields) "is more akin to a method of warfare than to a law enforcement purpose."[164]

4.4.3 Bacteriological and biological weapons

The prohibition on gas warfare for IAC found in the 1925 Geneva Gas Protocol extends "to the use of bacteriological methods of warfare."[165] The United Nations General Assembly produced the 1972 Convention on the Prohibition of the Development, Production and Stockpiling of Bacteriological (Biological) and Toxin Weapons and on Their Destruction (BWC),[166] which "is arguably, the first treaty to have prohibited entirely a category of weapons."[167] The BWC has not been viewed as effective as the 1993 Chemical Weapons Convention because it lacks a verification supervisory mechanism.[168] Biological weapons are not referred to in the 1998 Rome Statute, however, "it is indisputable that the prohibition of use of biological weapons . . . constitutes an integral part of customary international law."[169] As the ICRC *Customary Humanitarian Law Study* notes, State "[p]ractice is in conformity with the rule's applicability in both international and non-international armed conflicts."[170]

4.4.4 Nuclear weapons

As the International Court of Justice noted in the *Nuclear Weapons Case*, there "is in neither customary nor conventional international law any comprehensive and universal prohibition of the threat or use of nuclear weapons as such."[171] However, any use of such weapons needs to be considered in the context that "the threat or use of nuclear weapons would generally be contrary to the rules of international law applicable in armed conflict, and in particular the principles and rules of humanitarian law."[172] Further, the court held:

> States must never make civilians the object of attack and must consequently never use weapons that are incapable of distinguishing between civilian and military targets. According to the second principle, it is prohibited to cause unnecessary suffering to combatants: it is accordingly prohibited to use weapons causing them such harm or uselessly aggravating their suffering. In application of that second principle, States do not have unlimited freedom of choice of means in the weapons they use.[173]

Additionally, the court held:

> [N]one of the States advocating the legality of the use of nuclear weapons under certain circumstances, including the "clean" use of smaller, low yield, tactical nuclear weapons, has indicated what, supposing such limited use were feasible, would be the precise circumstances justifying such use; nor whether such limited use would not tend to escalate into the all-out use of high yield nuclear weapons. This being so, the Court does not consider that it has a sufficient basis for a determination on the validity of this view.[174]

The United States has specifically noted that "[t]he law of war governs the use of nuclear weapons, just as it governs the use of conventional weapons" and that "attacks using nuclear weapons must not be conducted when the expected incidental harm to civilians is excessive compared to the military advantage expected to be gained."[175] Notably, in 2017, over 120 countries voted to ban nuclear weapons, approving the Treaty on the Prohibition of Nuclear Weapons. However, since all nuclear States and NATO countries (except for the Netherlands) boycotted the negotiations, the long-term impact of the treaty is unclear.[176]

4.5   Cyber weapons

Cyber warfare involves both cyber weapons and cyber weapons systems. Cyber means of warfare "include any cyber device, materiel, instrument, mechanism, equipment or software used, designed or intended to be used to conduct a cyber attack."[177] A *cyber attack* is defined as a "cyber operation, whether offensive or defensive, that is reasonably expected to cause injury or death to persons or damage or destruction to objects."[178] For example, if a "CNA [computer network attack] were to cause severe damage to property or even human fatalities (as a result, e.g., of the shutdown of computers controlling waterworks and damns, leading to the flooding of inhabited areas), it would qualify as an armed attack."[179] Cyber weapons' capacity to cause damage was demonstrated in the 2011 Stuxnet attack on the gas centrifuges used in the Iranian uranium enrichment program.[180] Other offensive uses of force can include distributed denial-of-services attacks or "[a] kill-program might be planed enabling, for example, data to be corrupted or the target system to be shut down."[181]

Like all weapons, cyber weapons cannot be employed if they are of a nature to cause superfluous injury or unnecessary suffering.[182] Similarly, it is prohibited to employ means or methods of cyber warfare that are indiscriminate in nature, such as when they cannot be directed at a specific military objective, or limited in their effects as required under IHL.[183] Weapons law rules relating to the environment are equally applicable.[184] Such weapons must also be the subject of a legal review to ensure they comply with humanitarian law rules where the States study, develop, acquire, or adopt a new means or method of cyber warfare or when required by AP I or by another other rule of international law.[185]

4.6 Autonomous weapons

Technological advances have always driven the development of new weapons systems. One area of growing interest is the use of lethal autonomous weapon systems, or LAWS. It has been suggested that "[a]utonomous weapons systems differ from automated ones in that they can understand higher-level intent and direction . . . [s]o autonomous systems independently identify and decide to engage targets."[186] A crucial aspect of a weapon becoming autonomous is artificial intelligence, "in which the weapons system learns and then makes decisions based on what it has learned."[187]

The idea that machines may make human-like decisions causing the death of civilians or destruction of civilian property without a human in the loop controlling the use of force is viewed as particularly problematic. In other words, a weapons system capable of various degrees of independent artificial intelligence attack judgments could breach the requirement that weapons must not cause unnecessary suffering or superfluous injury, be indiscriminate, deny quarter, or cause widespread and severe damage to the natural environment. Arguments against permitting autonomous weapons include concerns that "machine programming will never reach the point of satisfying the fundamental ethical and legal principles required to field a lawful autonomous lethal weapon"; "it is simply wrong per se to take the human moral agent entirely out of the ring loop"; the lack of human involvement undermines the possibility of holding anyone accountable for a war crime; and "by removing human soldiers from risk and reducing harm to civilians through greater precision, the disincentive to resort to armed force is diminished."[188]

However, the reality is that autonomous weapons systems already exist, and have for some time. For example, the Phalanx Close-In Weapon System (CIWS) (anti-missile defense), has been in continuous production since 1978[189] and is used by the U.S. Navy and 24 other countries.[190] A land-based variant, using self-destructing rounds to limit collateral damage, is designed to intercept rockets, artillery, and mortar rounds in the air prior to impact.[191] Other autonomous weapons include the U.S. Patriot and Israeli Iron Dome anti-missile systems.[192] The nature of technologically driven threats, whether missiles, artillery rounds, or cyber weapons, will inevitably push defenses to become more automated. This is evident in the realm of cyber warfare regarding discussions about active cyber defense and the degree to which a threatened State can or should be able to take pre-emptive, preventive cyber counter-operations.[193]

It should be noted that the existing autonomous weapon systems mentioned above are normally employed pursuant to well-defined parameters posing minimal risk to civilians and civilian property. The LAWS developmental process, however, will not necessarily produce systems sharing these characteristics. Accordingly, autonomous weapons systems raise complex legal and ethical issues. It has also been suggested that "it is highly improbable that moral *jus in bello* [IHL] principles of military necessity, discrimination, and proportionality could ever be programmed into robots."[194]

There have been calls for fully autonomous weapons to be banned outright and the proposing of a requirement of meaningful human control.[195] The position set out in the U.S. *DoD Law of War Manual* is that humanitarian law does "not impose obligations on the weapons themselves; of course, an inanimate object could not assume an 'obligation' in any event."[196] Rather, it is humans who are responsible, and "the obligation on the person using the weapon to take feasible precautions in order to reduce the risk of civilian casualties may be more significant when the person uses weapon systems with more sophisticated autonomous functions."[197] Such feasible precautions may not involve direct control, but rather "monitoring the operation of the weapon system or programming or building mechanisms for the weapon to deactivate automatically after a certain period of time."[198] As William Boothby suggests, "an outright ban of autonomy is premature and inappropriate, difficult to enforce and perhaps easy to circumvent. Existing law should be applied to this as to any other technology in warfare."[199]

4.7 Nanotechnology

The regulation of nanotechnology is another area that IHL will have to address in the coming years. *Nanotechnology* has been defined as "the ability to measure, organize and manipulate matter at the atomic and molecular levels."[200] Its weaponized uses might include increased efficiency of laser weapons, "enhanced or tailored blast and detonation parameters of blast weapons," miniaturized drones using swarm intelligence technology, and the controlled delivery of bio-chemical agents.[201] It has been noted that "[t]here is no specific international law rule relating to nanotechnology as such and arms control provisions in relation to nanotechnology seem very unlikely."[202] However, weapons using nanotechnology will be subject to the relevant treaty and customary law governing method and means of warfare.

5 Tactics

As can be seen in Article 23 of the 1907 Hague Land Warfare Regulations, certain tactics to gain an operational advantage, such as the use of poison weapons, the employing of weapons calculated to cause unnecessary suffering, the improper use of flags of truce, or the military uniforms/insignia of an enemy, the denial of quarter, and the killing of persons who are *hors de combat* have long been prohibited. Contemporary operations, particularly as they concern fighting non-State actors, continue to raise legal issues concerning the legality of methods of warfare and what restraint must be exercised in fighting an enemy. The two issues that are the subject of analysis in this section are treacherous or perfidious action and whether in certain circumstances there is a legal obligation to capture rather than kill an otherwise lawful target.

5.1 Treachery

Treachery, or *perfidy* as it is often referred to, relates to acts carried out in a deceitful or untrustworthy manner. As is set out in Article 37(1) of AP I, such acts invite "the confidence of an adversary to lead him to believe that he [or she] is entitled to, or is obliged to accord, protection under the rules of international law applicable in armed conflict, with intent to betray that confidence." This provision of the Protocol prohibits the killing, injuring, or capturing of an adversary by resort to perfidy, such as the feigning of surrender, feigning incapacitation through wounds or sickness, feigning civilian status, or falsely claiming a protected status by use of United Nations markings or those of neutral or other States not involved in the conflict.

Perfidy can be a challenging legal concept to deal with. The Article 37 wording incorporating *capture* represents a broadening of the 1907 Hague Land Warfare Regulations, which limited the prohibition to the treacherous *killing* or *wounding* of an adversary.[203] The 1998 Rome Statute only makes the "[k]illing or wounding treacherously individuals belonging to the hostile nation or army" a war crime in IAC.[204] Similarly, in NIAC the offense is "[k]illing or wounding treacherously a combatant adversary."[205] Notably, neither of the criminal offenses extends to the capture of an enemy. In terms of customary law, the ICRC *Customary Humanitarian Law Study* states that the "[k]illing, injuring or capturing an adversary by resort to perfidy is prohibited,"[206] and "capturing by resort to perfidy is illegal under customary international law but that only acts that result in serious bodily injury, namely killing or injuring, would constitute a war crime."[207] In contrast, the U.S. Department of Defense "has not interpreted customary international law to prohibit U.S. forces from seeking to capture by resort to perfidy."[208]

One type of perfidy relates to uniforms. This can arise in two ways: the misuse of an enemy uniform, or not using a uniform at all. Article 39(2) of AP I indicates that "[i]t is prohibited to make use of the flags or military emblems, insignia or uniforms of adverse Parties while engaging in attacks or in order to shield, favour, protect or impede military operations." This offers a more detailed prohibition of *improper use*, which was referred to in Article 23(f) of the 1907 Hague Land Warfare Regulations. The need for greater specificity resulted from "the controversial Skorzeny trial of 1947, in which a U.S. Military Court acquitted

German soldiers who—in the course of the Battle of the Bulge in December 1944—had dressed in American uniforms prior to engaging in combat."[209]

However, there remains a State reluctance to fully embrace the wide-ranging prohibition suggested in AP I. This is reflected in the ICRC *Customary Humanitarian Law Study*, where the customary rule is referred to as the "*[i]mproper use* of the flags or military emblems, insignia or uniforms of the adversary is prohibited,"[210] and in the Canadian reservation to AP I, which indicates that the country did "not intend to be bound by the prohibitions contained in paragraph 2 of Article 39 to make use of military emblems, insignia or uniforms of adverse parties in order to shield, favour, protect or impede military operations."[211] U.S. personnel are not subject to the restrictive rule found in Article 39(2).[212] Rather, the U.S. interpretation is focused on *not fighting* in an enemy uniform, indicating that use of enemy uniforms to facilitate movements or infiltrations of enemy lines is considered permissible. The UK's *Manual of The Law of Armed Conflict* indicates that members of commando or reconnaissance forces using enemy forces would contravene the Additional Protocol rule but "would not forfeit prisoner of war status."[213]

Further, the rules regarding treachery would not affect existing international law relating to spying. In that respect, "a spy who succeeds in rejoining his own forces cannot, if subsequently captured, be tried for his earlier spying offences. That means that he [or she] could not be punished for wearing enemy uniform while committing those offences."[214]

A more frequent concern in contemporary conflict, given its asymmetrical nature, is the feigning of civilian status. The wearing of a uniform or a fixed distinctive sign or carrying arms openly has long been a critical element of distinction, a constitutive principle of IHL. During IAC, even where these distinguishing requirements are relaxed in the limited circumstances set out in Article 44(3) of AP I (*see* Chapter 3, 2.1.3: *Additional Protocol I*), it remained that a combatant was required to carry arms openly during an attack, or while engaged in a deployment prior to an attack. To engage in armed conflict without meeting the legal requirements of belligerency exposed a person to trial under the domestic law of the capturing State, and possibly to allegations of a war crime (*see* Chapter 3, 2.2: *Unlawful or unprivileged belligerents*). Even in NIAC, where there is no lawful combatant status, feigning civilian status while engaging in hostilities leaves the person involved subject to prosecution for perfidious conduct (*see* Chapter 3, 3: *Non-international armed conflict*).

However, conflict against non-State actors in a counterinsurgency and counter-terrorism context raises a number of challenging issues regarding uniforms, and whether wearing civilian clothing constitutes perfidy. This can occur, in part, because of the law enforcement functions that security forces may be required to perform, whether in IAC or NIAC. It is permissible under human rights law for police and other security forces to carry out law enforcement duties in civilian clothes, and even with an undercover status. However, this may bring those security forces into contact with insurgent forces because of that latter group's involvement in ordinary criminal acts (e.g., bank theft, hostage taking) or because the security forces are the public face of the governing authority (e.g., manning vehicle checkpoints). This can lead to exchanges of fire while those security forces are operating in civilian clothes. In other situations, the wearing of local garb might arise as a result of special forces units mentoring local police and security forces during counterinsurgency, as occurred in Afghanistan.[215]

Another challenging aspect of contemporary conflict is terrorism, and the determination about whether counterterrorism operations are taking in the context of an armed conflict. Perfidy is a humanitarian law concept, and as such requires the existence of an armed conflict. This can be an issue particularly during the initial stages of violence against organized armed groups, or in the context of an unexpected armed attack by a non-State actor, prompting military action to be taken by a State in self-defense. Each of these situations raise the issue of the threshold for the existence of a NIAC. Absent an armed conflict, there is no obligation to distinguish oneself from the civilian population. Attacking State security forces outside of an armed conflict will almost always amount to a serious domestic criminal law offense, subjecting the terrorists to prosecution. The important difference is that an act of perfidy subjects the individual to prosecution for a violation of international law (a war crime), which may allow for prosecution by different tribunals with different consequences.

Finally, the disguising of military and police forces as members of an organized armed group, or recruiting captured or surrendered insurgents to work for security forces, in the context of pseudo-ops has occurred in counterinsurgency operations, particularly in Africa.[216] Further analysis needs to be done regarding what activity is prohibited in respect of pseudo-operations given the inclusion of treacherous killing and wounding of an opponent as a war crime in the 1998 Rome Statute.[217]

5.2 Capture rather than kill

The prohibition against killing an enemy who is *hors de combat* (or, in other words, "to kill or wound an enemy who, having laid down his arms, or having no longer means of defence, has surrendered at discretion") is not only reflected in Article 23(c) the 1907 Hague Land Warfare Regulations, Article 41 of AP I, and Common Article 3 of the 1949 Geneva Conventions (i.e., protection of persons taking no active part in hostilities) but is also a long-standing rule of customary international law.[218] Consideration of that principle, along with the prohibition against unnecessary suffering and superfluous injury, has been the genesis of a discussion as to whether there is, in certain circumstances, outside of traditional *hors de combat* situations (e.g., under an enemy's power, surrender, wounds, or injury) an obligation to capture rather than kill an enemy belligerent when capture is a tactically feasible alternative.

At the heart of the issue of an expanded obligation to capture an opponent is whether it is lawful to target an unarmed or non-threatening enemy belligerent who is not otherwise *hors de combat* based solely on a status determination. The killing of an unarmed enemy has been the subject of ethical debate.[219]

A broad authority to kill was rejected by Jean Pictet of the ICRC in his famous statement that:

> if we can put a soldier out of action by capturing him we should not wound him, if we can obtain the same result by wounding him, we must not kill him, if there are two means to achieve the same military advantage we must choose the one which causes the lesser evil.[220]

It also provided an underpinning for an argument presented by the ICRC in Part IX of the Interpretive Guidance on the Notion of Direct Participation in Hostilities Under International Humanitarian Law[221] that an obligation not to use any more force than is necessary means that, depending on the circumstances, the armed or police forces of the government may be required to give an opponent an opportunity to surrender "where there manifestly is no necessity for the use of lethal force."[222] However, this is one area where the Interpretive Guidance has been the subject of criticism by military experts who worked on its development[223] (*see also* Chapter 6, 3: *Targeting persons*).

It has been suggested there is a requirement to use least restrictive means (LRM) based, in part, on an expanded notion of *hors de combat* and the prohibition on unnecessary suffering and superfluous injury.[224] In effect this reflects the transformation into a *legal obligation* "of Sun Tzu's statement that 'to capture the enemy is better than to destroy it . . . [t]o subdue the enemy without fighting is the acme of skill.'"[225] However, the LRM theory has attracted considerable criticism.[226] As one analysis has noted, "Article 35 [of AP I] deals with unnecessary suffering, not unnecessary killing, which are two very different ideas."[227] In this regard, "[h]istorically and presently, the concept of military necessity permits lethal force against lawful targets, even when non-lethal force might be sufficient as a first resort.[228]

6   Conclusion

Weapons are regulated by a combination of treaty and customary international law. A key principle in assessing the legality of a weapon or weapons system is whether it causes superfluous injury or unnecessary suffering. That in turn requires consideration of whether weapons, projectiles, and methods and means of warfare are of a nature to cause such injury or suffering. Since the 1970s, the international community has increased its efforts to prohibit specific weapons. The areas of regulation or prohibition reflect the impact of advances in technology on the conduct of warfare. These include expanding bullets; protection of the environment; mines, booby-traps, and improvised explosive devices; cluster munitions; poison, chemical, bacteriological, and nuclear weapons; cyber weapons; autonomous weapons and the use of nanotechnology. The regulation of methods of warfare extends to the use of treachery, and increasingly the issue of the capture rather than killing an opponent. The effort to control, or prohibit certain methods and means of warfare is an essential part of IHL. This is an area of law that raises complex issues. However, in the final analysis, the words of Joseph Kunz nearly 70 years ago perhaps best identify the solution to this regulatory challenge: "[w]eapons, however terrible, however destructive, however automatic, are in themselves dead machines; everything depends on the heart of men that use them."[229]

Notes

1 Carl von Clausewitz, *On War* 75 (Michael Howard & Peter Paret eds and trans., 1989).
2 Protocol (I) Additional to the Geneva Conventions of 12 August 1949, and Relating to the Protection of Victims of International Armed Conflicts, 8 June 1977, 1125 U.N.T.S. 3 [hereinafter AP I] (entered into force 7 December 1978) (signed by the United States 12 December 1977, not transmitted to U.S. Senate, *see* S. Treaty Doc. No. 100–2 (1987)).
3 Jean S. Pictet et al., Commentary on the Additional Protocols of 8 June 1977 to the Geneva Conventions of 12 August 1949 (ICRC, 1987), para 1402 [hereinafter AP Commentary].
4 AP I, Art 35(2).
5 AP I, Art 35(3).
6 Adam Roberts & Richard Guelff, *Documents on the Laws of War* 53 (3rd edn, 2003).
7 W. Hays Parks, *Conventional Weapons and Weapons Reviews*, 8 Y.B. Int'l L. 55, 67–8 (2005).
8 *Id.* at 68.
9 Convention (IV) Respecting the Laws and Customs of War on Land and its annex: Regulations concerning the Laws and Customs of War on Land, 18 October 1907, 36 Stat. 2277, 3 Martens Nouveau Recueil (ser. 3) 461 [hereinafter 1907 Hague IV Regulations].
10 Parks, *supra* note 7, at 68. *See also* Roberts & Guelff, *supra* note 6, at 77 n.3 (where it is noted that the authentic French text of the 1899 Regulations referred to *superfluous injury*).
11 Parks, *supra* note 7, at 69.
12 *Id.* at 69–70.
13 AP I, Art 35(2).
14 AP I, Art 35(3).
15 AP I, Art 36.
16 Convention on the Prohibition of Military or Any Other Hostile Use of Environmental Modification Techniques, 10 December 1976, 1108 U.N.T.S. 151 (1978).
17 Convention on Prohibitions or Restrictions on the Use of Certain Conventional Weapons Which May be Deemed to be Excessively Injurious or to Have Indiscriminate Effects, 10 October 1980, 1342 U.N.T.S. 137 [hereinafter CCW].
18 Convention on the Prohibition of the Development, Production, Stockpiling and Use of Chemical Weapons and on Their Destruction, 13 January 1993, 1974 U.N.T.S. 317 [hereinafter CWC].
19 Convention on the Prohibition of the Use, Stockpiling, Production and Transfer of Anti-Personnel Mines and on Their Destruction, 18 September 1997, 2056 U.N.T.S. 241 [hereinafter Ottawa Convention].
20 Rome Statute of the International Criminal Court, 17 July 1998, 2187 U.N.T.S. 90 [hereinafter Rome Statute].
21 Convention on Cluster Munitions, 30 May 2008, 48 I.L.M. 357 [hereinafter CCM].
22 *Customary International Humanitarian Law Study* (Jean-Marie Henckaerts & Louise Doswald-Beck eds, 2005) [hereinafter ICRC *Customary Humanitarian Law Study*].

23 Secretary-General's Bulletin: Observance by United Nations Forces of International Humanitarian Law, in Bruce Oswald, Helen Durham, & Adrian Bates, *Documents on the Law of UN Peace Operations* 201–5 (2010) [hereinafter Secretary-General's Bulletin]. *See* William H. Boothby, *Weapons and the Law of Armed Conflict* 31–3 (2nd edn, 2016) (for a discussion of the ICRC *Customary International Humanitarian Law Study* and the Secretary-General's Bulletin).

24 Boothby, *supra* note 23, at 58.

25 *Id.* at 320.

26 *Id.*

27 *Id.*

28 *Id.* However, *see Tagayeva v. Russia*, Application no. 26562/07 and 6 other applications, Eur. Ct. H. R. para 589, at 138 (2017), *available at* http://hudoc.echr.coe. int/eng?i=001-172660 (where the European Court of Human Rights incorporates IHL concepts of indiscriminate weapons in its analysis).

29 *Id.* at 4.

30 AP I, Art 49(1).

31 Samantha Power, *"A Problem From Hell": America and the Age of Genocide* 334 (2002).

32 *Tallinn Manual on the International Law Applicable to Cyber Operations* (Michael N. Schmitt ed., 2013) [hereinafter *Tallinn 1.0*].

33 *Id.* at 141–2.

34 *Id.* at 142.

35 Yoram Dinstein, *The Conduct of Hostilities Under the Law of International Armed Conflict* 64 (2nd edn, 2010).

36 Leslie Green, *The Contemporary Law of Armed Conflict* 151 (3rd edn, 2008).

37 Dinstein, *supra* note 35, at 64.

38 Parks, *supra* note 7, at 86–7 n.123.

39 Boothby, *supra* note 23, at 49. *See also* William J. Fenrick, *The Conventional Weapons Convention: A Modest but Useful Treaty*, 279 Int'l. Rev. Red Cross 498, 500 (1990) ("A weapon causes unnecessary suffering when in practice it inevitably causes injury or suffering disproportionate to its military effectiveness. In determining the military effectiveness of a weapon, one looks at the primary purpose for which it was designed.").

40 Boothby, *supra* note 23, at 53.

41 *Id.* at 4.

42 Dinstein, *supra* note 35, at 65.

43 *Id.* at 65.

44 Judith Gardam, *Necessity, Proportionality and the Use of Force by States* 67–75 (2004).

45 ICRC *Customary Humanitarian Law Study*, at 240 (emphasis added).

46 *Manual of the Law of Armed Conflict*, para 2.6.1 (UK Ministry of Defence ed., 2004) [hereinafter *UK LOAC Manual*].

47 Dinstein, *supra* note 35, at 65; Henri Meyrowitz, *The Principle of Superfluous Injury or Unnecessary Suffering from the Declaration of St. Petersburg of 1868 to Additional Protocol I of 1977*, 34 Int'l Rev. Red Cross 98, 109–10 (1994).

48 Dinstein, *supra* note 35, at 65.

49 Geoffrey S. Corn, Laurie R. Blank, Chris Jenks, & Eric Talbot Jensen, *Belligerent Targeting and the Invalidity of a Least Harmful Means Rule*, 89 Int'l L. Stud. 536, 601–7 (2013).

50 Thomas M. Franck, *On Proportionality of Countermeasures in International Law*, 102 Am. J. Int'l L. 715, 716 (2008) ("the principle of proportionality has mostly eluded definition in any but the most general terms.").

51 Parks, *supra* note 7, at 104.

52 *Id.*; *UK LOAC Manual*, para 6.1.2.

53 Dinstein, *supra* note 35, at 65.
54 Corn et al., *supra* note 49, at 601–3.
55 Boothby, *supra* note 23, at 58; Legality of the Threat or Use of Nuclear Weapons, Advisory Opinion, 1996 I.C.J. 226, para 78, at 257 (8 July).
56 Boothby, *supra* note 23, at 58.
57 *Id.*
58 Legality of the Threat or Use of Nuclear Weapons, Advisory Opinion, 1996 I.C.J. 226, para 78, at 257 (8 July).
59 AP Commentary, para 1968.
60 AP I, Art 51(5)(a).
61 AP Commentary, para 1958.
62 *Palestine/Israel: Indiscriminate Palestinian Rocket Attacks,* Human Rights Watch (9 July 2014), *available at* www.hrw.org/news/2014/07/09/palestine/israel-indiscriminate-palestinian-rocket-attacks (the unguided rockets launched by Gaza armed groups are inherently indiscriminate and incapable of being targeted at possible military targets in or near Israeli population centers).
63 Boothby, *supra* note 23, at 66.
64 *Id.* at 67.
65 AP I, Art 51(5)(b).
66 Boothby, *supra* note 23, at 67.
67 Stefan Oeter, "Methods and Means of Combat," in *The Handbook of International Humanitarian Law* 119, 131 (Dieter Fleck ed., 2008).
68 Roberts & Guelff, *supra* note 6, at 407.
69 Oeter, *supra* note 67, at 131–2.
70 A.P.V. Rogers, *Law on the Battlefield* 168 (2004).
71 Oeter, *supra* note 67, at 132–3.
72 Roberts & Guelff, *supra* note 6, at 408.
73 Boothby, *supra* note 23, at 83.
74 Oeter, *supra* note 67, at 133.
75 *Id.*
76 Boothby, *supra* note 23, at 84.
77 ICRC *Customary Humanitarian Law Study*, at 143–6.
78 *Id.* 147–51.
79 *Id.* 151–7.
80 Boothby, *supra* note 23, at 89.
81 ICRC *Customary Humanitarian Law Study*, at 153–4.
82 Legality of the Threat or Use of Nuclear Weapons, Advisory Opinion, 1996 I.C.J. 226, para 31, at 242 (8 July).
83 U.S. Dep't of Def., *Law of War Manual* 6.10.3.1 (June 2015, updated December 2016) [hereinafter *DoD Law of War Manual*].
84 *See* A Guide to the Legal Review of New Weapons, Means and Methods of Warfare: Measures to Implement Article 36 of Additional Protocol I of 1977, Int'l Comm. of the Red Cross (January 2006), *available at* https://app.icrc.org/e-briefing/new-tech-modern-battlefield/media/documents/12-A-Guide-to-the-Legal-Review-of-New-Weapons.pdf. But *see* Boothby, *supra* note 23, at 349–52 (for a critique of the ICRC Guide).
85 Boothby, *supra* note 23, at 342–3.
86 Parks, *supra* note 7, at 106.
87 *Id.* at 107; Boothby, *supra* note 23, at 344.
88 Boothby, *supra* note 23, at 345.
89 Dinstein, *supra* note 35, at 88.
90 Boothby, *supra* note 23, at 347–8.
91 Parks, *supra* note 7, at 129.

92   Declaration (IV, 3) Concerning the Prohibition of the Use of Expanding Bullets, 29 July 1899, 26 Martens Nouveau Recueil (ser. 2) 1002, 187 Consol. T.S. 459.
93   Boothby, *supra* note 23, at 138–9.
94   Rome Statute, Art 8(2)(b)(xix).
95   *Id*. Art 8(2)(e)(xv).
96   ICRC *Customary Humanitarian Law Study*, at 268.
97   *DoD Law of War Manual*, 6.5.4.4.
98   Rev. Conf. of the Rome Statute, 13th plenary meeting, 11 June 2010, ICC Doc. RC/Res. 5 (advance version) (16 June 2010), preambular para 9; Boothby, *supra* note 23, at 143.
99   Watkin, *Chemical Agents and "Expanding" Bullets: Limited Law Enforcement Exceptions or Unwarranted Handcuffs*, 82 Int'l L. Stud. 193, 199 (2006).
100 Geneva Convention Relative to the Protection of Civilian Persons in Time of War Art, 64, 12 August 1949, 6 U.S.T. 3516, 75 U.N.T.S. 973 (emphasis added).
101 *The U. S. Army, Marine Corps, Counterinsurgency Field Manual*, paras 6–90, at 229 (2007) [hereinafter *Counterinsurgency Manual*] ("the primary frontline COIN force is often the police—not the military.").
102 Watkin, *Fighting at the Legal Boundaries: Controlling the Use of Force in Contemporary Conflict* 486–91 (2016).
103 Watkin, *supra* note 99, at 208.
104 *DoD Law of War Manual*, 6.5.4.4.
105 James Pettifer, *The Kosova Liberation Army: Underground War to Balkan Insurgency, 1948–2001*, at 70 (2013).
106 Protocol (II) on Prohibitions or Restrictions on the Use of Mines, Booby-Traps and Other Devices, Annexed to the Convention on Prohibitions or Restrictions on the Use of Certain Conventional Weapons Which May be Deemed to be Excessively Injurious or to Have Indiscriminate Effects, 10 October 1980, 19 ILM 1523 [hereinafter CCW Protocol II].
107 Protocol (II) on Prohibitions or Restrictions on the Use of Mines, Booby-Traps and Other Devices, as Amended on 3 May 1996, Annexed to the Convention on Prohibitions or Restrictions on the Use of Certain Conventional Weapons Which May be Deemed to be Excessively Injurious or to Have Indiscriminate Effects, 3 May 1996, 2048 U.N.T.S. 93 [hereinafter 1996 Amended CCW Protocol II].
108 *See* Ottawa Convention.
109 *See* Boothby, *supra* note 23, at 149.
110 Convention (VIII) Relative to the Laying of Automatic Submarine Contact Mines, 18 October 1907, 36 Stat. 2332.
111 Dinstein, *supra* note 35, at 75.
112 Wolff Heintschel von Heinegg, "The Law of Armed Conflict at Sea," in *The Handbook of International Humanitarian* Law 475, 520 (Dieter Fleck ed., 2nd edn, 2008).
113 CCW Protocol II, Art 2(1).
114 Ottawa Convention, Art 2(1).
115 1996 Amended CCW Protocol II, Art 2(2).
116 *See, e.g.*, Dinstein, *supra* note 35, at 74.
117 ICRC *Customary Humanitarian Law Study*, at 280.
118 *Id*. at 283.
119 *Id*. at 285.
120 Boothby, *supra* note 23, at 173.
121 Kenneth Anderson, *The Ottawa Convention Banning Landmines, the Role of International Non-governmental Organizations and the Idea of International Civil Society*, 11 Eur. J. Int'l. L. 91, 92 (2000).
122 Canada Landmine Foundation, *available at* http://canadianlandmine.org/the-issues/the-treaty

123 Ottawa Convention, Art 1(1)(c).

124 *See, e.g., UK LOAC Manual,* para 6.13. *See also* the Understanding submitted by Canada:

> Understanding:
>
> It is the understanding of the Government of Canada that, in the context of operations, exercises or other military activity sanctioned by the United Nations or otherwise conducted in accordance with international law, the mere participation by the Canadian Forces, or individual Canadians, in operations, exercises or other military activity conducted in combination with the armed forces of States not party to the Convention which engage in activity prohibited under the Convention would not, by itself, be considered to be assistance, encouragement or inducement in accordance with the meaning of those terms in article 1, paragraph 1 (c).
>
> Convention on the Prohibition of the Use, Stockpiling, Production and Transfer of Anti-Personnel Mines and on their Destruction, 18 September 1997, Understanding Submitted by Canada, ICRC, *available at* https://ihl-databases.icrc.org/applic/ihl/ ihl.nsf/Notification.xsp?action=openDocument&documentId= 93A8C30465E5CBC54125658500490529

125 Boothby, *supra* note 23, at 150.

126 *Id.* at 187.

127 *Id.* at 150.

128 *DoD Law of War Manual,* 6.12.14.

129 1996 Amended Protocol II, Art 2(2).

130 *Id.* Art 6.

131 Dinstein, *supra* note 35, at 71.

132 *Id.* at 71.

133 ICRC *Customary Humanitarian Law Study,* at 278.

134 1996 Amended Protocol II, Art 2(5).

135 Thomas E. Ricks, *Fiasco: The American Military Adventure in Iraq* 217 (2007).

136 A. J. Bosker, *IEDs Will Remain "Weapon of Choice" for Decades,* Joint IED Defeat Organization News Service (26 September 2012), *available at* www.army.mil/ article/87833/Congress_told_IEDs_will_remain__weapon_of_choice__for_decades

137 Boothby, *supra* note 23, at 169.

138 *See* CCM.

139 *Id.* Art 2.

140 Boothby, *supra* note 23, at 265.

141 *Id.* at 264–5.

142 Dinstein, *supra* note 35, at 80.

143 Boothby, *supra* note 23, at 266.

144 States Parties and Signatories by Region, The Convention on Cluster Munitions, *available at* www.clusterconvention.org/the-convention/convention-status/

145 *DoD Law of War Manual,* 6.13.3.

146 CCM, Art 21(3).

147 Jeff Abramson, *Treaty Analysis: The Convention on Cluster Munitions,* Arms Control Association (4 December 2008), *available at* www.armscontrol.org/act/2008_12/ CCM

148 Green, *supra* note 36, at 167.

149 Dinstein, *supra* note 35, at 68.

150 *Id.* at 69.

151 Declaration (IV, 2) Concerning the Prohibition of the Use of Projectiles Diffusing Asphyxiating Gases, 29 July 1899, 26 Martens Nouveau Recueil (ser. 2) 998, 187 Consol. T.S. 453.

152   Protocol for the Prohibition of the Use in War of Asphyxiating, Poisonous, or Other Gases, and of Bacteriological Methods of Warfare, 17 June 1925, 26 U.S.T. 571, 94 L.N.T.S. 65.

153   Rome Statute, Art 8(2)(b)(xvii).

154   Boothby, *supra* note 23, at 123.

155   ICRC *Customary Humanitarian Law Study*, at 261–3.

156   *Prosecutor v. Tadić*, Case No. IT-94-1-A, Decision on The Defence Motion For Interlocutory Appeal On Jurisdiction, para 124 (Int'l Crim. Trib. for the former Yugoslavia 2 October 1995).

157   *Id*. paras 121–4.

158   Boothby, *supra* note 23, at 124.

159   Eric Schmitt, *ISIS Used Chemical Arms at Least 52 Times in Syria and Iraq, Report Says, N.Y. Times* (21 November 2016), *available at* www.nytimes.com/2016/11/21/world/middleeast/isis-chemical-weapons-syria-iraq-mosul.html?_r=0

160   CWC, Art 1(5), 2(9)(d).

161   *Finogenov v. Russia*, 2001-VI Eur. Ct. H.R. 365.

162   Watkin, *supra* note 99, at 206.

163   *DoD Law of War Manual*, 6.16.2.

164   David P. Fidler, *The Meaning of Moscow: "Non-lethal" Weapons and International Law in the Early 21st Century*, 87 Int'l Rev. Red Cross 525, 546 (2005).

165   Dinstein, *supra* note 35, at 82.

166   Convention on the Prohibition of the Development, Production and Stockpiling of Bacteriological (Biological) and Toxin Weapons and on Their Destruction, 10 April 1972, 1015 U.N.T.S. 163.

167   Boothby, *supra* note 23, at 112.

168   Dinstein, *supra* note 35, at 83.

169   *Id*.

170   ICRC *Customary Humanitarian Law Study*, at 258 (Rule 73).

171   *Legality of the Threat or Use of Nuclear Weapons*, Advisory Opinion, 1996 I.C.J. 226, para 105, at 242 (8 July).

172   *Id*.

173   *Id*. para 78, at 257.

174   *Id*. para 94, at 262. *See also* Green, *supra* note 36, at 156.

175   *DoD Law of War Manual*, 6.18.

176   *122 Countries Adopt "Historic" UN Treaty to Ban Nuclear Weapons*, CBC News (7 July 2017), *available at* www.cbc.ca/news/world/un-treaty-ban-nuclear-weapons-1.4192761

177   *Tallinn 1.0*, at 142.

178   *Id*. at 106.

179   Dinstein, *War, Aggression and Self-Defence* 212 (5th edn, 2011).

180   Andrew C. Foltz, *Stuxnet, Schmitt Analysis, and the Cyber "Use-of-Force" Debate*, 67 Joint Force Quarterly 40, 43–4 (2012).

181   Boothby, *supra* note 23, at 239.

182   *Tallinn 1.0*, at 143–4.

183   *Id*. at 144–6.

184   Boothby, *supra* note 23, at 240.

185   *Tallinn 1.0*, at 153–6.

186   Boothby, *supra* note 23, at 248.

187   *Id*. at 251.

188   Ken Anderson & Mathew C. Waxman, *Law and Ethics for Autonomous Weapon Systems: Why a Ban Won't Work and How the Laws of War Can*, American University Washington College of Law Research Paper No. 2013–11, Columbia Public Law Research Paper 14–18 (2013), *available at* https://unoda-web.s3-accelerate.

amazonaws.com/wp-content/uploads/assets/media/702327CF5F68E71D
C1257CC2004245BE/file/LawandEthicsforAutonomousWeaponSystems_Why
abanwontworkandhowthelawsofwarcan_Waxman%2Banderson.pdf

189 *US Navy Awards $287.9M Close-In Weapon System Contract, Naval Today* (5 August
2016), *available at* http://navaltoday.com/2016/08/05/us-navy-awards-287–9m-
close-in-weapon-system-contract/

190 *Phalanx Close-In Weapon System*, Raytheon, *available at* www.raytheon.com/
capabilities/products/phalanx/

191 *Counter-Rocket, Artillery, Mortar (C-RAM) Intercept Land-Based Phalanx Weapon
System (LPWS)*, United States Army Acquisition Support Center, *available at* http://
asc.army.mil/web/portfolio-item/ms-c-ram_lpws/

192 Anderson & Waxman, *supra* note 188, at 1.

193 *Tallinn 1.0*, at 257 (where *active cyber defence* is defined as: "A proactive measure
for detecting or obtaining information as to a cyber intrusion, cyber attack, or
impending cyber operation, or for determining the origin of an operation that
involves launching a pre-emptive, preventative or cyber counter-operation against
the source."). *See also* Gordon Corerra, *UK Moves to "Active Cyber-Defence,"* BBC
News (13 September 2016), *available at* www.bbc.com/news/technology-37353
835 (the UK's focus on defense is distinguished "from the US use of the term,
which relates to pursuing hackers into their networks.").

194 Seumas Miller, *Shooting to Kill: The Ethics of Police and Military Use of Force* 283
(2016).

195 *Killer Robots and the Concept of Meaningful Human Control: Memorandum to
Convention on Conventional Weapons (CCW) Delegates*, Human Rights Watch (April
2016), *available at* www.hrw.org/sites/default/files/supporting_resources/robots_
meaningful_human_control_final.pdf

196 *DoD Law of War Manual*, 6.5.9.3.

197 *Id.*

198 *Id.*

199 Boothby, *supra* note 23, at 248. *See also* Anderson & Waxman, *supra* note 188,
at 27.

200 S.E. Miller, *A New Renaissance: Tech, Science, Engineering and Medicine are Becoming
One*, 7 N.Y.L.J. 5 (2003), referred to in Boothby, *supra* note 23, at 258 n. 178.

201 Hitoshi Nasu, *Nanotechnology and the Future of the Law of Weaponry*, 91 Int'l. L.
Stud. 486, 487 (2015).

202 Boothby, *supra* note 23, at 261.

203 1907 Hague IV Regulations, Art 23(b).

204 Rome Statute, Art 8(2)(b)(xi).

205 *Id.* Art 8(2)(e)(ix).

206 ICRC *Customary Humanitarian Law Study*, at 221.

207 *Id.* at 225.

208 *DoD Law of War Manual*, 5.22.2.1.

209 Dinstein, *supra* note 35, at 237.

210 ICRC *Customary Humanitarian Law Study*, at 213 (emphasis added).

211 Reservations Made at Time of Ratification, Canada, *available at* https://ihl-databases.
icrc.org/applic/ihl/ihl.nsf/Notification.xsp?action=openDocument&documentId=
172FFEC04ADC80F2C1256402003FB314

212 *DoD Law of War Manual*, 5.23.3.

213 *UK LOAC Manual*, para 5.11.1.

214 *Id.* para 5.11 n.47.

215 Ann Scott Tyson, *American Spartan: The Promise, The Mission, and the Betrayal of
Special Forces Major Jim Gant* 156–7, 162, 228–9 (2014); Hays Parks, *Special
Forces' Wear of Non-Standard Uniforms*, 4 Chic. J. Int'l. L. 493 (2003).

216   *See* Huw Bennett, *Fighting the Mau Mau: The British Army and Counter-Insurgency in the Kenya Emergency* 152–8 (2013); Piet Nortje, *Battalion: The Inside Story of South Africa's Elite Fighting Unit* 113–14 (2003); Jugdep S. Chima, "The Punjab Police and Counterinsurgency against Sikh Militants in India," in *Policing Insurgencies: Cops as Counterinsurgents* 258, 280–1, 283–4 (C. Christine Fair & Sumit Ganguly eds, 2014); Randall Wilson, *Blue Fish in a Dark Sea: Police Intelligence in a Counterinsurgency* 121–33 (2013). *See also* Eeben Barlow, *Composite Warfare: The Conduct of Successful Ground Operations in Africa*, Appendix 1, 506–9 (2016) (for an outline given to an African army regarding the use of pseudo-operations to armed anti-government forces and terrorists).

217   *See generally* Wilson, *supra* note 216.

218   ICRC *Customary Humanitarian Law Study*, at 163–70.

219   Michael Walzer, *Just and Unjust Wars* 138–43 (3rd edn, 1977).

220   N. Melzer, Interpretive Guidance on the Notion of Direct Participation in Hostilities Under International Humanitarian Law (2009) [hereinafter the Interpretive Guidance] (quoting J. Pictet, *Development and Principles of International Humanitarian Law* 75 (1985)).

221   *Id. See also* Jamie A. Williamson, *Challenges of Twenty-First Century Conflicts: A Look at Direct Participation in Hostilities*, 20 Duke J. Comp. & Int'l L. 457 (2010).

222   Interpretive Guidance, at 81, 82 n.221.

223   For critiques of the *Interpretative Guidance*, and a reply by its main author *see* Schmitt, *Deconstructing Direct Participation in Hostilities*, 42 N.Y.U.J. Int'l L. & Pol. 697 (2010); Boothby, *"And for Such Time as": The Time Dimension to Direct Participation in Hostilities*, 42 N.Y.U.J. Int'l L. & Pol. 741 (2010); Watkin, *Opportunity Lost: Organized Armed Groups and the ICRC "Direct Participation in Hostilities" Interpretive Guidance*, 42 N.Y.U. J. Int'l L. & Pol. 641, 642 (2010); Parks, *Part IX of the ICRC "Direct Participation in Hostilities" Study: No Mandate, No Expertise, and Legally Incorrect*, 42 N.Y.U. J. Int'l L. & Pol. 769 (2010). *See also* Melzer, *Keeping the Balance Between Military Necessity and Humanity: A Response to Four Critiques of the ICRC's Interpretive Guidance on the Notion of Direct Participation in Hostilities*, 42 N.Y.U.J. Int'l L. & Pol. 831 (2010).

224   Ryan Goodman, *The Power to Kill or Capture Enemy Combatants*, 24 Eur. J. Int'l L. 819, 830–52 (2013).

225   Green, *supra* note 36, at 151.

226   Corn et al., *supra* note 49, at 536; Michael N. Schmitt, *Wound, Capture, or Kill: A Reply to Ryan Goodman's "The Power to Kill or Capture Enemy Combatants,"* 24 Eur. J. Int'l L. 855, 857 (2013).

227   Jens David Ohlin & Larry May, *Necessity in International Law* 225 (2016).

228   *Id.* at 229.

229   Josef L. Kunz, *The Chaotic Status of the Laws of War and the Urgent Necessity for Their Revision*, 45 Am. J. Int'l L. 37, 41 (1951).

8   Neutrality and naval warfare

1   Introduction

International law regulates the use of sea power by States at all times. During peacetime, a complex mosaic of treaty and customary international law—the law of the sea—governs the activities of State and private activities on and beneath the seas. But, during armed conflict, specialized rules for the regulation of hostilities come into force. It is important to note that, while these IHL naval warfare rules will often trump or qualify the general laws of the sea, the peacetime laws remain in effect even during armed conflict.

During the course of armed conflict, military operations will frequently take place on or from the seas. These actions may take many forms: from a projection of military power to land from the sea, to combat between the naval forces of opposing parties, to actions to interdict seaborne traffic headed to or from enemy ports.[1] As a general rule, IHL principles and rules applicable to land warfare—military necessity, humanity, precautions, and proportionality—also apply to naval warfare.[2] However, over time additional specialized IHL rules evolved to address unique aspects of naval operations. These rules specifically regulate naval hostilities, protect the wounded, sick, and shipwrecked, and address the deployment of undersea mines and torpedoes. Furthermore, because international waters serve as transportation routes for belligerent and neutral States alike, the law of neutrality complements the law of war and provides a legal framework intended to reconcile the interests of belligerents and neutrals.[3]

The international law of the sea regime is a relevant source of law during both peacetime and during armed conflict, and applies to the high seas and other international waters (like international straits). This law regulates the activities of naval power whenever States project such power beyond the waters of their national territory. This national territory includes territorial seas—the areas of the sea within the 12-mile nautical limit of national land borders. While it is often complex to determine exactly where the territorial sea baseline is properly drawn (especially for neighboring States with territorial ambitions over the same areas of adjacent seas), this issue is beyond the scope of this chapter. This is because IHL takes a more practical approach to the scope of application for the law of naval warfare, focusing instead on the seaborne nature of the operations or the use of the sea to support military operations. For example, though the law of the sea has no impact on the use of internal waters, such as lakes and rivers, projecting military power onto such waters would implicate the laws of naval warfare. Just imagine an IAC between Bolivia and Peru involving naval engagements on Lake Titicaca: although occurring on an internal body of water, IHL naval warfare rules would apply because of the nature of the hostilities.

2 An introduction to the sources of law applicable during naval warfare

Like land warfare, the conduct of naval operations is regulated by IHL principles. Furthermore, targeting rules (*see* Chapter 6: *Targeting*) and rules regarding the legality of weapons (*see* Chapter 7: *Weapons, means, and methods*) apply to seaborne platforms whenever combat power is projected from the sea to the land.[4] For example, if a naval vessel launches a cruise missile or a naval gunfire attack on a land-based target, the legality of the attack must be assessed pursuant to IHL targeting principles and rules applicable to land warfare.

When naval operations are confined to the sea, there is a much greater likelihood of an intersection of the interests in the use of the seas between neutral and belligerent States. Accordingly, the law of neutrality—though not limited in its application to naval warfare—is especially relevant to this domain of armed conflict. The law of neutrality defines the rights and obligations of neutral States vis-à-vis belligerent States, and the rights and obligations of belligerent States vis-à-vis the neutral. Therefore, like IHL itself, the law of neutrality reflects a rational balance between competing State interests. Neutrality law also protects the sovereign right that all States share to use the high seas. During armed conflict, the law also functions to ensure that neutral States do not unjustifiably interfere with belligerent efforts or provide a military advantage to one belligerent party to the detriment of the other.

There are also certain provisions of IHL that apply exclusively to the domain of naval warfare. These rules have developed over time in response to the unique issues related to naval hostilities. Examples of such issues include how to limit the risk created by sea mines to neutral shipping and post-conflict sea commerce, and how to deal with the humanitarian needs of shipwrecked aircraft and ship crews. Like the regulation of land warfare, almost all of these IHL rules were originally developed to apply exclusively during IAC. But, also like land warfare, naval warfare issues often transcend the inter-State context and enter the intra-State context of NIACs. While neither Common Article 3 of the four Geneva Conventions nor AP II includes provisions specifically focused on naval warfare during NIAC, it would be erroneous to assume that IHL plays no role in regulating such activities. First, as will be noted below, NIAC-specific treaty provisions may be implicated by naval operations. For example, rescuing shipwrecked enemy personnel may not be an express NIAC treaty obligation, but it certainly falls within the scope of Common Article 3's humane treatment mandate. Second, the more specific rules developed to regulate naval warfare in IAC will often extend to analogous operations during NIACs as a matter of customary international law.

Whether dealing with an IAC or a NIAC, issues related to naval warfare will often turn on *where* the operations take place. This, in turn, implicates another branch of international law—the law of the sea. This law defines the limits of national sovereignty on the high seas, and addresses numerous other issues related to international waters and their use by nations. It is necessary to begin with a brief overview of these delineations.

3   The law of the sea: classification of and conduct within the world's waters

International law divides the oceans, seas, and other waters into national and international waters. *National waters* are those over which States enjoy exclusive sovereign rights.[5] *International waters* are those over which no State has *complete* sovereignty, although States may assert limited rights in such waters.[6]

National waters include a State's territorial seas, the area of the ocean extending 12 nautical miles from what is deemed the baseline of State land territory.[7] National waters also include internal waters, waters within the territorial boundary of the State.[8] International waters are all ocean areas that are not subject to the territorial sovereignty of any State. International waters include contiguous zones, exclusive economic zones, and the high seas,[9] all of which are defined, directly or indirectly, in applicable law of the sea treaties.[10]

A State's authority and control over national waters of an internal nature (inside the State's land borders) is absolute—the State exercises complete national jurisdiction in such areas and may restrict or prohibit use of such waters by other States.[11] However, the relationship a sovereign enjoys over its territorial seas (the 12-mile sea) is significantly different. Because a State's territorial seas are considered to fall within its sovereign territory as national waters, the State may exercise jurisdiction and control over such areas. However, international law also allows other States to utilize such waters pursuant to a series of strict limitations.

The most important of these is the concept known as *innocent passage*.[12] During peacetime, innocent passage allows foreign vessels, including military vessels, to pass through territorial waters continuously and expeditiously in order to travel: (1) from/to one part of international waters to/from another, (2) to reach the internal waters of the vessel's home country, or (3) to reach internal waters of another country.[13] However, to constitute innocent passage the vessel's transit through territorial waters must not be prejudicial to peace, good order, or the security of the coastal State.[14] Two of the more significant activities that disqualify innocent passage qualification are overflights and subsurface passage.[15]

Another important concept of the sea navigation waters is *transit passage*, which applies to international straits used by international navigation to travel from one part of international waters to another.[16] Transit passage affords transiting vessels greater rights than innocent passage. Belligerent vessels under transit passage are permitted to take defensive measures consistent with their security, including launching and recovering aircraft, screen formation steaming, and acoustic and electronic surveillance.[17] However, these vessels may not conduct offensive operations against enemy forces, or use such international straits as a place of sanctuary or as a base of operations.[18] Rather, vessels are required to proceed without delay and must refrain from threatening or using force against the territorial integrity and independence of the neutral State or States abutting the strait.[19]

If a State is involved in an armed conflict, naval operations will often extend to the belligerent's respective territorial and even internal national waters. Parties to a conflict will often seek to project their military naval and air forces into such waters belonging to the opponent in order to execute military operations. Obviously, belligerent parties may take action to counter this threat, to include launching attacks against any enemy vessel it identifies in its territorial or national waters, including those overlapping with international straits, or on the high seas (but normally not if the enemy vessel is located in neutral territorial waters). International law also allows States involved in an armed conflict to suspend the right of neutrals to use territorial waters for innocent passage.[20] Neutral rights to use international straits or archipelagic sea lanes, however, may not be impaired.[21] Neutral States are also granted the authority to suspend innocent passage through their territorial waters, but they must apply any restrictions equally to all belligerents.[22] Neutrals may not, however, suspend, hamper, or otherwise impede the right of belligerent vessels exercising transit passage.[23]

Waters beyond the territorial seas are considered international waters and include the oceans, as well as some bodies of water that are not considered to be part of an ocean (e.g., the Mediterranean Sea). All States share an equal right to utilize international waters for navigation or overflight and even to conduct military operations during armed conflicts.[24] There are also two additional zones that extend beyond territorial seas into international waters, although these are relevant primarily for assessing economic and resource exploitation rights: contiguous zones and exclusive economic zones (EEZs).[25] These zones give coastal States certain additional rights in international waters, and place specific limitations on the conduct permissible by other States operating in these waters.

3.1 Status of vessels and aircraft under international law

During armed conflict, IHL regulates permissible actions against a vessel or aircraft operating on, under, or above the high seas. The legality of such actions requires assessing the status of the vessel/aircraft and the accordant authority provided by IHL vis-à-vis such vessel/aircraft. This analysis begins with the vessel's categorization pursuant to the peacetime law of the sea.

Warships are vessels: (1) belonging to the armed forces of a State; (2) bearing external markings that distinguish the character and nationality of the vessels from civilian vessels and aircraft, including civilian vessels and aircraft engaged in non-military government service; (3) under the command of an officer duly commissioned by the government of that State and duly listed as being in its military service; and (4) manned by a crew under regular armed forces discipline.[26] Merchant vessels are vessels other than warships or other non-commercial State vessels.[27] Hospital ships are military or civilian vessels exclusively engaged in the collection, transportation, and treatment of the wounded and sick.[28]

Like warships, all other vessels and aircraft operating in, under, or over international waters should bear markings and, if possible, should be internationally registered. This marking/registration enables both private and public vessels or aircraft to be identified with the State under whose flag it operates. The flag and type of vessel or aircraft trigger specific consequences during armed conflict:

- All vessels and aircraft flagged to a belligerent state may be treated as enemy vessels and aircraft by the opposing belligerent state.[29]
- All such *enemy* vessels (warships), whether private or public, may be captured.[30]
- Enemy warships (and merchant vessels in a convoy protected by enemy warships) may be attacked and sunk.[31]
- Neutral vessels may be stopped and inspected when operating in belligerent territorial waters or in international waters, and if determined to be in violation of their neutrality obligation, may be seized and confiscated.[32]
- Neutral merchant vessels are not subject to attack or capture by a belligerent unless they either take action that renders them a military objective (e.g., by making an effective contribution to an enemy's military capabilities).[33]
- Neutral warships are protected from being made the object of attack unless and for such time as they engage in conduct resulting in a loss of that protection.[34]
- Enemy merchant vessels may be captured and confiscated by the enemy so long as the capture occurs outside neutral waters.[35]
- Enemy merchant vessels are normally protected from attack, unless they engage in activities that render them military objectives.[36]
- Hospital ships and medical aircraft exclusively engaged in their designated humanitarian functions are protected from attack, but measures may be taken to verify their protected status, to include inspection.[37]

During armed conflict, it should be obvious that vessels determined to belong to an enemy State will be treated much differently from vessels determined to belong to a neutral State. In a very general sense, these determinations trigger important presumptions: enemy vessels are subject to capture and/or attack; neutral vessels are protected from unjustified interference. But these presumptions are not conclusive and are subject to being rebutted by certain actions or conduct. These presumptions and rebuttal considerations will be addressed below.

4 The law of neutrality

4.1 An introduction to neutrality

The law of neutrality is a branch of international law that complements IHL by facilitating international discourse between belligerent States and neutral States in a manner that does not favor one belligerent over the other. The principal international legal right of the neutral State is that of inviolability; its principal duties are those of abstention (from participation in hostilities) and impartiality (in dealing with each side of the conflict).[38] Conversely, it is the duty of a belligerent to respect the inviolability of the neutral while at the same time insisting that neutrals strictly comply with their obligations of abstention and impartiality.[39] Understanding the relationship between neutral and belligerent States is essential, because States routinely refrain from becoming involved in armed conflicts involving other States by declaring or otherwise assuming neutral status. Indeed, in the increasingly rare situations of IACs, this will be the position of most States in the international community.[40]

Like its 1907 counterpart codifying the laws and customs of war, the process of codifying the law of neutrality began at the same time as the codification of the laws and customs of war in the 1907 Hague Convention (XIII) Respecting the Rights and Duties of Neutral Powers in Naval War. Article 1 of Hague XIII reflects the core principle of neutrality:

> Belligerents are bound to respect the sovereign rights of neutral Powers and to abstain, in neutral territory or neutral waters, from any act which would, if knowingly permitted by any Power, constitute a violation of neutrality.[41]

Pursuant to this law, belligerents may continue to engage in commerce and other international discourse with neutral States, and vice versa. Furthermore, neutral States have a right to continue to utilize international waters and airspace without interference by belligerents.

In order to maintain their neutrality, neutral States must refrain from aiding a belligerent's military activities, most notably by preventing the belligerent from using its national territory or territorial waters, and by limiting commercial intercourse to commodities that do not directly contribute to the belligerent's war efforts.[42] Accordingly, in order to ensure compliance with these neutrality obligations, belligerents are granted the right to verify compliance by neutral vessels and aircraft even when using international waters and airspace.

Neutrality obligations extend well beyond commercial intercourse between neutrals and belligerents. For example, a neutral State has an affirmative obligation to prevent belligerents from using its territory or airspace for military operations, to include the obligation to intern for the duration of hostilities members of belligerent armed forces who enter their territory.[43] However, it is in the realm of international commerce and the use of the high seas to facilitate this commerce where the law of neutrality has the most common impact. This point is emphasized by the U.S. Navy's *Commander's Handbook on the Law of Naval Warfare*:

> A principal purpose of the law of neutrality is the regulation of belligerent activities with respect to neutral commerce. For purposes of this publication, neutral commerce comprises all commerce between one neutral nation and another not involving materials of war or armaments ultimately destined for a belligerent nation, and all commerce between a neutral nation and a belligerent that does not involve the carriage of contraband or otherwise contribute to the belligerent's war-fighting/war-sustaining capability.[44]

4.2   The rights and obligations of neutral States

There are three key pillars of neutrality obligation. First, a neutral cannot provide material support to either belligerent's ability to pursue the armed conflict against the other. For example, a neutral State cannot permit belligerents to move troops and war materials through its territory, to use its territory for military operations or communications, or to recruit troops from its territory.[45] Further, a neutral cannot supply "warships, ammunition, or war material of any kind" to belligerents, although it can supply food and non-military goods, and can continue to trade in non-contraband items.[46] Second, a neutral must maintain impartiality in its dealings with belligerents.[47] Thus, if a neutral State elects to open its ports to one belligerent, it must also open its ports to the other. Similarly, if it elects to close its territorial seas to belligerents, it must close them equally to all belligerents. Third, a neutral must strictly enforce its neutral status.[48] Thus, if a belligerent enters a neutral's territorial sea in a manner inconsistent with the rules of innocent passage, the neutral State must take action to put an end to the violation of its neutrality.[49]

While neutral shipping has the right to utilize international waters, there are situations where belligerents may legitimately interfere with this right. First, restrictions on neutral shipping is permissible to protect the security of a naval force or to minimize the risk of collateral damage to neutral vessels as a consequence of naval hostilities. Second, international law permits a belligerent to impose a blockade of the ports of its enemy as a measure of warfare, which requires completely cutting off all sea intercourse on a non-discriminatory basis.[50] Thus, by its very nature, a blockade will interfere with neutral access to the ports of the belligerent subjected to blockade.

Third, because engaging in activities that contribute to the war-fighting capability of one belligerent violates the neutrality obligation, the other belligerent is authorized to take necessary responsive measures. This will often manifest itself in relation to international commercial shipping and measures taken by the armed forces of the warring parties to verify that neutral vessels are in fact in compliance with neutrality obligations: inspection of papers and in some cases cargo. This is referred to as the right of *visit and search*, which applies only to international waters or a belligerent's territorial seas (not in neutral territorial seas).[51] And, when a neutral vessel refuses to submit to a visit and search, it may be subjected to capture or attack.[52]

With the exception of the right to visit and search, before taking any action inconsistent with a neutral State's neutrality, a belligerent must first demand that the neutral State terminate the violation.[53] However, because a neutral must ensure compliance with its obligations, it may be compelled to use its own military forces against a belligerent to prevent or terminate actions by that belligerent in violation of its neutrality. When a neutral uses military force for this purpose, it is not considered an act inconsistent with its obligation as a neutral, and therefore may not be treated as a breach of neutrality.[54] This is a manifestation that neutrality involves not only passive obligations (like refraining from engaging in commerce involving restricted materials) but also an active obligation of neutrality enforcement.

4.3   The rights and obligations of belligerent States regarding interaction with neutral States

The principal obligation imposed on belligerents by the law of neutrality is to respect the inviolability of neutral territory, including the neutral's national and territorial waters.[55] Because neutral States are not obligated to close their ports and territory to belligerent States, this means that it is not uncommon for belligerents engaged in an IAC to visit neutral territorial waters and ports. As a result, the naval or air forces of one belligerent may observe enemy military assets in neutral territorial waters or territory. Because belligerents are permitted to enter neutral territory subject to certain conditions, the presence of enemy ships, aircraft, or personnel in neutral territory does not provide an automatic right of the opposing State to take responsive action. Instead, because belligerent States must respect neutral territory, in such cases belligerents are presumptively prohibited from conducting military operations directed against each other when one belligerent identifies enemy assets in neutral territory (such as an enemy ship coming to or from a neutral port).[56] Belligerents are also presumptively prohibited from conducting visit and search of shipping in neutral territorial waters.

This does not mean that enemy vessels, aircraft, or personnel may use neutral territory to conduct their own operations or remain in neutral territory indefinitely. Such a rule would be inconsistent with the very notion of neutrality. Accordingly, belligerent warships are prohibited from remaining in a neutral port in excess of 24 hours, and the neutral must notify any such naval vessels of the obligation to depart its territory upon the outbreak of armed conflict.[57] A neutral may extend this time period based on an assessment that compliance is not feasible owing to weather or the fact that the ship is not seaworthy, but in such cases the neutral State must intern the warship and its crew.[58] Finally, belligerents may use only those ports and roadsteads made available by the neutral and must respect all limitations on such use imposed by the neutral.[59] And, while use of such ports is permissible when authorized, belligerents may not enter neutral territory if the neutral chooses to close its ports to belligerents (with the exception of a belligerent ship in distress as the result of damage or weather).[60]

There are also significant limitations on permissible activities of belligerent ships authorized to use neutral ports. Most notably, belligerent warships may not use a visit to replenish supplies of war materials or to augment or reinforce a crew.[61] Other supplies may be procured, even by warships, but the amount is limited by what is referred to in Article 19 of Hague XIII as the *peace standard*: a limit intended to prevent access to the neutral and its resources to be used to sustain combat operations.[62] However, there is no clear definition of this standard, and in practice the neutral will establish the permissible extent of non-military resupply, such as food, water, and fuel.[63]

Finally, to avoid the risk that authorized visits by ships from opposing belligerents will trigger hostilities in neutral territory, the neutral will require at least 24 hours between visits by opposing belligerent naval ships.[64] A similar 24-hour or more rule applies to the coordination of visits by merchant ships of one belligerent and naval ships of the other.

4.4 Special rules related to neutral shipping

Neutrality does not require a complete severance of commercial activities with belligerents. Instead, neutral States may engage in trade with the belligerents, and neutral flagged vessels may transport cargo and persons from a belligerent State for transportation to the neutral State or to other destinations. Obviously, this authority cannot extend to the movement of military personnel (combatants) and/or military equipment, the type of activities routinely performed by vessels belonging to a belligerent. If this occurs, the neutral vessel will acquire enemy character, subjecting the vessel to the same risks as enemy vessels (the ship may be seized, cargo confiscated, and if the activity amounts to participation in hostilities the ship may be attacked).[65] Accordingly, neutral vessels and aircraft may engage in commerce with belligerents, but may not facilitate the trade in or movement of what is designated as contraband.

The method by which neutrals are provided notice of contraband and belligerents verify compliance with contraband restrictions, and the consequences of violating these restrictions, is explained in the following excerpt from the *Law of Armed Conflict: An Operational Approach*:

> Contraband consists of goods destined for the enemy of a belligerent that may be susceptible to use in armed conflict.[66] Traditionally, contraband has been divided into two categories: absolute and conditional. Absolute contraband consisted of goods the character of which made it obvious that they were destined for use in armed conflict, such as munitions, weapons, uniforms, and the like. Conditional contraband consisted of goods equally susceptible to either peaceful or warlike purposes, such as foodstuffs, construction materials, and fuel.[67] Goods that are not on the contraband list are treated as "free goods" that are exempt from being treated as contraband,

including medical supplies, religious articles, and items for prisoners of war that must be treated as free goods under international law.[68]

Belligerents are required to publish their lists of contraband, with sufficient specificity so that neutrals are aware of what is to be treated as contraband.[69] If a State's contraband list is particularly long, it may seek to meet its obligation by listing the goods that are not contraband, rather than providing a list of contraband goods.[70]

The visit and search authority granted to belligerents is a common method for belligerents to ensure neutrals are in compliance with contraband prohibitions, as explained in the same text:

> All neutral merchant vessels are subject to "visit and search" by belligerent warships to determine if suspected of being subject to capture, e.g., by carrying contraband.[71] . . . If a neutral [s]tate vessel subject to visit and search is carrying contraband, it can be seized and condemned (i.e. taken as enemy property without compensation or destroyed) . . .
>
> The risks to vessel owners are great, because a neutral vessel found to be carrying contraband may be condemned, although only after hearing before the capturing [s]tate's prize court . . .
>
> The carriage of contraband is not the only reason for which a neutral merchant vessel may be captured. It also can be captured if the vessel:
>
> - Is "especially undertaken" (e.g., chartered) to carry individuals who are part of the enemy's armed forces;
> - Is operating under enemy control, orders, charter, employment, or direction;
> - Presents to the visit and search boarding party, irregular or fraudulent documents; lacks necessary documents; or destroys, defaces, or conceals documents;
> - Violates regulations of a belligerent in immediate area of military operations; or
> - Engages in, or attempts to engage in, a breach of a blockade.[72]
>
> Further, a neutral merchant vessel can be attacked or captured if it:
>
> - Is believed on reasonable grounds to be carrying contraband or breaching a blockade and, after warning, intentionally and clearly refuses to stop or intentionally and clearly resists visit and search;
> - Engages in belligerent acts on behalf of a belligerent's enemy, e.g., is incorporated into, or assists, the enemy's intelligence system;
> - Acts as an auxiliary (e.g., as a transport) to the enemy's armed forces;
> - Sails under convoy of enemy warships or enemy military aircraft; or
> - Otherwise makes an effective contribution to the enemy's military action and it is not feasible to first place passengers and crew in a place of safety. A warning should be given if circumstances permit.[73]

5   Applicability of international humanitarian law during naval warfare

Belligerent naval forces may often engage in operations to ensure that neutral shipping complies with neutrality obligations, but their primary mission is to destroy, disrupt, or disable enemy naval forces. Accomplishing this objective involves operations on, above, and below the sea, and these operations are subject to certain IHL rules specifically developed to regulate naval hostilities and protect victims of naval warfare. These rules are, in many respects, identical to IHL rules applicable to land hostilities. The remainder of this chapter will focus on the unique aspects of the law of naval warfare.

There are several relevant treaties and provisions specific to naval warfare;[74] however, with the exception of the 1949 Geneva Convention for the Amelioration of the Condition of Wounded, Sick and Shipwrecked Members of Armed Forces at Sea (GWS-Sea), they are quite limited in scope.[75] There is, however, a substantial body of customary international law applicable to naval warfare. Two especially important sources for assessing this law are the *Oxford Manual on the Laws of Naval War Governing the Relations Between Belligerents* of 1913, and the *San Remo Manual on International Law Applicable to Armed Conflicts at Sea*.[76] Certain military manuals also provide important insight into national assessments of customary international law, most notably the U.S. *DoD Law of War Manual* and the U.S. Navy's *Commander's Handbook on the Law of Naval Operations*, which was most recently updated in 2007.

As noted above, general IHL principles apply to naval operations, and whenever an attack is launched from the sea against land targets, the law of land warfare regulates the attack.[77] There are, however, specific rules that apply only to naval warfare. One example is related to conduct that might, if engaged in during land warfare, qualify as perfidy. Pursuant to the customary law of naval warfare, a belligerent warship may lawfully fly false colors and even disguise its outward appearance in order to deceive the enemy into believing it is a merchant ship or even a neutral merchant ship. This deception is lawful so long as the true identity of the warship is revealed prior to an actual engagement.[78] This rule allows a warship to cloak itself as a *civilian* merchant ship in order to gain a tactical advantage over the enemy; analogous conduct is not a permissible tactic during land warfare. Another example is the authority to seize and confiscate enemy merchant/civilian vessels.[79] No analogous authority extends to enemy civilian property on land.

The law of piracy may also be implicated during naval warfare. Private individuals may not engage in armed conflict at sea, and doing so may qualify as piracy, one of the oldest violations of international law. Because the law applicable to NIAC does not expressly address naval warfare, it is unclear how members of non-State organized belligerent groups involved in a NIAC and engaging in naval operations would be characterized. It is possible the capturing State may treat them as pirates. However, it is more likely they would be characterized and treated no differently than had they engaged in land operations—either as civilians who directly participated in hostilities or as unprivileged belligerents.[80]

Like land warfare, a State may utilize only warships and military aircraft to conduct naval operations, and these platforms that are subject to attack or capture by the enemy based solely on their status. These are ships and aircraft that are treated analogously to enemy combatants and military equipment on land, and include enemy warships (including auxiliaries),[81] and enemy military aircraft. Like land warfare, some enemy military vessels are exempted from this attack authority, namely medical transports, vessels that have surrendered, life rafts, and life boats, as well as others.[82]

Another very significant difference between land and naval warfare is that the law of naval warfare allows the capture and confiscation of enemy *merchant* vessels and their cargo based solely on the fact that they are flagged to the enemy nation.[83] No analogous authority to seize civilian property applies to land warfare. In some situations, destruction of the property is also authorized.[84]

Any merchant vessel flying the flag of the enemy State, or any civil aircraft that bears the markings of the enemy State, is considered to have enemy character. Enemy character also can be determined by the registration, ownership, charter, or other criteria that indicate that the vessel or aircraft is under enemy control. This does not require enemy government ownership; so long as the vessel or aircraft is registered to, chartered by, or owned by a citizen of the enemy State, or flies the enemy flag, it is considered an enemy vessel. Neutral vessels do not fall within this status-based seizure authority. However, a neutral's merchant vessels and civil aircraft may become subject to seizure or even attack by carrying contraband or engaging in other hostile acts; any vessel forfeits protection from attack if it engages in activity that qualifies as direct participation in hostilities or renders itself a military objective.[85]

As noted above, enemy merchant vessels may be captured and confiscated based solely on their status (although this authority does not extend to captures when an enemy vessel is in neutral waters). Once captured, these vessels are subject to *prize* proceedings in court, in which cargo owners from neutral States may seek to recover non-contraband cargo or receive fair compensation. Cargo owned by enemy citizens, and the enemy merchant vessel itself, are subject to condemnation without compensation. Civilian crews of such vessels must be either repatriated or interned as civilians. Civilian merchant crews may be detained as prisoners of war. However, they may under certain circumstances be treated as unprivileged belligerents subject to domestic criminal sanction if they directly participate in hostilities prior to capture.[86] Neutral State nationals should be promptly repatriated.

6 Naval warfare: special tactics

6.1 Blockade

A blockade is a military operation to deny shipping access to enemy territory or a certain enemy port, regardless of whether those vessels and aircraft are enemy or neutral in character, with no regard to the nature of goods they carry.[87]

A blockade is therefore far more restrictive than a visit and search regime used to monitor compliance with contraband restrictions. To be valid under international law, a blockade must be both effective and non-discriminatory.[88] Furthermore, the State imposing the blockade is required to issue a formal declaration of blockade that provides notice of location, duration, and any permitted exceptions.[89] This serves to provide notice to neutral States. Finally, a blockade must be reasonable in scope so as not to interfere with neutral commerce unrelated to the blockaded enemy.[90]

Blockades may be uncommon in contemporary military operations, but there certainly may be situations in the future where States utilize this naval warfare tactic. A blockade does not, however, nullify the State's humanitarian obligations.[91] Like all measures of warfare, a blockade is justified only to weaken enemy forces, not inflict suffering on the civilian population. According to the *San Remo Manual,* the same proportionality rule that applies to attacking an enemy military objective is applicable to assessing whether the impact on civilians anticipated from a blockade would be excessive compared to the anticipated military advantage.[92] As a result, one important consideration for any future blockade will be ensuring compliance with the prohibition against using starvation of the civilian population as a method of warfare, as reflected in Article 54(1) of AP I.[93] Even where the objective of the blockade is to deprive the enemy armed forces of essential supplies (including food), the collateral consequences of the blockade must be considered. These consequences may implicate the right of humanitarian relief access, reflected in Article 70 of AP I.[94] As a result, the blockading State may be obligated to allow passage of neutral ships and aircraft delivering such supplies, subject to inspection and monitoring to ensure that the supplies are not diverted to enemy use.[95]

While the use of surface ships is the traditional method of imposing a blockade, the naval forces may have other options. A close-in blockade is one that cuts off specific enemy ports instead of the entire coastline, a logical tactic to restrict enemy access to heavy shipping carrying military supplies. For example, during the Vietnam War the United States successfully implemented a close-in blockade against the North Vietnamese harbor at Haiphong using underwater mines. Designated Operation Pocket Monkey, the activation of the underwater mines was delayed to allow for the advanced notice required, and mine locations were tracked to enable removal at the end of hostilities.[96]

A blockade is not analogous to a quarantine or an embargo, neither of which is a method of naval warfare. Unlike a blockade, a quarantine interdicts specific types of goods, and may be authorized during both peacetime and armed conflict. For example, the United States imposed a quarantine on Cuba during the Cuban missile crisis, but asserted that this was not a use of force triggering Cuba's inherent right of self-defense.[97] Embargos prohibit the shipment of certain goods to one or more targeted countries as an international sanction. An embargo is an enforcement measure short of the use of force normally authorized by the United Nations Security Council acting pursuant to Chapter VII of the Charter.

6.2   *Naval exclusion zones*

Naval commanders conducting combat operations against enemy forces on land and/or on sea obviously have a strong interest in minimizing the presence of neutral shipping in the conflict area. Lowering the probability of such shipping will clarify naval targeting judgments, lower the risk of accidental attack on neutral shipping, and ultimately increase the effectiveness of operations.[98] The mechanism for achieving this objective is the imposition of naval exclusion zones or other special restrictions on vessels entering into the immediate area of naval operations during armed conflict, with such areas often reaching out several miles or even farther, depending upon the military capabilities of the enemy.[99]

There are several important aspects of a naval exclusion zone. First, if the zone extends to international waters, neutrals are not obligated to respect it.[100] Second, violation of an exclusion zone does not automatically justify attack—while the presence in the zone may influence the distinction judgment, commanders are not relieved of the obligation to make individualized judgments as to the legality of a potential target. The fact that a civilian or neutral ship entered the zone without permission does not per se justify targeting the ship before first ascertaining whether it is a military objective.

Third, the imposition of an exclusion zone does not indicate that enemy ships and aircraft *will not* be attacked outside the zone. Enemy ships and aircraft are subject to attack at all times and places, unless lawfully within neutral territory. The misconception associated with attacking an enemy outside of a naval exclusion zone was exposed during the Falklands War. During the opening phase of hostilities, the Argentine warship *General Belgrano* was lawfully attacked and sunk by the UK submarine HMS *Conqueror* while cruising toward the Falkland Islands but prior to entering the UK maritime exclusion zone.

6.3   *Submarine warfare*

Submarines are subject to IHL targeting rules like any other warship. Torpedoes are often associated with submarine operations, although torpedoes may also be employed by surface ships and aircraft. Torpedoes are lawful weapons that may be used in accordance with IHL targeting principles. However, if used, torpedoes must become harmless if they miss their mark.[101]

Submarines are bound like other warships by the humanitarian obligations established by Article 18 of the GWS-Sea to search for and collect the wounded, sick, and shipwrecked at sea.[102] However, unlike surface ships, the limited capability of submarines to take on such victims of war, coupled with the inherent risk associated with surface operations, means that feasibility considerations will often prevent active search and collection. Because the Article 18 obligation is qualified by the phrase "all possible measures," a submarine may lawfully forgo such action when the commander reasonably assesses that search and collection will expose the submarine to undue additional hazard or prevent it from accomplishing its military mission.[103] Nonetheless, the submarine should alert a surface vessel or shore facility to the location of shipwrecked survivors as soon as possible to facilitate their rescue.[104]

Submarines will rarely be in a position to capture and take enemy merchant vessels into port. As a result, destruction will often be justified as a necessary measure. However, prior to destroying a merchant vessel, submarines should ensure the safety of the passengers, crew, and ship's papers, normally by issuing a warning that the ship will be sunk and providing a reasonable time to evacuate.[105] No such warning is required, however, when the merchant vessel persistently refuses to stop after being duly summoned, or actively resists the submarine. Some States, like the United States, do not interpret these warning requirements to apply to merchant vessels assessed as military objectives (based on any of the circumstances recognized by the *San Remo Manual* as grounds for attack on a merchant vessel discussed above).[106]

6.4 Sea mines

Anti-ship mines today are fairly advanced, capable of remote control activation and deactivation, neutralization, or detonation based on very specific ship signatures. Anti-ship mines can be deployed by ships or aircraft, and even by submarines. Most of the IHL rules related to mines are focused on protecting shipping from accidental destruction. Thus, for example, free-floating contact mines must become harmless within one hour of loss of control by the laying party.[107] In contrast, anchored mines are required to become harmless only when they break away from their mooring.[108]

The 1907 Hague Convention (VIII) relative to the Laying of Automatic Submarine Contact Mines specifically prohibits the laying of contact mines off the coast and ports of an enemy "with the sole object of intercepting commercial shipping."[109] Thus, a minefield may not be employed for the exclusive purpose of facilitating a visit and search regime for neutral shipping. This same treaty imposes other obligations intended to protect neutral commercial shipping: notification of the mine location to neutrals; an obligation to render the mines harmless "within a limited time"; and an obligation to remove the mines after the conflict.[110] Interestingly, this same treaty provides that neutral States may lay mines off their coasts to protect their neutrality. However, belligerents may not lay a minefield in neutral territorial or internal waters, but only in international or enemy waters.[111] These mine specific rules are summarized in the following excerpt from the U.S. Navy's *Commander's Handbook on the Law of Naval Operations*:

> Naval mines may be lawfully employed by parties to an armed conflict subject to the following restrictions:
>
> 1. International notification of the location of emplaced mines must be made as soon as military exigencies permit.
> 2. Mines may not be emplaced by belligerents in neutral waters.

3. Anchored mines must become harmless as soon as they have broken their moorings.

4. Unanchored mines not otherwise affixed or imbedded in the bottom must become harmless within an hour after loss of control over them.

5. The location of minefields must be carefully recorded to ensure accurate notification and to facilitate subsequent removal and/or deactivation.

6. Naval mines may be employed to channelize neutral shipping, but not in a manner to deny transit passage of international straits or archipelagic sea lanes passage of archipelagic waters by such shipping.

7. Naval mines may not be emplaced off the coasts and ports of the enemy with the sole objective of intercepting commercial shipping, but may otherwise be employed in the strategic blockade of enemy ports, coasts, and waterways.

8. Mining of areas of indefinite extent in international waters is prohibited. Reasonably limited barred areas may be established by naval mines, provided neutral shipping retains an alternate route around or through such an area with reasonable assurance of safety.[112]

7　Protecting the wounded, sick, and shipwrecked during naval warfare

GWS-Sea is devoted specifically to the protection of members of the armed forces and associated civilian crewmembers who are at sea and are wounded, sick, or shipwrecked. GWS-Sea is nearly identical to the first of the Conventions, the Geneva Convention for the Amelioration of the Condition of the Wounded and Sick in Armed Forces in the Field (GWS), except that it also addresses the plight of the shipwrecked.[113] As a general matter, the GWS-Sea can be viewed as the sea version of the GWS, as the obligations are generally analogous, only extended to shipwrecked crews and passengers of ships, or crews and passengers of aircraft that crash into the sea or eject from their aircraft over the sea.[114]

The protections of the GWS-Sea apply to all individuals who qualify for prisoner of war status pursuant to Article 4 of the GPW (*see* Chapter 5: *Prisoners of war and other detainees*). Importantly, this includes "[m]embers of crews, including masters, pilots and apprentices, of the merchant marine and the crews of civil aircraft of the Parties to the conflict, who do not benefit by more favourable treatment under any other provisions of international law."[115] Like the GWS, Article 12 of the GWS-Sea establishes the fundamental obligation to respect and protect victims of naval warfare and to ensure their humane treatment. Specifically, the Article provides:

Members of the armed forces and other persons mentioned in the following Article, who are at sea and who are wounded, sick or shipwrecked, shall be respected and protected in all circumstances, it being understood that the term "shipwreck" means shipwreck from any cause and includes forced landings at sea by or from aircraft.[116]

The GWS-Sea also imposes an obligation to search for and collect the wounded, sick, and shipwrecked. Accordingly, parties to an IAC must "take all possible measures to search for and collect the shipwrecked, wounded and sick, to protect them against pillage and ill-treatment, to ensure their adequate care, and to search for the dead and prevent their being despoiled."[117] The parties also may ask neutral craft, including yachts, to take on board and care for the wounded, sick, or shipwrecked persons.[118]

Like the GWS, the GWS-Sea extends protection to: (1) religious, medical, and hospital personnel on board ships who are assigned to provide medical or spiritual care to the sick, wounded, and shipwrecked;[119] (2) specially equipped and marked hospital ships, the crews of such ships, and the religious, medical, and hospital personnel on board such ships, dedicated to assisting and transporting the wounded, sick, and shipwrecked;[120] (3) ships chartered to transport equipment for treatment of the sick and wounded, or for the prevention of disease;[121] and (4) "medical aircraft . . . while flying at heights, at times and on routes specifically agreed upon between the Parties to the conflict concerned."[122]

The GWS-Sea does not include civilians (other than authorized members of merchant crews or civil aircraft, or authorized to accompany the armed forces) within the scope of its protection. However, AP I explicitly extended the humanitarian protections of the GWS-Sea to such individuals when they are wounded, sick, or shipwrecked. AP I also expanded the scope of humanitarian protections to include a broader array of vessels and aircraft that rescue, assist, treat, and transport the wounded, sick, and shipwrecked at sea. Accordingly, any individuals shipwrecked and/or wounded and sick at sea during an armed conflict are protected by the basic respect and protect humanitarian obligation, to include coming to their aid and providing care.[123] Although AP I is not universally ratified, these provisions are generally understood as reflections of customary international law applicable to both IACs and NIACs. This is reflected in a number of obligations included in the ICRC's *Customary International Law Study*, specifically: whenever circumstances permit, prompt searching for and collecting shipwrecked, wounded, and sick, especially after each engagement; prompt medical treatment of the wounded and sick prioritized on medical considerations only; and protection of the wounded and sick against ill-treatment or pillage.[124] The customary nature of these obligations is reinforced by their inclusion in the *DoD Law of War Manual*.[125]

Consistent with the protection of medical facilities and personnel during land warfare, military hospital ships are protected from attack unless they engage in activity inconsistent with their exclusive humanitarian function that harms an enemy. And, like the rule applicable to land warfare, an attacking force must provide a cease and desist warning with a reasonable time to comply, and attack the ship only in the case of non-compliance.[126] According to Article 35, the fact that crewmembers are armed for self-defense or defense of the wounded and sick, that weapons belonging to the wounded and sick are found stored on the ship, or that the ship is transporting medical supplies and equipment in excess of that needed on the ship *may not* justify attack as they do not indicate activities inconsistent with the ship's exclusive humanitarian mission.

Even where protected by the GWS-Sea, rescued individuals become prisoners of war upon capture if they fall within the scope of Article 4 of the GPW. Indeed, this will often be the outcome of the capture or rescue of enemy personnel during naval warfare—they will be considered prisoners of war upon rescue but will also be provided with the treatment and care required by the GWS-Sea (or the GWS once they reach land). In fact, an enemy warship encountering a hospital ship may require that all enemy military wounded, sick, and shipwrecked persons on board the hospital ship be turned over to them to be detained as prisoners of war, provided that these persons are fit to move and the capturing warship has facilities to care for them.[127] Similarly, where wounded, sick, and shipwrecked personnel of a belligerent, who would be prisoners of war in the hands of their enemy, are taken aboard neutral ships or military aircraft, or are landed in neutral territory, the neutral State must take steps to ensure that such personnel cannot again take part in the armed conflict.[128]

8   Conclusion

Naval operations will almost always be an important component of contemporary armed conflicts. Even when one State has total sea dominance, or is engaged in hostilities against non-State actors with no naval capability, naval assets will often be used as power projection platforms, to conduct attacks, protect lines of communication, and deprive the enemy of important resources. IHL and the law of neutrality provide vital regulation of naval operations, balancing the interests of belligerents and neutrals, and protecting victims of naval hostilities.

Notes

1   *See* Jean S. Pictet, Geneva Convention for the Amelioration of the Condition of the Wounded, Sick and Shipwrecked Members of Armed Forces at Sea: Commentary (ICRC, 1960), 39–41 [hereinafter Commentary GWS-Sea].

2   *See San Remo Manual on International Law Applicable to Armed Conflicts at Sea* para 4 (Louise Doswald-Beck ed., 1995) [hereinafter *San Remo Manual*] ("[t]he principles of necessity and proportionality apply equally to armed conflict at sea").

3   *Cf.* United Nations Convention on the Law of the Sea Preamble, 10 December 1982, 1833 U.N.T.S. 396 [hereinafter UNCLOS].

4   *See* Commentary GWS-Sea, at 39–41.

5   U.S. Dep't of Def., *Law of War Manual* 13.2.2 (June 2015, updated December 2016) [hereinafter, *DoD Law of War Manual*].

6   *Id.* at 13.2.3. The distinction between national and international waters is not found in UNCLOS, but is made in the *DoD Law of War Manual*. According to the *DoD Law of War Manual*:

> Waters are often divided analytically between *national waters* (*i.e.*, internal waters, territorial seas, and archipelagic waters), which are subject to the sovereignty of a State, and *international waters*, which are not subject to the sovereignty of any State. In addition, special rules apply to international straits and archipelagic sea lanes.

Id. at 13.2

7   *See Id.* at 13.2.2.2. The United States and most States claim their territorial seas extend to a distance of 12 nautical miles from the baseline.

8   *Id.* at 13.2.2.1. National waters of the internal sort include rivers and lakes inside a State's national territory. Two examples are the Mississippi River and the Great Salt Lake.

9   *Id.* at 13.2.3.

10 *See* UNCLOS, Art 33 (contiguous zone), Arts 55–7 (exclusive economic zone (EEZ)), Art 86 (high seas).

11 *Id.* Art 18; *DoD Law of War Manual*, 13.2.2.

12 *DoD Law of War Manual*, 13.2.2.4.

13 UNCLOS, Art 18; *DoD Law of War Manual*, 13.2.2.

14 UNCLOS, Art 19.

15 *Id.* The restriction against overflights means that aircraft may not be launched or recovered from vessels engaged in innocent passage. The restriction on subsurface passage means that all submarines must surface during the duration they are in innocent passage.

16 *DoD Law of War Manual*, 15.8.

17 *San Remo Manual*, para 30

18 *Id.*

19 *Id.*

20 *Id.* para 32.

21 *Id.* paras 27, 33. The right to use archipelagic sea lanes also may not be impeded.

22 *Id.* paras 19, 29, 31, 33. However for neutrals, transit through international straits and archipelagic sea lanes may not be impeded. *Id.* paras 29, 33.

23 *Id.* paras 29.

24 *See* UNCLOS, Art 87; *San Remo Manual*, para 10.

25 A contiguous zone is an area extending to a maximum of 24 nautical miles from the baseline of a coastal State. The zone provides the coastal State with rights to "exercise control necessary to prevent or punish infringement of its customs, fiscal, immigration, and sanitary laws and regulations." *DoD Law of War Manual*, 13.2.3.2. An EEZ is "a zone of limited, generally resource-related rights and jurisdiction adjacent to the territorial sea," extending to a maximum of 200 nautical miles from the baseline of a coastal nation. *Id.* at 13.2.3.3.

26 UNCLOS, Art 30; *San Remo Manual*, para 13(g). There is a corresponding category for military aircraft in the *San Remo Manual*. *Id.* para 13(j).

27 *San Remo Manual*, para 13(i).

28 Geneva Convention for the Amelioration of the Condition of Wounded, Sick, and Shipwrecked Members of the Armed Forces at Sea, Art 22, 12 August 1949, 6 U.S.T. 3217, 75 U.N.T.S. 971 [hereinafter GWS-Sea]; *San Remo Manual*, para 13(e).

29 *E.g.*, *San Remo Manual*, para 112.

30 *Id.* para 135.

31 *See, e.g.*, *Id.* paras 40, 60 (discussing military objectives).

32 *Id.* para 118.

33 *Id.* para 67.

34 *See, e.g.*, *Id.* para 67.

35 *Id.* para 135. Certain categories of enemy vessels are exempt from capture. These include vessels transporting the sick or wounded, vessels transporting cultural property, vessels designed exclusively for and responding directly to incidents in the marine environment, and of supreme importance, small coastal fishing vessels. *Id.* para 136 (providing a more complete list).

36 *Id.* paras 59–60.

37 *See, e.g.*, *Id.* para 47.

38 *DoD Law of War Manual*, 15.3.1.
39 *Id*. at 15.3.1.2.
40 *See, e.g., Id*. at 15.1.2, 15.3.1. The law of neutrality presupposes the existence of an IAC, as it provides the basis for distinguishing between belligerent States and neutral States. Because a NIAC does not involve armed conflict between two or more States, the notion of applying neutrality law in relation to such conflicts seems odd. However, principles of State responsibility may impose analogous obligations on States not involved in the NIAC.
41 Convention (XIII) Concerning the Rights and Duties of Neutral Powers in Naval War, 18 October 1907, Art 1, 36 Stat. 2415 [hereinafter 1907 Hague XIII].
42 *See, e.g., DoD Law of War Manual*, 15.3 (discussing the reciprocal rights and duties of the law of neutrality).
43 *See San Remo Manual*, para 18.
44 U.S. Dep't of Navy, NWP 1–14M, *Commander's Handbook on the Law of Naval Operations* 7.4 (July 2007) [hereinafter NWP 1–14M].
45 However, a neutral power is not responsible to prevent persons from crossing the frontier separately to offer their services to one of the belligerents. *See* Convention (V) Respecting the Rights and Duties of Neutral Powers and Persons in Case of War on Land, 18 October 2007, Art 6, 36 Stat. 2310 [hereinafter 1907 Hague V].
46 1907 Hague XIII, Art 6.
47 *Id*. Art 9.
48 *See Id*. Art 26.
49 A neutral can permit mere passage of belligerent warships through its territorial waters. *Id*. Art 10. A neutral may even allow belligerents to employ the neutral's licensed pilots. *Id*. Art 11.
50 *See San Remo Manual*, paras 93–104.
51 *Id*. para 118.
52 *Id*. para 67(a).
53 *See, e.g., DoD Law of War Manual*, 15.4 (discussing the various remedies and procedure for addressing violations of the law of neutrality).
54 1907 Hague XIII, Art 26.
55 1907 Hague V, Art 1; 1907 Hague XIII, Art 1. *See also DoD Law of War Manual*, 15.3.
56 *See DoD Law of War Manual*, 15.7 (discussing neutral waters and the conduct of those operating in them).
57 *San Remo Manual*, para 21 (belligerent warships devoted exclusively to humanitarian, religious, or non-military scientific purposes, such as a naval hospital ship, are exempted from this restriction).
58 1907 Hague XIII.
59 *See Id*. Art 15 (in the absence of express regulations, no more than three ships may be present in a neutral port at any given time).
60 NWP 1–14M, 7.3.2.
61 *See DoD Law of War Manual*, 15.3.2.1.
62 *See* 1907 Hague XIII, Art 19.
63 According to the U.S. Navy's *Commander's Handbook on the Law of Naval Operations*, the amount of food and fuel a belligerent ship may take on is decided by the neutral State. NWP 1–14M, 7.3.2.2. This section of the *Commander's Handbook* also discusses the scope of repairs to belligerent warships that can occur in neutral ports. *Id*.
64 1907 Hague XIII, Art 16.
65 *San Remo Manual*, paras 67, 146.
66 *Id*. para 148.
67 *See* NWP 1–14M, 7.4 (for a discussion of contraband).

68 *San Remo Manual*, para 150.
69 *Id.* para 149.
70 NWP 1–14M, 7.4.1; Geoffrey S. Corn et al., *The Law of Armed Conflict: An Operational Approach* 435–6 (2012) [hereinafter Corn et al.].
71 *San Remo Manual*, para 118.
72 *San Remo Manual*, para 146.
73 *Id.* para 67.
74 The Paris Declaration Respecting Maritime Law of April 1856 abolished the authorization of privateering (granting private ships authority to engage in hostilities on behalf of the State). *See generally* Declaration Respecting Maritime Law, 16 April 1856, LXI B.S.P. 155, 155–8 (1856) [hereinafter Paris Declaration].
75 *See generally* GWS-Sea.
76 *See generally San Remo Manual.*
77 *See* Protocol (I) Additional to the Geneva Conventions of 12 August 1949, and Relating to the Protection of Victims of International Armed Conflicts, 8 June 1977, 1125 U.N.T.S. 3 [hereinafter AP I] (entered into force 7 December 1978) (signed by the United States 12 December 1977, not transmitted to U.S. Senate, *see* S. Treaty Doc. No. 100–2 (1987)); Commentary GWS-Sea, 39–41.
78 *San Remo Manual*, paras 109–11. *See also* DoD *Law of War Manual*, 13.13 (discussing the use of deception by naval forces).
79 *See San Remo Manual*, paras 135–40 (discussing the capture of enemy vessels and goods, and the concept of *prize*, specifically).
80 *Cf. DoD Law of War Manual*, 4.18, 4.19.
81 For example, civilian vessels chartered to serve as military transports and military cargo ships.
82 *San Remo Manual*, para 47. Various additional types of enemy vessels are exempt from capture, including hospital ships, small coastal rescue craft, and small coastal fishing vessels. *Id.*
83 *Id.* para 135. Neutral vessels may be taken only for conduct that results in a loss of protection.
84 *Id.* paras 139–40. Specifically, paragraphs 139 and 140 provide: "[C]aptured enemy merchant vessels may, as an exceptional measure, be destroyed when military circumstances preclude taking or sending such a vessel for adjudication as an enemy prize," provided the safety of passengers and crew is provided for, documents and papers of the ship are saved, and if feasible crew and passenger personal effects are saved. *Id.*
85 *See Id.* para 41. According to the *San Remo Manual*, a merchant vessel may become a military objective and thereby subject to attack by:

> (a) engaging in acts of war on behalf of the enemy, e.g., laying mines, minesweeping, laying or monitoring acoustic sensors, engaging in electronic warfare, intercepting or attacking other civil aircraft, or providing targeting information to enemy forces;
> (b) acting as an auxiliary aircraft to an enemy's armed forces, e.g., transporting troops or military cargo, or refueling military aircraft;
> (c) being incorporated into or assisting the enemy's intelligence-gathering system, e.g., engaging in reconnaissance, early warning, surveillance, or command, control, and communications missions;
> (d) sailing under the protection of accompanying enemy warships or military aircraft;
> (e) refusing an order to identify itself, divert from its track, or proceed for "visit and search" to a belligerent airfield that is safe for the type of aircraft involved and reasonably accessible, or operating fire control equipment that could

reasonably be construed to be part of an aircraft weapon system, or on being intercepted clearly maneuvering to attack the intercepting belligerent military aircraft;

(f) being armed with air-to-air or air-to-surface weapons; or

(g) otherwise making an effective contribution to military action.

Id. para 60

86 NWP 1–14M, 5.4.1.1.

87 *See San Remo Manual,* paras 93–104. For a recent in-depth analysis of the law of blockade, *see* Phillip Drew, *The Law of Maritime Blockade: Past Present and Future* (2017).

88 *San Remo Manual,* para 95.

89 *Id.* para 94.

90 *See Id.* paras 93–101. The only treaty provisions that specifically address the international law requirements for a blockade can be found in the Paris Declaration Respecting Maritime Law of April 1856. *See* Paris Declaration.

91 *See San Remo Manual,* para 103.

92 *Id.* para 102(b). *See* Drew, *supra* note 87, at 107–10 (for a critique of the application of the proportionality test in this context).

93 *See* AP I, Art 54(1).

94 *See Id.* Art 70.

95 *San Remo Manual,* para 103.

96 NWP 1–14M, 7.7.5. However, *see* Drew, *supra* note 87, at 54–5 (where it is noted that the idea that a blockade can be enforced by mines alone is controversial with many experts taking the view a blockade cannot be supported by weapons systems alone).

97 *See* A. Chayes, *The Legal Case for U.S. Action on Cuba,* 47 Dep't State Bull. 763, 765 (19 November 1962).

98 Naval exclusion zones assist targeting assessments by indicating with a high probability that an unidentified vessel or aircraft in the zone is enemy.

99 *See* NWP 1–14M, 7.8.

100 *See DoD Law of War Manual,* 13.9.4.

101 *San Remo Manual,* para 79.

102 GWS-Sea, Art 18.

103 *Id.*

104 The Commentary to Article 18 of GWS-Sea states:

> Generally speaking, one cannot lay down an absolute rule that the commander of a warship must engage in rescue operations if, by doing so, he would expose the vessel to attack. The "possible measures" which may be taken by the belligerents to collect the shipwrecked are, on the other hand, many and varied and in nearly all cases they should enable the purpose of the present paragraph to be achieved.
>
> Commentary GWS-Sea, 131

105 *See DoD Law of War Manual,* 13.7; *San Remo Manual,* para 60.

106 *Id.* at 13.7.1.

107 Convention (VIII) relative to the Laying of Automatic Submarine ContactMines, 18 October 1907, Art 1(1), 36 Stat. 2332.

108 *Id.* Art 1(2).

109 *Id.* Art 2.

110 *Id.* Art 3.

111 Armed mines may not be emplaced in international straits or archipelagic sealanes during peacetime.

112 NWP 1–14M, 9.2.3.

113 Members of the armed forces and other persons mentioned in the following Article, who are at sea and who are wounded, sick or shipwrecked, shall be respected and protected in all circumstances, it being understood that the term "shipwreck" means shipwreck from any cause and includes forced landings at sea by or from aircraft.

GWS-Sea, Art 12

Downed airmen over water are considered shipwrecked, and are therefore entitled to the protection of GWS-Sea. Pictet et al., Commentary on the Additional Protocols of 8 June 1977 to the Geneva Conventions of 12 August 1949 (ICRC, 1987), para 1637.

114 *See Id.* (discussing how downed airmen over sea are considered shipwrecked).

115 GWS-Sea, Art 13(5).

116 *Id.* Art 12.

117 *Id.* Art 18.

118 *Id.* Art 21.

119 *Id.* Arts 36–7.

120 *Id.* Art 25. Hospital ships typically are part of a State's navy, although GWS-Sea also provides for the protection of hospital ships operated by a humanitarian organization such as the Red Cross.

121 *Id.* Art 38.

122 *Id.* Art 39.

123 Aside from Article 3 of the Geneva Conventions, neither AP I nor the GWS-Sea expressly apply to NIACs. However, customary international law would apply to such conflicts. *See San Remo Manual*, para 2.

124 Jean-Marie Henckaerts & Louise Doswald-Beck, *Customary International Humanitarian Law* 396–405 (2009).

125 *DoD Law of War Manual*, 7.4 (discussing the obligation to search for, collect and evacuate the wounded, sick, and shipwrecked), 7.5 (discussing the humane treatment obligation and the requisite care demanded for enemy military wounded, sick, and shipwrecked), 7.4.2 (discussing the obligation to protect wounded, sick, and shipwrecked from pillage or ill-treatment by *any* person).

126 GWS-Sea, Art 34.

127 *Id.* Arts 14, 16.

128 *Id.* Arts 15, 17 (e.g., they must be interned). The Commentary to Article 17 of GWS-Sea makes clear that *landed* means the situation where a ship elects to leave behind in neutral territory wounded, sick, or shipwrecked persons with the consent of the neutral. Commentary GWS-Sea, at 116–29.

9 Air and missile warfare

1 Introduction

In 1952, the renowned international lawyer Sir Hersch Lauterpacht noted in his review of the problems facing the international community concerning the revision of the laws of war in the post–World War II era that it was unprofitable to inquire into the practice of aerial bombardment during that conflict.[1] That was because there was "no rule firmly grounded in the past on which we can place reliance—for aerial bombardment is a new weapon which raises new problems."[2] From the late nineteenth century until the end of the 1945, the world had witnessed the advent of total war between States. This form of warfare developed during an era of tremendous technological advancement. It was the introduction of airplanes and air power doctrine that perhaps best represented the quantum shift that was occurring in how wars were fought. This resulted in an asymmetric extension of conflict beyond traditional battlefields to the home front, particularly with the goal of attacking economic targets and, controversially, enemy morale.[3] Adding to the regulatory challenge was the use of aerial-delivered nuclear weapons at the close of World War II, and the beginning of the Cold War between major superpowers.

Given the pace of change, it is perhaps not surprising that the first half of the twentieth century was a period where international law struggled to regulate inter-State conflict and, with it, aerial warfare. Unfortunately, there was and remains little treaty law developed to specifically regulate aerial conflict, although treaties such as the 1949 Geneva Conventions and their two Additional Protocols do have applicability to aerial warfare. The 1923 Hague Rules of Air Warfare,[4] although "never embodied in a treaty, or officially declared to constitute a statement of law," did gain some recognition as constituting rules of customary law.[5] However, over the last seven decades there has been a concerted effort by the international community to better regulate the use of airpower, and by extension the use of missiles. In part, this has occurred because of emphasis being placed on the targeting provisions of AP I,[6] which are applicable to air warfare. Elsewhere it is evidenced in the efforts of the international community to produce manuals explaining the general understanding of the law, such as the Commentary on the *HPCR Manual on International Law Applicable to Air and Missile Warfare.*[7]

This chapter will explore unique aspects of aerial warfare. It encompasses not only the use of aircraft but also missiles. The latter weapons system has been defined as "self-propelled unmanned weapons—launched from aircraft, warships or land-based launchers—that are either guided or ballistic."[8] Dealing with missiles as well as aircraft highlights the technological change that has long underpinned this area of legal conflict regulation. The analysis will look at the competing tensions that exist between those seeking to use a means of warfare that has proven itself to be an essential component of successful military operations, and humanitarian and human rights advocates working to limit the most destructive effects of these aerial weapons of war.

The chapter is divided into four parts. The first part looks at the development of air power theory, contemporary air warfare doctrine, and its impact on how wars are fought. Included in this analysis will be an outline of the scope of air operations, extending from high-intensity inter-State warfare to counterinsurgency and counterterrorism. The second part addresses the inherent tension between a broad application of air power, and the conflicting goal of limiting the negative humanitarian effects of such operations. In its modern manifestation, such resistance is reflected in the contemporary efforts to restrict the use of airpower in urban areas. The third part of this chapter focuses on unique aspects of the law governing aerial warfare, including the status of aircraft and aircrews, the protection of civilian aircraft, the conduct of operations, and the use of no-fly zones and aerial blockades. Finally, the last part of this chapter will address the use of missiles and the technological advances that increasingly cause them to be looked upon in the same manner as air dropped munitions, even when delivered by ground artillery units.

2   Theory, doctrine, and the use of airpower

The use of air power has proven to be a dominant force in the conduct of military operations. Often identified with how hostilities are carried out by the United States,[9] it is key to the military success of any State armed forces. Indeed, some non-State armed groups, such as Hamas, Hezbollah, and the Islamic State, have developed rudimentary drone capabilities.[10] It has been noted that "[t]heory alone would suggest that surface warfare cannot possibly succeed if the surface forces and their support are under constant attack by enemy aircraft."[11] However, it has been the ability of air power to strike at the "enemy's great industrial and governing centers" that has particularly distinguished this form of warfare.[12] Between the two great wars of the twentieth century, a number of early air power theorists developed a vision for airpower that saw it as a war-winning technology that reduced sea and land warfare to a sideshow.[13] Such thinking on strategic bombing has more recently been linked to the twenty-first-century counterterrorism strategy of kinetic operations, which "seeks 'quick and easy' outcomes that avoid the uncomfortable fact that air strikes destroy but do not reclaim territory, secure, or re-build."[14] While the use of strategic bombing did not unilaterally win World War II, it is clear that the use of airpower was a decisive aspect of the Allied victory. Tremendous destruction was brought about by using airpower as part of strategic air campaigns, as well as tactically in support of ground forces. It was the strategic use of airpower, in contrast to its tactical use, that represented a significant departure from how wars had previously been fought. However, while conceived as a method of warfare that would decisively and quickly end wars, it came to represent attritional warfare.[15]

Of note, conventional warfare has been less prevalent in the post–World War II period. States have largely engaged in low-intensity conflicts. Although the United States conducted a strategic bombing campaign in Vietnam,[16] it was in non-strike roles (e.g., reconnaissance, transport) that airpower proved particularly effective during the so-called small wars of the 1960s and 1970s.[17] The post-Vietnam-era conflicts did see a change in focus for airpower theorists. Led by an American theorist, John Warden, that focus moved from targeting war-supporting industry to war-supporting command.[18] It was an approach that systematically matched "*ends* (political objectives), *ways* (strategies to attain those ends), and *means* (identifying specific targets to execute the chosen strategy)."[19] This emphasis on strategic warfare has at times even created an ideological conflict within military forces between strategic airpower enthusiasts, and those advocating more direct support to ground forces.[20] However, treating the enemy in a systemic fashion remains a critical part of air warfare targeting doctrine. It is referred to as *effects-based targeting*,[21] an approach which looks for specific effects to fulfill strategic objectives.[22] It has also been integrated into joint targeting doctrine, which means it is applied beyond an air force context to land- and sea-based uses of force.[23]

A strategic approach, and the emphasis placed on effects-based operations, is reflected in U.S. military doctrine, which contains the "[f]undamental principles that guide the employment of United States military forces in coordinated action toward a common objective."[24] The procedural framework developed for targeting is an essential part of military operations because of the potentially large number of attacks that must be planned and conducted during any armed conflict, whether directed at another State or a non-State actor. For example, during the 2003 Iraq War, the Coalition forces flew nearly 50,000 fixed-wing missions between 19–20 March and 25 April 2003. Of those missions, 36 percent were strike sorties dropping 28,820 munitions.[25] Similarly, during the 2006 Second Lebanon War between Israel and Hezbollah, there were 18,900 sorties carried out, which struck 7,000 targets. In 2008, in a 23-day conflict between Israel and Hamas in Gaza, 3,430 targets were hit, with 5,650 sorties being carried out.[26] This rate of sorties highlights that individual drone strikes, which have caught much of the attention of the international community in the post-9/11 period, is not nearly representative of how air power is used, and therefore ultimately how it has to be controlled by IHL.

These examples all highlight the reality that in the twenty-first century most conflicts do not involve inter-State warfare but rather States acting against non-State actors. Non-State groups, and even nascent State governments, tend not to present as many strategic targets as developed nation-states. As was noted in respect of operations against the Taliban in 2001, that group, while nominally a State government, did not have a conventionally organized military or supporting infrastructure to strike. As a result, attacking "fixed military targets such as supply depots, vehicle repair facilities and rear-area military installations, would have little or no impact."[27] This means that strategic targeting will not take place in a non-State actor context. The targeting of oil production facilities and money storage depots by the United States occurred in the fight against the Islamic State on the basis that such targets were war-sustaining (*see* Chapter 6, 4.2: *Military action and war sustaining*).[28] However, what must be emphasized is that counterinsurgency and counterterrorism predominately involve military forces fighting among the people.[29] A particular goal is to maintain the support of the local population. The result is that the military advantage to be gained from limiting collateral civilian casualties and deaths can result in a requirement for an even more tightly controlled use of airpower (*see* Chapter 6, 4.4.2: *Excessive collateral casualties and damage*).

Nonetheless, States and their armed forces must be prepared to employ airpower during high-intensity inter-State armed conflicts. While less frequent, these conflicts when they did occur have reinforced the critical role of airpower. For example, the strategic air campaign against North Vietnam conducted by the United States in 1972, the so-called Christmas bombing, is credited by many historians as the event that finally compelled North Vietnam to agree to repatriate U.S. POWs, the final hurdle to securing an agreement to end U.S. involvement in the war. And, when the United Kingdom conducted its operation to reclaim the Falkland Islands from Argentina in 1982, Argentine air attacks on the British fleet, and the ability of British aircraft to defeat those attacks, proved a decisive factor in the ultimate victory.

The result is that airpower may be used in a variety of ways, from strategic attacks directed at war-supporting industry, to close air support in villages where terrorists use civilians and civilian infrastructure to screen their activities. However, in every case the targeting process is focused on producing effects that achieve the commander's objectives. It is the exceptional breadth of the potential uses of airpower that frequently creates a tension between armed forces seeking of a military advantage, and the humanitarian desire to control the effects of such operations on the civilian population. This has made the use of airpower a focus of efforts to limit the effects of the use of military force. It is to that issue that the analysis now turns.

3   Airpower: a unique challenge

Airpower has presented a unique set of challenges to those seeking to limits its destructive effects. At the extremes were those seeking to maximize its utility as a war-winning weapon, and conversely those adopting a pacifist, almost utopian viewpoint.[30] While the pacifist movements that developed in the aftermath of World War I failed to eliminate war, they did have a real impact such that early "expressions regarding the immorality of indiscriminate target area bombing have now been incorporated into IHL."[31] In humanitarian law terms, the discord regarding the use of airpower is reflected in the debate between using a narrow or broad interpretation of what constitutes a military objective (Chapter 6, 4.1: *Military objects*).

Added to these pacifist, narrow (tactical) and broad (strategic) influences on interpretations of the law governing air warfare, there is an increasing focus on how human rights law affects military operations, especially in the context of NIACs. This is evident in the approach taken by regional human rights tribunals toward the use of force in circumstances that in both fact and law involve armed conflict, but are assessed under a uniquely human rights regulatory framework. For example, in the European Court of Human Rights decision in *Kerimova v. Russia*, the court applied human rights law standards, such as a compelling test of necessity, that any force be strictly proportionate to its aims, and no more force than is absolutely necessary be used when assessing air strikes.[32] Similarly, in the *Targeted Killing Case* the Israeli Supreme Court applied human rights norms in interpreting a requirement that consideration be made to capture prior to killing an opponent.[33]

In addition, some analyses treat airpower as something qualitatively and quantitatively different from other uses of violence during armed conflict. This can be seen in *Finogenov v. Russia*,[34] where the European Court of Human Rights made a distinction between the use of Fentyal gas during the 2004 Moscow theater counterterrorist operation, and the use of "airborne bombs to destroy a rebel group which was hiding in a village full of civilians" in the *Isayeva II* case.[35] The latter was viewed as being an indiscriminate use of force.[36] Similarly, the court stated, "the choice of means (gas) by the authorities was less dangerous than in *Isayeva* (bombs),"[37] notwithstanding the fact that 129 hostages died as a result of that operation.[38] A distinction regarding the use of airpower is also evident in the International Committee of the Red Cross treatment of voluntary human shields in their Interpretive Guidance on the Notion of Direct Participation in Hostilities under International Humanitarian Law.[39] In that Guidance, it is suggested that, unlike the situation of ground operations, the presence of such civilians would not constitute direct participation in hostilities since "in operations involving more powerful weaponry, such as artillery or air attacks, the presence of voluntary human shields often has no adverse impact on the capacity of the attacker to identify and destroy the shielded military objective."[40] In this discussion, it is the high-explosive nature of aerial-delivered weapons and their destructive effect that underpins the suggested distinction.

There is no doubt that airpower can deliver significant destructive force. From a humanitarian perspective, the use of such force in an urban environment or other areas with concentrations of civilians can be particularly problematic. The potential adverse humanitarian impact of an aerial bombing campaign was evident in the operations undertaken by the Syrian Government and their Russian allies to take control of Aleppo, leading to allegations of war crimes.[41] Attempts to limit the destructive effect of air-delivered weapons is reflected in the tactical directive issued by military commanders in Afghanistan, which limited "[t]he use of air-to ground munitions and indirect fire [artillery and mortars] against residential compounds."[42] The changing nature of conflict can also impact on a proportionality assessment, with the military advantage derived from maintaining the support of the people in a counterinsurgency leading to more restrictive permissible collateral impact in an urban environment (*see* Chapter 6, 4.4.2: *Excessive collateral casualties and damage*).[43]

As explained in Chapter 7, "explosive weapons—like bombs, rockets and shells —are not prohibited as such under humanitarian law."[44] Nonetheless, it has also been noted that

> due to the significant likelihood of indiscriminate effects and despite the absence of an express legal prohibition for specific types of weapons, the ICRC considers that explosive weapons with a wide impact area should be avoided in densely populated areas.[45]

A key factor is the ability to target those taking a direct part in hostilities, and the practical measures taken to mitigate the humanitarian effects of using explosive weapons in an urban environment. As was evident in the Iraqi efforts to gain control of Mosul in 2017, the use of aerial-delivered ordnance may be justified by military necessity, even in an urban environment, if the enemy is to be defeated without subjecting ground forces to unacceptable risk.[46] The issue is not that aerial bombing should be uniquely restricted, or that special air-centric rules should be developed to curb its use. Precision munitions and low-yield warheads highlight that airpower can be applied effectively in many operational situations, including in cities. Artillery- and missile-delivered munitions present a similar challenge to aerial bombing. The rules governing targeting have universal application regardless of the type of weapon system, with an assessment of the results of any attack being dependent on a number of factual considerations that can be very context-dependent. Indeed, there may be situations where, in accordance with Article 57 of AP I, use of airpower in an urban area is a required attack option because alternate options, such as a ground attack, would pose increased risk to the civilian population.

4 Aerial warfare

4.1 *Status of aircraft and aircrew*

4.1.1 *Military aircraft and aircrew*

As with other forms of warfare, the principle of distinction has a fundamental application to aerial conflict. As a result, a key requirement is to distinguish between military and civilian aircraft, as well as establishing whether aircrew are lawful combatants entitled to the POW status. The term *aircraft* encompasses both fixed or rotary winged vehicles, but also extends to balloons, blimps, and dirigibles. Further aircraft may be manned or unmanned, clearly encompassing the use of drones.[47] Military aircraft have been defined as ones:

(i) operated by the armed forces of a State; (ii) bearing the military markings of that State; (iii) commanded by a member of the armed forces; and (iv) controlled, manned or preprogrammed by a crew subject to regular armed forces discipline.[48]

Only military aircraft can engage in attacks, conduct interception, and enforce blockades as the exercise of belligerent rights.[49] State aircraft other than military aircraft (e.g., police and customs aircraft) have no entitlement to exercise belligerent rights. Therefore, those aircraft are not lawful targets unless they become involved in activities that render them to be considered military objectives.[50]

During IAC, military aircrew are entitled to the status of POWs. However, if an aircraft taking a part in hostilities is not marked, thus not making it distinguishable to an adverse party, its crew members may be punished as criminals even if they are wearing uniforms.[51] When an aircraft is properly marked, it is not necessary that the aircrew be wearing uniforms, since "the wearing of the uniform is generally not apparent to the enemy, and because the military aircraft's marking allows sufficient identification."[52] In contrast, "[a]ircrews conducting combat operations on land or on water—outside their aircraft—must distinguish themselves from the civilian population, as required by the law of international armed conflict."[53] If a military aircraft is carrying civilian officials, it remains a military aircraft, although the presence of civilians would impact on a targeting proportionality assessment assuming the attacking force knew or reasonably should have known of such presence.[54]

Aircrew may attempt to surrender their aircraft, and it is prohibited to deny them quarter, or to kill an enemy that is wounded or surrendering. However, "it must be recognized that this prohibition is sometimes difficult to observe in aerial combat," although "[i]f enemy crew are clearly offering to surrender, that offer must be respected."[55] Otherwise, disabled aircraft can be pursued to their destruction to prevent them from returning to their home base.[56] A person parachuting from an aircraft in distress cannot be made the object of attack during his or her descent.[57] Upon reaching the ground, they must be given an opportunity to surrender, unless they are engaging in a hostile act.[58] Examples of hostile acts include attempting to destroy the aircraft or its equipment.[59] The prohibition on attacking parachuting aircrew does not extend to airborne troops, or paratroopers, who unlike a disabled aircrew member use the parachute descent as a tactic to engage in hostilities.[60]

4.1.2 Civilian aircraft and aircrew

Civilian aircraft are those that are neither military nor other State aircraft,[61] although State aircraft are normally regarded as civil.[62] Civilian or other State aircraft must be protected from attack,[63] however they may become military objectives because of their use or purpose.[64] Civilian aircraft should be generally "presumed to be carrying civilians, who may not be made the object of direct attack."[65] Such aircraft are liable to be intercepted and inspected, and may be captured as a prize (a concept derived from naval warfare whereby the capturing State may sell the aircraft and cargo and retain the proceeds).[66] Similarly, neutral aircraft "may not be attacked unless they become military objectives."[67] Neutral civilian aircraft are also subject to capture as a prize outside of neutral airspace under a variety of circumstances.[68]

Considering the events of 9/11, where hijacked civilian airliners were used to make attacks on the World Trade Center and the Pentagon, as well as an intended strike on the Capitol Building or the White House in Washington, D.C.,[69] such civilian aircraft have come under special consideration. The *HPCR Air and Missile Warfare Manual* Commentary notes that civilian airliners "are but a category of 'civilian aircraft,'" however they "benefit from particular care in terms of precautions in view of their world-wide employment in carrying civilian passengers in international air navigation, and in view of the vast risks to innocent passengers in areas of armed conflict."[70]

The civilian status of an aircraft or its aircrew does not necessarily render an aircraft immune from attack, for example if civilian aircraft were used to ferry military personnel. Similarly, transporting military supplies or engaging in intelligence gathering would make the aircraft liable to attack.[71] During World War II, unarmed transport aircraft flown by civilian aircrew in order to bring them from their production facilities in North America to the United Kingdom were legitimate targets that could be attacked.[72]

Under limited circumstances, civilian aircrew may quality for POW status. Pursuant to Article 4(A)(4) of the Third Geneva Convention, POW status is provided upon capture to *"civilian members of military aircraft crews,* war correspondents, supply contractors, members of labour units or of services responsible for the welfare of the armed forces."[73] Similarly, in Article 4(A)(5), "[m]embers of crews, including masters, pilots and apprentices, of the merchant marine and the *crews of civil aircraft* of the Parties to the conflict, who do not benefit by more favourable treatment under any other provisions of international law" are also provided prisoner of war status.[74] The activities performed by those civilians have historically been connected to supply, logistics and support functions.[75] However, they may engage in activities that amount to taking a direct part in hostilities, such as performing offensive operations, that could cause them to be considered unprivileged belligerents by the capturing State. As a result, the capturing State may also deny them POW status (*see* Chapter 3, 2.1.2: *In the aftermath of World War II*).

4.1.3 Protected status

Medical aircraft are generally immune from attack, as explained in Chapter 4. However, to ensure protection they must be properly marked with the protective emblem and exclusively engaged in the humanitarian function.[76] Technically, protection may also require overflight agreements between the parties to the conflict, although in reality this will rarely be the case. Accordingly, a warning and opportunity to comply is required before such an aircraft may be attacked. If they perform acts harmful to the enemy (e.g., also carrying combatants to a military objective), they may become lawful military objectives, but the warning and compliance opportunity is still required.[77] By agreement between belligerents, special protection can be provided to *cartel aircraft* (e.g., transporting wounded or exchanging prisoners).[78] Search-and-rescue aircraft—meaning aircraft that are equipped for combat and not exclusively engaged in a humanitarian function—are not specially protected unless the enemy consents to their operations.[79] Further, "[a]ircraft involved in civil defence functions, humanitarian relief, or UN activities (other than those which qualify them as a party to an armed conflict) are entitled to special protection."[80] (*see* Chapter 4, 4.1.7: *Medical aircraft*).

4.2   *Conduct of operations*

Although it is the kinetic aspect of targeting and the potential collateral impact on the civilian population that have garnered most contemporary attention concerning aerial warfare, it encompasses a broader range of activities. Military aircraft may provide direct support to land and sea forces, carryout interdiction operations, or be used "for reconnaissance, as transports for airborne troops, for bringing up reinforcements of men and supplies, as a strategic strike force, to bombard enemy forces to induce their surrender, for anti-naval activities or to enforce a blockade."[81] Air operations can also involve refueling, command and control, special operations, combat search and rescue, navigation, and weather services. Aircraft may also be used to disseminate propaganda.[82] Air and missile warfare particularly raises the issue of the use of nuclear weapons. In the Advisory Opinion on the Legality of the Threat or Use of Nuclear Weapons, the International Court of Justice held that IHL applied to nuclear weapons.[83] This included the principles of distinction and unnecessary suffering,[84] as well as proportionality and the protection of the environment.[85]

Military aircraft are "the only aircraft allowed to engaged in attacks (or otherwise exercise belligerent rights) against enemy lawful targets."[86] State aircraft are not entitled to exercise such rights.[87] Military aircraft are, except for medical or cartel aircraft, lawful military objectives.[88] When an attack is made on a military aircraft, all targeting rules that function to protect civilians and civilian property and other specially protected objects, to include distinction, precautions, and the targeting proportionality principle, must be complied with (*see* Chapter 6, 3: *Targeting persons*).[89] One challenge that arises because of the capabilities of aircraft and air-delivered missiles is targeting beyond visual range. Such targeting is permissible if appropriate steps are taken to determine that the intended object of attack is a lawful military objective. Verification that the target is a lawful military objective will normally be based on a variety of information including radar, electronic signals, flight formations, tracks, speed and signatures.[90]

The conduct of air and missile operations raises numerous other legal issues. As with warfare in other environments, belligerent aircraft may be used to conduct ruses but are prohibited from carrying out perfidious action.[91] Lawful ruses include the conduct of feint attacks, disinformation, the use of false military codes and false electronic optical or acoustic means, using decoys, and the use of camouflage.[92] Even when a plane is camouflaged, there is still a requirement for aircraft to have distinguishing national markings.[93] It is not lawful to feign distress by wrongful use of international recognized symbols, such as the International Committee of the Red Cross, the United Nations, or cartel aircraft.[94] Further, feigning the status of civilian or neutral aircraft as a means to kill or injure an adversary is prohibited.[95] For AP I countries, perfidy extends to betraying the confidence of an adversary to capture an opponent.[96] The improper use of distress codes are also prohibited.[97]

Espionage from aerial platforms is not prohibited under IHL, however captured military personnel who are engaged in espionage from an air platform to gather information of military value may be prosecuted under the domestic laws of the capturing power.[98] If military personnel engaged in espionage successfully return to their lines and are subsequently captured, they cannot be prosecuted for their prior acts of spying.[99] If an aircraft is properly marked, it is not considered to be engaged in espionage. Aircrew of a properly marked aircraft do not have to wear a uniform, however misunderstanding may occur regard their status if they do not and are captured.[100] If uniformed aircrew are flying a civilian aircraft (or an aircraft not properly marked) then they are at risk for being treated as having engaged in espionage since "the uniform worn in no way diminishes the covert ('clandestine') nature of the operation."[101]

4.3   No-fly zones and aerial blockades

4.3.1   No-fly zones

A belligerent may establish an exclusion or *no-fly zone* that is enforced wholly, or in part, by air forces. Such zones are distinguished from blockades.[102] As has been noted in the *HPCR Air and Missile Warfare Manual* Commentary, "[w]ith blockades, the focus lies on the horizontal line (or 'curtain') marking the outer limits of the blockaded area."[103] In contrast, exclusion zones and no-fly zones are focused on "the three dimensional area/space within the declared borderline."[104] Exclusion or no-fly zones may be created to defend military assets, protect civilians, or seek to geographically contain hostilities.[105] These zones provide a form of warning to aircraft.[106] Belligerents are also entitled, for reasons of military necessity, to prohibit aircraft from operating within a certain vicinity, "or prescribe set routes for passage."[107]

The establishment of such zones must be properly notified to all civil aviation (e.g., through the use of NOTAMs).[108] While these zones are intended to reduce the likelihood that aircraft will enter the airspace, it is critical to emphasize that declaration of a zone *does not* absolve the belligerent party seeking to enforce it from complying with its obligations under IHL.[109] At most, "entry into the properly identified and announced zone by an aircraft merely creates a presumption it is engaged in non-innocent activities."[110] This presumption may not, however, ever be treated as exclusive, but instead is always rebuttable. In other words, even when an aircraft enters an exclusion zone, the military forces tasked to enforce the zone may not launch an attack on the aircraft if they know that the aircraft is not in fact a lawful object of attack. They are not free-fire zones, and belligerents must confirm that targeted aircraft are valid military objectives.[111]

4.3.2   Aerial blockades

Blockades traditionally have occurred in a naval context, however they are also contemplated as purely air-based activity. Regarding aerial blockades "the belligerents should apply the general principles of a sea blockade."[112] The law governing blockade applies to IAC, although States may similarly impose restrictions regarding access to its own territory during NIAC.[113] A blockade must be declared and requires adequate notification to all States.[114] The enforcement of naval blockades may involve the use of air power, as occurred when the Israel Defense Forces used helicopters to land naval commandoes on the deck of a ship during its 2010 enforcement of its blockade of Gaza.[115] As the *HPCR Air and Missile Warfare Manual* Commentary states, an aerial blockade is "a belligerent operation to prevent aircraft (including UAVs/UCAVs) from entering or exiting specified airfields or coastal areas belonging to, occupied by, or under the control of the enemy."[116] An aerial blockade may be supported by both naval and land forces, particularly through the use of surface to air missiles.[117]

A blockade must be effective to be considered lawful. In this respect, it must be impartially enforced against all aircraft,[118] although "aircraft in distress must be permitted to enter the blockaded area when necessary."[119] Effectiveness requires that "civilian aircraft believed on reasonable grounds to be breaching, or attempting to breach, an aerial blockade, be forced to land, inspected, captured or diverted."[120] This does not mean that every aircraft must be stopped. Rather, "an aerial blockade is to be considered effective if any attempt to leave or enter the blockaded area proves to be a hazardous undertaking."[121] Blockades are meant to be enforced through capture, however, "if that is not possible, by the destruction of the alleged blockade runner."[122] Special care in terms of precautions must be taken regarding civilian airliners.[123]

5   Missile warfare

Missile (and rocket) warfare encompasses a broad range of weapons ranging from inter-continental ballistic missiles to cruise missiles (e.g., Russian SSC-8),[124] to artillery-based multiple-tube launch systems (e.g., the United States' Multiple Rocket Launch System (MRLS)[125] and High Mobility Artillery Rocket

(HIMARS)).[126] They may be guided by rocket or jet engines, however they "are to be distinguished from munitions propelled by external force, such as a mortar or artillery shell."[127] Missiles may be air-, land-, or sea-launched, and may be offensive or defensive (e.g., Russia's S-400,[128] the United States' Terminal High Altitude Area Defense (THAAD) missiles,[129] Israel's Iron Dome system)[130] in nature. As with aerial bombing, missile warfare is regulated by IHL. This includes when missiles carry nuclear warheads.

Historically, the use of missiles has prompted allegations of their being indiscriminate weapons. As has been noted, the "first employment of modern missiles in warfare—that of the German V-1s and V-2s in World War II—was the epitome of an indiscriminate attack."[131] Similarly, the Scud missiles fired by Iraq during the 1991 Gulf War were viewed as too imprecise and therefore incompatible with humanitarian law.[132] However, the development of precision guidance systems, even for artillery launched systems such as the HIMARS, has radically changed their effectiveness as a weapons system. Even tactically deployed missiles can reach targets far beyond what might normally be considered the front lines of a conflict. For example, the U.S. Army Tactical Missile System (ATACMS) can strike targets up to 300 kilometers away.[133] This means that those weapons could potentially be directed at strategic targets. Further, artillery-based missiles are used not only in conventional warfare but also during counterinsurgencies against non-State actors (e.g., the Taliban, the Islamic State).[134]

The result is that missiles, like that of other weapons in aerial warfare, are likely to be put under increasing scrutiny as their role changes and the frequency of their use increases. However, so long as they are employed consistent with IHL targeting rules, there is no reason why a rocket or missile should be considered per se unlawful. Two key considerations in assessing this compliance, as noted in Chapter 7, are whether the missile can be adequately directed against a specific military objective, and whether once fired it can be expected to strike the intended target. Accordingly, using missiles as substitutes for World War II–type carpet bombing attacks on densely populated areas is clearly inconsistent with humanitarian law.

6 Conclusion

While the use of airpower has not proven to be a war-winning capability on its own, aerial warfare is a dominant aspect of contemporary armed conflict. Some analysts have sought to treat air and missile warfare as quantitatively and qualitatively different from other forms of violence during armed conflict. There is no doubt that there are unique aspects of air warfare, including the status of aircrew and aircraft and the use of no-fly zones and aerial blockades. Missiles are also being placed under increased scrutiny as their role changes and they become more frequently used. However, in the final analysis the rules governing air and missile warfare, and in particular targeting, are those of international application regardless of the type of weapon system that is employed.

Notes

1 Hersch Lauterpacht, *The Problem of the Revision of the Law of War*, 29 Brit. Y.B. Int'l L. 360, 365–6 (1952).
2 *Id.*
3 Richard Overy, "Total War II: The Second World War," in *The Oxford History of Modern War* 138, 148 (Charles Townshend ed., 2005) ("Bombing strategy was deliberately aimed not at forces in the field but at the war-willingness and productive capacity of the society behind them.").
4 *Hague Rules of Air Warfare*, 1923, 32 Am. J. Int'l L. Supp. 12 (1938).
5 Leslie Green, *The Contemporary Law of Armed Conflict* 208 (3rd edn, 2008).
6 Protocol (I) Additional to the Geneva Conventions of 12 August 1949, and Relating to the Protection of Victims of International Armed Conflicts, 8 June 1977, 1125 U.N.T.S. 3 [hereinafter AP I] (entered into force 7 December 1978) (signed by the United States 12 December 1977, not transmitted to U.S. Senate, *see* S. Treaty Doc. No. 100–2 (1987)); Protocol (II) Additional to the Geneva Conventions of 12 August 1949, and Relating to the Protection of Victims of Non-International Armed Conflicts, Art 6(5), 8 June 1977, 1125 U.N.T.S. 609 [hereinafter AP II] (entered into force 7 December 1978) (signed by the United States 12 December 1977, transmitted to the U.S. Senate 29 January 1987, still pending action as S. Treaty Doc. No. 100–2 (1987)).
7 Program on Humanitarian Policy and Conflict Research (HPCR) at Harvard University, Commentary on the *HPCR Manual on International Law Applicable to Air and Missile Warfare* (2009) [hereinafter the *HPCR Air and Missile Warfare Manual* Commentary]. *See also San Remo Manual on International Law Applicable to Armed Conflicts at Sea* (Louise Doswald-Beck ed., 1995) [hereinafter *San Remo Manual*] (which also addresses air warfare at sea).
8 *HPCR Air and Missile Warfare Manual* Commentary, r. 1(z).
9 William Murray & Robert H. Scales, Jr., *The Iraq War* 180 (2003) ("[a]ir superiority has allowed U.S. ground forces the freedom to maneuver audaciously.").
10 *See, e.g.*, Michael S. Schmidt & Eric Schmitt, *Pentagon Confronts a New Threat From ISIS: Exploding Drones*, *N.Y. Times* (11 October 2016), *available at* www.nytimes.com/2016/10/12/world/middleeast/iraq-drones-isis.html?_r=0
11 John Warden III, *The Air Campaign: Planning for Combat* 14 (1988).
12 James M. Spaight, *Air Power and War Rights* Ch. X, 14 (3rd edn, 1947).
13 Kenneth Watkin, *Targeting in Air Warfare*, 44 Isr. Y.B. on Hum. Rts 1, 10–11 (2014).
14 Nadia Schadlow, *War and the Art of Governance: Consolidating Combat Success into Political Victory* 277 (2017).
15 B.H. Liddell Hart, *Strategy* 322 (2nd edn, 1991) ("with perhaps less killing more devastation than the 1914–1918 form").
16 John Andreas Olsen, *John Warden and the Renaissance of American Air Power* 78 (2007) (where reference is made to American theorist John Warden's view that Vietnam was not lost until after the United States withdrew its airpower).
17 James S. Corum & Wray R. Johnson, *Airpower in Small Wars: Fighting Insurgents and Terrorists* 427 (2003).
18 D.S. Fadok, John Boyd, & John Warden, "Airpower's Quest for Strategic Paralysis," in *The Paths of Heaven: The Evolution of Airpower Theory* 385 (P.S. Meilinger ed., 1997).
19 Olsen, *supra* note 16, at 79.
20 Michael W. Lewis, *The Law of Aerial Bombardment in the 1991 Gulf War*, 97 Am. J. Int'l L. 481, 484–5 (2003).
21 David Deptula, *Effects Based Operations: Change in the Nature of Warfare* 5 (2001).

22 Michael N. Schmitt, *Effects-Based Operations and the Law of Aerial Warfare*, 5 Wash. Glob. Stud. L. Rev. 274 (2006).

23 Geoffrey S. Corn & Gary P. Corn, *The Law of Operational Targeting: Viewing the LOAC Through an Operational Lens*, 47 Tex. Int'l L. J. 337, 341–3 (2012).

24 U.S. Dep't of Defense, *Dictionary of Military and Associated Terms* 127 (June 2017), *available at* www.dtic.mil/doctrine/new_pubs/dictionary.pdf (definition of joint doctrine).

25 Walther Boyne, *The Influence of Airpower upon History* 379 (2005).

26 Benjamin S. Lambeth, *Air Operations in Israel's War Against Hezbollah: Learning from Lebanon and Getting It Right in Gaza*, Rand Project Air Force 251 (2011), *available at* www.rand.org/content/dam/rand/pubs/monographs/2011/RAND_MG835.pdf

27 Gary C. Schroen, *First In: An Insider's Account of How the CIA Spearheaded the War on Terror in Afghanistan* 146 (2005).

28 *See* Watkin, *Reflections on Targeting: Looking in the Mirror, Just Security* (2016), *available at* www.justsecurity.org/31513/reflections-targeting-mirror/

29 Rupert Smith, *The Utility of Force: The Art of War In The Modern World* 3–5 (2007).

30 Joseph L. Kunz, *The Chaotic Status of the Laws of War and the Urgent Necessity for their Revision*, 45 Am. J. Int'l. L. 37, 39 (1951).

31 AP I, Art 51(5)(a). *See also* Kenneth Watkin, *Assessing Proportionality: Moral Complexity and Legal Rules*, 8 Y.B. Int'l Hum. L. 1, 32–4 (2005).

32 *Kerimova v. Russia*, App. Nos. 17170/04, 20792/04, 22448/04, 23360/04, 5681/05 and 5684/05 Eur. Ct. H. R. para 246 (3 May 2011), *available at* http://hudoc.echr.coe.int/sites/eng/pages/search.aspx?i=001-104662

33 HCJ 769/02 *Pub. Comm. against Torture in Isr. v. Gov't of Isr.* 57(6) PD 285, para 40 [2005].

34 *Finogenov v. Russia*, 2011-IV Eur. Ct. H. R. Rep. 365 (extracts).

35 *Isayeva v. Russia*, App. No. 57959/00, Eur. Ct. H. R., para 175 (2005), *available at* http://hudoc.echr.coe.int/eng?i=001-68381

36 *Finogenov v. Russia*, 2011-IV Eur. Ct. H. R. Rep. 365, 408, para 232 (extracts).

37 *Id.* para 216, at 404.

38 Mark Galeotti, *Russian Security Forces and Paramilitary Forces since 1991* (2013).

39 N. Melzer, Interpretive Guidance on the Notion of Direct Participation in Hostilities Under International Humanitarian Law (2009).

40 *Id.* at 57.

41 *Russia/Syria: War Crimes in Month of Bombing Aleppo*, Human Rights Watch (1 December 2016), *available at* www.hrw.org/news/2016/12/01/russia/syria-war-crimes-month-bombing-aleppo

42 Daniel P. Bolger, *Why We Lost: A General's Inside Account of the Iraq and Afghanistan Wars* 305 (2014).

43 Watkin, *Fighting at the Legal Boundaries: Controlling the Use of Force in Contemporary Conflict* 254–61 (2016).

44 Vincent Bernard, *War in Cities: The Spectre of Total War*, 98 Int'l Rev. Red Cross 1, 7–8 (2016).

45 ICRC, International Humanitarian Law and the Challenges of Contemporary Armed Conflicts: Report, October 2011, at 42, *available at* www.icrc.org/eng/assets/files/red-cross-crescent-movement/31st-international-conference/31-int-conference-ihl-challenges-report-11-5-1-2-en.pdf

46 Paul D. Shinkman, *Top General Defends Air Campaign After Mosul Bombing*, U.S. *News* (31 March 2017), *available at* www.usnews.com/news/national-news/articles/2017-03-23/us-general-pushes-back-against-claims-of-indiscriminate-bombing-in-mosul

47 *HPCR Air and Missile Warfare Manual* Commentary, r. 1(d).

48 *Id*. r. 1(x).
49 Schmitt, "Air Law and Military Operations," in *The Handbook of Military Law and Operations* 303, 312–13 (2010).
50 *HPCR Air and Missile Warfare Manual* Commentary, r. 1(cc).
51 Green, *supra* note 5, at 211.
52 *HPCR Air and Missile Warfare Manual* Commentary, r. 123.
53 *Id*. r. 117.
54 Schmitt, *supra* note 49, at 313; AP I, Art 57(2).
55 Green, *supra* note 5, at 214. *See also HPCR Air and Missile Warfare Manual* Commentary, rr. 125–6.
56 Green, *supra* note 5, at 215.
57 AP I, Art 42(1).
58 *Id*. Art 42(2).
59 Green, *supra* note 5, at 215.
60 *Id. See also* AP I, Art 42(3).
61 *HPCR Air and Missile Warfare Manual* Commentary, r. 1(h).
62 Green, *supra* note 5, at 209. *See also* Yoram Dinstein, *The Conduct of Hostilities Under the Law of International Armed Conflict* 117 (2nd edn, 2010).
63 *HPCR Air and Missile Warfare Manual* Commentary, r. 1(h).
64 Schmitt, *supra* note 49, at 313.
65 Green, *supra* note 5, at 216.
66 *HPCR Air and Missile Warfare Manual* Commentary, r. 1(h).
67 Schmitt, *supra* note 49, at 321.
68 *HPCR Air and Missile Warfare Manual* Commentary, r. 140 (if they are carrying contraband, are specifically undertaking to fly members of the enemy armed forces, are operating under enemy control, present or do not have proper papers, violate regulations established by the parties to a conflict in the vicinity of military operations, or are engaged in the breach of an aerial blockade).
69 The 9/11 Commission Report: Final Report of the National Commission on Terrorist Attacks Upon the United States 7–14 (2004).
70 *HPCR Air and Missile Warfare Manual* Commentary, r. 1(i); Schmitt, *supra* note 49, at 318–19.
71 Schmitt, *supra* note 49, at 313.
72 Green, *supra* note 5, at 215.
73 Geneva Convention Relative to the Treatment of Prisoners of War, Art 4.A(4), 12 August 1949, Art 4, 6 U.S.T. 3316, 75 U.N.T.S. 972 [hereinafter GPW] (emphasis added).
74 GPW, Art 4(A)(5) (emphasis added).
75 *See* U.S. Dep't of Def., *Law of War Manual* 6.10.3.1 (June 2015, updated December 2016) [hereinafter *DoD Law of War Manual*], where it is indicated that

> civilian members of military aircrews are entitled to POW status if they fall into the power of the enemy during international armed conflict, and they have legal immunity from the enemy's domestic law *for providing authorized support services to the armed forces.*

76 Green, *supra* note 5, at 215.
77 Schmitt, *supra* note 49, at 316–17.
78 Green, *supra* note 5, at 215–16.
79 Schmitt, *supra* note 49, at 317.
80 *Id*. at 317.
81 Green, *supra* note 5, at 215–16.
82 *Id*. at 211.

83 Legality of the Threat or Use of Nuclear Weapons, Advisory Opinion, 1996 I.C.J. 226, para 85, at 259 (8 July) [hereinafter Nuclear Weapons Case]. *See also HPCR Air and Missile Warfare Manual* Commentary, r. 7.

84 *Nuclear Weapons Case*, para 78, at 257.

85 *Id.* at 30, at 242.

86 Dinstein, *supra* note 62, at 116.

87 *Id.*

88 Schmitt, *supra* note 49, at 313.

89 *Id.* at 313.

90 *Id.*

91 AP I, Art 37(1).

92 *HPCR Air and Missile Warfare Manual* Commentary, r. 116.

93 Green, *supra* note 5, at 214.

94 *HPCR Air and Missile Warfare Manual* Commentary, r. 114(d). *See also* Green, *supra* note 5, at 214.

95 *Id.* r. 114(b)-(c).

96 AP I, Art 37(1).

97 *HPCR Air and Missile Warfare Manual* Commentary, r. 115(a).

98 Richard R. Baxter, "So-called 'Unprivileged Belligerency': Spies, Guerrillas, and Saboteurs," in *Humanizing the Laws of War: Selected Writings of Richard Baxter* 37, 42–6 (Detlev F. Vagts et al. eds, 2013).

99 AP I, Art 46(4).

100 *HPCR Air and Missile Warfare Manual* Commentary, r. 120.

101 *Id.* Section P.

102 *Id.*

103 *Id.* Section P(9).

104 *Id.* Section P.

105 *Id.* Schmitt, *supra* note 49, at 315.

106 Dinstein, *supra* note 62, at 229. *See also* Schmitt, *supra* note 49, at 314 (where it is suggested exclusion and no-fly zones are not warning zones, "which are force protection measures that merely serve to warn off aircraft approaching the vicinity of military operations or facilities"; however, it is also noted "[a]ircraft, other than enemy belligerent aircraft, approaching the zone must be appropriately notified and warned away.").

107 Schmitt, *supra* note 49, at 314.

108 *Id.* at 315.

109 *HPCR Air and Missile Warfare Manual* Commentary, r. 114(b); Schmitt, *supra* note 49, at 314.

110 Schmitt, *supra* note 49, r. 18.15.

111 *Id.*

112 *San Remo Manual*, at 177.

113 *HPCR Air and Missile Warfare Manual* Commentary, para 7, at 287. *See also* 1 Public Commission to Examine the Maritime Incident of 31 May 2010, para 42 at 47–8 (2011) [hereinafter First Turkel Report] (for a discussion of the applicability of blockade law to NIACs).

114 *HPCR Air and Missile Warfare Manual* Commentary, r. 148(a).

115 First Turkel Report, para 182 at 286.

116 *HPCR Air and Missile Warfare Manual* Commentary, r. 147.

117 *Syria: Minimizing Civilian Harm During Military Intervention,* Roundtable Outcome Document, Center for Civilians in Conflict 7–8 (February 2013), *available at* http://civiliansinconflict.org/uploads/files/publications/Syria_Roundtable_brief_Feb_2013.pdf (for a discussion of the use of Patriot missile batteries to enforce a

no-fly zone in Syria). *See also HPCR Air and Missile Warfare Manual* Commentary, r. 153(a).

118 *HPCR Air and Missile Warfare Manual* Commentary, r. 155.

119 *Id.* r. 153(b).

120 *Id.* r. 156.

121 *Id.* r. 151.

122 Green, *supra* note 5, at 214.

123 *HPCR Air and Missile Warfare Manual Commentary*, r. 158; Schmitt, *supra* note 49, at 318–19.

124 *This Is the Ground-Launched Cruise Missile that Russia Has Reportedly Just Deployed*, *Washington Post* (15 February 2017), *available at* www.washingtonpost.com/ news/checkpoint/wp/2017/02/15/this-is-the-ground-launched-cruise-missile-that-russia-has-reportedly-just-deployed/?utm_term=.4edeeccba4fc

125 Multiple Launch Rocket System M270, *available at* www.lockheedmartin.ca/ us/products/MLRSM270.html ("[T]he crew of three can fire up to 12 MLRS rockets or two Army Tactical Missile System (ATACMS)," and "[m]ore than 10,000 rockets and 32 ATACMS fired in combat during Desert Storm.") *See also* Kris Osborn, *US Army's Guided Multiple Launch Rocket System Is Getting a New Warhead*, *The National Interest* (20 September 2016), *available at* http://nationalinterest.org/ blog/the-buzz/us-armys-guided-multiple-launch-rocket-system-getting-new-17774

126 Kyle Mizokami, *Meet the U.S. Military's Globetrotting Rocket Launcher*, *Popular Mechanics* (17 June 2016), *available at* www.popularmechanics.com/military/ weapons/a20415/the-us-militarys-busy-truck-mounted-rocket-launcher/.

127 *HPCR Air and Missile Warfare Manual* Commentary, r. 158.

128 Shashank Shantanu, *Russia to Supply S-400 Missile System to India: Why Pakistan, China Should Worry*, *India Today* (2 June 2017), *available at* http://indiatoday. intoday.in/story/russia-to-supply-s-400-missile-system-to-india-modi-putin/1/ 969057.html

129 Ankit Panda, *What Is THAAD, What Does It Do, and Why Is China Mad About It?*, *The Diplomat* (16 February 2016), *available at* http://thediplomat.com/2016/ 02/what-is-thaad-what-does-it-do-and-why-is-china-mad-about-it/

130 *Israel Successfully Tests Improved Version of Iron Dome*, *Jerusalem Post* (23 February 2017), *available at* www.timesofisrael.com/army-successfully-tests-improved-version-of-iron-dome/

131 Dinstein, *supra* note 62, at 128.

132 *Id.*

133 *See generally* Mizokami, *supra* note 126.

134 *Id. See also, e.g.*, Michael R. Gordon, *U.S. Forces Play Crucial Role Against ISIS in Mosul*, *N.Y. Times* (26 February 2017), *available at* www.nytimes.com/2017/02/ 26/world/middleeast/mosul-iraq-american-military-role-islamic-state.html?_r=0

10 Command responsibility

1 Introduction

The roles and responsibilities of commanders are central to ensuring the respect of IHL.[1] Commanders are expected to lead by example by disseminating IHL among their troops and overseeing the actions of their subordinates.[2] As with any other individual, commanders in their individual capacity can be held criminally responsible for war crimes they commit or are complicit in committing. Additionally, in their command capacity, they can be held responsible for the violations committed by their subordinates, either by the failure to prevent the occurrence of the violations or by the failure to punish those who committed violations.

Where evidence indicates that a commander, military or, where relevant, civilian ordered, encouraged, or incited a subordinate's commission of a war crime, the well-established doctrine of accomplice liability renders the commander criminally responsible for the war crime as if it had been committed by his or her own hand. The more complicated question of accountability arises when a commander's failure to discharge his or her duties of leadership set the conditions for a war crime committed by the subordinate. In such cases, a mere breach of duty, whereby the commander has not fulfilled the responsibilities expected of his or her rank, is usually dealt with through disciplinary action. However, where a commander, military or civilian, fails to prevent or punish violations of IHL by subordinates, criminal responsibility for that failure is likely and the punishment to be meted out will reflect the gravity and nature of the crime committed by the subordinate. This additional layer of accountability for commanders is understandable given their position of responsibility and influence over the actions and conduct of troops and other subordinates. In short, when a causal connection is established between a commander's failure to responsibly ensure that subordinates respect IHL, the commander becomes criminally responsible for the foreseeable war crimes reasonably attributable to that failure.

Commanders therefore have an affirmative duty to act in preventing and punishing violations of IHL by their subordinates. In essence, the commander acquires liability by omission.[3] Having evaded the leadership responsibility as a superior to intervene in ensuring the respect of IHL, the commander will be seen as accountable for the offenses of subordinates and, in certain circumstances, as even more culpable than them. This does not mean that subordinates are absolved from all blame, as they too will be held individually accountable for the violations they perpetrate.

This chapter will consider the evolution of the principle of command responsibility, before turning to its constitutive elements. These are, essentially: (1) the existence of a superior–subordinate relationship, (2) the knowledge of the potential or actual offenses, and (3) the measures that a commander is expected to take to prevent and punish the actions of his or her subordinates. Finally, this chapter will summarily consider issues regarding manifestly illegal orders and the defense of superior orders.

2   A settled principle

The principle of *command responsibility* is solidified in jurisprudence stemming from the post–World War II trials of captured Axis commanders. One of the seminal cases was that of General Tomuyuki Yamashita, which was reviewed by the U.S. Supreme Court in 1946. In this case, Yamashita, commander of the Japanese forces in the Philippines during 1944 and 1945, was convicted for the numerous murders committed by his subordinates based on his failure to discharge his duty to control the operations of persons under his command who had violated the laws of war. The majority judgment, delivered by Chief Justice Stone, emphasized that the laws of war impose upon an army commander a duty to take such appropriate measures as are within his power to control the troops under his command and prevent them from committing violations of the laws of war. In the view of the court, the absence of such an affirmative duty for commanders to prevent violations of the laws of war would defeat the very purpose of those laws. To quote the court:

> It is evident that the conduct of military operations by troops whose excesses are unrestrained by the orders or efforts of their commander would almost certainly result in violations which it is the purpose of the law of war to prevent. Its purpose to protect civilian populations and prisoners of war from brutality would largely be defeated if the commander of an invading army could with impunity neglect to take reasonable measures for their protection. Hence the law of war presupposes that its violation is to be avoided through the control of the operations of war by commanders who are to some extent responsible for their subordinates.

The court thus concluded that commanders like Yamashita were deemed to have a clear responsibility to control subordinates and to ensure that they respected IHL. The failure to do so, along with the resulting foreseeable IHL violations by those subordinates, rendered the commander criminally liable for those war crimes, warranting penal action and punishment befitting the crimes. This was similarly iterated in the case of the *United States v. Wilhelm von Leeb et al.* (*High Command Case*), where the U.S. Military Tribunal at Nuremberg stated that

> under basic principles of command authority and responsibility, an officer who merely stands by while his subordinates execute a criminal order of his superiors which he knows is criminal violates a moral obligation under international law. By doing nothing he cannot wash his hands of international responsibility.[4]

It took over 30 years to have these principles codified into treaty law. The precedents set by the post–World War II cases, including the above and others from the International Military Tribunal for the Far East (Tokyo Tribunal) and the U.S. Military Tribunal at Nuremberg, heavily influenced the drafting of the text of Article 86 (failure to act) of the 1977 Protocol I Additional to the 1949 Geneva Conventions, which reads:

1. The High Contracting Parties and the Parties to the conflict shall repress grave breaches, and take measures necessary to suppress all other breaches, of the Conventions or of this Protocol which result from a failure to act when under a duty to do so.
2. The fact that a breach of the Conventions or of this Protocol was committed by a subordinate does not absolve his superiors from penal or disciplinary responsibility, as the case may be, if they knew, or had information which should have enabled them to conclude in the circumstances at the time, that he was committing or was going to commit such a breach and if they did not take all feasible measures within their power to prevent or repress the breach.

The main reason for the development of this form of responsibility, notably in the international criminal arena, lies in the recognition that it is often the low-level subordinate—the soldier on the ground—who actually commits war crimes by pulling the trigger. Article 86 reflected an endorsement of the post–World War II command responsibility jurisprudence, and the general agreement that command responsibility is necessary to enable prosecutions beyond the direct perpetrators of the crimes. Without this mode of responsibility for the war crimes committed by subordinates, superiors could all too often absolve themselves of any wrongdoing based on an inability to satisfy the traditional requirements for accomplice liability by arguing that the subordinates were not following orders when they committed crimes, or that the superior was at no time at the scene of the violations and therefore could not be credibly accused of encouraging or inciting the violations.[5]

Today the law is clear: a commander is duty-bound to intervene and to prevent or repress acts of subordinates when he or she knew or should have known that these acts constituted or would constitute violations of IHL. Failure to discharge this duty may, accordingly, lead to command accountability for the violations.

Command responsibility is now recognized in many national military manuals and has been the subject of further developments in particular by the various international criminal tribunals, both in their constitutive documents and in their jurisprudence.[6] Furthermore, the doctrine has evolved to cover both military and well as civilian superiors. Holding military and civilian commanders accountable for the war crimes committed by their subordinates pursuant to this doctrine has concretized into international customary law.[7]

3   Conditions for establishing command responsibility

3.1   *Superior-subordinate relationship*

Military as well as civilian leaders can be held responsible as commanders under IHL. The existence of a superior–subordinate relationship must first be established between the commander and his or her subordinates. This relationship can be de jure or de facto, based on authority or command. It is traditionally easier to demonstrate the existence of this relationship in a military environment, where a clearly defined and more formal hierarchal system exists, than in civilian settings. With this in mind, case law, in particular at the international level, provides important guidance on how this relationship is established, absent proof of a formal chain of command.

The International Criminal Court (ICC) has defined the term *command* as "authority, especially over armed forces," and the term *authority* as the "power or right to give orders and enforce obedience."[8] The position of authority and/or command alone is insufficient to lead to criminal accountability based on the command responsibility doctrine. It must come with the exercise of *effective control* over the subordinate(s) who committed the underlying offenses.[9] Therefore, a commander will not be held responsible for the acts of all his or her subordinates that result in IHL violations. Only when the violations are committed by subordinates over whom the commander exercises effective control—and where he or she failed to intervene, subject to the *knowledge requirement* discussed below being met as well—will the doctrine expose the commander to liability for those war crimes. Furthermore, a commander is justified in the expectation that subordinates will implement orders in accordance with IHL, unless he or she is aware or should be aware of circumstances that indicate such an assumption is invalid. When such circumstances exist, the commander's failure to prevent a war crime he or she was aware would occur, or where he or she should have known such a war crime would occur, results in criminal responsibility. In the *High Command Case*, the Nuremberg Tribunal explained:

> A high commander cannot keep completely informed of the details of military operations of subordinates and most assuredly not of every administrative measure. He has the right to assume that details entrusted to responsible subordinates will be legally executed. The President of the United States is Commander in Chief of its military forces. Criminal acts committed by those

forces cannot in themselves be charged to him on the theory of subordination. The same is true of other high commanders in the chain of command.

Criminality does not attach to every individual in this chain of command from that fact alone. There must be a personal dereliction. That can occur only where the act is directly traceable to him or where his failure to properly supervise his subordinates constitutes criminal negligence on his part. In the latter case it must be a personal neglect amounting to a wanton, immoral disregard of the action of his subordinates amounting to acquiescence. Any other interpretation of international law would go far beyond the basic principles of criminal law as known to civilized nations.[10]

Notably the High Command Case introduced a "should have known" standard rather than the "must have known" standard applied in Yamashita, and that became the generally accepted international standard.[11]

Likewise, the ICRC Commentary on Article 86 of AP I, explains,

we are concerned only with the superior who has a personal responsibility with regard to the perpetrator of the acts concerned because the latter, being his subordinate, is under his control. . . . The concept of the superior . . . should be seen in terms of a hierarchy encompassing the concept of control.

The ICC has explained that effective control for military commanders or persons effectively acting as military commanders requires that the "commander have the material ability to prevent or repress the commission of the crimes or to submit the matter to the competent authorities," and that anything less than effective control "such as the ability to exercise influence—even substantial influence—over the forces who committed the crimes would be insufficient to establish command responsibility."[12]

The meaning and assessment of effective control is primarily a factual question, focusing on the superior's power to prevent, punish, or initiate relevant proceedings against his or her alleged subordinates. It must be shown, at a minimum, that the commander had "the material ability to prevent and punish the commission" of relevant offenses.[13] This material ability can take a variety of forms and be based on a range of factors, including the capacity to issue orders, whether orders are in fact followed, the authority to issue disciplinary measures, and the power to terminate the employment of subordinates.[14]

This last factor is particularly relevant in the case of civilian superiors and subordinates, as illustrated in the ICTR case against Alfred Musema, a tea factory director in Gisovu, Rwanda, during the 1994 massacres. The accusations against him included the failure to prevent and punish offenses committed by his subordinates, namely his tea factory employees. The failings alleged were not that he did not physically prevent his subordinates in the act of committing crimes. Instead, the focus of the court's reasoning was that, as their employer, he exercised "legal and financial control" over them and could have taken "reasonable measures, such as removing, or threatening to remove, an individual

from his or her position at the Tea Factory if he or she was identified as a perpetrator" of crimes. The court also reasoned, given that tea factory vehicles were
used to transport tea factory workers in uniform to carry out rapes and killings
of Tutsi, that he could have taken "reasonable measures to attempt to prevent
or to punish the use of Tea Factory vehicles, uniforms or other Tea Factory
property in the commission of such crimes."[15] Although he was not ultimately
convicted as a superior, the court concluded that he exercised both de jure
authority, as well as de facto control, over his employees and factory resources.

3.2 *The knowledge requirement*

For liability to be attached to a commander, it must be shown that he or she
knew or had reason to know that his or her subordinate(s) committed or were
about to commit offenses, and failed to act.[16] Article 86(2) of AP I, building on
the post-World War II jurisprudence, confirms important aspects of this concept:
commanders will be deemed responsible if they had information that should have
enabled them to conclude, in the circumstances at the time, that their subordinates
were committing or were going to commit a breach.[17] It should be noted,
though, as discussed below, that the ICC introduces a distinction in the required
knowledge between civilian and military commanders.

The commander need not have actual knowledge of the offenses and actions of
his or her subordinates. An implicit or constructive knowledge of the actions will
suffice. As the ICTY has explained, a superior may be deemed to possess sufficient
knowledge where he or she has

> information of a nature, which at the least, would put him on notice of the
> risk of . . . offences . . . indicating the need for additional investigation in
> order to ascertain whether such crimes were committed or were about to
> be committed by his subordinates.[18]

In other words, the information available to the commander need not contain
"extensive or specific details about the unlawful acts committed or about to be
committed,"[19] nor the identity of each subordinate.[20] The commander must,
however, be in a position that would allow a reasonable commander in the same
or similar position to actually understand that the anticipated unlawful conduct
of the subordinates would amount to a war crime.[21] Article 82 of AP I goes as
far as to suggest that expert advice is available to the commander in this regard.[22]

A review of relevant case law on the scope of the knowledge requirement
demonstrates that, traditionally, no distinction was made between military or
civilian commanders (for instance ministers, mayors, and directors of factories),
irrespective of office held. While it may be easier to establish knowledge in
military settings than in civilian contexts, the test remained the same. Rule 153
of the ICRC's *Customary Law Study* reflects this: for both categories of superiors to attract liability, it had to be shown that the superior either knew or had
reason to know.

Like any other crime, the mental element of command responsibility need not be established by direct evidence (like a confession). Instead, the required knowledge of the commander can be inferred from circumstantial evidence. A number of factors have been taken into account by the courts to assess the extent of the commander's actual knowledge or whether the commander reasonably should have known of expectant war crimes. These include actions such as the giving of orders or instructions, the widespread nature of the offenses, public reports and media coverage, and the number of subordinates engaged in acts of ill-discipline.[23]

In contrast to this broad notion of the knowledge element, the ICC Statute has introduced a clear distinction between civilian and military commanders. For the former, Article 28 introduces a *willful blindness* standard, requiring that the superior either *knew or consciously disregarded information which clearly indicated* that the subordinates were committing or about to commit war crimes.[24] In the case of military commanders, a higher standard is expected. Accordingly, their criminal liability for war crimes committed by subordinates is not limited to the same situations that result in civilian superior responsibility. Instead, the knowledge element of command responsibility will be satisfied if the military commander or superior either *knew or, owing to the circumstances at the time, should have known* that the forces were committing or about to commit such crimes.

It could be argued that these two distinct standards incorporated into the ICC Statute are warranted, given that military commanders operate in much more formal and hierarchical structures than most civilian superiors, and given that military commanders are primarily responsible for developing subordinates who understand and implement their IHL obligations. Thus, limiting the "should have known" test to military commanders reflects the duty of the military commander to properly supervise subordinates. Moreover, as described above, IHL gives additional responsibilities to military commanders for the instruction and dissemination of the law among subordinates, and for ensuring the respect of IHL at all times. With these clear responsibilities, it is natural to expect the military commander to take positive actions to remain informed of the actions of subordinates, and equally natural to condemn the commander when dereliction of this vital command duty renders war crimes by subordinates foreseeable. Subjecting a civilian commander to this same broad notion of criminal responsibility for the crimes of another—the notion that resulted in General Yamashita's conviction and execution—will rarely be justified, as the civilian superior will almost never stand in a similar command/subordinate relationship with the soldier.

Application of the ICC's "knew or consciously disregarded" standard for civilians is still evolving through the court's jurisprudence. It does beg both legal as well as policy questions, if it is conceded that one of the principal aims of superior responsibility is to punish those individuals higher up the hierarchical ladder who, while not the direct weapon wielders, are deemed nonetheless to be criminally responsible for failing to act appropriately in controlling and punishing subordinates. Indeed, superior responsibility has proved to be a particularly vital weapon in the prosecutor's arsenal at the international tribunals in bringing to trial heads of government, ministers, and other civilian superiors. These are often defendants who, in their leadership capacity, allegedly played a substantial role in overseeing and directing violations of IHL, crimes against humanity, and genocide, without necessarily setting foot in the arena of combat or where the crimes were committed. It is a more demanding standard for prosecutors to be required under Article 28 of the Statute to show that non-military defendants consciously disregarded—as opposed to should have known—clearly indicative information. This may ultimately make it more difficult to effectively prosecute non-military superiors for violations of IHL through the doctrine of command responsibility.[25]

3.3 *To prevent and to punish*

Finally, to be held accountable as a commander or superior for the actions of subordinates it must be shown that there was a failure to take appropriate measures to prevent or punish the commission of the IHL violations by the subordinates.

Under Article 86(2) of AP I, superiors are required to take all feasible measures within their power to prevent or repress a breach of IHL by their subordinates. The commander is not presumed to be able to do the impossible but, instead, the circumstances prevailing at the time frame the assessment of what is or is not feasible. As the ICRC Commentary on this Article explains, the language "reasonably restricts the obligation upon superiors to 'feasible' measures, since it is not always possible to prevent a breach or punish the perpetrators."[26] In addition, it is a matter of common sense that the measures concerned are described as those "'within their power' and only those."[27] In the context of international criminal law, as in many domestic legal systems, the terminology that has been slightly modified from "feasible" to "necessary and reasonable measures" within the power of the superior to prevent or repress the commission of the crimes by his or her subordinates.[28]

Evaluating post facto what measures a commander could and should have taken in response to ill-discipline and misconduct among his or her subordinates—whether in the form of an investigation or a criminal trial—is particularly challenging. Justice Murphy, in his *Yamashita* dissent, reasoned:

> [d]uties, as well as ability to control troops, vary according to the nature and intensity of the particular battle. To find an unlawful deviation from duty under battle conditions requires difficult and speculative calculations. Such calculations become highly untrustworthy when they are made by the victor in relation to the actions of a vanquished actor. Objective and realistic norms of conduct are then extremely unlikely to be used in forming a judgment as to deviations from duty.[29]

The complexity of contemporary armed conflicts and the inevitable fog of war associated with any situation of hostilities naturally make any assessment of the measures that superiors or commanders could and should have taken in the circumstances a challenging exercise. The courts tasked with adjudicating allegations of command responsibility have been conscious of the risk of expecting more than that which is within the reasonable capacity of a superior at the time of the violations, and have been pragmatic in their approach. In *Čelebići*, the ICTY underscored that it must "be recognised that international law cannot oblige a superior to perform the impossible. Hence, a superior may only be held criminally responsible for failing to take such measures within his powers [or] within his material possibility."[30] In *Blaskic*, the ICTY Appeals Chamber added that "necessary and reasonable measures are such that can be taken within the competence of a commander as evidenced by the degree of effective control he wielded over his subordinates."[31] Similarly, in *Bemba*, that Chamber noted that " 'necessary' measures are those appropriate for the commander to discharge his obligation, and 'reasonable' measures are those reasonably falling within the commander's material power."[32]

Examples of measures that could be considered as falling within the powers of a commander are varied, and to be assessed on a case-by-case basis. In *Musema*, for instance, the judges considered reasonable measures to be the "removing, or threatening to remove, an individual from his or her position at the Tea Factory if he or she was identified as a perpetrator of crimes" or "to attempt to prevent or to punish the use of Tea Factory vehicles, uniforms or other Tea Factory property in the commission of such crimes."[33] Other preventive and punitive measures include: adequate IHL training of subordinates, the issuance of clear orders, the taking of disciplinary action in response to acts of misconduct, referral of incidents to the competent prosecutorial authorities, initiating courts martial, removing or redeploying at-risk subordinates, making strong policy statements on the importance of respecting IHL, regular after-action reviews, reviewing and amending tactical directives, and suspending military operations.[34] One thing does seem clear: any commander who is made aware of ill-discipline resulting in IHL violations by members of his or her unit, and then ignores these reports and fails to take any meaningful corrective action, creates great risk that more serious war crimes will be committed and that he or she will be held accountable for essentially setting the conditions for those war crimes.

In conclusion, if it is found that the superior has taken all the necessary and reasonable measures within his or her powers to either prevent or punish the actions of his or her subordinates, he or she cannot be held accountable under the theory of command responsibility.

4   Manifestly illegal orders and superior orders

The "knew or should have known" theory of command responsibility is premised on the assumption that the commander did not order the war crime for which he or she is being held accountable. Where the evidence indicates that such an order was issued, traditional notions of accomplice liability render the commander equally accountable for the war crime as the subordinate that committed the unlawful act. But if such an order is issued, will the subordinate who obeys it be absolved of individual criminal responsibility based on the fact that he or she was obeying superior orders? The answer depends on how obvious it was that adherence to the order required an IHL violation, therefore rendering it unlawful.

It is axiomatic that military effectiveness and good order and discipline necessitate obedience to orders by subordinates. Indeed, obedience to orders, no matter how dangerous or unpleasant the duty to be performed may be, is the essence of military service. However, where the order is *manifestly illegal*, the execution of which would amount to a war crime, obedience to the order will not absolve the subordinate from war crimes liability, and both the commander and subordinate may be convicted. For his or her part, the commander, military or civilian, can be held criminally responsible for having ordered the commission of the unlawful acts.[35] Where the order requires an act that any soldier would immediately recognize violates IHL, such as murdering a POW or physically abusing a civilian, the subordinate will have no defense to a war crime. The subordinate will also be held responsible for having obeyed the order by committing the unlawful act. However, where the nature of the violation is less certain, obedience to the order may provide a defense.

Under the theory of *superior orders*, a subordinate who carried out an order that resulted in a war crime may raise the obedience to orders defense, and as a consequence should be discharged of any wrongdoing—the argument being that the subordinate was simply following orders issued by his or her commander which he or she is duty-bound to execute. After all, the failure to do so could result in disciplinary action, reprimand, court martial, or even discharge. Yet in situations where the order is deemed to be manifestly illegal, a subordinate will find it difficult if not impossible to prevail in such a defense theory. The effect of the defense will turn ultimately on whether the court determines any reasonable subordinate in the same or similar situation would have realized the order was unlawful. If so, the defense fails; if not, the obedience to the order is a complete defense. However, even when the defense is ineffective, the fact that the subordinate acted pursuant to an order, even an unlawful order, may be considered as a mitigating factor in determining an appropriate sentence.

4.1   What is manifestly illegal?

As explained in the U.S. *DoD Law of War Manual*:

> In cases in which the illegality of the order is not apparent, the subordinate might lack the wrongful intent necessary to the commission of the crime. Subordinates, absent specific knowledge to the contrary, may presume orders to be lawful. The acts of a subordinate done in compliance with an unlawful order given by a superior are generally excused unless the superior's order is one that a person of ordinary sense and understanding would, under the circumstances, know to be unlawful (e.g., to torture or murder a detainee), or if the order in question is actually known to the accused to be unlawful.[36]

Elsewhere it has been said that above a manifestly illegal order "should fly, like a black flag, a warning sign saying 'Prohibited!'".[37]

To be sure, in the fog of war, the line between right and wrong under IHL may be difficult to ascertain.[38] In these circumstances, a subordinate could have a strong defense. For instance, in *Dover Castle*, a German submarine commander who torpedoed a British hospital ship successfully raised the defense of superior orders on the basis that German Government and Admiralty memoranda had been communicated, indicating that hospital ships were being used for military purposes in violation of the laws of war. Thus, the commander reasonably believed the attack order was lawful under the circumstances, and the evidence failed to establish that the order was *manifestly* unlawful, as the memoranda suggested that the ships were legitimate targets.[39]

However, there will be instances where the illegality of the order is undeniable, and its execution is highly likely to result in the commission of a war crime. In these situations, where the order is deemed manifestly illegal, the subordinate's position is much weaker and it will be difficult for him to escape liability. Thus, for example, in *Llandovery Castle*—a case arising out of German torpedo attacks during World War I—the court rejected the defense of obedience to orders for two subordinates who followed their submarine commander's order to open fire on the survivors of a torpedoed hospital ship seeking refuge in their lifeboats. Here, the order was seen to be manifestly unlawful, in violation of a universally known rule of international law. Therefore, the subordinates could not claim their ignorance of the illegality.[40]

Today, a manifestly illegal order is understood to be one that offends the conscience of every reasonable, right-thinking person, and which is patently and obviously wrong. For example, the pattern jury instruction used by the U.S. Army in cases where a soldier raises the obedience to orders defense provides:

> Obedience to an unlawful order does not necessarily result in criminal responsibility of the person obeying the order. The acts of the accused if done in obedience to an unlawful order are excused and carry no criminal responsibility unless the accused knew that the order was unlawful or unless the order was one which a person of ordinary common sense, under the circumstances, would know to be unlawful.

Thus, a subordinate must treat all orders as *presumptively* lawful, but this presumption is not conclusive. Where the order is blatantly unlawful, leaving no reasonable doubt as to its unlawfulness, the subordinate actually has a duty to *disobey* the order.[41] This is similarly reflected in Rule 155 of the ICRC's *Customary Law Study*, whereby criminal responsibility remains if the manifest illegality of the order was known: "[o]beying a superior order does not relieve a subordinate of criminal responsibility if the subordinate knew that the act ordered was unlawful and should have known because of the manifestly unlawful nature of the act ordered."[42]

4.2 The defense of superior orders

The majority trend in post–World War II case law has been to deny the defense of superior orders where a subordinate has a *moral choice* to obey or disobey the order. The Nuremberg Principles echoed this standard: "[t]he fact that a person acted pursuant to order of his Government or of a superior does not relieve him from responsibility under international law, provided that a moral choice was in fact possible to him."[43] Along this line, in the Canadian case of *Finta*, the Supreme Court noted that a defense of superior orders could only be raised in certain circumstances, in particular where the subordinate has no moral choice, or was acting under duress:

> The defence of obedience to superior orders and the peace officer defence are available to members of the military or police forces in prosecutions for war crimes and crimes against humanity. Those defences are subject to the manifest illegality test: the defences are not available where the orders in question were manifestly unlawful. Even where the orders were manifestly unlawful, the defence of obedience to superior orders and the peace officer defence will be available in those circumstances where the accused had no moral choice as to whether to follow the orders. There can be no moral choice where there was such an air of compulsion and threat to the accused that he or she had no alternative but to obey the orders.[44]

The ad hoc UN international criminal jurisdictions struck out the possibility of raising the defense of superior orders, allowing only for its consideration at sentencing.[45] The ICC has likewise ruled out raising the defense of superior orders for genocide and crimes against humanity.[46]

5 Conclusion

Commanders, be they civilian or military, have been assigned an additional layer of responsibility under IHL. By virtue of their position, they are expected to lead by example and ensure respect at all times for IHL by their subordinates. By failing to do so, they can be held accountable as if they had themselves pulled the trigger. Therefore, the development of the principle of command responsibility has been instrumental in ensuring that all individuals irrespective of rank are held accountable for war crimes.

Notes

1 The term *commanders* and *superiors* are used interchangeably in this chapter, as are the terms *command responsibility* and *superior responsibility*.

2 On the role of commanders: In the first place, they are on the spot and able to exercise control over the troops and the weapons which they use. They have the authority, and more than anyone else they can prevent breaches by creating

the appropriate frame of mind, ensuring the rational use of the means of combat and by maintaining discipline. Their role obliges them to be constantly informed of the way in which their subordinates carry out the tasks entrusted them, and to take the necessary measures for this purpose. Finally, they are in a position to establish or ensure the establishment of the facts, which would be the starting point for any action to suppress or punish a breach.

> Jean S. Pictet et al., Commentary on the Additional Protocols of 8 June 1977 to the Geneva Conventions of 12 August 1949 (ICRC, 1987), para 3555 [hereinafter AP Commentary]

3 Also described a form of derivate imputed liability, distinct from strict vicarious liability. *See* Chapter 14: "Command Responsibility and Compliance Mechanisms," in Geoffrey S. Corn et al., *The Law of Armed Conflict: An Operational Approach* (2012).

4 *U.S. v. Wilhelm von Leeb et al. (The High Command Case)*, 10 T.W.C. 2, 1230, 1303 (1950).

5 U.S. Dep't of Def., *Law of War Manual* 18.23.3.2 (June 2015, updated December 2016) [hereinafter *DoD Law of War Manual*]

> The commander's personal dereliction must have contributed to or failed to prevent the offense; there must be a personal neglect amounting to a wanton, immoral disregard of the action of his or her subordinates amounting to acquiescence in the crimes.

6 Statute of the International Criminal Tribunal for Rwanda, Art 6(3), 8 November 1994, 33 I.L.M. 1598 [hereinafter ICTR Statute]; Statute of the International Tribunal for the Prosecution of Persons Responsible for Serious Violations of International Humanitarian Law Committed in the Territory of the Former Yugoslavia since 1991 Art 7(3), 25 May 1993, 32 I.L.M. 1203 [hereinafter ICTY Statute]. Both the ICTR and ICTY Statutes read:

> The fact that any of the acts referred to in . . . the present Statute was committed by a subordinate does not relieve his or her superior of criminal responsibility if he or she knew or had reason to know that the subordinate was about to commit such acts or had done so and the superior failed to take the necessary and reasonable measures to prevent such acts or to punish the perpetrators thereof.
>
> ICTR Statute, Art 6(3); ICTY Statute, Art 7(3)

7 *See* Jean-Marie Henckaerts & Louise Doswald-Beck, *Customary International Humanitarian Law* 556–63 (2009) (*see* Rules 152 and 153).

8 *Prosecutor v. Jean Pierre Bemba Combo*, Case No. ICC-01/05-01/08-3343, Trial Chamber III Judgment, para 180 (21 March 2016).

9 Rome Statute of the International Criminal Court, Art 28, 17 July 1998, 2187 U.N.T.S. 90 [hereinafter Rome Statute]. Article 28 addresses the "Responsibility of commanders and other superiors." The text is as follows:

> In addition to other grounds of criminal responsibility under this Statute for crimes within the jurisdiction of the Court:
>
> (a) A military commander or person effectively acting as a military commander shall be criminally responsible for crimes within the jurisdiction of the Court committed by forces under his or her effective command and control, or effective authority and control as the case may be, as a result of his or her failure to exercise control properly over such forces, where:
>
> (i) That military commander or person either knew or, owing to the circumstances at the time, should have known that the forces were committing or about to commit such crimes; and

    (ii) That military commander or person failed to take all necessary and reasonable measures within his or her power to prevent or repress their commission or to submit the matter to the competent authorities for investigation and prosecution.

(b) With respect to superior and subordinate relationships not described in paragraph (a), a superior shall be criminally responsible for crimes within the jurisdiction of the Court committed by subordinates under his or her effective authority and control, as a result of his or her failure to exercise control properly over such subordinates, where:

    (i) The superior either knew, or consciously disregarded information which clearly indicated, that the subordinates were committing or about to commit such crimes;

    (ii) The crimes concerned activities that were within the effective responsibility and control of the superior; and

    (iii) The superior failed to take all necessary and reasonable measures within his or her power to prevent or repress their commission or to submit the matter to the competent authorities for investigation and prosecution.

Id.

10 *U.S. v. Wilhelm von Leeb et al. (The High Command Case)*, 10 T.W.C. 2, 543 (1950).

11 Gary D. Solis, *The Law of Armed Conflict: International Humanitarian Law in War* 387 (2010).

12 *Prosecutor v. Jean Pierre Bemba Combo*, Case No. ICC-01/05-01/08-3343, Trial Chamber III Judgment, para 183 (21 March 2016).

13 *Prosecutor v. Delalic & Mucic (aka "Pavo") & Delic & Landzo (aka "Zenga") (Čelebići Case)*, Case No. IT-96-21-A, Appeals Judgment, para 198 (Int'l Crim. Trib. for the former Yugoslavia 20 February 2001).

14 *See Prosecutor v. Karadžić*, Case No. IT-95-5/18-T, Judgment, paras 581–2 (Int'l Crim. Trib. for the former Yugoslavia 24 March 2016). Additionally, the *Bemba* judgment provides a fairly comprehensive summary of relevant factors considered in international jurisprudence:

> There are a number of factors that may indicate the existence of "effective control", which requires the material ability to prevent or repress the commission of crimes or to submit the matter to the competent authorities; these have been properly considered as "more a matter of evidence than of substantive law." These factors may include: (i) the official position of the commander within the military structure and the actual tasks that he carried out; (ii) his power to issue orders, including his capacity to order forces or units under his command, whether under his immediate command or at lower levels, to engage in hostilities; (iii) his capacity to ensure compliance with orders including consideration of whether the orders were actually followed; (iv) his capacity to re-subordinate units or make changes to command structure; (v) his power to promote, replace, remove, or discipline any member of the forces, and to initiate investigations; (vi) his authority to send forces to locations where hostilities take place and withdraw them at any given moment; (vii) his independent access to, and control over, the means to wage war, such as communication equipment and weapons; (viii) his control over finances; (ix) the capacity to represent the forces in negotiations or interact with external bodies or individuals on behalf of the group; and (x) whether he represents the ideology of the movement to which the subordinates adhere and has a certain level of profile, manifested through public appearances and statements.
>
> *Prosecutor v. Jean Pierre Bemba Combo*, Case No. ICC-01/05-01/08-3343,
> Trial Chamber III Judgment, para 188 (21 March 2016)

15 *Prosecutor v. Alfred Musema*, Judgment, Case No. ICTR-96-13-T, para 880, 27 January 2000).

16 *See also* 10 U.S.C. Section 950q ("Any person is punishable under this chapter who ... (3) is a superior commander who, with regard to acts punishable under this chapter, knew, had reason to know, or should have known, that a subordinate was about to commit such acts or had done so and who failed to take the necessary and reasonable measures to prevent such acts or to punish the perpetrators thereof, is a principal.").

17 Similarly, Karshoven and Zegveld explain:

> Clearly, a superior cannot be held responsible for just any form of criminal behaviour exhibited by his subordinates: he must have had prior knowledge, or the very least, the necessary information, and have failed to do what could be expected of him to prevent or repress the crime.
>
> Frits Kalsoven & Liesbeth Zegveld, *Constraints on the Waging of War* 134 (3rd edn, 2001)

18 *Prosecutor v. Delalic & Mucic (aka "Pavo") & Delic & Landzo (aka "Zenga") (Čelebići Case)*, Case No. IT-96-21-T, Judgment, para 383 (Int'l Crim. Trib. for the former Yugoslavia 16 November 1998). On the difference between the "knew" and "had reason to know" standards, *see Prosecutor v. Bagilishema*, Case No. ICTR-95-1A-A, Appeals Judgment, para 28 (3 July 2002):

> After considering the Appellant's arguments, the Appeals Chamber holds, for the reasons set out below, that the Trial Chamber actually examined the "had reason to know" standard. However, the distinction between the "knowledge" and "had reason to know" standards could have been expressed more clearly by the Trial Chamber. The "had reason to know" standard does not require that actual knowledge, either explicit or circumstantial, be established. Nor does it require that the Chamber be satisfied that the accused actually knew that crimes had been committed or were about to be committed. It merely requires that the Chamber be satisfied that the accused had "some general information in his possession, which would put him on notice of possible unlawful acts by his subordinates."

19 *Prosecutor v. Karadžić*, Case No. IT-95-5/18-T, Judgment, para 586 (Int'l Crim. Trib. for the former Yugoslavia 24 March 2016).

20 *Prosecutor v. Jean Pierre Bemba Combo*, Case No. ICC-01/05-01/08-3343, Trial Chamber III Judgment, para 194 (21 March 2016):

> Article 28 does not require that the commander knew the identities of the specific individuals who committed the crimes. In addition, it is unnecessary to establish that the accused mastered every detail of each crime committed by the forces, an issue that becomes increasingly difficult as one goes up the military hierarchy.

21 *See* Karshoven & Zegveld, *supra* note 16, at 134:

> In this respect, it is of major importance for military commanders to be able to know with a sufficient measure of certainty what conduct will be regarded as amounting to a "breach" of these instruments. Given their complex structure, the commanders will often be in need of expert advice on their correct (or, at least, acceptable interpretation).

22 Protocol (I) Additional to the Geneva Conventions of 12 August 1949, and Relating to the Protection of Victims of International Armed Conflicts, Art 82, 8 June 1977, 1125 U.N.T.S. 3 [hereinafter AP I] (entered into force 7 December 1978) (signed by the United States 12 December 1977, not transmitted to U.S. Senate, *see* S. Treaty Doc. No. 100–2 (1987)) (which states that "[t]he High Contracting Parties at all times, and the Parties to the conflict in time of armed conflict, shall ensure that legal

advisers are available, when necessary, to advise military commanders at the appropriate level on the application of the Conventions and this Protocol and on the appropriate instruction to be given to the armed forces on this subject.").

23 *Prosecutor v. Jean Pierre Bemba Combo*, Case No. ICC-01/05-01/08-3343, Trial Chamber III Judgment, para 193 (21 March 2016):

> Relevant factors that may indicate knowledge include any orders to commit crimes, or the fact that the accused was informed personally that his forces were involved in criminal activity. Other indicia include the number, nature, scope, location, and timing of the illegal acts, and other prevailing circumstances; the type and number of forces involved; the means of available communication; the modus operandi of similar acts; the scope and nature of the commander's position and responsibility in the hierarchical structure; the location of the command at the time; and the notoriety of illegal acts, such as whether they were reported in media coverage of which the accused was aware. Such awareness may be established by evidence suggesting that, as a result of these reports, the commander took some kind of action.

24 This approach was followed by the ICTR in *Kayishema & Ruzindana*, despite the wording of Article 6(3) of the ICTR Statute. The Trial Chamber, having cited ICC Article 28 approvingly, stated with regard to the command responsibility of civilian superiors:

> In light of the objective of Article 6(3) which is to ascertain the individual criminal responsibility for crimes as serious as genocide, crimes against humanity and violations of Common Article 3 to the Geneva Conventions and Additional Protocol II thereto, the Chamber finds that the Prosecution must prove that the accused in this case either knew, or consciously disregarded information which clearly indicated or put him on notice that his subordinates had committed, or were about to commit acts in breach of Articles 2 to 4 of this Tribunal's Statute.
> *Prosecutor v. Kayishema & Ruzindana*, Case No. ICTR-95-1-T, Judgment, para 228 (21 May 1999)

25 Further developed in Jamie Allan Williamson, *Some Considerations on Command Responsibility and Criminal Liability*, 90 Int'l Rev. Red Cross 870, 303 (June 2008).

26 AP Commentary, para 3548.

27 *Id.*

28 *See* ICTR Statute, Art 6(3); ICTY Statute, Art 7(3). *See also DoD Law of War Manual,* 18.23.3:

> Commanders have duties to take necessary and reasonable measures to ensure that their subordinates do not commit violations of the law of war. Failures by commanders of their duties to take necessary and reasonable measures to ensure that their subordinates do not commit violations of the law of war can result in criminal responsibility.

29 *In Re Yamashita*, 327 U.S. 1 (1946).

30 *Prosecutor v. Delalic & Mucic (aka "Pavo") & Delic & Landzo (aka "Zenga") (Čelebići Case)*, Case No. IT-96-21-T, Judgment, para 395 (Int'l Crim. Trib. for the former Yugoslavia 16 November 1998).

31 *Prosecutor v. Blaskic*, Appeals Judgment, Case No. IT-95-14-A, para 72 (Int'l Crim. Trib. for the former Yugoslavia 29 July 2004).

32 *Prosecutor v. Jean Pierre Bemba Combo*, Case No. ICC-01/05-01/08-3343, Trial Chamber III Judgment, para 198 (21 March 2016).

33 *Prosecutor v. Alfred Musema*, Judgment, Case No. ICTR-96-13-T, para 880 (27 January 2000).

34 *See Prosecutor v. Jean Pierre Bemba Combo*, Case No. ICC-01/05-01/08-3343, Trial Chamber III Judgment, paras 202–9 (21 March 2016).

35 *DoD Law of War Manual*, 23.1:

> A person who orders another person to commit an offense is generally punishable as though that person had committed the offense directly. Note, that to be held responsible under Article 6(1) of the Statute for ordering a crime, on the contrary, it is sufficient that the accused have authority over the perpetrator of the crime, and that his order have a direct and substantial effect on the commission of the illegal act.

> *See also Prosecutor v. Jean de Dieu Kamuhanda*, Appeals Judgment, Case No. ICTR-99-54A-A, para 75 (19 September 2005).

36 *DoD Law of War Manual*, 18.22.4.

37 Ronen Bergman, *Rise and Kill First: The Secret History of Israel's Targeted Assassinations* 274 (2018) (quoting Judge Havlevy in the Israeli case, *Prosecutor v. Major Malinki, et. al.* 1957).

38 *See U.S. v. Calley*, 22 C.M.A. 534, 543–4 (1973)

> In the stress of combat, a member of the armed forces cannot reasonably be expected to make a refined legal judgment and be held criminally responsible if he guesses wrong on a question as to which there may considerable disagreement.

39 *Dover Castle (1921)*, Supreme Court of Leipzig, 16 Am. J. Int'l L. 704 (1922). *See also U.S. v. List (The Hostage Case)*, 11 T.W.C. 757 (1950). Dicta from *The Hostage Case*:

> We are of the view, however, that if the illegality of the order was not known to the inferior, and he could not reasonably have been expected to know of its illegality, no wrongful intent necessary to the commission of a crime exists and the interior [sic] will be protected. But the general rule is that members of the armed forces are bound to obey only the lawful orders of their commanding officers and they cannot escape criminal liability by obeying a command which violates international law and outrages fundamental concepts of justice.

40 Llandovery Castle (1921), *Supreme Court of Leipzig*, 16 Am. J. Int'l L. 708 (1922).

41 *See* MC (Central) 3/57 *The Chief Military Prosecutor v. Lance Corporal Ofer, Major Malinki Shmuel and Others*, Case concerning the events of 29 October 1956 in Kafr Qassem, PM 5718(2) 90 (1958) (Isr.):

> The identifying mark of a "manifestly unlawful" order must wave like a black flag above the order given, as a warning saying: "forbidden." It is . . . not unlawfulness that is detectable only by legal experts . . . but an overt and salient violation, a certain and obvious unlawfulness that stems from the order itself, . . . an unlawfulness that pierces the eye and agitates the heart, if the eye be not blind nor the heart closed or corrupt.

42 *See* Henckaerts & Doswald-Beck, *Customary International Humanitarian Law*, Rule 155.

43 *Principles of International Law Recognized in the Charter of the Nürnberg Tribunal and in the Judgment of the Tribunal*, Yrbk Int'l L. Comm'n, 1950, Vol. II, paras 95–127.

44 *R. v. Finta* [1994] 1 S.C.R. 701 (Can.).

45 Both the ICTR and ICTY Statutes read, in part:

> The fact that an accused person acted pursuant to an order of a government or of a superior shall not relieve him or her of criminal responsibility, but may be considered in mitigation of punishment if the International Tribunal for Rwanda determines that justice so requires.
>
> ICTR Statute, Art 6(4); ICTY Statute, Art 7(4)

46 Rome Statute, Art 33:

> 1. The fact that a crime within the jurisdiction of the Court has been committed by a person pursuant to an order of a Government or of a superior, whether military or civilian, shall not relieve that person of criminal responsibility unless: a) The person was under a legal obligation to obey orders of the Government or the superior in question; b) The person did not know that the order was unlawful; and c) The order was not manifestly unlawful. 2. For the purposes of this article, orders to commit genocide or crimes against humanity are manifestly unlawful.

The exclusion of war crimes from Article 33(2) of the ICC Statute has been criticized as being at odds with customary international law. *See Cassese's International Criminal Law* Sec. II, "Fundamentals of International Criminal Responsibility" (P. Gaeta, L. Baig, M. Fan, C. Gosnell, & A. Whiting eds, 3rd edn, 2013).

11 International justice and compliance

1 Introduction

By becoming party to the Geneva Conventions and/or their two Additional Protocols, States have undertaken the obligation to ensure that any individual who commits war crimes is held accountable therefor. The enactment of criminal laws at the national level to allow for prosecuting violations of IHL is therefore required to fully implement the obligations imposed by these treaties. In addition, judicial mechanisms need to be provided with the appropriate competence to allow for prosecutions and trials at the national level. Various approaches have been taken by States to enable prosecutions domestically, either incorporating into their existing court system, civilian or military, or by creating specialized chambers with jurisdiction over such crimes.[1] There is no one preferred approach, though it is essential that, at a minimum, trials meet international standards before independent and competent bodies.

Notwithstanding their primary responsibility to try perpetrators of war crimes—especially members of their own armed forces and other nationals who are suspected of committing such crimes—there may be situations where, owing to lack of political will, lack of judicial and structural capacity, or the absence of necessary legislation, States are unable to fulfill this obligation. As this chapter will discuss, in certain circumstances the international community has responded to such situations by creating international or hybrid judicial bodies to bring to trial individuals often deemed to be those bearing senior responsibility for the most serious war crimes. Inspired in part by the legacies of the Nuremberg and Tokyo Tribunals—international military tribunals established by the Allies to try high-level Nazi and Japanese leaders at the end of World War II—the latter part of the twentieth century saw a proliferation of such bodies, which will be reviewed in this chapter. These include courts to try cases from Sierra Leone, Cambodia, the former Yugoslavia, and Rwanda. The pinnacle of international justice, in the eyes of many, was the creation of the International Criminal Court (ICC), a permanent treaty-based court with a potentially broad jurisdictional reach. The chapter will explain how the ICC, deemed a court of last resort, can exercise its jurisdiction. Finally, this chapter will consider other mechanisms that could possibly further compliance with IHL. While these alternate enforcement bodies are no substitute for criminal trials, they are nonetheless important to mitigate any limitations of domestic and international courts and the resulting impunity gap.

2   International criminal tribunals

Nearly half a century after the Nuremberg and Tokyo Tribunals, created to deal with crimes committed by the Nazi regime and Japanese forces during World War II, the international community came together to establish a number of international tribunals and hybrid courts to prosecute individuals for war crimes in both IACs and NIACs. The 1990s represented a genuine turning point in the fight against impunity for such violations of international law, which were largely immune from criminal sanction in the half-century following World War II. These new judicial mechanisms complemented the work of national jurisdictions, and importantly addressed a notable accountability gap for violations of war crimes that prevailed owing to a lack of capacity and political will in many contexts. In addition, they developed extensive jurisprudence strengthening the understanding of IHL, genocide, and crimes against humanity.

With the establishment of the two United Nations Ad Hoc International Criminal Tribunals for the former Yugoslavia and Rwanda (ICTY and ICTR, respectively), the United Nations opened this milestone era for international justice. These Tribunals were created in response to atrocities committed in the former Yugoslavia from 1991 onwards, and in Rwanda throughout 1994. On the basis of a number of reports by experts and special rapporteurs, the Security Council deemed that impunity for mass killings and violations of IHL in both conflicts constituted threats to international peace and security, one of the triggers for a Chapter VII resolution.[2] As a result, these tribunals came into being pursuant to UN Security Council Resolutions adopted under Chapter VII of the UN Charter.[3] In the view of the Security Council, prosecution of those involved would contribute to national reconciliation and the restoration and maintenance of peace in both contexts. The Security Council decided that the seat of the ICTR would be in Arusha, Tanzania, and that of the ICTY in The Hague, the Netherlands.[4]

While initiatives to bring war criminals to trial were welcomed by many, the authority of the UN Security Council to create tribunals was challenged in the early cases at both the ICTR and ICTY. The seminal decision confirming the competence of the Security Council, *Prosecutor v. Tadić*, was issued by the ICTY Appeals Chamber in October 1995.[5] In this decision, the Appeals Chamber, looking at the wording of Article 39 of the UN Charter, opined that armed conflicts, international as well as internal, could constitute threats to peace and breaches of peace.[6] It added that, once the Security Council has made a determination that a situation poses a threat to peace or that a breach of peace exists, "it enjoys a wide margin of discretion in choosing the course of action" to be taken in accordance with Articles 41 and 42 of the UN Charter,[7] albeit such "discretion is not unfettered."[8] Referring to Article 41 specifically, the Appeals Chamber reasoned that the measures set out in the Article were merely illustrative and not exhaustive.[9] The creation of a judicial body to provide for accountability for serious war crimes committed during such armed conflicts could therefore be contemplated by virtue of the wording "measures not involving the use of armed force" that contribute to the restoration of international peace and security. It went on to say that, in taking such measures, the United Nations could act through the intermediary of its members or "it can a fortiori undertake measures which it can implement directly via its organs, if it happens to have the resources to do so."[10]

As subsidiary bodies to the UN Security Council, one of the strengths of the ICTY and the ICTR was their jurisdictional primacy over domestic courts.[11] In practice, this meant that, while domestic courts could be concurrently competent to try cases falling within the mandate of the Tribunals, they would be expected to defer the case to the Tribunals if so requested by either of them. In the *Tadić* Appeals Decision, the Appeals Chamber confirmed that this primacy was essential to ensure that serious violations of IHL, genocide, and crimes against humanity were effectively prosecuted. In the view of the Appeals Chamber, absent primacy, these crimes risked being downgraded by the national courts to ordinary crimes[12] and there was a danger that domestic jurisdictions would design proceedings to shield those accused of such serious international crimes and fail to diligently prosecute the cases.[13] These concerns were particularly pertinent given that most of those accused by the ICTR and ICTY were high-ranking military and civilian officials.

The nature of these Tribunals as subsidiaries of the UN Security Council also had the positive effect of making it obligatory that all UN Member States cooperate with them and provide judicial assistance without undue delay. This was particularly important given the fact that the Tribunals did not possess their own police forces or domestic judicial capacities. Areas of assistance and cooperation included the identification and location of persons, the taking of testimony, the production of evidence, and the service of documents; the arrest or detention of persons; and the surrender or the transfer of the accused to the ICTR or ICTY.[14] In addition, on the basis of the obligations to cooperate and provide judicial assistance, Articles 28 (ICTR) and 29 (ICTY) of the statutes were deemed to "prevail over any legal impediment to the surrender or transfer of [an] accused or of a witness . . . which may exist under the national law or extradition treaties of the State concerned."[15] In cases of non-cooperation by States in failing to execute warrants of arrest or transfer orders for an accused, the Tribunals could notify the Security Council accordingly.[16] As the Tribunals had no long-term detention facilities, convicted individuals would serve their sentences in either Rwanda for the ICTR, or the former Yugoslavia for the ICTY, or alternatively in States that had indicated to the UN Security Council their willingness to accept convicted persons.[17]

Both the ICTY and the ICTR were mandated to prosecute individuals for war crimes, crimes against humanity, and genocide, if falling within the personal, geographical, and temporal jurisdictional parameters framed in their respective statutes. Accordingly, the ICTY was competent to try individuals for such crimes committed in the former Yugoslavia from 1992 onwards, whereas the ICTR was limited to such crimes committed only in 1994 in Rwanda by individuals of any nationality, and in neighboring countries only if the individual was a Rwandan citizen.

The scope of war crimes over which each Tribunal had competence was based on assessments made by UN-appointed experts on the nature of each of the armed conflicts. For the ICTR, the Independent Commission of Experts found that the armed conflict that occurred in Rwanda between 6 April and 15 July 1994 qualified as a NIAC, with the use of armed force having been carried out "within the territorial borders of Rwanda and did not involve the active participation of any other State." Any "third State involvement entailed peace-making and humanitarian functions rather than belligerent action."[18] As a consequence, the ICTR jurisdiction included war crimes committed in NIACs, namely serious violations of Common Article 3 to the four Geneva Conventions of 1949 and AP II.

In relation to the ICTY, the appointed Independent Commission of Experts chose not to determine the specific nature of the conflicts that occurred in the former Yugoslavia, preferring to leave this task to the Tribunal itself.[19] Nonetheless, it concluded that "the character and complexity of the armed conflicts concerned, combined with the web of agreements on humanitarian law that the parties have concluded among themselves" justified the application "of the law applicable in international armed conflicts to the entirety of the armed conflicts in the territory of the former Yugoslavia."[20] As a consequence, the Statute of the ICTY provided the Tribunal with competence to try individuals for grave breaches of the Geneva Conventions, as well as other violations of the laws or customs of war. The Commission of Experts explained that the customary law applicable to IACs included not only war crimes but also a "wide range of provisions also stated in Hague Convention IV of 1907, the Geneva Conventions of 1949 and, to some extent, the provisions of Additional Protocol I."[21] Interestingly, though, it underscored that "the violations of the laws or customs of war referred to in Article 3 of the Statute of the International Tribunal are offences when committed in international, but not in internal armed conflicts."[22]

As a result of this interpretation, the Commission of Experts had arguably limited the jurisdiction of the ICTY to war crimes that occurred only in IACs, excluding those committed in NIACs. This issue, as to be expected, was addressed at length by the ICTY Appeals Chamber in the *Tadić* decision on jurisdiction, where the Chamber ultimately concluded that:

> [i]n the light of the intent of the Security Council and the logical and sys-
> tematic interpretation of Article 3 as well as customary international law, the
> Appeals Chamber concludes that, under Article 3, the International Tribunal
> has jurisdiction over the acts alleged in the indictment, regardless of whether
> they occurred within an internal or an international armed conflict.[23]

In the view of the Appeals Chamber, Article 3 of the Statute was designed to function as a "residual clause designed to ensure that no serious violation of international humanitarian law is taken away from the jurisdiction of the International Tribunal."[24]

Both Tribunals operated for over two decades. The ICTR closed in 2012, having convicted and sentenced 62 and acquitted 14 individuals. The ICTY stopped most of its activities in 2013, having convicted and sentenced 83 and acquitted 19 individuals. The UN Security Council recognized that a number of key functions of the Tribunals would need to be managed after their closure. These included: the handling the trials of "the most senior leaders suspected of being the most responsible for crimes" who were still fugitives; the referral to national jurisdictions of individuals not deemed the most senior; retrials and reviews of cases completed by the ICTR and ICTY; and management of archives. To manage these functions, in 2010, the Security Council established the International Residual Mechanism for International Criminal Tribunals (MICT), which started operating on 1 July 2012 for the ICTR and 1 July 2013 for the ICTY, with branches in Arusha, Tanzania, and The Hague, the Netherlands, respectively.[25] The MICT was to function for an initial period of four years, with a possibility of two-year renewals as determined by the Security Council following reviews of progress reports.

The importance of the legacy of these two Tribunals in the fight against impunity for war crimes is undeniable. During their lifespans, they prosecuted nearly 200 individuals, developed extensive jurisprudence, and set importance precedents. In so doing, they brought a semblance of justice to affected communities in Rwanda and the former Yugoslavia. There were criticisms nonetheless. The ICTY and ICTR were seen as too expensive and burdened by UN bureaucracy, with trials taking too long to complete. Despite their strong outreach programs, their international constructs, criminal procedures, and staffing, compounded by being located outside of Rwanda and the former Yugoslavia, created a sense of detachment for many of the victims and survivors. There were also question marks over the limited number of perpetrators brought to trial compared to the number of victims in the contexts. History will judge. That which is certain notwithstanding, is that the creation of the ad hoc Tribunals by the UN Security Council in the early 1990s put the effective prosecution of war crimes at the forefront of the international community's agenda and, crucially, filled a vacuum that domestic criminal jurisdictions in neither Rwanda nor the former Yugoslavia could address on their own. It is probably no exaggeration to conclude that this resurrection of international war crimes jurisdiction resulted in a widespread expectation of meaningful accountability in future IAC and NIACs.

3   Hybrid courts

Building on the momentum created with the ICTR and ICTY, the late 1990s and early 2000s saw the establishment of mixed or hybrid courts to prosecute perpetrators of war crimes in Sierra Leone and Cambodia. The main differences between these bodies and the ad hoc UN Tribunals were (1) the legal basis of their establishment, (2) their blend of international and national procedures and composition, and (3) their location in the affected countries.

3.1   *The Special Court for Sierra Leone*

In January 2002, the United Nations and the Government of Sierra Leone signed an agreement to establish the Special Court for Sierra Leone (SCSL). Unlike the ICTR and the ICTY, the SCSL was constituted as a "treaty based sui generis court of mixed jurisdiction and composition" and not as a subsidiary body of the UN Security Council.[26] In part, this was a consequence of some of the criticisms mentioned above already being levied against the approach taken with the ad hoc Tribunals. The SCSL's hybrid design also stemmed from the preference put forward by the president of Sierra Leone in June 2000 in a letter addressed to the UN Security Council. In this communication, President Kebbah argued for the establishment of a court that would meet international standards for trials of criminal cases and have a mandate that could administer "a blend of international and domestic Sierra Leonean law on Sierra Leonean soil."[27] The aim of the court was to prosecute members of the Revolutionary United Front (RUF) and their accomplices for crimes committed against Sierra Leoneans and UN peacekeepers, following the conflict that occurred after the RUF reneged on the Lomé Peace Agreement, signed in 1999 between the Government of Sierra Leone and the RUF.

The framework of the court proposed by the Government of Sierra Leone envisioned a narrow mandate to prosecute "the most responsible violators and the leadership of the Revolutionary United Front," blending international and domestic Sierra Leonean law so as to "cast a wider web to catch the leaders of the violence and atrocities committed" and to root "the process in Sierra Leone," thereby making it "uniquely Sierra Leonean."[28] It was also suggested that the seat of the court should be in Sierra Leone, unless security constraints dictated otherwise; that judges should be drawn from West Africa; and that the Attorney General of Sierra Leone should act as the chief or co-chief prosecutor.

In his October 2000 report, the UN Secretary-General confirmed the need for both the mixed jurisdiction and the composition of the court. The applicable law was to include both international as well as national law of Sierra Leone, and the judges, prosecutors, and staff were to be international and Sierra Leoneans.[29] The court was to have jurisdiction for crimes against humanity and war crimes, as well as crimes under Sierra Leonean law committed after 30 November 1996,[30] the date of the conclusion of the Abidjan Peace Agreement, which was the first comprehensive peace agreement reached between the Government of Sierra Leone and the RUF.[31] With respect to the prosecutable war crimes, the Secretary-General recommended inclusion of serious violations of Common Article 3 and AP II, as well as other serious violations of IHL, namely:

(a) Intentionally directing attacks against the civilian population as such or against individual civilians not taking direct part in hostilities;

(b) Intentionally directing attacks against personnel, installations, material, units or vehicles involved in a humanitarian assistance or peacekeeping mission in accordance with the Charter of the United Nations, as long as they are entitled to the protection given to civilians or civilian objects under the international law of armed conflict;

(c) Conscripting or enlisting children under the age of 15 years into armed forces or groups or using them to participate actively in hostilities.

The reasoning for the inclusion of (a) and (b) was premised on the fact that such intentional attacks violated fundamental protections recognized under IHL, and that (a) and (b) were simply adding to existing international customary law crimes.[32] The Secretary-General's report was more circumspect with the regard to the addition of (c) on the conscription and enlistment of child soldiers. Although the report noted that the prohibition on child recruitment had acquired a status of customary international law, it also noted that "it is far less clear whether it is customarily recognized as a war crime entailing the individual criminal responsibility of the accused." A similar doubt was evoked as to the customary nature of the International Criminal Court crime of "conscription or enlistment, whether forced or voluntary, of children under the age of 15." As a consequence, the Secretary-General underscored that the terms *conscription* and *enlistment* should be understood as abduction, forced recruitment and "transformation of the child into, and its use as, among other degrading uses, a 'child-combatant.'"[33]

Although the Government of Sierra Leone had sought to limit personal jurisdiction to the RUF and their accomplices, based on the Secretary-General's report submitted to the UN Security Council, it was extended to refer simply to those persons who bore the greatest responsibility for the crimes covered under the Statute.[34] As a consequence, the SCSL was able to prosecute members of all of the parties to the conflict in Sierra Leone post–November 1996, notably the RUF, the Armed Revolutionary Council (AFRC), and the Civil Defense Force (CDF), as well Charles Taylor, then president of Liberia. Interestingly, though, it was decided that transgressions by UN peacekeepers and related personnel fell within the primary jurisdiction of the sending States (their State of nationality that provided the forces to support the peacekeeping mission). Jurisdiction by the SCSL could only be exercised over these cases where authorized by the Security Council on proposal of any State, if the sending States were unwilling or unable to handle or prosecute the cases themselves.

The SCSL functioned for nearly a decade, ceasing operation in 2013. It convicted and sentenced a total of nine individuals from the RUF, CDF, and AFRC, as well as Charles Taylor, the former president of Sierra Leone. Similar to the ICTR and the ICTY, a residual mechanism known as the Residual Special Court for Sierra Leone (RSCSL) was established pursuant to an agreement signed between the United Nations and the Government of Sierra Leone.[35] With its seat in Sierra Leone, it will ensure among other functions no double jeopardy and prevent the trial of any individual before the national courts of Sierra Leone if he or she has already been tried by the SCSL or RSCSL.

3.2   *The Extraordinary Chambers in the Courts of Cambodia*

The Extraordinary Chambers in the Courts of Cambodia (ECCC), also known as the Khmer Rouge Tribunal, was similar to the SCSL in its mixed composition and jurisdiction, however the ECCC was more integrated into the national system. Created in 2003 through an agreement between the United Nations and the Government of Cambodia, the ECCC is seen as a Cambodian court with international participation, applying international standards.[36]

The ECCC was established at the request of the then two prime ministers of Cambodia, in a letter addressed to the UN Secretary-General in June 1997. Based in part on Cambodia's own lack of resources and expertise in the field of international justice, they sought assistance from the United Nations and the international community to bring to justice those persons responsible for the genocide and crimes against humanity during the rule of the Khmer Rouge from 1975 to 1979.[37] Long negotiations then ensued before the United Nations and the Government of Cambodia could agree on the nature, structure, oversight, and jurisdiction of the ECCC.[38] Major concerns had been evoked by the United Nations Secretary-General about the lack of urgency and commitment being shown by the Government of Cambodia, and regarding that the initially proposed structure left ample scope for obstruction and delay in the conduct of proceedings.[39]

It was finally agreed that the ECCC would be a national Cambodian court, established within the court structure of Cambodia.[40] Trial, appellate, and investigating judges, as wells as prosecutors and co-prosecutors, are both international and Cambodian. The ECCC was vested with jurisdiction to try the "most senior leaders of the Democratic Kampuchea and those more responsible" for crimes within the tribunal's jurisdiction committed between 17 April 1975 and 6 January 1979.[41] In addition to a number of crimes under Cambodian law, the ECCC can prosecute individuals for certain violations of international law: genocide, crimes against humanity, and grave breaches of the Geneva Conventions of 1949.

Financial and political challenges beset the ECCC from its inception, with regular requests for subventions being submitted to the United Nations.[42] The ECCC plans to conclude its four cases by 2019, with a first conviction for war crimes and crimes against humanity having been issued against the former chairman of Phnom Penh's security prison S-21.

4   The permanent international criminal court

4.1   *Jurisdiction of the International Criminal Court*

The adoption of the Rome Statute of the International Criminal Court in July 1998 led to the creation of the International Criminal Court (ICC). Its creation is undeniably recognized as one of the most important landmarks in the developments of international justice and the fight against impunity for violations of IHL, genocide, and crimes against humanity.[43] As an international treaty, the Rome Statute came into effect in 2002, once ratified by 60 States. To date, more than 139 States are signatories and over 120 of those States have also ratified the Rome Statute. The United Nations acts as the depositary. By contrast to the ad hoc UN Tribunals and the hybrid courts discussed above, the ICC, which has its seat in the Netherlands, is a permanent body with a broad geographical and material jurisdiction for crimes committed after the entry of force of the Statute, or after the time the concerned State became party to the ICC.[44]

The ICC may exercise jurisdiction over States Parties or over a State not party if it has made a declaration accepting the ICC's competence, when (1) one or more of the States is either "the State on the territory of which the conduct in question occurred or, if the crime was committed on board a vessel or aircraft, the State of registration of that vessel or aircraft"; or (2) if the "the person accused of the crime is a national of the State."[45] The ICC's jurisdiction can be engaged by a State Party referring a situation to the ICC prosecutor *or* if the prosecutor decides to initiate an investigation into alleged crimes.[46]

Under the Rome Statute, the UN Security Council, acting under Chapter VII of the UN Charter, is also permitted to refer cases to ICC.[47] As a result, the Security Council can now utilize the ICC for situations that previously necessitated creation of an ad hoc tribunal. This will usually only be in situations falling outside the ICC's consent-based jurisdiction—suspected crimes concerning States not party to the ICC. And, as noted, this referral authority in essence dispenses with the Security Council having to establish any further international tribunals or hybrid courts to address atrocities committed in future armed conflicts.

The first such referral occurred in 2005, when the UN Security Council determined that the then ongoing situation in Sudan, in particular the atrocities committed in Darfur since July 2002, constituted a threat to international peace and security. Because Sudan had not ratified the Rome Statute or submitted to ICC jurisdiction, only referral by the Security Council could allow the ICC to pursue cases arising out of this situation. Eleven of the 15 Member States of the Security Council voted in favor of the referral, with Algeria, China, Brazil, and the United States abstaining.[48] In 2011, the Security Council, this time by unanimous vote, also referred to "the situation in the Libyan Arab Jamahiriya since 15 February 2011" to the ICC Prosecutor.[49]

While at face value the possibility for the Security Council to refer matters to the ICC is seen as an important advancement in the international community's efforts to end impunity, its success depends on alignment of political interests and consensus of the Council members. The Darfur referral may have succeeded but numerous other attempts to have the Security Council refer cases in other situations have fared less favorably, as exemplified by the debates concerning accountability for serious and quite blatant international law violations committed during the armed conflict in Syria.

In terms of the crimes over which it has material jurisdiction, the Rome Statute provides the ICC with competence to try crimes against humanity, genocide, war crimes, and the crime of aggression, the latter only being added to as a crime at the 2010 Kampala Review Conference.[50] Prosecutable war crimes listed in Article 8 of the ICC Statute include grave breaches of the Geneva Conventions of 12 August 1949, serious violations of Common Article 3 to the four Geneva Conventions of 12 August 1949, and other serious violations of the laws and customs applicable in IAC and NIACs.[51] It should be noted that Article 8 of the ICC Statute specifies that the court will have jurisdiction for war crimes "in particular when committed as part of a plan or policy or as part of a large-scale commission of such crimes." Although not a precondition for the admissibility of war crimes prosecutions, this wording may raise the bar as to which cases can be investigated.[52]

4.2 A gravity threshold

In terms of who can be prosecuted, the focus is not on those most responsible or senior, or similar language found in the statutes of the ICTY, ICTR, SCSL, and ECCC. Instead, the approach taken by the ICC is to exercise jurisdiction "over persons for the most serious crimes of international concern,"[53] effectively creating a threshold of seriousness based on the circumstances and not only the accused's status. In line with Article 17 of the ICC Statute, the ICC prosecutor will consider the gravity of the crimes which includes making "an assessment of the scale, nature, manner of commission of the crimes, and their impact."[54] The ICC has explained that determining sufficient gravity

> involves a generic assessment (general in nature and compatible with the fact that an investigation is yet to be opened) of whether the groups of persons that are likely to form the object of the investigation capture those who may bear the greatest responsibility for the alleged crimes committed.

It must also be "assessed from both a 'quantitative' and 'qualitative' viewpoint and factors such as nature, scale, and manner of commission of the alleged crimes, as well as their impact on victims, are indicators of the gravity of a given case."[55]

The criterion for making this critical gravity determination—the determination that triggers jurisdiction—has been a contentious issue before the ICC. This issue was especially controversial during investigations into cases seen as politically charged by critics, including those concerning Kenya and the attack on a humanitarian aid flotilla by the Israeli Defense Force on 31 May 2010. In particular, the *Flotilla* situation gave rise to substantial scrutiny as to the elements that had to be taken into consideration by the prosecutor in deciding whether to open investigations following a referral. The initial referral of May 2013 was submitted to the Office of the ICC Prosecutor by the Government of the Comoros, a State Party to the ICC.[56] The Comoros asserted jurisdiction of the ICC on the basis that one of the eight ships forming part of a humanitarian flotilla sailing to Gaza and attacked by Israel was the MV *Mavi Mara*, a Comoros-registered vessel. According to the referral, the majority of the alleged crimes occurred on this vessel.

In November 2014, following a preliminary examination of the referral, the ICC prosecutor concluded that "the potential case(s) likely arising from an investigation into this incident would not be of 'sufficient gravity' to justify further action by the ICC."[57] Nonetheless, the prosecutor noted that there was a "reasonable basis to believe that war crimes under the Court's jurisdiction ha[d] been committed in the context of interception and takeover of the *Mavi Marmara* by IDF soldiers on 31 May 2010." However, the prosecutor's office concluded that the loss of 10 lives and injuries to 50–55 other passengers on the *Mavi Marmara*, while resulting from serious violations of international law, were insufficiently grave to trigger ICC jurisdiction.[58] Factors that led to this conclusion included:

- The limited number of victims in comparison to other cases before the court.
- The fact that the IDF did not subject passengers to torture or inhuman treatment.
- The fact that the impact of the violations was limited to the actual victims.
- The fact that this was a single and isolated incident, and not one in a more pervasive practice of legal violations.

On review at the request of the Comoros, the Pre-Trial Chamber found that the prosecutor had failed to consider certain critical factors in deciding not to proceed, including the use of live fire by the IDF prior to boarding the *Mavi Mamara* and the alleged cruel and abusive treatment of detained passengers in Israel. The judges opined that there

> appear[ed] to be no reason . . . to consider that an investigation . . . could not lead to the prosecution of those persons who have the greatest responsibility for the identified crimes committed during the seizure of the *Mavi Marmara* by the IDF,

to include senior IDF commanders and Israeli political leaders.[59] Accordingly, the Pre-Trial Chamber requested reconsideration by the prosecutor.[60] On 30 November 2017, following a review of all relevant information, including new material provided between 2015 and 2017, the ICC Prosecutor issued a statement communicating her decision to close the preliminary examination. In reaching her decision, she noted that whilst "there is a reasonable basis to believe that war crimes were committed by some members of the Israel Defence Forces during and after the boarding of the *Mavi Marmara* on 30 May 2010," there was no potential case of sufficient gravity to be admissible before the ICC.

The *Flotilla* litigation demonstrates that the ICC will only assert jurisdiction over those crimes which are sufficiently grave in terms of number, nature, impact, and potential perpetrators, and will give a preference to those committed as part of a plan or policy or as part of a large-scale commission of such crimes. Even if the prosecutor concludes that serious war crimes were committed, this alone does not seem sufficient for the case to be pursued by this court.

4.3   *A court of last resort*

In contrast to the UN Ad Hoc Tribunals, the ICC was not established with the objective to exercise primacy over national courts. Instead, the ICC was intended to function as a court of last resort, exercising its jurisdiction only when States are either unwilling or unable to credibly prosecute individuals over whom the ICC may also exercise jurisdiction. In other words, the ICC will only step in or be seized by the UN Security Council when States fail to fulfill their pre-existing obligations under international law to bring to justice perpetrators of serious violations of IHL, crimes against humanity, and genocide. As explained by Luis Moreno-Ocampo, the first prosecutor of the ICC:

> The Court is complementary to national systems. This means that whenever there is genuine State action, the court cannot and will not intervene. But States not only have the right, but also the primary responsibility to prevent, control and prosecute atrocities. Complementarity protects national sovereignty and at the same time promotes state action.
>
> The effectiveness of the International Criminal Court should not be measured by the number of cases that reach it. On the contrary, complementarity implies that the absence of trials before this Court, as a consequence of the regular functioning of national institutions, would be a major success.[61]

The concept of complementarity can be both a stick as well as a carrot. As a stick, the ICC can use complementarity to take over prosecutions in cases where national authorities purport to pursue prosecutions against individuals for violations of IHL and other crimes falling within the jurisdiction of the ICC, yet are in fact shielding their nationals from meaningful accountability and even using their national process as a fig leaf. This could occur, for example, when the accused is still a serving member of the sitting government or in a leadership position of influence in the concerned country. Similarly, the government may want to give the impression that it has put in place the necessary mechanisms to try crimes of interest to the ICC, when in fact they are of limited ICC relevance or even mere empty shells.[62]

Or it may be the situation that the nature of the domestic level prosecution fell short of internationally recognized standards of credible justice. This may occur, for instance, in situations where there has been regime change, and the new authorities have little regard to due process as they seek to expedite trials against member of the deposed government.[63] This became a particularly sensitive issue in Libya, after the cases of Saif Gaddafi were referred to the ICC by the UN Security Council. Gaddafi had been sentenced to death in July 2015 by the Tripoli Court of Assize for crimes committed during the 2011 uprising in Libya. The ICC prosecutor noted that various organizations, including the Office of the United Nations High Commissioner for Human Rights (OHCHR), had criticized the quality of the trial in Libya and expressed discomfort with the verdicts and sentences. Concerns were evoked that international fair trial standards were not met in those trials.[64] As a consequence of these shortcomings, the prosecutor filed a request before the court seeking an order for surrender of Saif Gaddafi to the ICC and a reporting of the death sentence.[65]

As a carrot, the court's ability to exercise jurisdiction can act as an incentive to national authorities to initiate or carry out further investigations themselves into alleged violations and perpetrators, with a view to possible trials at domestic level. The risk of ICC intervention creates an important incentive for national authorities to demonstrate that they have the willingness and ability to proceed with the cases, and that any decision not to pursue a case is based on objectively credible considerations.[66] As part of its strategy, the ICC has also made available its resources and expertise to develop the local capacity of States requiring support with potential national proceedings, including in areas of witness protection and training of judges and counsel.[67]

5 Alternative compliance mechanisms

5.1 A compliance gap

The various criminal accountability mechanisms reviewed above are all essential components in the overall system of preventing impunity for violations of IHL. To date, though, trials of war criminals, be they at the domestic or international level, have been few and far between. Indeed, they have been in minute proportion in comparison to the number of war crimes that have been allegedly perpetrated in past and contemporary conflicts. This status quo is unlikely to be resolved in future conflicts unless greater judicial capacity and political will are generated to effectively close the impunity gap.

Criminal prosecution of war criminals should therefore be seen as part of a broader system to ensure the respect of IHL. As described in other sections of this book, IHL provides a robust, wide-ranging, and detailed legal framework to facilitate the protection of civilians in armed conflicts by limiting the suffering of war, regulating the means and methods of warfare, and guaranteeing humane treatment as a minimum for all persons not actively participating in hostilities. A second part of this system is, as such, the integration of IHL into all aspects of military operations, doctrine development, education and training of combatants and others responsible for implementing the law, and ensuring leaders understand and embrace their responsibility to ensure that subordinates comply with the law and investigate alleged violations.

Ideally, a third component would be the existence of a compliance mechanism within the Geneva Conventions with the power to truly compel the parties to the conflict to comply with IHL and, for example, to have IHL violations halted immediately. This, unfortunately is one of the main weaknesses of current IHL.[68]

Compared to many IHRL conventions, there is nothing in IHL providing for the creation of a strong monitoring body, or compliance procedures, be it for States, armed forces, other organized armed groups, or individuals.[69] Attempts have been made to include within the Geneva Conventions and their Protocols varying forms of IHL compliance oversight mechanisms. However, for a number of reasons, they have never been fully utilized or effective. These include protecting powers, enquiry procedures, and the International Humanitarian Fact-Finding Commission.

Under the Geneva Conventions, each State Party to an IAC can designate by agreement of the other side, as a *protecting power*, a neutral State to safeguard its humanitarian interests.[70] The function of the protecting power is to monitor compliance with the Conventions and other IHL obligations and act as an intermediary between the parties to the conflict to address compliance concerns. Unfortunately, protecting powers have rarely been called upon to act because parties to IACs have been unable to reach agreement on this issue.[71] However, it should be noted that the ICRC is authorized to fulfill this function in the absence of an agreed-upon protecting power, and has done so frequently. Furthermore, while the protecting power concept is technically only applicable during IACs, the ICRC performs an analogous function during NIACs.

Enquiry procedures, applicable only in IACs, were originally envisaged in Article 30 of the 1929 Geneva Convention for the Amelioration of the Condition of the Wounded and Sick in Armed Forces in the Field, and also included in the four Geneva Conventions of 1949.[72] An enquiry procedure into alleged violations of IHL can be instituted at the request of a party to the conflict, in agreement with the other party. If they are unable to agree on the modalities of the enquiry, they can appoint an umpire who will decide on the procedure to be followed. Following the enquiry, and if a violation is established, as with any violations, the parties to the conflict are to put an end to it and shall repress it with the least possible delay. On paper, these procedures, if fully executed, could bring about both an end to the incriminated conduct as well as lead to criminal accountability. Unfortunately, as with the protecting powers, the use of enquiry procedures has been virtually non-existent.

The International Humanitarian Fact-Finding Commission (IHFFC), established pursuant to Article 90 of AP I, is composed of 15 members of high moral standing and acknowledged impartiality. The IHFCC is notably competent to enquire into any facts alleged to be grave breaches and other serious violations of the Geneva Conventions and AP I. However, it can only act where a State has made a declaration to that effect in relation to another State Party accepting the same obligation, or on an ad hoc basis, again subject to the consent of all the parties involved. The Commission can also offer its good offices to facilitate the restoration of an attitude of respect for the Conventions and AP I.[73] Again, as with the enquiry procedures and protecting powers, States have rarely utilized the IHFFC.[74]

5.2   A new compliance mechanism?

As a consequence of the palpable compliance gap within IHL instruments, the 31st International Conference of the Red Cross and Red Crescent, held in Geneva in 2011, invited the ICRC, in cooperation with States, to identify and propose a range of options and recommendations to "enhance and ensure the effectiveness of mechanisms of compliance with international humanitarian law."[75] During the four years of consultations leading up to the 32nd International Conference, in 2015, numerous inter-State meetings and consultations were hosted by the ICRC and the Swiss Government. The issues debated during these sessions were indicative of the inherent complexity in defining a mechanism able to successfully enhance compliance with IHL.

Between 2011 and 2015, a number of proposals were considered by States and the ICRC to improve IHL compliance. These included: (1) periodic reporting, to allow for self-assessment and exchanges among States on their practical experiences in IHL implementation, (2) thematic discussions on, *inter alia*, States' legal and policy positions on current and emerging IHL, (3) fact-finding, with a possible role for the IHFFC, and (4) a meeting of States Parties to allow for a regular dialogue among States on IHL. While the proposals gave rise to divergent views on key issues, States did agree that any compliance system must be devoid of politicization, has to be State-driven and consensus-based, and must not duplicate other compliance systems (such as the Universal Periodic Review or the Human Rights Special Procedures).[76]

At the outcome of the 32nd International Conference, held in Geneva in December 2015, States were unable to come to an agreement on the nature and structure of a possible compliance structure.[77] The ICRC president was quite critical of the result, and voiced his disappointment: "International humanitarian law is flouted almost every day, in every conflict around the world. By failing to support this initiative, States missed an opportunity to help to protect millions of people." It was resolved nonetheless to continue considering the best way forward, in the lead up to the 33rd International Conference, scheduled for 2019.[78]

Thus, despite incorporation of compliance enhancement mechanisms into existing treaties and ongoing efforts to develop consensus on other mechanisms, very little *international* progress has been made on this front. However, many States have devoted substantial effort to compliance enhancement within their armed forces, and even non-State organized armed groups periodically implement measures to enhance compliance within their ranks. Integration of legal advisors into military units, integration of IHL into military doctrine and training, emphasizing the responsibility of individual service-members to comply with the law and conducting credible investigations and disciplinary proceedings in response to alleged IHL violations—these mechanisms will hopefully continue to blossom in the future, reducing the gap between the ideal and the reality of IHL.

6 Conclusion

Repeatedly throughout history, war has proven to be a corrosive agent on the moral compasses of the men and women who fight in them. This very chapter and the necessity for the creation of the Tribunals discussed in it are evidence of that fact. But as will be discussed further in the next chapter, war is not a justi-fication for combatants to kill or otherwise act against another person at any time for any reason. Therefore, the IHL framework—and the international and national justice mechanisms that help comprise a strong enforcement apparatus—are essential to the preservation of human dignity during and after war.

Notes

1 For instance, the Kosovo Specialist Chambers, established in August 2015, the International Crimes Division within the High Court of Uganda, established in 2008, the War Crimes Chamber of the Court of Bosnia and Herzegovina, established in 2002, and the Military Law Commissions at Guantanamo Bay, established in 2001.
2 Charter of the United Nations, Art 39, 26 June 1945, 59 Stat. 1031 [hereinafter UN Charter]. Article 39 of the United Nations Charter reads:

> The Security Council shall determine the existence of any threat to the peace, breach of the peace, or act of aggression and shall make recommendations, or decide what measures shall be taken in accordance with Articles 41 and 42, to maintain or restore international peace and security.

3 S.C. Res. 827, UN Doc. S/RES/827 (25 May 1993) (establishing the International Criminal Tribunal for the former Yugoslavia); S.C. Res. 955, U.N.Doc. S/RES 955 (8 November 1994) (establishing the International Criminal Tribunal for Rwanda).
4 S.C. Res. 827, UN Doc. S/RES/827 (25 May 1993); S.C. Res. 955, U.N.Doc. S/RES 955 (8 November 1994).
5 *Prosecutor v. Tadić*, Case No. IT-94-1-AR72, Decision on Defence Motion for Interlocutory Appeal on Jurisdiction (Int'l Crim. Trib. for the former Yugoslavia 2 October 1995) [hereinafter Tadić Appeals Decision].
6 Tadić Appeals Decision, paras 28–30.
7 UN Charter, Art 41. Article 41 of the United Nations Charter:

> The Security Council may decide what measures not involving the use of armed force are to be employed to give effect to its decisions, and it may call upon the Members of the United Nations to apply such measures. These may include complete or partial interruption of economic relations and of rail, sea, air, postal, telegraphic, radio, and other means of communication, and the severance of diplomatic relations." Article 42 of the United Nations Charter: "Should the Security Council consider that measures provided for in Article 41 would be inadequate or have proved to be inadequate, it may take such action by air, sea, or land forces as may be necessary to maintain or restore international peace and security. Such action may include demonstrations, blockade, and other operations by air, sea, or land forces of Members of the United Nations.

8 Tadić Appeals Decision, paras 31–2.
9 UN Charter, Art 41.
10 Tadić Appeals Decision, paras 35–6.
11 Statute of the International Tribunal for the Prosecution of Persons Responsible for Serious Violations of International Humanitarian Law Committed in the Territory of the Former Yugoslavia since 1991 Art 8–9, 25 May 1993, 32 I.L.M. 1203 [hereinafter ICTY Statute]. Article 9 (Concurrent jurisdiction) of the ICTY Statute reads:

> 1. The International Tribunal and national courts shall have concurrent jurisdiction to prosecute persons for serious violations of international humanitarian law committed in the territory of the former Yugoslavia since

1 January 1991. 2. The International Tribunal shall have primacy over national courts. At any stage of the procedure, the International Tribunal may formally request national courts to defer to the competence of the International Tribunal in accordance with the present Statute and the Rules of Procedure and Evidence of the International Tribunal.

Article 8 of the ICTR Statute is identical except that the ICTR primacy concerns cases arising "in the territory of Rwanda and Rwandan citizens for such violations committed in the territory of the neighbouring States, between 1 January 1994 and 31 December 1994."

12 Tadić Appeals Decision, para 59. Concurring, the Appeals Chamber cited the Trial Chamber:

> Before leaving this question relating to the violation of the sovereignty of States, it should be noted that the crimes which the International Tribunal has been called upon to try are not crimes of a purely domestic nature. They are really crimes which are universal in nature, well recognised in international law as serious breaches of international humanitarian law, and transcending the interest of any one State. The Trial Chamber agrees that in such circumstances, the sovereign rights of States cannot and should not take precedence over the right of the international community to act appropriately as they affect the whole of mankind and shock the conscience of all nations of the world. There can therefore be no objection to an international tribunal properly constituted trying these crimes on behalf of the international community.

13 *Id*. paras 58–9.

14 ICTY Statute, Arts 28–9.

15 *See* American Society for International Law, International Tribunal for the Prosecution of Persons Responsible for Serious Violations of International Humanitarian Law Committed in the Territory of the Former Yugoslavia since 1991: Rules of Evidence and Procedure, r. 58, 33 I.L.M. 484, 505 (1994) [hereinafter ICTY Rules of Evidence and Procedure] (National Extradition Provisions).

16 *See Id*. r. 59 (Failure to execute a warrant of arrest or Transfer Order).

17 Statute of the International Criminal Tribunal for Rwanda, Art 26, 8 November 1994, 33 I.L.M. 1598 [hereinafter ICTR Statute]; ICTY Statute, Art 27.

18 Preliminary report of the Independent Comm'n of Experts established in accordance with Security Council Res. 935 (1994), para 91, annexed to the letter dated 1 October 1994 from the Secretary-General addressed to President of the Security Council, UN Doc. S/1994/1125 (4 October 1994).

19 Final Report of the Comm'n of Experts Established in Accordance with Security Council Res. 780 (1992), para 43, annexed to the Letter dated 27 May 1994 from the Secretary-General addressed to President of the Security Council, UN Doc. S/1994/674 (27 May 1994):

> [T]he major conflicts in the territory of the former Yugoslavia have occurred in Croatia and in Bosnia and Herzegovina. Determining when these conflicts are internal and when they are international is a difficult task because the legally relevant facts are not yet generally agreed upon. This task is one which must be performed by the International Tribunal.

20 *Id*. para 44.

21 *Id*. para 52.

22 *Id*. para 54.

23 Tadić Appeals Decision, para 137.

24 *Id*. para 91.

25 S.C. Res. 1966, UN Doc. S/RES/1966 (22 December 2010).

26 Report of the Secretary-General on the establishment of a Special Court for Sierra Leone, UN Doc S/2000/915 (4 October 2000).

27 Letter dated Aug. 9, 2000 from the Permanent Rep. of Sierra Leone to the UN addressed to the President of the Security Council, UN Doc S/2000/786 (10 August 2000).

28 *Id.* (Enclosure framework for the Special Court for Sierra Leone).

29 Report of the Secretary-General on the establishment of a Special Court for Sierra Leone, para 9, UN Doc S/2000/915, 4 October 2000).

30 Statute of the Special Court for Sierra Leone Arts 2–5, 16 January 2002, 2178 U.N.T.S. 145 [hereinafter SCSL Statute].

31 Report of the Secretary-General on the establishment of a Special Court for Sierra Leone, paras 26–8, UN Doc S/2000/915, 4 October 2000).

32 *Id.* paras 15–16.

33 *Id.* paras 17–18. In 2004, the SCSL Appeals Chamber confirmed that the recruitment of child soldiers had been "criminalized before it was explicitly set out as a criminal prohibition in treaty law and certainly by November 1996," in *Prosecutor against Sam Hinga Norman*, Case No. SCSL 2004-14-AR72(E), Decision on Preliminary Motion Based on Lack of Jurisdiction (Child Recruitment), para 53 (31 May 2004).

34 SCSL Statute, Art 1.

35 Agreement between the United Nations and the Government of Sierra Leone on the Establishment of a Residual Special Court for Sierra Leone.

36 Agreement between the United Nations and the Royal Government of Cambodia concerning the prosecution under Cambodian law of crimes committed during the period of Democratic Kampuchea. Phnom Penh (6 June 2003).

37 Letter dated June 21, 1997 from the First and Second Prime Ministers of Cambodia addressed to the Secretary-General, UN Doc A/51/930 S/1997/488 (24 June 1997).

38 Report of the Secretary-General on Khmer Rouge trials, UN Doc A/57/769 (31 March 2003).

39 *Id.* paras 14–15.

40 *Id.* para 31.

41 Agreement between the United Nations and the Royal Government of Cambodia concerning the prosecution under Cambodian law of crimes committed during the period of Democratic Kampuchea. Phnom Penh, Art 1 (6 June 2003).

42 *See* Request for a subvention to the Extraordinary Chambers in the Courts of Cambodia, UN Doc A/71/338 (16 August 2016).

43 Rome Statute of the International Criminal Court, 17 July 1998, 2187 U.N.T.S. 90. [hereinafter Rome Statute].

44 *Id.* Art 10.

45 *Id.* Art 12.

46 *Id.* Arts 13–15.

47 *Id.* Art 13.

48 S.C. Res. 1593, UN Doc S/RES/1593 (31 March 2005).

49 S.C. Res. 1970, UN Doc S/RES/1970 (26 February 2011).

50 The Review Conference of the Rome Statute, held in Kampala, Uganda, from 31 May to 11 June 2010 adopted the amendments on the crime of aggression on 11 June 2010 by Resolution RC/Res. 6. R.C. Res. 6 (11 June 2010).

51 Rome Statute, Art 8.

52 *See* Statement of the Prosecutor of the International Criminal Court, Fatou Bensouda, on concluding the preliminary examination of the situation referred by the Union of Comoros, para 23 (6 November 2014) ("Rome Statute legal requirements have not been met. . . . Although this threshold is not a prerequisite for jurisdiction, it does,

however, provide statutory guidance indicating that the Court should focus on cases meeting these requirements.").

53 Rome Statute, Art 1.

54 *See* First Report of the Prosecutor of the International Criminal Court to the UN Security Council pursuant to UNSCR 1970 (2011).

55 ICC Decision on the request of the Union of the Comoros to review the prosecutor's decision not to initiate an investigation, in the situation on the registered vessels of the Union of the Comoros. *The Hellenic Republic and the Kingdom of Cambodia*, Case No. ICC-01/13, para 21 (16 July 2015).

56 Referral of the Union of the Comoros with respect to the 31 May 2010, Israeli raid on the humanitarian aid flotilla bound for Gaza Strip, requesting the prosecutor of the International Criminal Court pursuant to Articles 12, 13, and 14 of the Rome Statute to initiate an investigation into the crimes committed within the court's jurisdiction, arising from this raid (14 May 2013).

57 Statement of the Prosecutor of the International Criminal Court, Fatou Bensouda, on concluding the preliminary examination of the situation referred by the Union of Comoros (6 November 2014) ("Rome Statute legal requirements have not been met").

58 *Id.* para 138.

59 *Id.* para 24.

60 Statement of ICC Prosecutor, Fatou Bensouda, on the Situation on registered vessels of the Union of the Comoros et al. (30 November 2017), *available at* www.icc-cpi. int/Pages/item.aspx?name=171130_OTP_Comoros

61 Statement by Mr. Luis Moreno-Ocampo, Ceremony for the solemn undertaking of the chief prosecutor of the International Criminal Court at The Peace Palace, The Hague, the Netherlands (16 June 2003).

62 For instance, look to the numerous reports of the Prosecutor of the ICC to the UN Security Council pursuant to UNSCR 1593 (2005). In the Third Report, dated 14 June 2006, the prosecutor noted:

> The Darfur Special Court has been presented by the Government of the Sudan as an alternative to the prosecution of cases by the International Criminal Court – invoking the complementarity framework underpinning the Rome Statute. At the time of the establishment of the first Darfur Special Court, the President of the Court highlighted that the subject-matter jurisdiction of the Court would include crimes against humanity and war crimes and that the Court would deal with any perpetrators, regardless of rank or affiliation. Moreover, the Government of the Sudan announced that approximately 160 suspects had been identified for investigation and possible prosecution: 92 from South Darfur, 38 from North Darfur and 32 from West Darfur. With regard to the work of the first Darfur Special Court, there are no significant changes since the last report of the Prosecutor to the Security Council. So far the Special Court has conducted six trials of fewer than 30 suspects. The cases include four incidents of armed robbery, one incident of receipt of stolen goods, two cases of possession of firearms without a licence, one case of intentional wounding, two cases of murder and one case of rape. Eighteen of the defendants were low-ranking military officials (including eight members of the Popular Defence Forces); the remainder appear to be civilians. The President of the Special Court has Stated that no cases involving serious violations of international humanitarian law were ready for trial and that the six cases selected were in fact chosen from the case files lying before the ordinary Courts.

63 *See* Decision on the Admissibility of the Case against Abdullah Al-Senussi, Case No. ICC-01/11-01/11-466-Red, Judgment on the appeal of Mr. Abdullah Al-Senussi against the decision of Pre-Trial Chamber I, para 3 (11 October 2013):

However, there may be circumstances, depending on the facts of the individual case, whereby violations of the rights of the suspect are so egregious that the proceedings can no longer be regarded as being capable of providing any genuine form of justice to the suspect so that they should be deemed, in those circumstances, to be "inconsistent with an intent to bring the person to justice."

64 Tenth report of the Prosecutor of the International Criminal Court to the United Nations Security Council pursuant to UNSCR 1970 (2011), *available at* www.icc-cpi.int/iccdocs/otp/otp-rep-unsc-05–11–2016-Eng.pdf

65 *See* Situation in Libya: In the Case of The Prosecutor v. Saif Al-Islam Gaddafi, Case No. ICC-01/11-01/11-611, Prosecution Request for an Order to Libya to Refrain from Executing Saif Al-Islam Gaddafi, Immediately Surrender Him to the Court, and Report His Death Sentence to the United Nations Security Council (30 July 2015), *available at* www.icc-cpi.int/Pages/record.aspx?docNo=ICC-01/11–01/11–611

66 *See* ICC Prosecutorial Strategy 2009–2012, paras 16–17 (1 February 2010):

In this design, intervention by the Office is exceptional—it will only step in when States fail to conduct genuine investigations and prosecutions. This principle of complementarity has two dimensions: (i) the admissibility test, *i.e.* how to assess the existence of national proceedings and their genuineness, which is a judicial issue; and (ii) the positive complementarity concept, *i.e.* a proactive policy of cooperation aimed at promoting national proceedings. The positive approach to complementarity means that the Office will encourage genuine national proceedings where possible, including in situation countries, relying on its various networks of cooperation, but without involving the Office directly in capacity building or financial or technical assistance.

67 Focal points' compilation of examples of projects aimed at strengthening domestic jurisdictions to deal with Rome Statute Crimes, Review Conference of the Rome Statute, RC/ST/CM/INF.2, Kampala (31 May–11 June 2010).

68 *See* ICRC, Strengthening Legal Protection for Victims of Armed Conflicts, report prepared by the ICRC for the 31st International Conf. of the Red Cross and Red Crescent in Geneva, Switzerland (October 2011); Strengthening IHL Protecting Persons Deprived of Their Liberty in Relation to Armed Conflict, ICRC (1 April 2017), *available at* https://ihl-databases.icrc.org/applic/ihl/ihl.nsf/vwTreatiesByCountry.xsp

69 *Cf.* Convention Against Torture and Other Cruel, Inhuman or Degrading Treatment or Punishment, 10 December 1984, 1465 U.N.T.S. 85.

70 Geneva Convention for the Amelioration of the Condition of the Wounded and Sick in Armed Forces in the Field, Art 8, 12 August 1949, 6 U.S.T. 3114, 75 U.N.T.S. 970 [hereinafter GWS]; Geneva Convention for the Amelioration of the Condition of Wounded, Sick, and Shipwrecked Members of the Armed Forces at Sea, Art 8, 12 August 1949, 6 U.S.T. 3217, 75 U.N.T.S. 971 [hereinafter GWS-Sea]; Geneva Convention Relative to the Treatment of Prisoners of War, Art 8, 12 August 1949, 6 U.S.T. 3316, 75 U.N.T.S. 972 [hereinafter GPW]; Geneva Convention Relative to the Protection of Civilian Persons in Time of War, Art 9, 12 August 1949, 6 U.S.T. 3516, 75 U.N.T.S. 973 [hereinafter GC].

71 The last reported use of the protecting power occurred during the 1982 conflict between the United Kingdom and Argentina. *See* Background Document for the Working Group Meeting on Strengthening Compliance with IHL, Geneva, 4 (October 2012), *available at* www.icrc.org/eng/assets/files/2013/2012-11-strenghtening-ihl-and-chairs-conclusions-meeting-states-november-2012.pdf. For more on the role of the protecting power, *see* the ICRC Commentary to Articles 8 and 9 of Geneva Conventions I–IV respectively, Commentary on the First Geneva Convention: Convention

(I) for the Amelioration of the Condition of the Wounded and Sick in Armed Forces in the Field (2nd edn, 2016), paras 1003–119, *available at* www.icrc.org/applic/ihl/ihl.nsf/Treaty.xsp?action=openDocument&documentId=4825657B0C7E6BF0C12563CD002D6B0B

72 *See* GWS, Art 52; GWS-Sea, Art 53; GPW, Art 132; GC, Art 149.

73 For more on the activities of the IHFFC, *see* IHFFC, *available at* www.ihffc.org/index.asp?Language=EN&page=home

74 Note that in May 2017 the IHFFC was asked by the OSCE to lead an independent forensic investigation in relation to the incident of 23 April 2017. The incident, in Pryshyb, Luhansk Province, resulted in the death of a paramedic and the injury of two monitors of the OSCE Special Monitoring Mission to Ukraine.

75 Resolution 1 on Strengthening Legal Protection for Victims of Armed Conflicts, adopted at the 31st Int'l Conf. of the Red Cross and Red Crescent in Geneva, Switzerland (28 November–1 December 2011).

76 All background documents, reports and chair's conclusions are *available at* www.eda.admin.ch/eda/en/home/topics/intla/humlaw/icrc.html

77 Resolution 2 on Strengthening Compliance with International Humanitarian Law, adopted at the 32nd Int'l Conf. of the Red Cross and Red Crescent in Geneva, Switzerland, Doc. No. 32IC/15/R2 (8–10 December 2015).

78 *Id.*

12 War crimes and accountability

1 Introduction

IHL provides an extensive legal framework to ensure the protection of certain categories of individuals and property during armed conflict. As detailed in the earlier chapters of this book, numerous restrictions and prohibitions are provided for in IHL treaty and customary international law, most notably the Geneva Conventions and their Additional Protocols, to mitigate the effects of hostilities and to minimize suffering. IHL recognizes that even in times of war there are unqualified limits on the conduct of combatants and other belligerents, and many other rules that turn on the reasonableness of decisions.

As history has shown, there will be occasions when the protections afforded by IHL are violated, sometimes intentionally, sometimes as the result of carelessness, and sometimes as the result of genuine accident. In some circumstances where the parties to armed conflicts fail in their obligations, this can have particularly serious consequences for the people, places, and objects this body of law is intended to protect. These violations, upon reaching a particular threshold, will qualify as war crimes, and their repression is a core component of IHL enforcement. Without the ability to hold those responsible for war crimes criminally accountable, the protection and guarantees that this body of law provides will be undermined.

From a military perspective, the prosecution of war crimes is also seen as essential in preserving good order and discipline within the force and legitimacy of the operation, which ultimately contributes to mission accomplishment. Holding individuals accountable for war crimes they commit or are complicit in conveys a strong signal to the troops, hopefully deterring other potential perpetrators, stamping out ill-discipline and ultimately strengthening respect for the laws of war. It also signals to the local populace and the wider public that commitment to rule of law is central to the armed forces conducting a mission.

This chapter will provide an overview of the constitutive elements of war crimes, noting the distinction between grave breaches and other serious violations of IHL. It will then consider under what circumstances an individual can be held criminally responsible for war crimes.

2   What is a war crime?

The term *war crime* is to be understood broadly. Essentially, war crimes cover those IHL violations reaching a certain threshold of harm committed in armed conflicts, whether international or non-international. The London Charter of the Nuremberg Tribunal and the Charter of the International Military Tribunal for the Far East (Tokyo Tribunal) defined war crimes simply as violations of the laws or customs of war.[1] Over time, this definition has evolved to reflect the terminology of the 1949 Geneva Conventions and the development of IHL:

> The expression "violations of the laws or customs of war" is a traditional term of art used in the past, when the concepts of "war" and "laws of warfare" still prevailed, before they were largely replaced by two broader notions: (i) that of "armed conflict", essentially introduced by the 1949 Geneva Conventions; and (ii) the correlative notion of "international law of armed conflict", or the more recent and comprehensive notion of "international humanitarian law", which has emerged as a result of the influence of human rights doctrines on the law of armed conflict.[2]

Through case law and international treaties, and the work of the UN Ad Hoc Tribunals, hybrid courts, and the ICC,[3] the labeling of an act as a war crime is a threshold question in that it must be seen to "endanger protected persons or objects or if they breach important values."[4] Violations that meet that threshold will be viewed as war crimes deserving of criminal repression.[5] This position is best reflected in language used by the ICTY in *Tadić*:

> [T]he violation must be serious, that is to say, it must constitute a breach of a rule protecting important values, and the breach must involve grave consequences for the victim. Thus for instance, the fact of a combatant simply appropriating a loaf of bread in an occupied village would not amount to a "serious violation of international humanitarian law" although it may be regarded as falling foul of the basic principle laid down in Article 46, paragraph 1, of the Hague Regulations (and the corresponding rule of International Humanitarian law) whereby "private property must be respected" by an any army occupying an enemy territory.[6]

The focus on the seriousness of the violation rather than the context in which it occurred is reflected by the list of crimes contained in Article 8 of the ICC Statute, which can be committed in both IAC and NIAC. At the ICC Kampala Review Conference in 2010, amendments were brought to Article 8 of the Statute to give the court jurisdiction over additional crimes when committed in NIAC.[7] This enumeration of war crimes is perhaps the most comprehensive indication of State consensus on what IHL violations rise to that level. Similarly, a large number of the 161 rules identified in the ICRC's *Customary Law Study*, many of which would constitute war crimes if violated, are common to both types of armed conflict. Accordingly, while there may not be a complete mirroring, and while grave breaches are restricted to IAC, most IHL violations deemed sufficiently reprehensible will qualify for war crime prosecution irrespective the nature of the conflict.

In this vein, the *DoD Law of War Manual* notes that the term *war crime* is used to refer to "particularly serious violations of the law of war." It goes on to explain that "this usage of 'war crime' is understood to exclude minor violations of the law of war."[8] For example, if during an IAC military medical personnel perform their duties while wearing an armlet displaying the distinctive emblem affixed to their right arm—rather than to their left arm, as specified by Article 40 of the GWS—these personnel may be said to be violating the law of war. However, under this usage of war crime, such violations generally would not be regarded as a war crime.[9]

Violations of IHL that fall below this seriousness threshold may still warrant punishment, but not necessarily criminal sanction. Action to suppress them is required by States. The response by States may, though need not, be criminal in nature, and could take the form of administrative or disciplinary measures. The ICRC's 2016 GWS Commentary explains:

> States Parties will determine the best way to fulfil these obligations, for example by instituting judicial or disciplinary proceedings for violations of the Conventions other than grave breaches, or by taking a range of administrative or other regulatory measures or issuing instructions to subordinates. The measures chosen will depend on the gravity and the circumstances of the violation in question, in accordance with the general principle that every punishment should be proportional to the severity of the breach.[10]

It should be underscored that, as with any act to be deemed criminal and prosecutable as such at the domestic level, the State must enact law that provides for such prosecution. How the State chooses to do so is within its discretion, and could include enumerating war crimes, incorporating international law by reference, or enumerating domestic crimes that address the same misconduct as war crimes (for example, prosecuting the grave breach of murder of a protected person as murder in violation of domestic law). In this sense, misconduct deemed to constitute war crimes must be introduced into national law and regulations, and defined accordingly. Courts, be they civilian or military, need also to be given the necessary jurisdiction to try cases of war crimes. For many countries, the range of war crimes over which their courts will have jurisdiction will be determined by their own military tradition and be guided by the international treaties to which they are party. The scope of domestic war crimes jurisdiction vested in courts of a State Party to the Additional Protocols of 1977 and to the ICC will in all likelihood cover a broader range of war crimes than countries party only to the four Geneva Conventions, although a country not party to these treaties may certainly include war crimes established by them in its domestic law. In addition to treaties, war crimes considered to be part of customary international law will also normally form part of national law.

Ideally, the definition of offenses deemed to be war crimes incorporated into domestic law should reflect those war crimes commonly accepted in international instruments and practice. This may not always be the case. For instance, the U.S. War Crimes Act of 1996 uses the term *grave breaches* of Common Article 3 for violations committed in the context of and in association with NIAC.[11] The prohibited conduct covered by the definition of grave breaches are: torture, cruel or inhuman treatment; performing biological experiments; murder; mutilation or maiming; intentionally causing serious bodily injury; rape, sexual assault, or abuse; and taking hostages.[12] Labeling such acts as grave breaches, despite not being committed in IACs, is confusing and inconsistent with the war crimes structure established by the Geneva Conventions and customary international law. While it is laudable that the United States has enacted domestic law to allow for prosecution of violations of Common Article 3, aligning the terminology of domestic law with international law would eliminate unfortunate confusion.

However, the United States was of the view that since Common Article 3 "protects persons against some of the acts described as grave breaches ... the obligations created by the grave breaches provisions could apply also to violations of Common Article 3."[13] While admittedly this reasoning may not reflect the true intent of the drafters of the Conventions when deciding to create the grave breaches regime, it nonetheless reflects a contemporary trend referred to above of looking at the seriousness of an action rather than the context of its commission to determine whether to criminalize. If this was indeed the motivation for enactment of the law, it would have been more logical to simply refer to serious violations of Common Article 3. However, as noted earlier, while the obligations created by the grave breaches do require enactment of legislation necessary to provide effective penal sanctions for persons committing, or ordering to be committed, any of the grave breaches of the 1949 Geneva Conventions, that *obligation* is simply not applicable to violations of Common Article 3.

In addition, the War Crimes Act of 1996 does not include as grave breaches other possible offenses covered by Common Article 3, namely outrages upon personal dignity, in particular humiliating and degrading treatment, and the passing of sentences and the carrying out of executions without previous judgment pronounced by a regularly constituted court affording all the judicial guarantees. This omission could be criticized as having downgraded certain types of conduct not considered a grave breach by the United States, thus creating a two-tiered system. At the time, the United States noted though that, "regardless of whether the obligations in the grave breaches provisions apply with respect to violations of Common Article 3, serious violations of Common Article 3 may nonetheless be punishable."[14]

At the international level, as discussed in Chapter 12, the jurisdiction for war crimes of the UN and hybrid courts varied, each being tailored to reflect the specific nature of the context for which they were established. For example, the ICTR had jurisdiction only over war crimes committed in Rwanda and neighboring countries in 1994, in a context deemed to be non-international.[15] The crimes covered therefore were "serious violations of Article 3 common to the Geneva Conventions of 12 August 1949 for the Protection of War Victims, and of Additional Protocol II thereto of 8 June 1977."[16] Article 3 of the SCSL Statute similarly mandated the court to prosecute persons for serious violations of Common Article 3 and AP II in relation to the NIACs that occurred in Sierra Leone after 30 November 1996.[17] The ICTY, which had to deal with a mix of IACs and NIACs after the breakup of Yugoslavia in 1990, was competent to deal with war crimes covered by the laws and customs of war in relation to both types of conflicts.[18]

The ICC is competent to investigate and try offenses committed in IAC or NIAC. War crimes within its jurisdiction are

> grave breaches of the Geneva Conventions of 12 August 1949, namely, any of the following acts against persons or property protected under the provisions of the relevant Geneva Convention . . . in the case of an armed conflict not of an international character, serious violations of Article 3 common to the four Geneva Conventions of 12 August 1949, namely, any of the following acts committed against persons taking no active part in the hostilities, including members of armed forces who have laid down their arms and those placed hors de combat by sickness, wounds, detention or any other cause, and other serious violations of the laws and customs applicable in IAC and NIAC within the established framework of international law.[19]

As noted above, the Rome Statute enumerated a list of war crimes the States Parties to the treaty agreed should be within the competence of a permanent international war crimes tribunal. This list of ICC war crimes is included as an Appendix to this chapter. These crimes are derived from treaty provisions, ad hoc tribunal jurisprudence, and customary international law. They are an important and perhaps most authoritative reflection of internationally accepted war crimes, and include war crimes that may arise in both IAC and NIAC. The authoritative nature of this listing of war crimes is bolstered by the fact that even States that chose not to join the ICC, most notably the United States, participated in the development of this list and generally supported the ultimate outcome. This does not necessarily mean that these are the only war crimes a State may seek to punish, but it is fair to say that this list is the best contemporary touchstone for assessing what a State should consider a war crime. For example, challenges to the broader scope of war crimes jurisdiction established by the United States for trials by military commission of detainees at Guantanamo often point to the divergence from the ICC list of war crimes as evidence of government overreach.

3   The grave breaches regime under international law

Under the Geneva Conventions and their Protocols, a distinction is made between the most serious treaty violations, called *grave breaches*, and other treaty violations.

Grave breaches can only be committed during IAC and are specifically defined in the four Geneva Conventions of 1949 and AP I.[20] Other treaty violations, and all violations during NIAC, may qualify as war crimes, but they are not grave breaches.

The drafters of the 1949 Geneva Conventions chose to speak of *breaches* rather than crimes given that countries attached a different legal meaning to the term *crimes*.[21] They also wanted to draw public attention to the list of these most serious breaches, which included specific categories on conduct of hostilities, went beyond those covered by Common Article 3, which is limited to a few prohibited acts against persons taking no active part in hostilities. The same approach was followed in the 1977 Additional Protocols. AP II, applicable in NIAC, outlines a few protections,[22] whereas AP I, applicable in IAC, added a number of grave breaches in supplement to those contained in the four Geneva Conventions.[23]

The main distinction between the grave breaches regime and other serious violations of IHL lies in the obligations imposed by the treaties on States Parties to the Geneva Conventions and AP I. For grave breaches, this obligation requires States to take positive action to prosecute any person within the States jurisdiction suspected of having committed such an offense, or turn the individual over to another State willing to prosecute, irrespective of where the alleged grave breach occurred and by whomsoever committed. Furthermore, under the grave breaches regime, States are obligated to take a certain number of additional measures to implement their treaty obligation, including the enactment of relevant national penal legislation and the taking of measures to search for and prosecute alleged perpetrators before their own courts. Grave breaches were deemed so serious that universal jurisdiction could be resorted to in ensuring their punishment, meaning that the prosecute or extradite obligation applies even if the State who finds a suspected war criminal in its jurisdiction had no connection to the armed conflict or the suspected war criminal.[24] This is why the Geneva Conventions obligate States Parties to enact the necessary domestic legislation to "provide effective penal sanctions for persons committing, or ordering to be committed" the grave breaches listed in four Conventions and Protocol I.[25] Only by so doing will the State be able to full implement its grave breach repression obligation.

Other violations not labeled grave breaches do not fall within the scope of these grave breach obligations. Nonetheless, States are still obligated to suppress acts contrary to provisions of the conventions and their protocols. Depending on the severity of the violation, suppression can take the form of penal repression or disciplinary action. Furthermore, as noted by the ICRC *Customary International Humanitarian Law Study*, as a matter of custom the authority of a State to exercise universal jurisdiction evolved to include these other war crimes committed in both IAC and NIAC.[26] The major difference is that, unlike grave breaches, prosecution of other war crimes is optional and not obligatory.

Today, it may seem odd that a distinction was made between different types of war crimes, and between crimes committed in IACs, compared to those committed in NIACs. After all, the willful killing, rape, or torture of a civilian is heinous irrespective of the nature of the armed conflict, and merits meaningful criminal sanction. This was not specifically questioned by States during the diplomatic conferences leading to the adoption of the Conventions and Protocols. Rather the main reason for the apparent disparity between the two regimes can be traced back to the nature of international relations at the time of the drafting of the conventions between 1947 and 1949. During this period, States were keen to protect their sovereignty and ensure non-interference in their internal affairs. NIACs were deemed domestic matters, and their regulation the business of the State and not the result of an obligation imposed through an international treaty. This historical context makes it is easier to appreciate why States gave greater importance to punishment of grave breaches in the Conventions. These violations were of international concern because of the inherently international nature of inter-State conflict, and because of the gravity of the violations.

The grave breach terminology is still applicable today, albeit its relevance is arguably limited to questions of State prosecutorial obligations and implementation of universal jurisdiction through national law. As has been confirmed in case law and legislation, the term *war crime* is now commonly accepted to describe *all* IHL violations resulting in individual criminal responsibility when committed during *any* armed conflict. If committed in IACs, though, States have a stronger footing to exercise universal jurisdiction over third-State nationals than if the violation occurred in a NIAC, or if the war crime did not amount to a grave breach.[27]

4   The trigger for war crimes accountability

4.1   *The existence of an armed conflict*

Step one to determining whether an act can constitute a war crime is demonstrating the existence of an armed conflict. Obvious as it may appear, it is good nonetheless to underscore that, absent an armed conflict, there can be no finding that war crimes have been committed. In the simplest terms, without a war there can be no war crime.

A war crime can only occur in times of armed conflict, international or non-international, where the proof indicates a nexus between the offense and the conflict. These *sine qua non* conditions distinguish war crimes from other international offenses, namely crimes against humanity and genocide. Neither of these international crimes requires the existence of an armed conflict for a prosecution to be successful, even though they may be committed during armed conflicts. The same act, for instance, of killing an unarmed civilian, could be labeled any one of the three, so long as the constitutive elements of each crime is proven. For genocide, it would have to be shown at a minimum that the perpetrator possessed the special intent to destroy in whole or in part a particular group on ethnic, religious, national, or racial grounds.[28] A crime against humanity can only be committed as part of a widespread or systematic attack against a civilian population,[29] whereas, for war crimes, it is the nexus with the armed conflict that is key. In the absence of an armed conflict, a prosecution for war crimes will fail, although it could still be successfully prosecuted for genocide or crimes against humanity or alternatively under general domestic criminal law.

As explained in Chapter 1, the existence of an armed conflict and qualification as either international or non-international is essentially a factual question. If the context where the offenses were committed in what is a clear and distinct armed conflict—for example, the IAC that occurred between the United Kingdom and Argentina in the Falkland Islands in 1982—then establishing this nexus is fairly straightforward factually. In many hostile and unstable environments, though, the facts can be quite complex, with genocide, widespread killing of civilians, and armed conflict seemingly all occurring at same time.

Indeed, many contemporary conflicts are fluid in nature, with ebbs and flows of violence sometimes rising to the level of military engagement and open hostilities, involving a range of different actors, including State armed forces, organized armed groups, criminal gangs, narco-traffickers, civilian defense groups, and private contractors. Any one context can give rise to a multitude of conflicts, violent encounters during situations that do not qualify as armed conflict, and a range of complex criminal jurisdiction issues. For prosecutors, judicial bodies, and commissions of inquiry, unraveling the facts to be able to make a determination that an armed conflict or armed conflicts occurred has on occasion proven to be a testing endeavor. Factors taken into account include the identity of the belligerents (State or non-State), the intensity of the violence and the duration of the hostilities, and the relationship between the violence and an ongoing armed conflict. Evidence of these factors can come from multiple sources, including: eye witnesses, expert testimony, reports of non-governmental organizations, international bodies such as UN Fact-Finding Commissions, UN Security Council Resolutions, decisions of international and domestic tribunals, and the media or records of national parliamentary inquiries and congressional hearings.

Establishing the existence and nature of an armed conflict is easier said than done, and peeling away all the layers to find the nexus with the armed conflict can be challenging. It is nonetheless an essential exercise in the prosecution of war crimes. The experience of the ICTR, discussed hereunder, is illustrative of the complexity of establishing to an evidentiary certainty these essential predicates for the exercise of war crimes jurisdiction.

As noted in Chapter 11, the ICTR was established in 1994 by the UN Security Council to prosecute individuals who committed genocide, crimes against humanity and war crimes, specifically serious violations of Common Article 3 and of AP II in Rwanda and neighboring countries in 1994.

The first three trials to be handled by the ICTR were against Rwandan civilians. None of them belonged to the State armed forces or the Rwandan Patriotic Front. Two of the accused, Georges Rutaganda and Obed Ruzindana, were businessmen based in Kigali and Kibuye, respectively; two more were local administration officials: Jean-Paul Akayesu was a mayor and Clément Kayishema a prefect. All had been charged with counts of genocide, crimes against humanity, and war crimes for their individual roles in the massacres that occurred in their regions between April and June 1994. Before being able to make any findings under these counts, the respective Trial Chambers had to first make sense of the context in which the alleged offenses were said to have been perpetrated. For some commentators, the massacres that occurred in Rwanda in 1994 were simply part of the genocide and widespread killings of members of the Tutsi ethnic group and had nothing to do with the armed conflict between the Rwandan Armed Forces and the Rwandan Patriotic Front. For others, they were only war crimes and not genocide or crimes against humanity. However, the Trial Chamber in *Akayesu* concluded the genocide and the armed conflict were intrinsically linked.[30]

The judges found that, as this NIAC met the threshold requirements of both Common Article 3 and AP II, these instruments would apply over the whole territory, "hence encompassing massacres which occurred away from the war front."[31] This reasoning would suggest then that any of the massacres committed as part of the genocide could also be considered as possible war crimes, given the entwining between the genocide and armed conflict.

However, in *Kayishema and Ruzindana* the court took a more restrictive position. It recognized that there existed in Rwanda a NIAC between the Rwandan Patriotic Front and the Rwandan Armed Forces, and also that a genocide against the Tutsi had been organized and launched by the Government of Rwanda. However, this Chamber concluded that the former was only a pretext to "unleash a policy of Genocide" without more. As no military operations had occurred in the Prefecture of Kibuye at the time of massacres, it concluded that there was an insufficient connection between the massacres and the armed conflict to find that war crimes had been committed.[32]

The Trial Chambers had both ruled that genocide and an armed conflict occurred in Rwanda. But they seemed to disagree on the nature of the link, and by implication, whether the acts of the accused, for instance the killing of Tutsi civilians, could constitute either or both war crimes and genocide. It was left ultimately to the Appeals Chamber to resolve the apparent contradiction, which they did, in line with the *Akayesu* findings. The genocide and the armed conflict were inextricably linked, and very difficult to dissociate.

Notwithstanding contextual challenges faced in the above examples, the cases were consistent in identifying the nexus with the armed conflict as being the crux of the matter. Determining its existence has to be assessed on a case-by-case basis. This careful approach to distinguishing when an act of violence can reasonably be included within the scope of war crimes jurisdiction, even in the context of an ongoing armed conflict, will likely be followed in future cases where the complexities of the overall situation defy a simple and generalized assumption that every *alleged* war crime is indeed linked to an armed conflict.

4.2   *What constitutes a nexus?*

As discussed above, once it has been established that an armed conflict exists, the second step is showing that the alleged misconduct was connected to the armed conflict—that there is a nexus. In the words of Professor Cassese—one of the most respected experts on international criminal law—the nexus standard "is objective in linking the armed conflict with the *crime*, not the criminal."[33] The judges in *Akayesu* and *Kayishema and Ruzindana* had recognized that there was a link between the genocidal massacres and the armed conflict. However, they were at odds when it came to their understanding of the nature of the nexus required to qualify any of the acts as war crimes.

The Appeals Chamber in *Rutaganda*, citing its jurisprudence in ICTY cases, attempted to bring more precision to the issue. Summarizing the case law, the judges explained that it must be shown that the offense is closely related to or connected with the armed conflict.[34] The judges relied especially on the ICTY Appeals Chamber decision in *Kunarac*, which emphasized that:

> What ultimately distinguishes a war crime from a purely domestic offence is that a war crime is shaped by or dependent upon the environment—the armed conflict—in which it is committed. It need not have been planned or supported by some form of policy. The armed conflict need not have been causal to the commission of the crime, but the existence of an armed conflict must, at a minimum, have played a substantial part in the perpetrator's ability to commit it, his decision to commit it, the manner in which it was committed or the purpose for which it was committed. Hence, if it can be established, as in the present case, that the perpetrator acted in furtherance of or under the guise of the armed conflict, it would be sufficient to conclude that his acts were closely related to the armed conflict.[35]

The *Rutaganda* judges further explained that the term *under the guise of* was more than simply taking advantage of the chaos and disorder caused by the armed conflict to murder a neighbor or commit a common law crime in no way related to the conflict. Instead, it was more akin to situations where for instance combatants "took advantage of their positions of military authority to rape individuals whose displacement was an express goal of the military campaign in which they took part."[36] It is not necessary to show that the alleged war crimes were perpetrated at the exact same time and place as the armed conflict or during open combat,[37] but only within the context of an armed conflict "irrespective of whether they took place contemporaneously with or proximate to intense fighting."[38]

While not a specific requirement, implicit in the jurisprudence of the UN Ad Hoc Tribunals on establishing a nexus is the fact that the accused in all likelihood *knew* that the conflict was ongoing. In this vein, the ICC has made "awareness of the factual circumstances that established the existence of an armed conflict," an element common to *all* war crimes covered under Article 8 of its Statute. In providing guidance on this element, the ICC's Elements of Crimes explains that: (1) there is no requirement for a legal evaluation by the perpetrator as to the existence of an armed conflict or its character as international or non-international; (2) in that context there is no requirement for awareness by the perpetrator of the facts that established the character of the conflict as international or non-international; and (3) there is only a requirement for the awareness of the factual circumstances that established the existence of an armed conflict that is implicit in the terms "took place in the context of and was associated with."

5   Who can be held responsible?

The concept of holding individual combatants and other belligerents criminally responsible for war crimes is well established under domestic law. Despite initial recognition during the Word War II Nuremberg and Tokyo Tribunals, it was really only with the creation of the ad hoc UN international tribunals in the 1990s that the principle of individual criminal responsibility at the international level truly took form.

As early as 1863, the Lieber Code, part of the Instructions for the Government of Armies of the United States in the Field, stipulated in its Article 71:

> Whoever intentionally inflicts additional wounds on an enemy already wholly disabled, or kills such an enemy, or who orders or encourages soldiers to do so, shall suffer death, if duly convicted, whether he belongs to the Army of the United States, or is an enemy captured after having committed his misdeed Lieber code.

Similarly, Principle 1 of the Nuremberg Principles, adopted by the Allies toward the end of World War II to lay the foundation for an international military tribunal to try high-level Axis war criminals, stated that "any person who commits an act which constitutes a crime under international law is responsible therefor and liable to punishment."[39] The 1954 Draft Code of Offences against Peace and Security of Mankind, prepared by the International Law Commission as the request of the UN General Assembly, which covers laws and customs of war, underscored in its Article 1 that "[o]ffences against the peace and security of mankind . . . are crimes under international law, for which the responsible individuals shall be punished."[40]

Notwithstanding the recognition that individuals can be held criminally accountable for war crimes, a question that did require some clarification was whether this accountability extended to civilians. The main reason for this to be an issue could be explained by the fact that IHL, broadly speaking, aims to regulate the conduct of combatants and other belligerents participating in hostilities, traditionally military or members of organized non-State groups. As such, criminal accountability of civilians for war crimes was not necessarily envisaged.

This presumptive exclusion of civilians from war crimes accountability began to change when the Allies sought to hold high-level Axis leaders responsible for their complicity in war crimes. Accordingly, there are a number of early examples of civilians being tried for war crimes following World War II. However, unlike the broad scope of war crimes accountability applicable to combatants and belligerents, accountability for civilians is a more limited concept. A review of some of these World War II cases indicates that a close connection with one of the parties to the armed conflict would be required for a civilian to be held responsible for war crimes. For example, the civilian defendant Hirota, as Japanese foreign minister, was officially part of the Government; in *Essen Lynching*, the civilians acted hand-in-hand with the escorting military unit in the killing of British airmen; and, in *Zyklon B*, the accused were German industrialists who provided poison to the Schutzstaffel (SS) used for killing interned Allied civilians.[41]

This extension of war crimes jurisdiction over civilians has been confirmed by the decisions of ad hoc war crimes tribunals. Furthermore, contemporary case law, notably from these ad hoc UN international tribunals, has clarified that, while in the majority of war crimes cases the perpetrators are likely to be those conducting the hostilities, namely the military or non-State belligerents, civilians can be held responsible irrespective of their belonging to or being closely connected with one of the parties to the armed conflict. The determining factor is whether a nexus can be established between the alleged crime and the armed conflict, rather than between the individual and a party to the armed conflict.

Perhaps the most significant contemporary authority related to the scope of war crimes liability applicable to civilians arose out of the NIAC in Rwanda. In the seminal ICTR *Akayesu* decision, the question of whether criminal accountability for war crimes was limited to a certain class of perpetrator was laid to rest. The accused, Jean-Paul Akayesu, was the mayor of the commune of Taba, Rwanda, during the massacres which occurred between April and July 1994. Charged with genocide, crimes against humanity, and war crimes, he was accused of having overseen the killing and raping of nearly 2,000 civilians, most of whom were Tutsi. The court was called upon to decide whether his civilian status was in any way an impediment to finding him responsible for war crimes. Indeed, as mayor (known as a *bourgmestre*), he was neither a member of the regular Rwandan armed forces nor within their chain of command. As the court explained:

> the duties of a bourgmestre were diverse. In short, he was in charge of the total life of the commune in terms of the economy, infrastructure, markets, medical care and the overall social life. . . . It is an executive civilian position in the territorial administrative subdivision of commune. The primary function of the bourgmestre is to execute the laws adopted by the communal legislature, i.e., the elected communal council.[42]

A mayor in Rwanda in 1994 had disciplinary jurisdiction over the communal police, as well as very little, if any, authority over the Gendarmerie Nationale, be it in time of peace or to intervene in times of war or national emergency, unless they were put at his disposal.[43]

In deciding if a civilian, such as *Akayesu*, could be held criminally responsible for war crimes, the Trial Chamber recalled that the Geneva Conventions and their Protocols were "primarily addressed to persons who by virtue of their authority, are responsible for the outbreak of, or are otherwise engaged in the conduct of hostilities." As such, the category of persons who would be held accountable for violations of their provisions "would in most cases be limited to commanders, combatants and other members of the armed forces." The Trial Chamber explained, in light of the overall protective nature of these instruments, that this category should be not be interpreted too restrictively. It went on to affirm, notably citing precedents from Tokyo and Nuremberg, that it had been established that civilians could also be held responsible for serious violations of the Conventions and Protocols where it was found that they "have a link or connection with a Party to the conflict."[44]

This was not to mean that only those with this link or connection could as such be held responsible. As the Appeals Chamber clarified, it is not necessary to show that an accused was acting as a public agent or government representative. For the court,

> international humanitarian law would be lessened and called into question if it were to be admitted that certain persons be exonerated from individual criminal responsibility for a violation of common Article 3 under the pretext that they did not belong to a specific category.[45]

As the court concluded, the existence of a special relationship is therefore not a condition precedent in finding individuals responsible for war crimes.[46]

This approach has been consistently followed by the ICC, which noted that

> although there is likely to be some relationship between a perpetrator and a party to the conflict, it is not necessarily the case that a perpetrator must him/herself be a member of a party to the conflict; rather, the emphasis is on the nexus between the crime and the armed conflict.[47]

Therefore, any individual, civilian or military, can be held responsible for war crimes. The determining factor is evidence that demonstrates the alleged war crimes were connected or tied to an armed conflict.

6   Amnesties

Pursuant to the 1977 AP II, States are encouraged "to grant the broadest possible amnesty to persons who have participated in the armed conflict, or those deprived of their liberty for reasons related to the armed conflict, whether they are interned or detained."[48] This provision is not geared toward providing amnesties for war crimes. It is instead aimed at limiting the criminal prosecution of individuals who took up arms and were active in a NIAC falling within the scope of AP II. The inclusion of this provision was motivated by the desire to foster reconciliation and restoration of peace and stability in the rebuilding of societies post-conflict, and especially responsive to the fact that, in this type of armed conflict, members of non-State armed groups are in no way protected by combatant immunity and therefore may be prosecuted domestically for taking up arms, even when their wartime conduct complied with IHL. Whether to grant an amnesty for participation in hostilities is left to the discretion of the responsible authorities and could also include pardons and commutation of sentences.[49]

There is no such provision for participation in IACs, and for good reason: unlike the AP II context, combatants who comply with IHL are immune from criminal sanction for those actions, and therefore as a matter of international law, criminal responsibility applies only to combatants whose conduct violates IHL. It would therefore be counterintuitive to encourage grants of amnesty for such misconduct.

Nonetheless, there are times when the interest of reconciliation may lead to a calculated policy decision to provide amnesty for war crimes. The law is still evolving when it relates to the provision of such amnesties. Some have argued that, for contexts coming out of war, which often ravages societies and sees the commission of war crimes, it is best to grant amnesties rather than to proceed with trials, which could give rise to further tensions and instability. Instead, alternative means of justice, for instance truth commissions, may be preferred to criminal prosecutions. The other school of thought is more skeptical at the value of amnesties. As Cassese surmised,

> it is doubtful that amnesty laws may heal open wounds. Particularly when very serious crimes have been committed involving members of ethnic religious, or political groups and eventually pitting one group against another, moral, and psychological wounds may fester if attempts are made to sweep past horrors sooner or later.[50]

Based on State practice, this seems to reflect the prevalent view. The ICRC *Customary Law Study* suggests that the prohibition on amnesty for war crimes is part of customary international law.[51] This makes sense when counterbalanced with the obligations placed upon States to ensure repression of grave breaches committed in IACs.[52]

The validity of amnesty provisions for war crimes was addressed by the SCSL following jurisdictional challenges by two accused, Morris Kallon and Ibrahim Bazzy Kamara.[53] In accordance with its Statute, the SCSL established that it was competent to prosecute persons who bear the greatest responsibility for serious violations of IHL and Sierra Leonean law committed in the territory of Sierra Leone since 30 November 1996.[54] Both defendants argued though that the SCSL could not assert jurisdiction for crimes committed prior to 1999, as the Government of Sierra Leone was bound to observe the amnesty granted under the Lomé Peace Agreement signed in June 1999 between the Government of Sierra Leone and the Revolutionary United Front of Sierra Leone (RUF). Article 9 of the Agreement was explicit:

> After the signing of the present Agreement, the Government of Sierra Leone shall also grant absolute and free pardon and reprieve to all combatants and collaborators in respect of anything done by them in pursuit of their objectives, up to the time of the signing of the present Agreement.

At first glance, Kallon and Kamara had a strong argument. The Article was quite broad in its wording, allowing for amnesties *in respect of anything done* by the combatants in the pursuit of their objectives. With no obvious caveats in the text, the defendants asserted that even war crimes were to be pardoned.

In anticipation of such challenges and recognizing a possible tension between international law and the Lomé Agreement, the drafters of the Statute, led by the United Nations, inserted a critical Article X in the Statute that specified that "an amnesty granted to any person falling within the jurisdiction of the Special Court in respect" of crimes against humanity, war crimes and other serious violations of IHL "shall not be a bar to prosecution."[55] In addressing the seeming contradiction between the Agreement and the SCSL's jurisdiction, the court opined that the Lomé Agreement was not an international treaty creating obligations under international law. The Agreement was more akin to a domestic accord restoring peace following an internal armed conflict, of which the UN Security Council could take note, but which did not create binding international obligations. The court further reasoned that the crimes covered by this Article X provision were international crimes which are subject to universal jurisdiction. As such, no State, by virtue of a domestic amnesty law, can "sweep such crimes into oblivion and forgetfulness which other States have jurisdiction to prosecute."[56]

The understanding of the function and limitations on amnesty provisions related to war crimes, while still in flux, is generally in accord with the SCSL's conclusion. Indeed, many international treaties, including the Geneva Conventions and their Protocols, do not provide for amnesties for international crimes. Even where States have sought to grant amnesty for such crimes, this cannot be a bar for other national or international jurisdictions to proceed with their prosecution.[57]

7　Conclusion

As this chapter has discussed, central to ensuring respect for IHL is holding individuals accountable for war crimes. At both the international and national levels, this principle has been engrained in legislation and practice. Case law has confirmed that individuals—civilians as well as combatants—can be held criminally responsible for war crimes committed in either IAC or NIAC. Still, further efforts are still required to make the prosecution of war criminals more widespread and systematic.

Notes

1 The violations included under this Article included but were not limited to murder, ill-treatment or deportation to slave labor or for any other purpose of civilian population of or in occupied territory, murder or ill-treatment of prisoners of war or persons on the seas, killing of hostages, plunder of public or private property, wanton destruction of cities, towns or villages, or devastation not justified by military necessity.

2 *Prosecutor v. Tadić*, Case No. IT-94-1-AR72, Decision on Defence Motion for Inter-locutory Appeal on Jurisdiction, para 94 (Int'l Crim. Trib. for the former Yugoslavia 2 October 1995).

3   One of the greatest achievements of the *ad hoc* tribunals has been to extend the reach of international law dealing with war crimes into the field of non-international conflicts (or civil wars). This reflects more general developments in international law, by which human rights and human security are no longer viewed as matters of purely national concern, sheltered from international oversight by notions of sovereignty and non-interference in internal affairs.

William A. Schabas, The UN International Criminal Tribunals: The former Yugoslavia, Rwanda and Sierra Leone 229 (Cambridge University Press, 2006)

4 Jean-Marie Henckaerts & Louise Doswald-Beck, Customary International Humani-tarian Law 568–603 (2009) [*CIL Study*]. Serious violations of IHL constitute war crimes. Also, *see* Cassese, who put forward a two-pronged test to determine when an offense can be considered a war crime, namely, it

(i) must have been perpetrated against persons who do not take part in hostilities or who no longer take part in such hostilities; and (ii) must have been committed to pursue the aims of the conflict or, alternatively, it must have been carried out with a view to somehow contributing to attaining the ultimate goals of a military campaign or, at a minimum, in unison with the military campaign.

Cassese's International Criminal Law Ch. 4 (P. Gaeta, L. Baig, M. Fan, C. Gosnell, & A. Whiting eds, 3rd edn, 2013) [hereinafter *Cassese*]

5 Note that as a matter of practice and under U.S. Military Doctrine any violation of the law of war is deemed to be a war crime. U.S. Dep't of Def., *Law of War Manual* 18.9.5.1 (June 2015, updated December 2016) [hereinafter *DoD Law of War Manual*].

6 *Prosecutor v. Tadić*, Case No. IT-94-1-AR72, Decision on Defence Motion for Inter-locutory Appeal on Jurisdiction, para 94 (Int'l Crim. Trib. for the former Yugoslavia 2 October 1995).

7 The amendments were as follows:

employing poison or poisoned weapons (article 8, paragraph 2 (b) (xvii)); employ-ing asphyxiating, poisonous or other gases, and all analogous liquids, materials and devices (article 8, paragraph 2 (b) (xviii)) and employing bullets which expand or flatten easily in the human body (article 8, paragraph 2 (b) (xix)).

Rome Statute Amendment Proposals: Report of the Working Group on Other Amendments, RC/11

8 *DoD Law of War Manual*, 18.9.5.2.

9 *Id.*

10 Commentary on the First Geneva Convention: Convention (I) for the Amelioration of the Condition of the Wounded and Sick in Armed Forces in the Field (2nd edn, 2016), para 2986, *available at* www.icrc.org/applic/ihl/ihl.nsf/Treaty.xsp?action=openDocument&documentId=4825657B0C7E6BF0C12563CD002D6B0B [hereinafter 2016 Commentary GWS].

11 As amended by the Military Commissions Act of 2006 and 2009. The original version of the U.S. War Crimes Act did not address any violations of Common Article 3. Another example of divergence with generally accepted international criminal law is that the War Crimes Act does not provide for universal jurisdiction over *actual* grave breaches of the four Geneva Conventions, but instead requires a nationality link between the war crime and the United States.

12 18 U.S.C. Section 2441 (2006).

13 *DoD Law of War Manual*, 18.9.3.3.

14 *Id.*

15 Letter from Secretary-General Boutros Boutros-Ghali to the President of the Security Council (4 October 1994), UN Doc. S/1994/1125, Annex [Preliminary Report of the Independent Commission of Experts Established in Accordance with Security Council Resolution 935, Para 91 (1994)]:

> The armed conflict between the period 6 April and 15 July 1994 qualifies as a non-international armed conflict. The use of armed force had been carried out within the territorial borders of Rwanda and did not involve the active participation of any other State. Third State involvement entailed peacemaking and humanitarian functions rather than belligerent action.

16 Statute of the International Criminal Tribunal for Rwanda, Art 4, 8 November 1994, 33 I.L.M. 1598.

17 Statute of the Special Court for Sierra Leone, Art 2, 16 January 2002, 2178 U.N.T.S. 145 [hereinafter SCSL Statute].

18 Statute of the International Tribunal for the Prosecution of Persons Responsible for Serious Violations of International Humanitarian Law Committed in the Territory of the Former Yugoslavia since 1991 Arts 2–3, 25 May 1993, 32 I.L.M. 1203.

19 Rome Statute of the International Criminal Court, Art 8, 17 July 1998, 2187 U.N.T.S. 90.

20 Geneva Convention for the Amelioration of the Condition of the Wounded and Sick in Armed Forces in the Field, Art 50, 12 August 1949, 6 U.S.T. 3114, 75 U.N.T.S. 970 [hereinafter GWS]; Geneva Convention for the Amelioration of the Condition of Wounded, Sick, and Shipwrecked Members of the Armed Forces at Sea, Art 51, 12 August 1949, 6 U.S.T. 3217, 75 U.N.T.S. 971 [hereinafter GWS-Sea]; Geneva Convention Relative to the Treatment of Prisoners of War, Art 130, 12 August 1949, 6 U.S.T. 3316, 75 U.N.T.S. 972; Geneva Convention Relative to the Protection of Civilian Persons in Time of War, Art 147, 12 August 1949, 6 U.S.T. 3516, 75 U.N.T.S. 973 [hereinafter GC]; Protocol (I) Additional to the Geneva Conventions of 12 August 1949, and Relating to the Protection of Victims of International Armed Conflicts, Arts 11 and 85, 8 June 1977, 1125 U.N.T.S. 3 [hereinafter AP I] (entered into force 7 December 1978) (signed by the United States 12 December 1977, not transmitted to U.S. Senate, *see* S. Treaty Doc. No. 100–2 (1987)).

21 2016 Commentary GWS, para 2917.

22 Protocol (II) Additional to the Geneva Conventions of 12 August 1949, and Relating to the Protection of Victims of Non-International Armed Conflicts, Art 4, 8 June 1977, 1125 U.N.T.S. 609 [hereinafter AP II] (entered into force 7 December 1978) (signed by the United States 12 December 1977, transmitted to the U.S. Senate 29 January 1987, still pending action as S. Treaty Doc. No. 100–2 (1987)) (regarding fundamental guarantees).

23 AP I, Art 85 (regarding repression of breaches).

24 Universal criminal jurisdiction is the assertion by one state of its jurisdiction over crimes allegedly committed in the territory of another state by nationals of another state against nationals of another state where the crime alleged poses no direct threat to the vital interests of the state asserting jurisdiction. In other

words, universal jurisdiction amounts to the claim by a state to prosecute crimes in circumstances where none of the traditional links of territoriality, nationality, passive personality or the protective principle exists at the time of the commission of the alleged offence.

> Council of the European Union, The AU–EU Expert Report on the Principle of Universal Jurisdiction, doc. 8672/1/09 Rev. 1, 7 (16 April 2009) [hereafter AU–EU report]

25 GWS, Art 49.

26 *See CIL Study*, at 604–7.

27 On the different approaches taken by States to incorporate universal jurisdiction into their domestic legal frameworks *see* ICRC, "Reflections on the Role of Universal Jurisdiction in Preventing and Repressing Violations of International Humanitarian Law and Other International Crimes," in *Report of the Third Universal meeting of National Committees for the Implementation of International Humanitarian Law, Preventing and Repressing International Crimes: Towards an Integrated Approach based on Domestic Practice, Vol. 1* (2013), *available at* www.icrc.org/eng/assets/files/publications/icrc-002-4138-1.pdf

28 Article II of the 1948 Genocide Convention reads: In the present Convention, genocide means any of the following acts committed with intent to destroy, in whole or in part, a national, ethnical, racial or religious group, as such: (1) Killing members of the group; (2) Causing serious bodily or mental harm to members of the group; (3) Deliberately inflicting on the group conditions of life calculated to bring about its physical destruction in whole or in part; (4) Imposing measures intended to prevent births within the group; (5) Forcibly transferring children of the group to another group.

29 Rome Statute, Art 7 reads as follows:

> 1. For the purpose of this Statute, "crime against humanity" means any of the following acts when committed as part of a widespread or systematic attack directed against any civilian population, with knowledge of the attack: (a) Murder; (b) Extermination; (c) Enslavement; (d) Deportation or forcible transfer of population; (e) Imprisonment or other severe deprivation of physical liberty in violation of fundamental rules of international law; (f) Torture; (g) Rape, sexual slavery, enforced prostitution, forced pregnancy, enforced sterilization, or any other form of sexual violence of comparable gravity; (h) Persecution against any identifiable group or collectivity on political, racial, national, ethnic, cultural, religious, gender as defined in paragraph 3, or other grounds that are universally recognized as impermissible under international law, in connection with any act referred to in this paragraph or any crime within the jurisdiction of the Court; (i) Enforced disappearance of persons; (j) The crime of apartheid; (k) Other inhumane acts of a similar character intentionally causing great suffering, or serious injury to body or to mental or physical health.

30 *See Prosecutor v. Akayesu*, Case No. ICTR-96-4-T, Judgment (2 September 1998).

31 *Id.* paras 636.

32 *Prosecutor v. Kayishema (Clément) & Ruzindana (Obed)*, Case No. ICTR-95-1-T, Judgment, para 603 (21 May 1999).

33 *See Cassese*, Ch. 4.

34 *Prosecutor v. Rutaganda*, Case No. ICTR-96-3-A, Judgment, para 569 (26 May 2003).

35 *Prosecutor v. Kunarac*, Case No. IT-96-23, IT-96-23/I-A, Judgment, paras 58–9 (Int'l Crim. Trib. for the former Yugoslavia 12 June 2002).

36 *Prosecutor v. Rutaganda*, Case No. ICTR-96-3-A, Judgment, para 570 (26 May 2003).

37 *Prosecutor v. Tadić*, Case No. IT-94-1-T, Opinion and Judgment, para 573 (Int'l Crim. Trib. for the former Yugoslavia 7 May 1997).

38 *Prosecutor v. Jean Pierre Bemba Combo*, Case No. ICC-01/05-01/08-3343, Trial Chamber III Judgment, para 144 (21 March 2016).

39 *Principles of International Law Recognized in the Charter of the Nürnberg Tribunal and in the Judgment of the Tribunal*, Yrbk Int'l L. Comm'n, 1950, Vol. II, paras 95–127.

40 *Draft Code of Offences against the Peace and Security of Mankind*, Yrbk Int'l L. Comm'n, 1951, Vol. II, paras 59ff.

41 *See* The Case of Kaki Hirota, sentenced to death for war crimes by the International Military Tribunal for the Far East; The Essen Lynching Case & The Zyklon B Case, Law Report of Trials of War Criminals, Selected and Prepared by the United Nations War Crimes Commission 1947–1949 Vol. 1 (1949).

42 *Prosecutor v. Akayesu*, Case No. ICTR-96-4-T, Judgment, paras 54, 66 (2 September 1998).

43 *Id.* paras 63–77.

44 *Id.* paras 630–4.

45 *Prosecutor v. Akayesu*, Case No. ICTR-96-4-A, Chamber, para 443 (1 June 2001).

46 *Id.* para 444.

47 *Prosecutor v. Jean Pierre Bemba Combo*, Case No. ICC-01/05-01/08-3343, Trial Chamber III Judgment, para 143 (21 March 2016).

48 AP II, Art 6(5).

49 Jean S. Pictet et al., Commentary on the Additional Protocols of 8 June 1977 to the Geneva Conventions of 12 August 1949 (ICRC, 1987), paras 4617–18.

50 *See Cassese*, Ch. 17.

51 *See CIL Study*, at 611–13.

52 *See* Letter from Head of the ICRC Legal Division to the Department of Law at the University of California (1997):

> The "*travaux préparatoires*" of Article 6(5) [of the 1977 AP II] indicate that this provision aims at encouraging amnesty, i.e., a sort of release at the end of hostilities. It does not aim at an amnesty for those having violated international humanitarian law. ... Anyway[,] States did not accept any rule in Protocol II obliging them to criminalize its violations. ... Conversely, one cannot either affirm that international humanitarian law absolutely excludes any amnesty including persons having committed violations of international humanitarian law, as long as the principle that those having committed grave breaches have to be either prosecuted or extradited is not voided of its substance.

53 *Prosecutor v. Kallon (Morris) & Kamara (Brima Bazzy)*, Case No. SCSL-2004-15-AR72(E), SCSL-2004-16-AR72(E), Decision on Challenge to Jurisdiction: Lomé Accord Amnesty (13 March 2004).

54 SCSL Statute, Art 1.

55 *Id.* Art 10.

56 *Prosecutor v. Kallon (Morris) & Kamara (Brima Bazzy)*, Case No. SCSL-2004-15-AR72(E), SCSL-2004-16-AR72(E), Decision on Challenge to Jurisdiction: Lomé Accord Amnesty, para 71 (13 March 2004).

57 *Cassese*, Ch. 17.

Appendix
Article 8 of the Rome Statute

Article 8 of the Statute of the International Criminal Court (ICC), as amended in 2010 at the Kampala Review Conference, today represents the most complete list of recognized war crimes:

(a) Grave breaches of the Geneva Conventions of 12 August 1949, namely, any of the following acts against persons or property protected under the provisions of the relevant Geneva Convention:
   (i)   Wilful killing;
   (ii) Torture or inhuman treatment, including biological experiments;
   (iii) Wilfully causing great suffering, or serious injury to body or health;
   (iv) Extensive destruction and appropriation of property, not justified by military necessity and carried out unlawfully and wantonly;
   (v)   Compelling a prisoner of war or other protected person to serve in the forces of a hostile Power;
   (vi) Wilfully depriving a prisoner of war or other protected person of the rights of fair and regular trial;
   (vii) Unlawful deportation or transfer or unlawful confinement;
   (viii) Taking of hostages.
(b) Other serious violations of the laws and customs applicable in international armed conflict, within the established framework of international law, namely, any of the following acts:
   (i)   Intentionally directing attacks against the civilian population as such or against individual civilians not taking direct part in hostilities;
   (ii) Intentionally directing attacks against civilian objects, that is, objects which are not military objectives;
   (iii) Intentionally directing attacks against personnel, installations, material, units or vehicles involved in a humanitarian assistance or peacekeeping mission in accordance with the Charter of the United Nations, as long as they are entitled to the protection given to civilians or civilian objects under the international law of armed conflict;
   (iv) Intentionally launching an attack in the knowledge that such attack will cause incidental loss of life or injury to civilians or damage to civilian objects or widespread, long-term and severe damage to the

natural environment which would be clearly excessive in relation to the concrete and direct overall military advantage anticipated;

(v) Attacking or bombarding, by whatever means, towns, villages, dwellings or buildings which are undefended and which are not military objectives;

(vi) Killing or wounding a combatant who, having laid down his arms or having no longer means of defence, has surrendered at discretion;

(vii) Making improper use of a flag of truce, of the flag or of the military insignia and uniform of the enemy or of the United Nations, as well as of the distinctive emblems of the Geneva Conventions, resulting in death or serious personal injury;

(viii) The transfer, directly or indirectly, by the Occupying Power of parts of its own civilian population into the territory it occupies, or the deportation or transfer of all or parts of the population of the occupied territory within or outside this territory;

(ix) Intentionally directing attacks against buildings dedicated to religion, education, art, science or charitable purposes, historic monuments, hospitals and places where the sick and wounded are collected, provided they are not military objectives;

(x) Subjecting persons who are in the power of an adverse party to physical mutilation or to medical or scientific experiments of any kind which are neither justified by the medical, dental or hospital treatment of the person concerned nor carried out in his or her interest, and which cause death to or seriously endanger the health of such person or persons;

(xi) Killing or wounding treacherously individuals belonging to the hostile nation or army;

(xii) Declaring that no quarter will be given;

(xiii) Destroying or seizing the enemy's property unless such destruction or seizure be imperatively demanded by the necessities of war;

(xiv) Declaring abolished, suspended or inadmissible in a court of law the rights and actions of the nationals of the hostile party;

(xv) Compelling the nationals of the hostile party to take part in the operations of war directed against their own country, even if they were in the belligerent's service before the commencement of the war;

(xvi) Pillaging a town or place, even when taken by assault;

(xvii) Employing poison or poisoned weapons;

(xviii) Employing asphyxiating, poisonous or other gases, and all analogous liquids, materials or devices;

(xix) Employing bullets which expand or flatten easily in the human body, such as bullets with a hard envelope which does not entirely cover the core or is pierced with incisions;

(xx) Employing weapons, projectiles and material and methods of warfare which are of a nature to cause superfluous injury or unnecessary suffering or which are inherently indiscriminate in violation of the international law of armed conflict, provided that such weapons, projectiles and material and methods of warfare are the subject of a comprehensive prohibition and are included in an annex to this Statute, by an amendment in accordance with the relevant provisions set forth in articles 121 and 123;

(xxi) Committing outrages upon personal dignity, in particular humiliating and degrading treatment;

(xxii) Committing rape, sexual slavery, enforced prostitution, forced pregnancy, as defined in article 7, paragraph 2 (f), enforced sterilization, or any other form of sexual violence also constituting a grave breach of the Geneva Conventions;

(xxiii) Utilizing the presence of a civilian or other protected person to render certain points, areas or military forces immune from military operations;

(xxiv) Intentionally directing attacks against buildings, material, medical units and transport, and personnel using the distinctive emblems of the Geneva Conventions in conformity with international law;

(xxv) Intentionally using starvation of civilians as a method of warfare by depriving them of objects indispensable to their survival, including wilfully impeding relief supplies as provided for under the Geneva Conventions;

(xxvi) Conscripting or enlisting children under the age of 15 years into the national armed forces or using them to participate actively in hostilities.

(c) In the case of an armed conflict not of an international character, serious violations of article 3 common to the four Geneva Conventions of 12 August 1949, namely, any of the following acts committed against persons taking no active part in the hostilities, including members of armed forces who have laid down their arms and those placed hors de combat by sickness, wounds, detention or any other cause:

(i) Violence to life and person, in particular murder of all kinds, mutilation, cruel treatment and torture;

(ii) Committing outrages upon personal dignity, in particular humiliating and degrading treatment;

(iii) Taking of hostages;

(iv) The passing of sentences and the carrying out of executions without previous judgement pronounced by a regularly constituted court, affording all judicial guarantees which are generally recognized as indispensable.

(d) Paragraph 2 (c) applies to armed conflicts not of an international character and thus does not apply to situations of internal disturbances and tensions, such as riots, isolated and sporadic acts of violence or other acts of a similar nature.

(e) Other serious violations of the laws and customs applicable in armed conflicts not of an international character, within the established framework of international law, namely, any of the following acts:

(i)   Intentionally directing attacks against the civilian population as such or against individual civilians not taking direct part in hostilities;

(ii)   Intentionally directing attacks against buildings, material, medical units and transport, and personnel using the distinctive emblems of the Geneva Conventions in conformity with international law;

(iii)   Intentionally directing attacks against personnel, installations, material, units or vehicles involved in a humanitarian assistance or peacekeeping mission in accordance with the Charter of the United Nations, as long as they are entitled to the protection given to civilians or civilian objects under the international law of armed conflict;

(iv)   Intentionally directing attacks against buildings dedicated to religion, education, art, science or charitable purposes, historic monuments, hospitals and places where the sick and wounded are collected, provided they are not military objectives;

(v)   Pillaging a town or place, even when taken by assault;

(vi)   Committing rape, sexual slavery, enforced prostitution, forced pregnancy, as defined in article 7, paragraph 2 (f), enforced sterilization, and any other form of sexual violence also constituting a serious violation of article 3 common to the four Geneva Conventions;

(vii)   Conscripting or enlisting children under the age of 15 years into armed forces or groups or using them to participate actively in hostilities;

(viii)   Ordering the displacement of the civilian population for reasons related to the conflict, unless the security of the civilians involved or imperative military reasons so demand;

(ix)   Killing or wounding treacherously a combatant adversary;

(x)   Declaring that no quarter will be given;

(xi)   Subjecting persons who are in the power of another party to the conflict to physical mutilation or to medical or scientific experiments of any kind which are neither justified by the medical, dental or hospital treatment of the person concerned nor carried out in his or her interest, and which cause death to or seriously endanger the health of such person or persons;

(xii)   Destroying or seizing the property of an adversary unless such destruction or seizure be imperatively demanded by the necessities of the conflict.

Index

Made in the USA
Las Vegas, NV
20 March 2022

46015892R00177